Carnegie Commission on Higher Education
Publications in Print

HIGHER EDUCATION IN NINE COUNTRIES:
A COMPARATIVE STUDY OF COLLEGES AND
UNIVERSITIES ABROAD
*Barbara B. Burn, Philip G. Altbach, Clark Kerr,
and James A. Perkins*

BRIDGES TO UNDERSTANDING:
INTERNATIONAL PROGRAMS OF AMERICAN
COLLEGES AND UNIVERSITIES
Irwin T. Sanders and Jennifer C. Ward

HIGHER EDUCATION AND THE NATION'S
HEALTH: POLICIES FOR MEDICAL AND
DENTAL EDUCATION
*a special report and recommendations by the
Commission*

GRADUATE AND PROFESSIONAL EDUCATION,
1980:
A SURVEY OF INSTITUTIONAL PLANS
Lewis B. Mayhew

THE AMERICAN COLLEGE AND AMERICAN
CULTURE:
SOCIALIZATION AS A FUNCTION OF HIGHER
EDUCATION
Oscar Handlin and Mary F. Handlin

RECENT ALUMNI AND HIGHER EDUCATION:
A SURVEY OF COLLEGE GRADUATES
Joe L. Spaeth and Andrew M. Greeley

CHANGE IN EDUCATIONAL POLICY:
SELF-STUDIES IN SELECTED COLLEGES AND
UNIVERSITIES
Dwight R. Ladd

THE OPEN-DOOR COLLEGES:
POLICIES FOR COMMUNITY COLLEGES
*a special report and recommendations by the
Commission*

QUALITY AND EQUALITY: REVISED
RECOMMENDATIONS
NEW LEVELS OF FEDERAL RESPONSIBILITY
FOR HIGHER EDUCATION
*a supplement to the 1968 special report by
the Commission*

STATE OFFICIALS AND HIGHER EDUCATION:
A SURVEY OF THE OPINIONS AND
EXPECTATIONS OF POLICY MAKERS IN NINE
STATES
Heinz Eulau and Harold Quinley

A CHANCE TO LEARN:
AN ACTION AGENDA FOR EQUAL
OPPORTUNITY IN HIGHER EDUCATION
*a special report and recommendations by the
Commission*

ACADEMIC DEGREE STRUCTURES:
INNOVATIVE APPROACHES
PRINCIPLES OF REFORM IN DEGREE
STRUCTURES IN THE UNITED STATES
Stephen H. Spurr

COLLEGES OF THE FORGOTTEN AMERICANS:
A PROFILE OF STATE COLLEGES AND
REGIONAL UNIVERSITIES
E. Alden Dunham

FROM BACKWATER TO MAINSTREAM:
A PROFILE OF CATHOLIC HIGHER
EDUCATION
Andrew M. Greeley

ALTERNATIVE METHODS OF FEDERAL
FUNDING FOR HIGHER EDUCATION
Ron Wolk

INVENTORY OF CURRENT RESEARCH ON
HIGHER EDUCATION 1968
Dale M. Heckman and Warren Bryan Martin

QUALITY AND EQUALITY:
NEW LEVELS OF FEDERAL RESPONSIBILITY
FOR HIGHER EDUCATION
*a special report and recommendations by the
Commission, with 1970 revisions*

*The following reprints are available from the Carnegie Commission on
Higher Education, 1947 Center Street, Berkeley, California 94704*

RESOURCES FOR HIGHER EDUCATION:
AN ECONOMIST'S VIEW
Theodore W. Schultz

STUDENT PROTEST—
AN INSTITUTIONAL AND NATIONAL PROFILE
Harold L. Hodgkinson

INDUSTRIAL RELATIONS AND UNIVERSITY
RELATIONS
Clark Kerr

WHAT'S BUGGING THE STUDENTS?
Kenneth Keniston

Higher Education in Nine Countries

A COMPARATIVE STUDY OF COLLEGES AND UNIVERSITIES ABROAD

by *Barbara B. Burn*

Director of International Programs,
University of Massachusetts, Amherst

with chapters by

Philip G. Altbach

Associate Professor of Educational Policy
Studies, University of Wisconsin

Clark Kerr

Chairman of the Carnegie Commission
on Higher Education

James A. Perkins

Chairman of the Board and Chief Executive Officer,
International Council for Educational Development

1971

A General Report Prepared for
The Carnegie Commission on Higher Education

MCGRAW-HILL BOOK COMPANY

New York   St. Louis   San Francisco   Düsseldorf
London   Sydney   Toronto   Mexico   Panama

The Carnegie Commission on Higher Education,
1947 Center Street, Berkeley, California 94704,
has sponsored preparation of this report as
part of a continuing effort to present significant
information and issues for public discussion.
The views expressed are those of the authors.

HIGHER EDUCATION IN NINE COUNTRIES

A Comparative Study of Colleges and Universities Abroad

Library of Congress catalog card number 79–132352

1 2 3 4 5 6 7 8 9 MAMM 7 9 8 7 6 5 4 3 2 1
07–010017–9

Foreword

It is one of the axioms of institutional evaluation that one does not proceed too far without examining the experiences of other institutions of a similar kind and purpose. Applied to higher education on a national scale, this means finding out what developments are taking place in other countries.

To obtain current information on colleges and universities abroad, the Carnegie Commission on Higher Education asked Dr. Barbara Burn, director of international programs at the University of Massachusetts, Amherst, to review higher education in eight industrial nations. Special attention was given to such matters as structure and organization, enrollment trends, financing, institutional government, relations of institutions to civil governments, students, and plans for the future. The results of her studies constitute the major portion of this volume. In order to contrast the experience of an economically less-developed nation—which also has the third largest system of higher education in the world—Philip Altbach, associate professor of educational policy studies at the University of Wisconsin, was invited to write a chapter on higher education in India. Still later, an introductory chapter suggesting ways in which national systems of higher education might be evaluated was added. Finally, James A. Perkins, a member of the Commission, and chairman of the board and chief executive officer of the International Council for Educational Development, provided a commentary on the significance of higher education developments abroad for colleges and universities in the United States.

As the manuscript neared completion, persons internationally regarded as experts on higher education in certain countries under discussion were invited to serve as critics. They are Sir Eric Ashby, the master, Clare College, Cambridge (Great Britain); Hellmut

Becker, professor, Institut für Bildungsforschung in der Max Planck Gesellshraft (West Germany); Claude Bissell, president, University of Toronto (Canada); Nicholas DeWitt, director, Center for Applied Manpower Studies and International Survey of Educational Development, Indiana University (Russia); Erik Lundberg, professor, The Stockholm School of Economics (Sweden); Michio Nagai, editorial writer, Asahi Press (Japan); Raymond Poignant, director, International Institute for Educational Planning, Paris (France); Amirik Singh, secretary, Interuniversity Board of India and Ceylon (India); and William Walker, professor, University of New England, Australia (Australia). The Carnegie Commission on Higher Education wishes to express thanks to these critics. Their assistance has made possible both currency and accuracy that could not have been obtained without their help.

The result of all these efforts is a description and discussion of higher education in nine important nations, a report that will prove useful for many years to come.

Clark Kerr

Chairman
The Carnegie Commission
on Higher Education

October, 1970

Contents

Higher Education in
Nine Countries

1. Introduction: The Evaluation of National Systems of Higher Education

by Clark Kerr

Knowledge knows no political or geographic boundaries, and the modern institutions that cultivate and disseminate learning share a heritage that can be traced to the ancient academies of Greece and, more directly, to medieval universities of Italy, France, and England. In each country, colleges and universities have been adapted to national conditions, customs, social structures, and political systems, but despite the resulting variations, vestiges of common antecedents are still visible everywhere.

To study the variations found in different countries is to appreciate the flexibility of the principles upon which all colleges and universities, including those in America, were founded. It also permits us to observe alternative solutions to common problems in higher education. This is important because the world's colleges and universities not only share a heritage but also are evolving in the same general directions.

In the next chapter, Barbara Burn outlines some of the most important trends: rapid enrollment growth and a movement toward providing universal access to higher education for the nations' youth; rising expenditures for higher education; increasing public— especially national—financial support for colleges and universities; greater involvement in society through research and continuing education; diversification of kinds of higher education to the extent that universities are no longer the only, or even the central, institutions of postsecondary education; and increased interest in centralized planning. She also observes that student activism and student disorders, which have come to occupy so much attention in the United States, are found nearly everywhere as students seek more participation in campus affairs, as a youth-oriented peer culture quite different from that of the surrounding society develops, and as certain political and philosophical movements challenge modern society.

Student unrest also has other components. One of them is the students' altered view of the purpose of education. Many no longer regard it as a career investment. Indeed, they expect it to be a rich life experience, and they empahsize the urgency of living now and not in the future. There also seems to be a revolt against science and research, activities that were popular in the 1950s and early 1960s. The subjects students favor now have more to do with human behavior, and sociology and psychology are at the top of the list.

Generally speaking, there is also restlessness among junior staff members. It is particularly dramatic in Germany, France, and Japan, where the ancient system continues of investing great authority in professors who hold chairs in their subjects. Junior staff members want more influence in their institutions and are challenging the chair system to get it. They also tend to join with the students in criticism of society and are inclined to believe that the campus should become a base for political action.

Some of these trends create difficult tensions. Within the campuses, there is tension between those who advocate major change and those who do not. There is also tension between those engaged in the favored subject fields of recent decades and those in the humanities and social sciences who seek more support for their own fields now. Finally, there is growing tension between campuses and the general public. It is seen in public hostility to students and intellectuals, to changes that are taking place in institutions of higher learning, and to attacks on society that originate on the campuses. In Russia, where the attacks are relatively mild, there is little obvious resentment. In Japan, France, and the United States, the attacks have often been violent, and the collision with the public has been severe.

Trends, of course, require adjustments and reactions. These are particularly evident — aside from those noted later by Barbara Burn — in five general directions:

1   In the distribution of authority, there is a tendency to give less of it to the chairs, particularly in France, Germany, and Japan, but also in Britain. Except in Japan, students are getting more representation on top policy-making councils and boards of their institutions. Because they are increasingly called upon to mediate internal disputes, answer to the public for student disturbances, and spearhead planning and innovation, the chief executives of colleges and universities throughout the world are being given

more authority. This movement is most pronounced in countries where these officers have historically been weak—Germany and Japan.

2 In places where faculty-student ratios have traditionally been unfavorable, as in France and Germany, improvement is noticeable. The general range is now between 1:8 and 1:16, with a tendency toward 1:12.

3 In matters of curriculum, there is greater emphasis on a broader liberal education for undergraduates and the development of new disciplines—like sociology and modern biology—and of interdisciplinary schools and programs.

4 There is more financial assistance available for low-income students, and loan programs are being extended to all students under favorable terms.

5 Finally, higher education planning that has characteristically been based upon national manpower requirements is receiving less emphasis, and more students, even in Russia, have more flexibility in choosing the types of institutions they will attend and the programs they will pursue.

It is clear, then, that much is happening in higher education throughout the world. Some of it advances the cause of colleges and universities, and some of it makes progress difficult. Not always so clear is the goal to be sought, the direction to be taken in developing systems of higher education for the future.

The purpose of studying higher education in other countries is not just to observe trends and differences, however. It is most useful as a means of learning how other nations have developed systems of education, have adapted them to the needs of their people, and have devised solutions to problems we Americans face in our own country—if not now, in the very near future. Applying this knowledge to planning higher education in the United States requires, first of all, a rational evaluation of the national systems described. It becomes necessary not only to know what is done but how well it has succeeded.

TESTS OF EF-
FECTIVENESS   To make sound evaluations, we must first have some idea of what constitutes a "good" system. Here we encounter several difficulties. Higher education involves many components and is capable of adjusting to many institutional forms. As a result, no single test can ever be fairly applied.

There are six possible universal tests that must or should be rejected:

1 *The net contribution of higher education to gross national product.* Were it possible to measure the contribution to the gross national product of

higher education and then subtract all the costs to get the net value added, this would be an important test. But as yet it has not been done, and, given the quality of statistics available, it is difficult to do.

2   *The contribution of higher education to the preservation and enhancement of the "cultural heritage."* The French rate this as a leading goal, perhaps *the* leading goal, of their system of education — but, then, they have a great heritage. The test cannot easily be applied to a tribal society trying to modernize, to a highly religious society that uses an "inquisition" to preserve its culture, to a once colonial nation, like India, where the imported higher education system ignored development of the national consciousness, or to a nation that has a rigid ideology that bans controversial thoughts. In short, the effectiveness of the test depends on the cultural heritage.

3   *The development of moral character.* This test, too, depends upon the meaning of what is being measured — in this case *moral character.*

4   *The integration of higher education with the total system of education.* The French and the Russians have prided themselves on having good articulation of all levels of education. The test is valid, however, only if the overall system is good. A poor system may be enabled to become better if it is loosely integrated or even in internal conflict.

5   *The dropout rate.* A system which has open access and which attracts many students with low maturation who just want to try higher education out will, of necessity, have a high dropout rate. On the other hand, an elite system that admits only the most able students to institutions of higher learning may have a very low dropout rate. The determining factor in this dropout rate, however, is not the quality of the institutions but the quality and policies of preparation for and admission to postsecondary institutions.

6   *The consistency of higher education with the surrounding society.* Any system of education must be reasonably consistent with its society. Otherwise, it will be changed or will change its society. In some societies there is much leeway for contrary tendencies, and in others — like Russia — almost none, but the leeway is never total. This is a law, not a test. It is not, of course, advisable for a "bad" society to have a "bad" educational system for the sake of consistency; but it is unlikely that there can be a "good" educational system in a "bad" society.

Rejection of these six tests does not leave us without other useful indexes. There are, in fact, eight tests that are generally useful in evaluating the quality of different higher education systems. They are as follows:

1   *The quality of scholarship in international competition.* This can be judged by the value placed on the published research of a nation's faculties in

worldwide intellectual circles and the general acceptance of the advanced degrees from the country's leading institutions.

2   *The ability to secure talent from the total population without regard to class or racial considerations.* This criterion is influenced by a country's total educational system and not higher education alone. The denial of opportunity in Latin America, for example, occurs at the secondary level. In India, higher education is now within reach of young people from diverse backgrounds. In fact, college education for students from the formerly untouchable castes and some tribal groups is now entirely free.

3   *The provision of technically trained persons to fill the needs of industry, agriculture, government, and the welfare services.*

4   *The provision of an opportunity for a liberal education,* appropriate to the times, to undergraduate students.

5   *The quality and balance of service* (consultation, policy, proposals, and so forth) to the several segments of society. In a developing country, much of this service comes under the heading of modernization; in a developed country, of improvement.

6   *The quality and balance of constructive criticism of society.*

7   *The effectiveness of the governance of higher education.* Ideally, higher education should be able to work out its problems without external interference or dominance or the use of internal force.

8   *The degree of popular support for higher education generally and from its alumni in particular.* Popular support is more meaningful in a democracy than in a one-party system or a dictatorship.

RANKING THE SYSTEMS   None of the countries reviewed in this volume would score high on all of the eight tests suggested. On the provision of service, for instance, none of them would measure up to the performance of higher education in the United States. But for each test, it is possible to indicate which of the systems surveyed rank the highest.

In terms of scholarship, Britian ranks high, but with lacks in certain of the social sciences. Russia also ranks well, but with major deficiencies in both the social sciences and humanities. For a country of its size, Sweden does remarkably well in a number of fields.

In the talent hunt, Canada and Russia rank high, with Australia rising rapidly.

In the training of persons with high-level skills, a number of countries have done well. The French, however, may have concentrated too much on teachers and civil servants and the British too little on business managers. The Russians and the Japanese have made enormous strides forward economically in recent times with the aid of the trained manpower supplied by their systems of higher education. India, by contrast, has supplied more lawyers and teachers and some other types of professionals than her society can absorb at its present stage of economic development.

In the provision of a liberal education, the British system, all levels of education considered, may be the best.

In the quality and balance of services, Sweden and Canada rank high, and Britain and Australia rank well.

In the quality of criticism, Sweden has an outstanding long-term record. Its university professors have had a constructive impact on the improvement of its society, particularly in the area of economic policy. Britain would also rate high. In Russia, the contribution, of necessity, is minimal.

In terms of governance, the British, Canadians, Australians, and Swedes have met their problems with the greatest flexibility, good-will, and pragmatism. Russia has no apparent problems, and there is little way they could become apparent if they do exist. It is the outstanding "law and order" society of those reviewed. Japan, France, and Germany have the greatest problems.

In popular support, there would appear to be the least difficulty today in exactly those countries with the best records in governance —Great Britain, Canada, Australia, and Sweden. Popular support, historically, has been very high in Japan but is declining. That France and Germany are facing difficulties is obvious. It is impossible to know about Russia. One key to popular support under modern conditions is clearly internal harmony.

Future events will undoubtedly change our evaluations of the systems of higher education in these countries. Although no country has yet managed a perfect score—and probably never will —it is clear that all of them are striving for progress and improvement. The chapters which follow indicate the directions and degrees of success.

No system of higher education, once it comes to serve large segments of a population and to cost substantial sums of money, can avoid being evaluated within its own nation by many people from many points of view. Increasingly, also, international comparisons will be made as national planners search out different approaches to common problems. The key question will no longer be *What kinds of systems are there?* but *How effective is each system?* The intent of this chapter has been to suggest ways of determining some of the answers.

2. General Trends in Higher Education in Eight Industrial Countries

Between August 1967, when this project began, and the summer of 1970, when it went to press, its interest—and complexity—mushroomed. France virtually transformed its university system. Japan and Germany, two countries where student violence drew attention to the stark inadequacies of traditional university systems, moved toward fundamental university reform. Britain and two countries whose higher education it partly influenced, Canada and Australia, strengthened nonuniversity institutions of higher education, taking the pressure off universities but also threatening their traditional role. In the last several years, Sweden has instituted reforms at critical points in its university system—in structures, staffing, examinations and degrees, and student participation in governance. The Soviet Union has made an about-face in its earlier emphasis on part-time relative to full-time study and is experiencing mounting pressure to broaden the extremely specialized training offered at higher education institutions. This change could rock the political foundations of the Soviet society by producing graduates more prone to question it.

Since 1950, higher education development in these eight countries has followed similar trends. The size of secondary school age groups and the proportion of them enrolling in university-oriented studies in secondary schools have increased, and the number of young people seeking higher education has multiplied severalfold. Universities in France, Australia, and Germany and the "free" faculties in Swedish universities by tradition automatically accepted all qualified secondary school graduates. They have experienced severe overcrowding, and as of 1969 only the French universities had not resorted to admissions quotas or other measures to restrict enrollment. In countries which place a hurdle between successful completion of academic secondary school and entry to higher education admission has become increasingly selective, and competition for entry is proportionately acute. Even though Australia, Britain, Canada, Japan, and Sweden have doubled their institutional capacities since 1950, they have had difficulty in keeping pace with enrollment demand. In Japan and the Soviet Union admissions pressure is particularly severe because universal secondary school attendance has been achieved rapidly and the higher education systems have accommodated a diminishing proportion of applicants.

Teachers college enrollments have also expanded, and the institutions training elementary school teachers have become more fully postsecondary (secondary school teachers are trained in universities or university-level institutions in all eight countries). Admissions requirements at teachers colleges have gone up, and periods of training have been lengthened. In some countries the teacher training institutions are becoming linked with universities and are more autonomous.

To meet the growing demand for higher education which cannot be handled by universities, six of the eight countries have recently launched or expanded other kinds of institutions. Germany and the Soviet Union have long had alternatives to academic universities.

These new institutions try to provide opportunity for higher education to students who are qualified for it but cannot gain admission to, or continue at, a university. They also try to offer more specialized or technically oriented training than the universities do and to provide higher education at a lower cost than the universities.

In all eight countries what may be called the "massification" of higher education has prompted reconsideration of what the functions of higher education should be. Who should have access? What should they study? Who should decide? Taxpayers, governments, and employers of graduates expect higher education institutions to produce highly trained people needed by the economy, and they call for relevance to social need. Students demand that their higher education be utilitarian not in terms of the world they see but in terms of the world they seek.

The high cost of mass higher education has prompted such questions as these: What should it cost and therefore what should it be? What share of the cost should be borne by students and their parents and by society at large? What share of the gross national prod-

uct should go to higher education? In all eight of the countries
except Japan, most of the costs of higher education are met by public funds. As the level of required support has risen, the institutions fear increasing government intervention in their affairs.
Higher education is not peripheral to society's concerns but essential to national development. Consequently, changes in the last
two decades have required new balances between the autonomy of
the institutions and their public accountability. In Australia,
Canada, and Germany, the three federal states where education
does not fall under the jurisdiction of the national government
but where national governments have moved into the financing of
higher education, there is the additional challenge of channeling
federal funds in ways compatible with the evolving federal-state
relationships.

Escalating enrollment demand and rising costs have prompted
efforts at educational planning. In democratic countries, the expansion of higher education is mainly determined by student
demand. These countries, therefore, try vainly to forecast student
demand and reconcile it with hypotheses about future needs of the
national economy. The basic tools of the democratic countries
include manpower forecasts and counseling mechanisms which
they hope will guide students into fields where the greatest employment needs and opportunities exist. In the Soviet Union students
can, in theory, be directed into priority fields, but as systems for
determining these priorities are inadequate, higher education planning in the Soviet Union has few advantages over that in the West —
and fewer alibis for its miscalculations.

Although student protest is increasing in all eight countries, it
varies in intensity. It occurs in part because of such grievances as
overcrowding within the higher education systems and in part because of the reciprocal reinforcement (and imitation) of student
protest from one country to another. Common to all student protest
is the present cultural revolution, of which it is one element.

The differences between students today and those of a generation
ago are a factor in student unrest. In most of the eight countries
entrants to higher education institutions are a year or more older
than their counterparts 20 years ago. They are therefore more
critical, less authority-oriented, more impatient. Although students
from different occupational segments of society do not enroll in
higher education in proportion to the size of these segments in the
national population, there is a better cross section today. More

than half the students are first-generation college or university matriculants. Their expectations of themselves and of their education are more diverse, unsettled, and pragmatic than those of the previous generation. The fact that higher education enrollments have at least tripled in the eight countries since 1950 also contributes to student unrest by giving students an awareness of their power and by intensifying their sense of alienation and of being engulfed in a faceless crowd.

Still another factor in student unrest is the emergence of the university as a vital instrument of national development. The university interacts with the world around it, and students plunge into this new interaction in pursuance of their own interests. In addition, students increasingly demand that the university be an instrument of social reform and not a tool of Establishment interests.

One last common denominator to higher education in the eight countries is mounting national concern. With the possible exception of the Soviet Union, on which information is limited, the countries either have undertaken or are in the process of preparing major studies of their higher education systems. Several of these studies examine higher education in the context of the higher education system of a given country. Among them are the Robbins Committee Report in Great Britain, the Martin Committee Report in Australia, and current studies in Japan, Canada, and Sweden by the National Institute for Educational Research, the Rowat-Hurtubise Commission, and the 1968 Education Committee, respectively.

Comparisons of different higher education systems are often misleading because of the need to apply common terminology to phenomena which, though seemingly similar, are in fact quite diverse. For example, bachelor's, master's, and doctoral degrees represent different amounts and kinds of education in the context of the British and Australian higher education systems. The foreign terms of the five non-English-language countries studied present additional challenge. Translations are not attempted for words like *Abitur, VUZy,* and *ronin.*

Statistical comparisons are difficult because available data relate to different assumptions and definitions. For example, staff-student ratios are calculated differently by different countries at different times. Recent statistics on seven of the countries were obtained in the course of visits to them, but even so they are not complete. Statistics on the Soviet Union, the one country not visited, are less recent.

3. Higher Education in France

With its "university of masters" at Paris, France provided a widely emulated model for the universities founded in Europe from the end of the twelfth to the middle of the sixteenth century. Only Italy and its famous Bologna were rival influences. Because the European institutions influenced by the University of Paris were themselves emulated by colonial colleges and universities established on other continents, traces of the French liberal arts tradition are found today in the higher education of much of the world.

However, because they were distracted and enfeebled by the civil and religious strife that accompanied the reformation and were abolished by the revolutionary National Convention in 1793, French universities lost much of their medieval luster.

Since the time of Napoleon I, the word *université* has referred to all public education, including primary, secondary, and higher education falling under the Ministry of National Education. Napoleon reorganized the universities into a single national institution directly administered by the government under the Grand Master in Paris. The faculties were not regrouped into universities until 1896. Although they were not independent corporations, they were given legal status and financial autonomy.

While it is still too early to see the total dimension of its impact, the Orientation of Higher Education Act of November 12, 1968,[1] passed in the wake of massive demonstrations of student discontent, provides for sweeping new reforms, many of which are not fully implemented as this chapter is written.

---

[1] See Orientation of Higher Education Act, no. 68–978, November 12, 1968, *Journal Officiel,* November 13, 1968, pp. 10579ff.

COMPONENTS OF THE SYSTEM Virtually all of higher education in France is at the university level. It includes:

1 The 626 unites d'enseignement et de recherche (UER, Education and Research Units) established under the Orientation of Higher Education Act of November 1968. Each UER consists of the professor and other teaching staff members together with students in a single discipline. A UER may choose to combine with several others to form a new university of an interdisciplinary nature. This process was under way in 1969 and was expected to take two or three years to stabilize. About 40 new universities were established in 1968–69.

2 The *grandes écoles* and other engineering schools.

3 Seven private universities, Catholic and Protestant, and various specialized technical establishments and private dental schools.

In addition, there are *grands établissements,* state institutions whose exclusive function is to promote knowledge through research and advanced seminars. Among them are the Collège de France, founded by Francis I in the sixteenth century, the National History Museum, and the Paris Observatory.

Most higher education in France is publicly sponsored; however, private universities and specialized establishments do exist and, under a law of 1959, are entitled to receive state aid.

Although they are under the Directorate of Secondary Education in the Ministry of National Education, special classes for *lycée* graduates preparing for the difficult competitive examinations for entrance to the *grandes écoles* are considered part of higher education. They last for two to three years.

The approximately 175 elementary teacher training institutions, *écoles normales primaires,* are not considered to be at university level. They overlap with upper secondary education and give an additional two years of postsecondary training.

Secondary school teachers are trained at the universities and at higher normal schools (*écoles normales supérieures*). The four higher normal schools are not really secondary training establishments in the usual sense because most of their students, after having passed the *agrégation,* prepare for a doctorate and ultimately go into higher education teaching positions or research.

The Universities France is divided into 23 educational districts known as *académies.* Before the 1968 act, each educational district could have only one public university. These universities embraced the five traditional faculties of law, sciences, humanities (*lettres*), pharmacy, and medicine. Only the University of Strasbourg had faculties of theology (Catholic and Protestant). The basic unit was the faculty, not the university. Also attached to the universities before 1968 was a complex of institutes, scientific and literary colleges, and other facilities. Some of these were attached to faculties; others were attached to universities. Institutes undertook research or offered practical or experimental teaching that could not be given by the traditional faculties. For instance, the only engineering training available at universities was offered by institutes known as ENSI (*écoles nationales supérieures d'ingénieurs*).

Beginning in 1957, and impelled by rising enrollments and congestion at the University of Paris, where one-third of all university students were enrolled, new branches and colleges of universities were set up at some distance from the parent institution. In that year, a faculty of science of the University of Paris was established at Orsay. In 1963, a faculty of humanities opened at Nanterre. Scientific university colleges, literary university colleges, juridical colleges, and medical schools have been established in the new provincial university towns since 1957. These colleges progressively transformed themselves into faculties and became the nucleus of seven new provincial universities that were established before the 1968 reforms. The requirement that educational districts have only one public university was abolished, and today all the *académies* have one university and some have more. These trends toward decentralization culminated in 1968 with the establishment of the UERs. University institutes are now commonly affiliated with these units. Some of the institutes and colleges formerly attached to faculties or universities are now UERs in their own right.

A major objective of the Orientation Act of 1968 was the establishment of multidisciplinary universities rather than new specialized institutions. Most of the universities formed in 1968–69 combine different disciplines, although some UERs in medicine and law were reluctant to join UERs in the social sciences because of the high proportion of student activists enrolled in those fields. One university in Nancy combines science, medicine, pharmacy, engineering, and technology; another combines law, humanities, economics, and commerce. In Grenoble, one university combines the former university faculties of science, pharmacy, and medicine and some science institutes; another combines letters, living languages, and phonetics; and the third combines the social science sections of the former law faculties, letters, political science, business administration, and urban studies.

Private Institutions

Not affected by the 1968 Orientation Act are five Catholic universities, two Protestant institutions, and about two dozen secular establishments run by individuals, professional bodies, and cultural organizations. Because state degrees traditionally have been given only by public higher education institutions, these private establishments not only have offered their own diplomas but also have entered their students for state awards. About two-thirds of their students, until recently, also enrolled in public higher education institutions. In April 1969 the government decreed that second-year diplomas awarded by faculties of law and science at private universities should be recognized as meeting the admission requirements for second- and third-year studies at public institutions. Modifications of the decree in September 1969 accorded such recognition subject to review of the transferring students' examination results by a jury composed of professors from public institutions. There was the possibility, discussed in late 1969, that some students might be required to submit to the regular end-of-year examinations. These new provisions may relieve enrollment pressures caused by university students in law and science who enroll concurrently in private and public institutions.

The Grandes Écoles

Also unaffected by the Orientation Act are the several hundred higher professional schools known as *grandes écoles*.[2] The most prestigious institutions of French higher education, the *grandes écoles* accept less than one-tenth of those who apply for admission and have demanding curricula. About half of their students are in schools under the Ministry of National Education. Foremost among these are the *écoles normales supérieures*. About one-fourth of the students in the *grandes écoles* are in schools under the other ministries, including those of agriculture, defense (the most famous of the *grandes écoles* is the *École Polytechnique*), industry and commerce, public works, and Atomic Energy Commission, and the *Présidence du Conseil*. The remainder are in establishments attached to private organizations. The *grandes écoles* train persons for senior staff positions in government, commerce and industry, and engineering.

[2] Although not all higher professional schools have *grandes écoles* status, they are designated as such in this study.

The Instituts Universitaires de Technologie Established under a 1966 decree, the *instituts universitaires de technologie* (IUTs) constitute a relatively new category of higher education institutions. Five of them began operating on an experimental basis in 1965, and in 1968, 30 IUTs were functioning in 19 *académies.* Their objective is to train people for positions in the upper technician levels in industry and in the tertiary sector to meet shortages of qualified personnel in these fields. In many cases, the IUTs developed out of preexisting post-*lycée* technical training programs. They offer two-year courses leading to a university diploma of technology in such fields as civil engineering, electronics, chemistry and automation, documentation and information techniques, applied biology, and management techniques. Their faculties include not only academics but also practicing professionals. Admission is open to students whose general record is deemed adequate, and half of the students admitted to the IUTs in 1966 did not have the *baccalauréat.*

Despite their shorter study period, different staffing, more flexible entrance requirements, and limited research activity, the IUTs are considered as university level and were converted to UERs by the Orientation Act of 1968. Some have now joined with the new universities. By 1972 it is expected that more than one-fourth of all students at university-level institutions in France will be enrolled in these new establishments.

National Institutes for Applied Sciences Somewhat older than the IUTs but still relatively new are the national institutes for applied sciences (INSAs). The first one was established in Lyon in 1957, and three more have been established since then. Admission is on the basis of the *baccalauréat* or entrance examination. The curriculum is of two kinds: a four-year course leading to an engineering diploma, and a shorter, more practical course of technical training leading to a certificate. These institutions were also converted to UERs in 1968.

New and Experimental Institutions Since the enactment of the Orientation Act, several new and experimental institutions of higher education have been established. The Institut Supérieur des Affaires, an advanced business school created by the Paris Chamber of Commerce and Industry, is patterned after American business schools. The university of sciences and techniques in Lille has close relations with local industry and teaches practical as well as theoretical knowledge. The experimental university center at Vincennes combines many features drawn from the American system: teaching organized on the basis of semesters and credits, a department structure, interdisciplinary studies, the substitution of small classes and discussion groups for the traditional large lectures (*cours magistrales*), grading based on class participation and written work, extensive audio-visual teaching assistance, and significant enrollments of adults and professional people in evening and Saturday afternoon courses. Vincennes also enrolls large numbers of non-*bacheliers,* and many of its teaching staff members are nonacademics and foreigners. Nurseries are provided for the children of both students and employees of this new center.

FUNCTIONS Increasingly, the functions of public university-level institutions extend beyond the training of people for the professions and for *lycée* teaching. About half of the research and development efforts in France are now carried out in the public sector by the UERs and *grandes établissements* and by institutes and centers of the Centre National de la Recherche Scientifique (CNRS). The CNRS promotes fundamental research, sponsoring it in its own centers, subsidizing many scientific workers in UERs, and seconding many of its staff members to industry and UER laboratories. Funds allocated in the annual budget to the CNRS doubled between 1962 and 1966. Allocations for university research increased tenfold between 1958 and 1966.

In the past, technical training was provided mainly by the Conservatoire National d'Arts et Métiers of Paris and its provincial centers and various professional schools, including INSA. It is an increasingly significant responsibility of university-level institutions, especially as a result of the establishment of the IUTs.

Engineering training has long been a function of the *grandes écoles,* the *écoles nationales supérieures des arts et métiers,* and other specialized institutions. Since 1947, however, when certain institutes attached to universities were transformed into higher engineering schools (ENSI), increasing numbers of engineers have been trained in these establishments.

The universities have played only a limited role in adult vocational education, although institutions associated with some of the universities offer part-time courses lasting three to four years and leading, in some cases, to an engineering diploma. Enrollments in these institutions, called *instituts de promotion supérieure du travail,* exceeded 4,000 in 1966–67. But the preponderance of adult education has been offered by government and private organizations. The 1968 Orientation of Higher Education Act calls on universities to strengthen their adult education programs in professional fields, and the University Center at Vincennes has been particularly active in this area.

ENROLLMENT TRENDS Statistics on higher education enrollments in France vary considerably. Some of them do not take into account the fact that about one-third of students in the *grandes écoles* and two-thirds of those in private universities enroll concurrently in faculties of the national universities (now UERs) so that they can attend certain lectures or prepare for state examinations. In the national universities, some students enroll concurrently in more than one faculty, and in 1968–69 an estimated 25,000 were in more than one UER. Moreover, some statistics do not include so-called nonenrolled students. These students have enrolled in courses given in university faculty institutes but not in the faculties and have constituted about 5 percent of all university enrollments. Another complication is that an estimated one-fifth of all students enrolled in sciences, humanities, and law are not effectively present. Many of these nonstudents *(étudiants fantômes)* enroll only so they can obtain economic benefits available to students. Others enroll but cannot attend most of their classes because they are working, usually as teachers.

Enrollments[3] in French universities increased from about 134,000 (enrolled only) in 1950–51 to about 500,000 in 1967–68 (enrolled and nonenrolled) and to about 650,000 in 1969–70 including the new UERs. About 30 percent of the total increase results from an expansion in the 20-year-old age group—612,900 in 1964–65 and expected to reach 851,700 in 1969–70 (Commissariat Général du Plan d'Équipement et de la Productivité, 1965, p. 37). The rest was largely the result of the increased proportion of the age group obtaining the *baccalauréat* or equivalent qualification. The proportion of women students has increased from about one-third to more than two-fifths since 1950–51.

Since 1950, enrollments in the *lycées* have tripled, and reforms in secondary education have extended the opportunity to socioeconomic groups previously little represented in higher education. The

---

[3] The statistics presented in this chapter attempt to include nonenrolled as well as enrolled students. They include foreign students unless otherwise specified but do not, unless specified, take account of double inscriptions. Nonstudents are also included.

proportion of working class and farm family children going to *lycées* or their equivalent has more than doubled since the early 1950s. The extension of compulsory schooling to age 16 in 1969–70 is resulting in a still larger percentage of students staying in school after that age. The number of *lycée* graduates has more than tripled since 1950 (Table 1), and the proportion of 18- to 23-year-olds enrolled in higher education is about 2½ times as large as it was in 1956–57 (Table 3). It is expected to reach 15.03 percent in 1972-73. A new system of university entrance examinations and simplification of admissions procedures for non-*bacheliers* is scheduled to go into effect in 1970. These changes are expected to further increase higher education enrollments in the 1970s.

According to a projection made in 1965, enrollment for 1972–73 will be 792,000 students, including 49,000 foreign students (Commissariat Général du Plan d'Équipement et de la Productivité, 1965, p. 40). Student capacity of the universities and *grandes écoles* in 1972 was projected to be 540,000, or 85,000 fewer places than students at that time. The students not enrolled at universities and *grandes écoles* are expected to be enrolled in the IUTs and in preparatory classes leading to *grandes écoles* (Commissariat Général du Plan d'Équipement et de la Productivité, 1965, pp. 63, 95).

TABLE 1 *Preparation and entrance of students in university-level institutions*

	1950–51	1955–56	1960–61	1964–65	1967–68
Percent of 15- to 17-year-olds in long-cycle (university preparatory) secondary education			22.6[a]	27.0[a]	32.6[a]
Baccalaureats awarded	31,700[b]	40,100[b]	61,100[b]	96,900[c]	169,300[d]
Bacheliers as a percentage of 18-year-olds	5.1[e]		10.9[e]	11.4[f]	19.9[f]
New entrants in public universities (not including grandes écoles)	23,600[b]	26,000[b]	45,600[b]		111,700[f]
New entrants in university-level institutions as percentage of 18- and 19-year olds (including grandes écoles)	4.6[g]		9.1[g]		14.7[f]

SOURCES: (a) Commissariat Général du Plan d'Équipement et de la Productivité, 1965, p. 32. (b) Rose Knight, "Trends in University Entry: An Inter-country Comparison," in *Social Objectives in Educational Planning,* OECD, Paris, 1967, p. 204. (c) Information supplied by the Ministry of National Education. (d) Ministry of National Education, France, *Informations Statistiques,* no. 95, September 1967. (e) Poignant, 1965, p. 78. (f) Raymond Poignant, communication to Carnegie Commission on Higher Education, October 1969. (g) Seymour Harris, "Student Financing and Enrollment in Higher Education," in *Financing of Education for Economic Growth,* OECD, Paris, 1966, p. 230.

TABLE 2   *Enrollment in higher education in France by type of institution*

	1955–56	1960–61	1965–66	1967–68	1972–73*
Preparatory classes for grandes écoles	15,125[a]	21,038[a]	24,814[b]		37,000[c]
Public universities	152,246[d]	214,672[d]	413,756[b]	494,063[e]	625,000[f]
Ministry of National Education grandes écoles	14,209[a]	20,951[a]	29,000[g]†		
Private universities	8,618[h]	12,500[h]			
IUTs				5,379[e]	125,000

*Estimated.

† An additional 14,000 students were enrolled in private *grandes écoles* in 1965-66. An estimated additional 15,000 were enrolled in private *grandes écoles* in 1966-67.

SOURCES: (a) Von Rundstedt, 1965, p. 18; includes French and French Community students in *grandes écoles* under the Ministry of National Education only. (b) Ministry of National Education, France, *Informations Statistiques,* no. 95, September 1967. Public classes only. (c) Commissariat Général du Plan d'Équipement et de la Productivité, 1965, p. 71. (d) Ministry of National Education, France, *Informations Statistiques,* no. 86, November 1966. Excludes nonenrolled students 1955-56 but includes them for 1960-61. (e) Ministry of National Education. (f) Commissariat Général du Plan d'Équipement et de la Productivité, 1965, pp. 63, 95. (g) Information supplied by French Office of Cultural Affairs, New York. (h) French Office of Cultural Affairs, *Education in France,* New York, October 1964, p. 18.

The percentage of all university students enrolled at the University of Paris decreased from 43.9 in 1950 to 32.5 in 1962-63. Before the enactment of the Orientation Act this proportion was expected to be 26 percent in 1973 (Commissariat Général du Plan d'Équipement et de la Productivité, 1965, p. 51).

Except in medicine and pharmacy, university students now begin with a two-year first cycle, receiving a diploma at the end of it.[4] In the second cycle, they may either study one year for the *licence,* or two years for the *maitrise,* a new degree required for entry into the third cycle. This third cycle is research-oriented and involves one year of preparation for the *agrégation,* two years toward a third-cycle doctorate, or longer for the *doctorat d'état,* the highest academic degree offered.

In the new first cycle defined by 1966 reforms, examinations are required at the end of the first and second years, thus introducing an organization of studies based on years rather than certificates.

The 1966 reforms also permit students who have a dean's approval to enroll as part-time students, taking two years for each year

[4] *L'Année Propédeutique* was eliminated in 1966 because of high failure rates at its conclusion and because it encouraged students to prolong study periods in order to pass examinations.

Year	Percent
1956-57	4.19
1960-61	5.24
1967-68	10.71
1972-73*	15.03

*Estimated.

SOURCE: Commissariat Général du Plan d'Équipement et de la Productivité, 1965.

in the first cycle if they need to do so because of their salaried professional activities. The new arrangement makes it easier for working students to attend the university. Another democratizing reform permits students to enter without the *baccalauréat* on the basis of special examinations. Admission in the sciences has been tightened up by requiring students entering those faculties to have mathematical training at the *lycée.*

A major concern of education planners in France is the need to increase the numbers of engineers and scientists that are trained. Enrollment in engineering schools and *grandes écoles* is projected to reach about 28,000 in 1972–73 (Commissariat Général du Plan d'Équipement et de la Productivité, 1965, p. 41). Establishment of the IUTs, it was hoped, would increase the proportion of all university students enrolled in the sciences to 42 percent (Commissariat Général du Plan d'Équipement et de la Productivité, 1965, pp. 62, 95), but only little more than one-fifth were enrolled in science in 1968, and it is unlikely that the 1972 goal will be achieved.

Persistence   The success rate for the *grandes écoles* and universities together in 1956–57 was about 57 percent. For the universities alone in the early 1960s it was 35 to 45 percent with the propedeutical year and 75 to 85 percent excluding it (Poignant, 1965, pp. 196–97). About 95 percent of the students who enter the *grandes écoles* complete their courses.

Study Periods   Until the reforms of 1966, study for the *licence* required three to four years, but many students spent five years or longer preparing for it. It takes four years, with examinations at the end of each year, to earn a first degree in law and economics. In 1960, the course for doctor of medicine was extended from five to six years. Courses in dental surgery and pharmacy each require five years.

Since 1966, study periods in the first cycle of university study in the sciences and humanities have been reduced to a maximum of three years because only one reexamination is now permitted in the two-year cycle. Since there is no such regulation for the second cycle, the two-year period may be exceeded. Study periods can also be extended in some disciplines because students who have enrolled in one faculty subsequently enroll in another.

In the *grandes écoles,* the study periods tend to be fixed. The curricula are structured, and repetition is not permitted.

Staff-Student Ratios

The size of the teaching staff at public universities increased from 7,901 in 1960–61 to 22,243 in 1967–68.[5] Between 1960 and 1967, the number of senior assistants *(maîtres-assistants)* and assistants increased from 4,549 to 16,044, or from about 57 percent to about 72 percent of the total teaching staff (*moniteurs,* advanced students who assist with classes devoted to practical work, are excluded from these figures). Professors and *maîtres de conference* teach three hours weekly, *maîtres-assistants* and *chefs de travaux* teach 7½ hours, and assistants teach 8 hours.

The university staff-student ratio in 1960 was 1:30 overall with variations from 1:14 in medicine to 1:51 in the law faculties (Robbins Committee, 1963, p. 70). The Commission d'Équipement cited the ratio in 1964-65 as 1:27.7, somewhat lower than the official goal of 1:15.9 (Commissariat Général du Plan d'Équipement et de la Productivité, 1965, p. 141).

In the *grandes écoles,* the ratio is about 1:3, and in the IUTs, it was 1:17.6 in 1966-67.

Projections of the Commission de l'Équipement have indicated that by 1972 there will be 37,445 university (UER) teaching staff members, about 17,000 more than there were in 1967–68 (Commissariat Général du Plan d'Équipement et de la Productivité, 1965, p. 141). This goal will be difficult to achieve without a substantial increase in the rate at which new teaching positions, particularly at the levels of *assistants* and *maîtres-assistants,* are created. While all teaching positions do not require the *doctorat d'état,* the supply of teaching staff with this qualification should increase as a result of reforms to decrease the time required to obtain it.

In the humanities, new teaching staff members are being recruited increasingly from among the *agrégés* teachers at the *lycées.* This practice is criticized, however, for lowering teaching standards

[5] Information supplied by the French Ministry of National Education.

and weakening the traditional unity between the *lycée* and university, linked in the past by the common body of *agrégés* teaching in both.

Prior to a decree published in the *Journal Officiel* of June 7, 1969, universities could not recruit teaching staff outside of the university system except for a special category, associate professor. The requirements that nonuniversity personnel recruited as associate professors teach full time, that they be recruited only at that level, and that their contracts be renewed annually have also limited the numbers recruited by the universities. Of the approximately 200 associate professors recruited in 1968–69, the majority were foreigners. The 1969 decree makes it possible to recruit nonuniversity personnel to teach at a variety of levels, to teach part time, and under contracts of longer duration than before, provided their number does not exceed 5 percent of full professors.

HIGHER EDUCATION AND CIVIL GOVERNMENT

Before November 1968, public higher education in France was almost completely centralized. The national government appointed professors, determined curricula, set examinations, and decided on the expansion of facilities and the magnitude and allocation of financial support. The universities were essentially a loose federation of mutually isolated faculties held together almost more by their common relationship to the Ministry of National Education than by their own central administrations.

One of the aims of the Orientation of Higher Education Act was to decentralize this system. The basic technique, as mentioned previously, was to break the faculties and their branches into small "education and research units," similar to departments in American universities. These are now coming together into independent and multidisciplinary universities and other "public institutions of a scientific nature." There were nearly 50 of these in the fall of 1969, and it was expected that there would be between 10 and 50 more by 1970. Reorganization of universities under the Orientation of Higher Education Act lagged conspicuously in the Paris area, and in early 1970 the Minister of Education made special efforts to speed reform there, setting a deadline of March 10 for the submission of proposals by Paris university administrators.

On March 20, 1970, the Minister of National Education announced the reorganization of universities in the Paris area. The plan called for replacing the five traditional faculties of the University of Paris with thirteen new universities, seven in central Paris, four in the suburbs, and two based on the existing institutions at Dauphine and Vincennes. The constituent UERs of the Sorbonne were to become three separate universities and the faculty of law and economics two universities. By January 1971 the faculties are to transfer all their powers, especially their financial authority, to the new universities.

All public higher education institutions except the *grandes écoles,* which fall under the other ministries, are still under the Ministry of National Education. But the Ministry's authority is sharply limited. A new National Board of Higher Education and Research (replacing an advisory body called the *Conseil Supérieur de l'Édu-cation Nationale)* has been established to plan the organization of higher education and research. One-third of its members are laymen who represent major national interests. They are chosen by elec-toral colleges consisting of the faculty and student members of the boards of the institutions. The National Board's work is done in part by 47 sections which represent groupings of academic disci-plines. The Ministry of National Education consults the new board on the financing of higher education institutions, on coordination between them, and on other important matters.

Within the *académies,* new regional boards of higher education whose composition parallels that of the National Board have mainly coordinating and advisory functions. The university rector presides over the regional board and represents the Ministry of National Education to the governing bodies of higher institutions that fall under the Ministry and are located in his *académie.* He may, for serious reasons, suspend the deliberations of these bodies pending a decision by the Ministry. Under the 1968 reforms, the university rector has become more an agent of the Ministry than of the univer-sity. Within the university, the rector is no longer the chief adminis-trative and executive official. The Orientation Act assigned this role to the president, a new position which cannot be held con-currently by the rector.

During the first year of the Orientation Act there was some doubt that the new UERs and universities would, in fact, be able to exer-cise the autonomy enshrined as a basic principle of the measure. If the state continued, for instance, to reserve the right to rule on degrees, programs, and examinations, the scope for autonomy would indeed be limited. In April 1969 a decree aimed at increasing the flexibility of faculties and university centers was accompanied by a government circular which proposed eliminating sociology as a field of concentration in first-cycle studies. Subsequent develop-ments made it clear that this circular was only making a recom-mendation, not setting forth a requirement, but the episode under-scored concern over the degree of autonomy that the UERs and university actually could claim in curriculum matters. Some ob-servers also see a contradiction in the fact that universities and UERs can exercise autonomy in their curricula and teaching meth-ods while a system continues of national diplomas, which requires each higher education unit to recognize diplomas awarded by other units despite differences in curricula and educational approaches. Others complain that the veritable avalanche of government decrees and rulings issued in 1968–69 seemed to render the basic princi-ples of autonomy and participation meaningless.

Despite such controls and influences, professors in France have great freedom. Within the limits of tolerance and objectivity, they can express themselves on any matter, including the current polit-ical regime, without fear of reprimand or adverse effects on their academic careers. Cases of academic discipline are judged by uni-versity tribunals and not by political authorities.

The Orientation Act did not enlarge the authority of higher educa-tion institutions with respect to research, and the act states ex-plicitly that its provisions do not affect the role of the CNRS. The only university research affected by the 1968 act is basic research "conducted . . . with a view towards maintaining education at the highest level of knowledge."

INTERNAL
GOVERNMENT
OF
INSTITUTIONS

The Orientation Act drastically changed the internal governance of higher education institutions. In the pre-reform system the rector was the chief executive but had little authority. Such authority as was held by the institutions lay with the faculties, especially with the holders of chairs. The basic unit of the university was the indi-vidual full professor, with his institute or laboratory, who was free to determine how to teach what he taught. Attempts to curtail the autonomy of professors and to coordinate their teaching and re-search in related disciplines by grouping chairs together into depart-ments made little headway. Student participation in university governance was marginal.

The Orientation Act enthroned autonomy and participation as key principles in the governance of higher education institutions. The chief governing units now are elected boards with no more than 80 members, and presidents. The boards are composed of faculty members, researchers, students, and nonteaching staff, plus a number of laymen who constitute between one-sixth and one-third of the board. The number of faculty representatives must at least equal that of student representatives, and a minimum of 60 percent of the faculty representatives must hold or be qualified for professorships or be *agrégés* who are recognized as qualified to teach in the institutions. The UERs have comparable boards with a maximum of 40 members. Representatives of the university and unit boards are elected by electoral colleges through secret ballot. Students may not vote in the elections of more than one education and research unit, and if less than 60 percent of enrolled students vote in an election, their representation on the board decreases proportionately. The Orientation Act provides that the composition of electoral colleges be defined later by government decree.

The university president is elected by the university board for a five-year term, and he cannot be immediately reelected. The legal representative of the institution, he cannot concurrently be director of a UER. If he is not a full professor, he must be elected by a two-thirds vote and approved by the Ministry of National Education. Among the functions of the president are the maintenance of order within the institution and authorization of expenditures as set forth in its budget.

Directors of UERs are elected for three years. If they are not chosen from among persons holding or qualified for professorships, or if they are not *agrégés* recognized as qualified to teach in the institution, they must receive a two-thirds vote of the unit board and approval of the Ministry before appointment.

In outlining the new governance system the Orientation Act set certain important limits to the autonomy of the boards of the UERs, the universities, and regional boards. Teaching staff members are chosen by other teaching staff, not by boards, and the national government still determines examination levels. Decision making in research concentrated in the CNRS is not affected by the new legislation. In contrast to the education and research units, research centers include on their boards only professors and *agrégés,* other researchers of these levels, and persons chosen for their scientific competence. The electoral colleges of research centers can include and elect only faculty, researchers, and third-cycle students who are already engaged in research. Only the science boards of the research centers can determine research curricula and the distribution of funds in these centers.

By April 1969 elections had been held in 534 of the 626 UERs. Some 65 percent of these institutions represent 67 percent of all students. The participation rate of students in the election varied from 42 percent in letters and 43 percent in sciences to 68 percent in medicine and pharmacy and 77 percent in university institutes of technology. Although the 60 percent participation prescribed by the act as the quorum was not achieved by most faculties, the student participation rate was considered relatively high, particularly because leftist student organizations had urged a student boycott of the elections.

The first elections to the councils of the UERs exceeded the expectations of some observers and failed the hopes of others. What was important was the spirit in which they were held. Most students, including leftists, participated despite the boycott recommended by leftist organizations. The anarchy predicted by the pessimists did not reign.

FINANCING HIGHER EDUCATION
Between 1958 and 1968, public expenditures on universities went up from about F 520 billion to F 3,375 billion. Of this amount, capital expenditures rose from about F 211 billion to F 961.7 billion, and recurrent expenses increased from F 309 billion to F 2,414 billion. Public expenditures on higher education as a proportion of the gross national product increased from 0.21 percent in 1958 to 0.5 percent in 1965. Between 80 and 90 percent of all expenditures on higher education in France are publicly financed.

Private institutions are financed mainly by student fees but receive some state funds to help them meet operating expenditures. In 1961, the budget of private universities was less than 5 percent of the total expenditures on higher education (Garcia, 1966, p. 157).[6]

The cost per student increased from F 1,062 in 1955 (Harris, 1966, 271)[7] to F 4,980 in 1965.[8]

In its 1966 report, the Commission de l'Équipement indicated a need for a F 6,305 billion investment in higher education between 1966 and 1970. When the government indicated that resources were too limited to meet that goal, the commission reduced its estimate to F 4,820 billion. Within that amount, it recommended

[6] All figures are in new francs.

[7] The cost per student varies among faculties. According to the Ministry of National Education, in 1963 the cost per student in the humanities was F 1,739 while it was F 4,952 in the sciences.

[8] Information supplied by UNESCO; United Nations, *Statistical Yearbook,* 1965.

TABLE 4
Public expenditures for higher education in France (in millions of new francs)

	1958	1960	1965	1968
Capital expenditures	211,510	400,800	733,000	961,700
Recurrent expenditures	309,141	554,539	1,608,168	2,414,185
TOTAL	520,651	955,339	2,341,168	3,375,885

SOURCE: Information supplied by Ministry of National Education.

allocation of F 47 billion to preparatory classes, F 1,255 billion to the IUTs and normal schools, and F 3,013 billion to the engineering schools. The total amount is a 150 percent increase over the sums authorized for expenditure between 1962 and 1965.

STUDENT FINANCE

Students attending a public university, UER, or other higher education institution in their home academy may apply for stipends accompanied by a waiver of fees. These fees, including tuition, were raised to F 140 per year as of 1969–70 but are not charged to holders of scholarships. In 1968-69 a total of 130,000 students in all higher education received scholarships. This number was expected to rise to 144,000 in 1969-70. In 1965, the maximum stipend for a student living away from home and receiving no financial aid from his family was F 2,664 for the first cycle, F 3,411 for the second, and F 4,230 for the third (Commissariat Général du Plan d'Équipement et de la Productivité, 1965, p. 161).

Interest-free loans, available to students with good scholastic records and suitable health reports, are repayable 10 years after the borrower completes his studies. The value of student loans increased from F 339,980 in 1950 to F 1.5 million in 1960 but still represented only a small fraction of total direct student aid (von Rundstedt, 1965, p. 92).

Students in the *écoles normales supérieures* in some other *grandes écoles,* and in teacher training programs in the *instituts de préparation à l'enseignement secondaire* (IPES) established in faculties of letters and faculties of science in 1957 obtain the equivalent of civil service trainee salaries if they commit themselves to 10 years of state employment after obtaining their qualifications. Public service scholarships *(bourse de service publique)* are offered to students in law, medicine, and pharmacy who commit themselves to public service for 5 to 10 years after obtaining their qualifications.

Other forms of student aid include subsidized meals in university restaurants, low-cost student housing for those students who can be accommodated in it, low-cost social security and health programs, low-cost travel of various kinds, and tax reductions for students' parents.

The percentage of students living in university residences increased from 8.4 in 1955 (von Rundstedt, 1965, p. 43) to 15 percent in 1965 (Commissariat Général du Plan d'Équipement et de la Productivité, 1965, p. 156). A goal of housing 25 percent by 1972 has been postponed for lack of funds.

The proportion of students who can take advantage of the low-cost meals in university restaurants reached 37.5 percent in 1962. Financial limitations have postponed plans to increase this proportion to 75 percent.

Students also benefit through the social security system (health insurance) paid for in modest contributions to the Mutuelle Générale des Étudiants de France, an offshoot of the National Union of French Students, which is heavily subsidized by the state.

A study conducted by the Mutuelle Générale des Étudiants de France showed that in 1964 about half of student expenditures in higher education institutions were financed by the students' families. Because the proportion of students in secondary schools who come from less affluent sectors of society is low, it is also low in institutions of higher education. In 1965, only 6.3 percent of the students in public higher education came from families categorized as agriculturalists and agricultural laborers (UNESCO, 1967, p. 104), and 9.5 percent came from manual worker families. The proportion of students from families headed by professional men, senior executives and intermediate management, and supervisory personnel decreased slightly, from 47.1 percent of all students in 1960 to 45.5 percent in 1965 (UNESCO, 1967, pp. 104–105).

STUDENTS Before the 1968 Orientation Act, student governance at French universities was typically organized on a faculty rather than university basis. Student representatives in each faculty were elected to negotiate with the university council and to sit on those committees (dealing with student discipline, for example) which included student representation. Student representation now is at the UER, university, regional board, and national board levels.

The principal national student organization is the Union of French Students (UNEF). After World War II, this organization attempted to operate as a trade union, pressuring the government to improve conditions within the universities and supporting programs to benefit its members. These included low-cost student insurance, cultural activities, job placement, informational services, reading rooms and libraries, and even the reproduction of lecture notes for students unable to attend overcrowded classes.

Until 1961, when UNEF organized large-scale demonstrations against the government's policy in Algeria, it received government subvention. After 1961, these subventions were given to a rival student organization, the Fédération Nationale des Étudiants de France (FNEF), which supported the government position. Although enrollment doubled between 1961 and 1968, membership in UNEF decreased by half, standing at about 50,000 in 1968. UNEF was also torn by internal disagreements between leftist factions in its leadership.

The intense and prolonged student disturbances of May 1968 drew attention to the inadequacy of the limited reforms that had been instituted in the previous few years. The UNEF played a leadership role in this disturbance although it was only one of the student groups involved. The others included the FNEF and the militant rightist *Orient,* whose violent encounter with leftist students at Nanterre in early May 1968 precipitated the closing of the faculty of humanities there. There were also several small leftist groups, including the anarchist movement of March 22, which led the initial disturbances at Nanterre; the Marxist-Leninist Union of Communist Students, which is theoretically linked to the Communist Party but in practice defies it; the Federation of Student Revolutionaries, which broke off from the Union of Communist Students; and the pro-Maoist and pro-Cuba Young Communist Revolutionaries. The fractionalization of these leftist movements and their inability to agree on positive goals for higher education or for society in general has made it virtually impossible for the government or university authorities to negotiate with them on a national basis.

On July 23, 1968, the new Minister of National Education, Edgar Faure, in addressing the National Assembly said that the May disturbances were the result of a "profound malaise" caused by "a faculty educational system that had become intolerable." His speech paved the way for reforms that resulted in greater democratization of access to higher education and an end to the universities' isolation from the rest of society.

At the same time that the government announced major reforms, it also indicated that it would not tolerate further student disruption. The Minister of Education announced that scholarships and military deferments of students would be withdrawn if the events of May 1968 were repeated. Student rallies and marches were forbidden. Since mid-December 1968, student militants and agitators have been threatened with summary expulsion from universities.

Student participation in institutional governance, as has been noted, was fairly strong in the early elections. But its success is in doubt. After elections held in June 1968 at the Institut d'Anglais of the Faculty of Letters of the former University of Paris, 18 students announced their resignation, objecting that they had no control over the execution or enforcement of decisions, especially when money was involved. They also protested against being held responsible for decisions with which they did not agree and commented that they had not participated in some of the decisions, such as faculty appointments, because of the lack of knowledge of the matters discussed. In a new election held in March 1969 only one-fourth of the students voted, and professors gained in representation on the council. In May 1969 the FNEF announced its intention to withdraw from the councils of the UERs. The reasons given were the councils' time-consuming discussions on trivial and irrelevant matters, their lack of jurisdiction in significant areas of concern still decided by the Ministry of National Education, and their failure to act with respect to the constitution of new universities, reformation of procedures for recruiting university staff, and adoption of planned priorities for improving material conditions of higher education institutions before they resumed in the fall of 1969.

In early 1969, UNEF Renewal, a relatively moderate Communist-sponsored faction of the UNEF initiated mainly by faculty of law students, appeared to be gaining ground among student protestors, and the more extreme students were being isolated. By then, the French were also learning to accept student strikes and sit-ins as a continuing phenomenon. The year 1968–69 was relatively calm as far as student unrest was concerned, but in 1969–70 student unrest began to increase. No single leader of leftist forces emerged, and the various leftist groups appeared to compete with each other. A general student impatience with the slow progress of reform was evident together with an inclination on the part of some leftist groups to sabotage contemplated reforms before they were agreed to; in short the outlook in 1969–70 was still uncertain.

CHANGES AND REFORMS Reforms that began in 1966 with the structuring of first- and second-cycle courses in the humanities and science faculties are still too new to evaluate, and the still newer reforms under the Orientation Act of 1968 will not be fully implemented until 1970 or even later.

In general the new reforms are aimed at modernizing curricula, reducing class size, and encouraging closer contact between teachers and students. For the first time faculty are required to live in the vicinity of their university or UER (in the past, many faculty members lived in Paris and commuted to their provincial universities). In 1968–69, the former universities were preoccupied with setting up the new system of UERs and electing their governing bodies. Reforms in curriculum and many other matters would have to await the completion of these changes. The control of the Ministry of Education over faculty appointments, promotion, curricula, examinations, discipline, and the allocation of public funds within higher education has been diminished although, as noted previously, the extent of decentralization is not yet clear.

Establishment of a new qualification (degree), the *maîtrise,* has caused concern that it might debase the traditional *agrégation.* The *agrégation* has, in fact, lost some of its significance as the usual qualification for *lycée* and university teachers at the level of *assistant* or *maître-assistant.* Some people argue, moreover, that the new *maîtrise* program does not adequately prepare secondary school teachers because it is too specialized and oriented mainly toward research. As Minister of National Education in 1968–69, Faure announced plans to do away with the *agrégation* and CAPES (Certificat d'Aptitude Pédagogique à l'Énseignement du Second Degré), but when Olivier Guichard became Minister of Education in June 1969, he withdrew these plans, stating that examinations for these awards would continue in 1969–70 but might still be changed after further study.

Pre-1968 reforms seemed to be developing a two-tiered scheme in which the first cycle would have relatively low persistence rates, high staff-student ratios, and an emphasis on teaching, while the second and third cycles would feature more research, close staff-student relations, and grooming of the intellectual elite. The 1968 reforms appear to give somewhat more emphasis to the demand for higher education than to the trained manpower needs of the nation as interpreted by planning bodies.[9]

---

[9] Article 22 of the Orientation Act urges that students be counseled on the relationship between their studies and career possibilities and that there be reciprocal adaptation between university curricula and the professional opportunities for university graduates.

HIGHER EDUCATION AND ECONOMIC PLANNING

France is now in its fifth four-year plan for social and economic development. The main planning body in education is the Commission de l'Équipement Scolaire, Universitaire et Sportif, which advises the Commissariat Général du Plan. Working closely with the Manpower Commission and other agencies, the Commission de l'Équipement estimates future needs for trained manpower. Beginning with the plan for 1962-1965, the commission also attempted to determine the proportion of students in higher education that should be enrolled in the various disciplines. It recommended, for example, that 42 percent of all university-level students be enrolled in science and technology by 1970. Using formulas involving capital costs per student, staff-student ratios, and enrollment demand, the commission sets targets for enrollment, makes recommendations on staff recruitment, and estimates the capital investment needed during the period covered by the plan. These recommendations are modified on the basis of available resources. The recommendations of the commission are submitted to the government which makes the final decisions submitted by the Commissariat Général du Plan to parliament.

The Commission de l'Équipement includes officials from the Ministry of National Education and other ministries that control schools affected by planning. Other members are the High Commissioner for Youth and Sports, and representatives of universities, teachers' associations, labor and employers' organizations, and parent associations. It has no direct responsibility for implementation of the plan that is ultimately adopted, as this is the role of the Ministry of Education, but it is responsible for making annual evaluations of its operation.

Planning Research

At the highest government level research planning is coordinated through the Committee of Ministers for Scientific and Technical Research. The prime minister is this committee's presiding officer. The committee is assisted by an Advisory Committee for Scientific and Technical Research made up of 12 scientists. The Committee of Ministers and the Advisory Committee are both served by the same secretariat, the General Delegation for Scientific and Technical Research (DGRST), which assembles all requests for funds for research (excluding military and nuclear research) into what is known as the "research block vote." This compendium is studied by the Advisory Committee before it is submitted to the Committee of Ministers.

The Commissariat Général du Plan includes a Commission on Scientific and Technical Research which prepares proposals for national science policy and makes recommendations for equipment and capital expenditures for public civil scientific research. Its recommendations are submitted by the commissariat to the Advisory Committee, which reviews them for submission to the Committee of Ministers. The members of the Advisory Committee are also members of the planning commission of the Commissariat du Plan. The general *rapporteur* of the commisson is the General Delegation for Scientific and Technical Research. Thus, the medium-term programs (five-year plan) and the annual programs (budgets) are closely examined. Since the Fourth Plan, 1962–1965, research has been given high priority in national social and economic planning.

THE BALANCE SHEET The principal difficulties confronting French higher education have stemmed from the inability of the traditional, centralized university system to cope with burgeoning enrollments, overcrowding, low staff-student ratios, diminishing time for professors to pursue research, inadequate supervision of students, protracted study periods, low survival rates, compartmentalization of knowledge, and resistance to new teaching techniques or new fields of knowledge. The system of faculty chairs and the dominance of individual professors over research institutes and laboratories is viewed by some critics as being responsible for many of these difficulties.

In 1966, a national colloquium of 300 reform-minded professors and higher education officials in Caen formulated a series of principles urging decentralization, diversity, and competition. Specifically, the colloquium also called for:

- Replacing professorial chairs and segregated faculties with departments headed by elected professors
- Appointing professors to the university instead of to a faculty
- Replacing the state-supported rector with a president elected by a professoriate
- Diversifying the sources of funds for research
- Developing closer associations between universities and industry in research
- Strengthening teacher education
- Expanding continuing education

The more radical of these recommendations were implemented in the reforms legislated in the fall of 1968.

The strengths of French higher education prior to 1968 were the reverse side of its weaknesses. Centralized administration assured equal standards at all public universities and made possible the relatively rapid introduction of comprehensive nationwide reforms. The liberty of the professor to determine how he teaches and to express his views gave him an academic freedom seldom equaled anywhere. The complex and increasingly detailed system for educational planning increasingly related higher education development to national economic growth. The training offered by the best of the *grandes écoles* assured a continuing flow of highly trained manpower to staff top positions in government and industry. And, finally, the research phase of French university education offered qualified students the opportunity for study in depth and for significant participation in the advancement of knowledge.

In less than a year, France moved rapidly to transform its higher education system. Some critics, however, note that the new structures of the UERs in effect permit the former faculties and the dominance by the professors to survive. An increasing number of critics have, in fact, called the reform legislation a failure because of the opposition to it of many university staff and the lack of student participation in new structures. Realizing the goals of the new legislation depends in the last analysis upon more substantial funding for higher staff-student ratios, enlarged facilities, and more generous scholarship provisions to democratize access. It also depends upon sustained momentum for reform. These difficulties cannot be minimized. But neither can the achievements. The experience of 1968–69 exceeded many expectations. In early 1970 optimism declined, and observers feared that the revival of student disorder, especially at Nanterre, might require the government to adopt a repressive policy toward students and university development.

THE FUTURE The future of higher education in France will be patterned largely on the reform legislation of 1968, assuming that it is successfully implemented. No new admissions hurdles are contemplated, and students passing the *baccalauréat* examinations will still be entitled to enter universities and UERs. Efforts will be made to expand the teaching staffs and raise staff-student ratios. There will be more decentraliztion and diversification; and staff members, students, and community leaders will have a greater share in decision making.

The major problems of the future will be finding enough qualified staff members and building enough physical facilities.[10]

The anxiety of university students about the professional opportunities open to them as graduates of universities was widely viewed as a major factor in student unrest in 1968. Now that university education seems to be more oriented toward student demand, the professional opportunities may be an even more important consideration in the future. Like other higher education systems, the French system has yet to find a practical compromise between orienting courses and methodology to student demand and at the same time directing students into pursuits needed by society.

In order to eliminate the present disequilibrium between the output of graduates and the needs of society, France must:

1 Prepare accurate forecasts of highly qualified personnel needs (as was done for 1978 by the Manpower Committee of the Fifth Plan)

2 Organize a liberal and flexible system of information and orientation based on the foreseeable structure of the future labor force

This second effort has not yet really been undertaken, and the law of November 12, 1968, commissioned the new universities to take urgent action in this field. At present universities are not equipped to perform such duties.

[10] These problems may become less acute as the result of the predicted leveling off in the number of students at the higher education level during the years immediately after 1972–73, consequent upon the leveling off observed during the past five years in enrollments in the second cycle at the secondary schools.

Universities and Institutions of Higher Education in France

THE NEW FRENCH UNIVERSITIES

Aix-Marseille I

Letters
Science
Observatory

Aix-Marseille II

Medicine
Law
Pharmacy
Technology
Business administration

Amiens

Medicine
Pharmacy
Science
Letters
Law
Technology

Angers

Medicine
Pharmacy
Science
Letters
Technology
Law

Besançon

Letters
Medicine

Pharmacy
Science
Technology
Observatory

Bordeaux I

Science
Law
Institute of political sciences

Bordeaux II

Medicine
Pharmacy
Letters
Science

Bordeaux III

Letters
Science
Sociology
Information

Brest

Medicine
Science
Letters
Technology

Caen

Medicine
Pharmacy

Law
Science
Technology
Data Processing

Chambéry

Science
Letters

Dijon

Medicine
Pharmacy
Law
Science
Technology
Observatory

Grenoble I

Medicine
Pharmacy
Law
Science
Letters
Technology

Grenoble II

Law
Technology

Grenoble III

Letters

Lille I

Business administration
Science
Technology
Data processing

Lille II

Medicine
Pharmacy
Dentistry
Law

Lille III

Letters

Limoges

Medicine
Pharmacy
Law
Letters
Technology

Lyon I

Science
Observatory
Technology
Medicine
Pharmacy

Lyon II

Letters
Law
Business administration

Le Mans

Science
Letters
Law
Technology

Metz

Letters
Science
Technology

Montpellier I

Law
Business administration
Medicine
Pharmacy
Dentistry

Montpellier II

Science
Technology
Business administration

Montpellier III

Letters

Mulhouse

Science
Letters
Technology

Nancy I

Medicine
Pharmacy
Dentistry
Science
Technology

Nancy II

Law
Letters

Nantes

Medicine
Pharmacy
Dentistry
Law
Letters
Technology

Nice

Medicine
Law
Letters
Technology
Business administration

Orléans

Law
Data processing
Technology

Paris I-XIII

Pau

Law
Letters
Science

Perpignan

Science

Poitiers

Medicine
Pharmacy
Law
Technology

Reims

Medicine
Pharmacy
Law
Letters
Technology

Rennes I

Law
Medicine
Pharmacy
Dentistry
Science
Technology

Rennes II

Letters

Rouen

Medicine
Pharmacy
Law
Letters
Technology

Sainte-Étienne

Science
Law
Letters
Technology
Medicine
Pharmacy
Dentistry

Strasbourg I

Science

Strasbourg II

Letters

Strasbourg III

Law
Journalism
Technology

Toulouse I

Law
Business administration
Data processing

Toulouse II

Letters
Management

Toulouse III

Science
Technology

Medicine
Pharmacy
Dentistry

Tours

Medicine
Pharmacy
Letters
Law
Technology

Valenciennes

Science
Technology

THE 13 UNIVERSITIES OF PARIS

Paris I

Major area of study: Economics and law

Economics
Public and administrative law
Business law
International and European relations
Philosophy of sciences
Modern languages

*Possible cooperative programs with the
Institut d'Études Politiques.

Paris II

Major area of study: Law

Civil law
Social psychology
Applied computer science
French Institute of the Press
Modern foreign languages

*Possible cooperative programs with the
Institut d'Études Politiques.

Paris III

Major area of study: Modern languages

Modern languages
School of interpreters
Law
Theatrical and cinematographic techniques
of expression and communication

*Possible cooperative programs with: École
Pratique des Hautes Études, Audio-visual
Center of Saint-Cloud, National Center of
Educational TV, Conservatoire National
des Arts et Métiers, Conservatoire National
d'art dramatique.

Paris IV

Major area of study: Classical studies

French language and literature
Latin
Greek
Languages and civilizations of Eastern
Europe

English, German, and Spanish studies
Applied sciences
Computer science applied to linguistics
History of philosophy
Aesthetics
Medieval studies
Applied literary and scientific studies

*Possible cooperative programs with: École
Pratique des Hautes Études, Institut
d'Études Politiques, École de Chartres,
Conservatoire de Musique, École des
Beaux-Arts.

Paris V

*Two major areas of study:
Medicine and human sciences*

Medicine
Human and experimental biology
Dental surgery
Pharmacy
Legal medicine
Psychology
Social sciences
Educational sciences
Mathematics
Formal logic and computer science
Physical education
University Institute of Technology
  (information, statistical computer
  sciences, marketing)

*Possible cooperative programs with: Institut
Pasteur, Museum of Natural History, École
Pratique des Hautes Études.

Paris VI

Major area of study: Sciences

Theoretical physics
Physical chemistry
Organic chemistry
Physiology
Earth sciences
Mathematics
Computer sciences and statistics
Institute of Programming
Modern languages
Geography (research)

Paris VII

Interdisciplinary university par excellence

Medicine
Biology
Genetics
Algebra and geometry
Physics
Chemistry
Anthropology
Human clinical sciences
Geography
Social sciences
English studies (Charles V)
Sciences of texts and documents
Linguistic research
Sciences of religion

*Possible cooperative program with: École
Pratique des Hautes Études, Museum of
Natural History, École Supérieure
d'Électricité, Institut National Agronomique

Paris VIII

*Study and research unit (U.E.R.) of
Vincennes*

Studies centered on contemporary problems
Modern languages
Human sciences

Paris IX

*Study and research unit (U.E.R.) of
Dauphine*

Management and applied economy
  (first cycle)
Sciences of organization (third cycle)
Computer sciences and management
Institute of Urbanism (will be ultimately
  transferred to Créteil)
Applied economics
Management (second cycle)

Paris X

*Study and research unit (U.E.R.) of
Vincennes*

Arts
Law

University Institute of Technology of
   Ville-d'Avray (electronics and mechanics)

Paris XI

Major area of study: Sciences

Medical studies (first cycle)
Biology (first cycle at Montrouge)
Institute of Nuclear Physics
University Institute of Cachan (chemistry,
   engineering, mechanics, electronics,
   computer science)
University Institute of Technology of Saclay-
   Orsay (chemistry)
Juridical and economical sciences
Therapeutic chemistry
Environmental sciences

*Possible cooperative programs with: École

Centrale des Arts et Manufactures, École
Supérieure de Chimie

Paris XII

Medicine (at Créteil)
Law and economics (at Saint-Maur)
Ecology
Medical computer sciences (second cycle)
Institute of Urbanism (subsequently)

Paris XIII

Still incomplete in mid-1970

Law and economics (future University of
   Villetaneuse)
Arts and human sciences (Villetaneuse)
University Institutes of Saint-Denis,
   Villetaneuse, Argenteuil (still in project)

References

Commissariat Général du Plan d'Équipement et de la Productivité, Ve Plan 1966-1970: *Rapport Général de la Commission de l'Équipement Scolaire, Universitaire et Sportif,* Imprimerie des Journaux Officiels, Paris, 1965.

Garcia, André: "The Financing of Education under a Centralized System," *Financing of Education for Economic Growth,* OECD, Paris, 1966.

Harris, Seymour: "Public Expenditures on Education," *Financing of Education for Economic Growth,* OECD, Paris, 1966.

Poignant, Raymond: *L'Enseignement Dans Les Pays du Marché Commun,* Institut Pedagogique National, Paris, 1965.

Robbins Committee: *Higher Education: Report of the Committee Appointed by the Prime Minister under the Chairmanship of Lord Robbins, 1961-63,* Cmnd. 2154, HMSO, London, 1963, appendix V.

UNESCO: *Factual Background Document on Access to Higher Education in Europe,* Conference of Ministers of Education of European Member States on Access to Higher Education, Vienna, November 20–25, 1967.

United Nations: *Statistical Yearbook,* New York, 1965.

von Rundstedt, Marianne: *Studien und Berichte: Die Studienforderung in Frankreich 1950–1962,* Institut für Bildungsforschung in der Max-Planck Gesellschaft, Berlin, 1965.

4. Higher Education in Great Britain

The origins of higher education in Great Britain date to the twelfth- and thirteenth-century foundations at Oxford and Cambridge, both strongly influenced by the universities in France. Uniquely English, however, has been the development of subunits called *colleges,* first as a means of providing dining and lodging for groups of students and later as academic units.

Like the universities of France, those of Great Britain traditionally have been highly selective in admitting students. A child's decision to prepare for entrance to a university must be made at the age of 11. Those who make the choice must pass a series of ordinary-level (O-level) examinations after 11 years of schooling and, after an additional two years, must pass advanced-level (A-level) examinations in at least three subjects before they can be admitted to a university. Although this system is beginning to change and is being subjected to increasing questioning, it still is common.

COMPONENTS OF HIGHER EDUCATION   The higher education system in Great Britain[1] includes 42 universities, about 175 colleges of education, which offer a basic three-year course, and a spectrum of specialized colleges and "further education" institutions, which offer a range of advanced and, in some cases, first-degree courses. Universities are autonomous, chartered corporations. All other institutions of higher education are public.

[1] This survey is mainly about higher education in England and Wales, which have a single system for all nonuniversity higher education. Discussions and statistics on universities, however, will include those for universities in Scotland because few available studies differentiate between universities of Great Britain and those of England and Wales. In 1967, eight of the universities in Great Britain were in Scotland. Northern Ireland has two universities, making a total of 44 for the United Kingdom.

The Universities

Universities in England and Wales include:

1 The ancient foundations of Oxford and Cambridge ("Oxbridge").

2 The University of London, founded in 1836. This institution is actually a federation of 33 self-governing schools and 13 institutes, some of which are as large as independent universities. In 1967 about 15 percent of all university students in Great Britain were enrolled at the University of London. It is the only British university offering external degrees. Students who are not enrolled in the University of London may earn a University of London degree by passing higher education courses following University of London syllabuses and pass University of London examinations.

3 The University of Wales, a federation of six schools and colleges.

4 The eight older civic or provincial ("red brick") universities of Durham, Newcastle (a division of Durham until 1963), Manchester, Birmingham, Liverpool, Leeds, Sheffield, and Bristol.

5 The six newer civic universities of Reading, Nottingham, Southampton, Hull, Exeter, and Leicester.

6 The eight universities founded since World War II, Keele, Sussex, York, East Anglia, Essex, Lancaster, Kent, and Warwick. Unlike other newly established universities, they were authorized to grant their own degrees as soon as established. Only Keele existed before 1960.

7 Ten former colleges of advanced technology (CATs), two of which are federated with the Universities of London and Wales.

Half of Scotland's eight universities were established after World War II.

Customarily, British universities have been viewed as a pyramid with "Oxbridge" dominating the system. But much of the current expansion, innovation, experimentation, and advanced work is taking place at both the civic and new universities, and the proportion of students at Oxford and Cambridge declined from 18.4 percent in 1953–54 to 11.6 percent in 1965–66.[2] In 1969 plans to establish a privately funded university, the Independent University, were under way. The proposed university, if established, would admit its first students around 1972 and would be funded through student fees, free of governmental controls.

Teacher Training Institutions

In 1967–68 teacher training programs were offered by 28 university departments of education, 16 art training centers, and 176 colleges of education. It normally takes three years for students at colleges

[2] University Grants Committee, 1966; see also Halsey, 1962.

of education to earn their certificates, but students with advanced or specialized qualifications may become "qualified teachers" with shorter courses. University graduates can become qualified teachers after serving for a probationary period in practical teaching. Many university graduates who plan to teach take a one-year professional training course at a college or in a university department of education. This route leads to a postgraduate certificate of education.

About two-thirds of the colleges of education are maintained by local education authorities (LEA). The others are maintained by voluntary, mainly denominational, organizations. Most of the colleges of education are general colleges, but 14 women's colleges in 1967–68 specialized in physical education or housecraft, and 4 colleges were devoted to technical education. The colleges of technical education provide a one-year course for students with qualifications in technical and general subjects. Their object is to prepare students for teaching in further education establishments (sub-university vocational and technical institutions). The art training centers offer teacher training to students with qualifications for entering colleges of education. Most of these programs are in colleges of art, but a few are associated with universities.

Colleges of education do not give degrees of their own and are not considered university-level institutions. Their entrance requirements are lower than those of universities and, until 1960, their general course lasted only two years. The study period is now the same as that for first-degree courses in universities, but the content of the courses is less academic and includes considerable practical and professional work.

Some colleges of education are associated with universities through institutes of education. These institutes, about 30 in number, are governed by bodies composed of representatives of colleges, the universities involved, LEAs and teacher associations. Their main responsibilities are to approve curricula in the colleges and to supervise examinations for the qualifying certificate. Only one college of education is not associated with a university. The reason for that exception is that Cambridge, which has conducted teacher training for a generation or more, has been reluctant to extend its help and prestige to the colleges of education in its vicinity.

An obstacle to the upgrading of teacher education for many years was the limited opportunity (through University of London external degrees only) for teacher trainees to get a university degree. With the affiliation of colleges of education with universities through schools or institutes of education, students in colleges of education may now take three years of college plus one year of university or, in a few cases, a combined four-year degree and training program leading to a university bachelor of education degree. Eligibility for the fourth-year program depends upon the student's record in the three-year certificate course or, in many universities, on his secondary school final examination results. By 1972–73 it is expected that about one-fourth of all entrants to colleges of education will take the four-year program. Alternatively, the colleges of education may develop their own degree-granting system.

The number of colleges of education increased from 136 in 1954 to 176 in 1967–68. Enrollments increased from about 22,000 in 1950 to about 95,000 in 1967 and are expected to reach 110,000 by 1971 (National Advisory Council on the Training and Supply of Teachers, 1965, p. 44).

Colleges of education are becoming more like universities. At entry, nearly half of their students have the minimum requirements for university matriculation; increasing numbers of their students are working toward the combined university degree and teacher's certificate; and current patterns of governance and financing make the distinctions between them and universities less acute. They draw students from all over the country and not only from their immediate geographic neighborhood. Recent trends make it not unlikely that some colleges of education will be turned into liberal arts colleges, capable of awarding degrees.

Further Education
A major study of higher education, the Robbins Committee Report (officially *Higher Education: Report of the Committee Appointed by the Prime Minister under the Chairmanship of Lord Robbins 1961–63*) described the *further education* institutions in England and Wales as "all the colleges providing post-school education that fall within the sphere of responsibility of the Ministry of Education, apart from the Training Colleges and the Colleges of Adult Education" (Robbins Committee, 1963, appendix II, p. 89). They include about 700 institutions: technical colleges, schools of art, colleges of commerce, agricultural colleges, and, most recently, polytechnics. They make up the bulk of postsecondary education establishments in the public sector. Most of them are under LEA control and offer mainly part-time and subuniversity education, but the most rapidly expanding enrollments at these institutions are in advanced courses.

Over the years, a four-tier system of further education has evolved in England and Wales. At the local level are some 300 *local colleges* that provide craft, technician, secretarial, and other courses, mostly on a part-time basis and at a nonadvanced level. These cannot be classified as institutions of higher education.

At the next level are 160 *area colleges,* which draw on a larger region for their students. In addition to offering part-time and non-advanced courses, the area colleges offer part-time advanced courses leading to the Higher National Certificate (described by the Robbins Committee as falling within its definition of higher education although not of university-degree level). They also offer sandwich courses (alternating three- to six-month periods in theoretical studies in colleges and professional training in industry) and full-time courses of university and near university-degree level. These are mainly courses for the Higher National Diploma.

At the third level are 25 *regional colleges,* which focus almost entirely upon advanced, including postgraduate, courses. These are mainly full-time or sandwich programs.

At the top of the system until 1965 were the *colleges of advanced technology* (CATs), which concentrated on advanced training. Before the creation of these schools in 1956, advanced training was given by a variety of colleges and there was a continuing controversy about whether technical training should be concentrated in certain institutions or should be available in a range of institutions offering nonadvanced as well as advanced training. The decision in 1956 favored concentration. In 1962, the CATs were removed from LEA control and became direct-grant institutions of the Ministry of Education. Three years later, they acquired full university status.

Additional nonuniversity institutions of higher education in the public sector include the 6 national-grant colleges set up since 1948 to provide advanced technological training in highly specialized fields such as aeronautics, horology, rubber technology, food technology, and foundry work; 5 colleges maintained by the military services; about 40 farm institutes giving mostly nonadvanced agricultural training; 5 agricultural colleges that moved under the aegis of the Department of Education and Science from the Ministry of Agriculture, Fisheries and Food in 1964; about 150 LEA-maintained art colleges, some 40 of which offer advanced courses for the diploma in art and design; and four direct-grant institutions in art, music, and drama.

The National Council for Awards in Art and Design, set up in 1961, approves art institution courses leading to a diploma of first-degree status in art and design.

The vacuum left at the top of the public sector of higher education when the CATs became universities is being filled by a new Council for National Academic Awards (CNAA), which, by royal charter in 1964, replaced the preexisting National Council for Technological Awards. The CNAA is an autonomous degree-awarding body which approves full-time or sandwich courses offered for first and higher degrees by further education institutions. By 1967, some 170 undergraduate and about half a dozen graduate courses enrolling over 10,000 students had been approved by the CNAA.

The CNAA degrees include bachelors in arts and science, both of honors standard (the B.Sc. has replaced the former diploma in technology); masters of arts, science, and philosophy; and doctorate in philosophy. Special academic regalia have been designed to represent CNAA degrees. Described by its chairman as a "disseminated university," the CNAA probably will become the largest degree-granting body in Great Britain. In 1968 it gave more first degrees than any other university except the University of London. Its degrees are not limited to technical and scientific fields but include business, law, foreign languages, social science, and arts. By the end of 1967, some 58 different subjects in arts and social sciences alone had been approved for CNAA awards.

In May 1966 (Department of Education and Science, 1966*a*) the establishment of 30 polytechnics was announced in a government white paper. They provide university and subuniversity courses that complement those of the universities and emphasize teaching rather than research. They are associated closely with business and industry and will eventually enroll at least 2,000 full-time students each. The new institutions are said to have grown out of Robbins Committee recommendations that some of the regional and teachers colleges be given university status and are forming what has been called (somewhat pejoratively) the new "state university system." Others see them as prototypes of a future "comprehensive university." The institutions given this new designation were selected by the government with the advice of the Regional Advisory Councils in mid-1968. In some cases they are former regional or other colleges of technology. In some cases, they are combinations of technical colleges with colleges of art and business.

It is likely that the polytechnics will be the main institutions of further education offering advanced work and that they will concentrate on offering CNAA-approved courses. They could therefore constitute a new top tier in the further education system. However, the polytechnics will not be the only institutions giving CNAA-approved courses. Over 50 other institutions are now giving these courses and are not likely to give them up.

The Robbins Committee recommended that British higher education be unified but internally differentiated, with colleges of education and technical colleges permitted, in some cases, to seek university status. This recommendation (which the government feared would lead to a proliferation of universities) was not accepted, and a *binary system* has emerged instead. The system is defended on the grounds that public sector institutions make "an equally distinguished but separate contribution," that they are not relegated to subdegrees and part-time work, that there is not a rat-race competition of nonuniversity institutions pursuing university status, and that the public institutions are under more direct social control than the autonomous universities.[3]

Critics of the binary system say that it unjustly implies that universities lack social responsibility and that university courses are less useful to society than the vocational and professional programs of the further education institutions. Critics also say that the government decided against permitting technical colleges to aspire to university status to avoid the political onus of wresting control of more of them from the LEAs. The decision was also motivated, critics say, by the government's desire to hold costs of higher education down (Lukes, 1967, pp. 6–46).

FUNCTIONS   Apart from the traditional functions of conserving, transmitting, and advancing knowledge and providing training for the professions, Britain's institutions of higher education participate in adult education, help develop the new technology, train persons in new fields, contribute to international education, and advance the cultural life of the nation.[4]

Scientific and Technological Training and Research   In 1965, more than 45 percent of all full-time first-degree or diploma university students were enrolled in courses of science and technology. The share of total national expenditures on research and development going to universities and technical colleges

[3] Speeches by Anthony Crosland, Secretary of State for Education and Science given at Woolwich, April 1965, and at the University of Lancaster, January 1967.

[4] Because support and encouragement of the arts is a responsibility of the Arts Council, financed by the Exchequer through the Department of Education and Science, the contribution of the university to the arts, varied and lively as it is, is not discussed in this section.

reached 7.2 percent in 1964–65. In monetary terms, expenditures in universities and technological colleges increased from £32.4 million to £55.9 million between 1961–62 and 1964–65 (Department of Education and Science, 1967, p. 8). But the amount of money spent on research conducted by universities is only about one-fifth as much as that spent on research conducted at government research departments.

In 1965–66, payments for research from government departments and other agencies to universities in Great Britain totaled about £17.8 million and constituted 10.8 percent of their total income (University Grants Committee, 1966, pp. 174–175).

Special studies in the past two decades have pointed up the importance of the universities' meeting the national need for graduates in science and technology. In response to these studies, the size of the Imperial College of Science and Technology was doubled in the 1950s; colleges of advanced technology were created; efforts were made to expand technological institutions in London, Glasgow, and Manchester; two-thirds of the new places in universities have been, in recent years, allocated to science and technology; and the polytechnics were established in 1968.

The percentage of all students enrolled in science and technology increased from 37 in 1950 to 45.9 in 1962 but declined in 1968. A major factor in this development was a decrease in the proportion of first-year, sixth-form (preparatory) students taking prerequisite courses in science and mathematics (Department of Education and Science, 1967b, 1968b, and 1968a, p. 93).[5]

National science policy in Great Britain involves several agencies, among them the Ministry of Technology, chiefly concerned with applied research, and the Secretary of State for Education and Science, responsible for five research councils and university research. The five research councils are autonomous agencies, funded mainly by government. They advise the government and provide support for research by their own institutes, by universities, and by various research organizations and associations. The Council for Scientific Policy (CSP), composed of leading scientists from industry and the universities, advises the Secretary of State on long-range policy and on support of the research councils. A Committee on Manpower Resources for Science and Technology, as-

[5] Sixth-form students planning to take A-level science and mathematics declined from 40 percent in 1963 (35,880 students) to 31.4 percent in 1967 (36,483 students).

sociated with both the Department of Education and Science (DES) and Ministry of Technology, is concerned with the training and utilization of manpower.

Several recent and current studies have import to the role of higher education in science and technology. Among them are the Dainton Report of 1968, which called attention to the decline in students entering science and technology courses; the Todd Report of 1968, which recommended that the intake of students into medical schools be doubled by 1990; a recent study on the support of scientific research in the universities; a study of the Working Group on Manpower for Scientific Growth, which reported scientists' and technicians' preference for fundamental research in universities and government as opposed to teaching school or working in industry; the Sutherland Report of 1967, which recommended closer liaison between universities and government research establishments (*Report of the Working Party on Liaison between Universities and Government Research Establishment,* 1967); and the Jones Report of 1967 on the "brain drain" (Committee on Manpower Resources for Science and Technology, 1967). The brain drain study indicated that net migration of scientists and technologists from the United Kingdom went up from 5 in 1961 to 2,695 in 1966 (Committee on Manpower Resources for Science and Technolgy, 1967, p. 80). It assigned some of the responsiblity to the lack of mobility for scientists and engineers between industry and university and to "the somewhat jaundiced attitude towards industry which is prevalent in some universities" (Committee on Manpower Resources for Science and Technology, 1967, p. 60).

Adult Education

All the older universities and most of the new ones have departments of adult education and extramural studies. These departments offer a considerable range of cultural, professional, and refresher courses that last from several weeks to three years. Most of the courses are given in the evening. Enrollment in extramural courses in England and Wales increased from about 100,000 in 1955–56 to about 137,000 in 1965–66 (University Grants Committee, 1957, p. 40 and Department of Education and Science, 1967*b*, vol. III, p. 69). The LEAs support a variety of liberal adult education courses presented in evening institutes held in schools and in further education establishments. The DES gives grants to "responsible bodies"—including the Workers' Education Association, the Welsh National Council of the Young Men's Christian

Associations, and the Cornwall Adult Education Joint Committee—
to support liberal education programs. Between 1957–58 and
1965–66 the total expenditures on adult education by universities,
LEAs, the Workers' Education Association, and other responsible
bodies in England and Wales doubled, and enrollments in these
programs increased from 159,611 to 223,528 (Department of
Education and Science, vol. V, 1967*b*, p. 23).

Public-sponsored adult education is also offered by about 20
residential colleges and by nine centers of adult education. There
were about 16,000 students in adult education courses in these
centers and colleges in England and Wales in 1965–66 (Department of Education and Science, vol. V, 1967*b*, p. 70).

In addition to the adult education programs of the public institutions, an enormous array of adult education courses is offered
by various national and local societies.

**External
Professional
Training**

Several fields of study commonly offered by universities in other
countries are offered in Great Britain, at least in part by institutions outside the formal higher educational system. Two notable
examples are architecture and law. There are some university
schools of architecture, but training for this profession is also available at various nonuniversity schools. One does not need university training in law in order to become a barrister or solicitor
in the United Kingdom. Qualification chiefly involves passing
examinations set by the profession and a period of practical training. However, many people do graduate in law and then take further
professional training. Candidates may pursue study through correspondence, cram schools, and, mainly for barristers, the Inns of
Court. Admission requirements for these programs are less stringent than those for a university. The Law Society oversees legal
training for solicitors, and the Council of Legal Education serves
this function for barristers. Changes in legal education are expected to result from the recommendations of a committee appointed in 1967 to review this field under the chairmanship of
Mr. Justice Omrod.

For other fields, mainly commercial, engineering, and technical,
some 100 associations determine requirements for acceptance to
the professions and set qualifying examinations for them. In some
cases completion of higher education courses may exempt candidates from examinations. In a few professions, entry is still accomplished through practical training with a qualified practitioner
rather than through formal courses of postsecondary education.

Vocationalism   The colleges of education and colleges of further education train students for specific occupations in programs that often include considerable practical experience. Industry cooperates actively, assisting the colleges in planning curricula and by developing a system of examinations required for membership in professional associations.

University-bound students pursue increasingly specialized courses of study from about the age of 14. There is little scope for general education in advanced secondary schools or, except at a few new ones, at a university. In the humanities and social sciences, the tradition that "the essential aim of a first degree course should be to teach the student how to think" (Robbins Committee, 1963, p. 90) persists, but the theory that university education produces generalists is breaking down in practice. There is a growing concern with the correlation between the production of graduates and the national needs for trained manpower. Students increasingly go to universities to learn a profession, and there is a widening awareness of the necessity for specialization in occupations for which the most qualified person, according to earlier views, was the "all-arounder." Reenforcing these changes is the fact that a growing number of students obtain their first degrees (CNAA) through the vocationally oriented further education route.

The Robbins Committee recommended more flexibility in university courses so that students could delay decisions on areas of concentration and pursue more than one subject. The University Grants Committee (UGC), in its report for 1966–67, also emphasized the need for breadth in first-degree programs. But, so far, there does not appear to be much general concern that intense specialization may not produce enough broadly trained people who can adapt to the rapidly changing demands of the technological age. Furthermore, midcareer or postexperience training programs have not acquired enough scope and acceptance to fulfill the refresher and retread needs that accompany technological change and the lack of general university training. In abandoning concepts of the all-arounder and amateur in favor of still more specialization, British higher education may further diminish the limited number of highly trained people who can move from one sector of employment to another.

New Fields of Study   Much of the impetus for initiating teaching and research in new fields comes from special government committees. For example, committees reported on dental, medical, veterinary, higher agricultural, area language, and social economic studies immediately after World War II. More recent committee recommendations have supported studies at selected universities in the social sciences, Latin America, and management. The close relations between further education colleges and local industrial firms and labor organizations help to ensure that new courses are initiated to meet local and regional needs at both the advanced and nonadvanced levels. One example of this response is seen in the field of computer technology. In 1967–68, on the invitation of the DES, some two dozen colleges of further education introduced short intensive courses in systems analysis, open to people in industry.

International Programs The Robbins Committee reported that, in 1962–63, full-time overseas students in British institutions of higher education totaled 63,730 (Robbins Committee, 1963, appendix XI*a*, p. 251). By 1965 the number had increased to about 68,000 (Central Office of Information, 1965, p. 1). Foreign (non-Commonwealth) students made up about one-third of all overseas students in 1965. Overseas students constituted 28.9 percent of all postgraduate students (excluding education) that year and 9.5 percent of total enrollments. In 1965 overseas students constituted 0.5 percent of all students in colleges of education in England and Wales and 13.6 percent of all students in further education (where the increase in overseas students has been most rapid in recent years).

A growing number of overseas students are financed by British sources, including the British Council and Commonwealth Scholarship and Fellowship Plan, and regional development programs such as the Colombo Plan. Overseas students are subsidized indirectly through the difference between their fees and the actual costs of full-time education annually. They pay £ 250 of the nearly £ 700 costs for an undergraduate and £ 900 for a graduate student. In 1967–68, when increased fees for overseas students went into effect, the number of foreign students at British universities decreased by 4,000 over the preceding year.

In the immediate postwar period, British universities provided assistance to colleges in the colonies through the Inter-University Council for Higher Education in the Colonies, and a number of colonial colleges entered into a special arrangement that permits colonial college students to work for University of London degrees. British universities provided expert advice and teaching and administrative staff members to the colonial colleges. As the colonies attained independence, the Inter-University Council for Higher

Education in the Colonies changed its name to the Inter-University Council for Education Overseas. It encourages cooperation in staff recruitment, consultative services, training programs, library services, and exchange visits between British universities and the universities in developing countries. The Association of Commonwealth Universities, in which British universities are members, promotes cooperation and provides assistance in staff recruitment. British university staff members also serve at overseas universities under international assistance programs of the Ministry of Overseas Development.

ENROLLMENT TRENDS

Enrollment in full-time higher education in Great Britain (including Scotland) increased from 122,000 in 1954 to about 439,000 in 1969. From 1954 to 1965 enrollments in England and Wales more than doubled in the universities, tripled in colleges of education, and increased more than fivefold in full-time advanced further education. By 1981 enrollments in full-time higher education are expected to be about 727,000 in England and Wales and over 800,000 including Scotland, over 40 percent more than the Robbins Committee estimate.

The targets of the Robbins Committee were to provide 173,000 places for students in universities in 1965; 204,000 by 1971; and 218,000 by 1972. In 1966–67, enrollments began to outstrip these projections, and the target for 1971 was revised to 220,000 to 225,000 students. In 1968–69, full-time university enrollment was already up to nearly 212,000. By 1982 it will be an estimated 450,000.

One explanation for these increases is that the proportion of the college-age population in England and Wales entering universities increased from 3.1 percent in 1954 (Robbins Committee, 1963, appendix I, p. 148) to 5.5 percent in 1965 (Department of Education and Science, part II, 1967a).[6] This rate of increase is expected to rise slowly until the middle of the 1970s and then to accelerate as the impact of the higher birth rate of the late 1950s is felt and with the anticipated advance in the school-leaving age from 15 in 1970 to 17 in the 1980s.

Enrollment in the colleges of education in England and Wales expanded to about 95,000 in 1967–68. In doing so, it prematurely exceeded the Robbins Committee Report projection for 1970–71 by 2,000 students. The greatest expansion, however, was in further

[6] Home initial entrants to universities in England and Wales including the CATs went up from 28,250 in 1961 to 43,250 in 1966.

education in England and Wales. In these institutions, the enrollment of an estimated 54,000 students in 1966 far exceeded the Robbins Committee Report projection of 40,000 for that year.

The Robbins Committee "assumed as an axiom that courses of higher education should be available for all those who are qualified by ability and attainment to pursue them and wish to do so" (Robbins Committee, 1963, p. 8). Contrary to this assumption, however, entry into universities has become more competitive. The number of students with theoretical and actual minimum entrance requirements for attending universities (two A-level passes and three or more A-level passes, respectively, in the General Certificate of Education examination) tripled between 1954 and 1965, but the percentage of students with the theoretical minimum qualifications who were actually admitted to universities dropped from 63 percent in 1961–62 to 55 percent in 1967 (Corbett, 1968, p. 23). Because the rate of expansion of the number of young people qualified for university admission exceeds the rate of increase of entrants, increasing numbers of students qualified for university admission now enter colleges of education and further education institutions. As a result, contrary to Robbins Committee recommendations, there seems to be faster expansion of nonuniversity higher education than there is of university education.

TABLE 5 *Enrollment by type of institution of higher education in Great Britain*

	1954-55	1960-61	1964-65	1966-67	1967-68
Further (advanced) education in England and Wales					
Full-time and sandwich	9,660[a]	26,770[a]	53,450[a]*	54,000[b]	
Total enrollments		104,260[a]	158,140	162,384[c]	
Colleges of education in England and Wales	24,300[d]	35,100[d]	66,000[b]	87,025[d]	95,000[c]†
Universities in Great Britain					
Full-time undergraduates	68,877[e]	88,957[e]	112,016[e]		164,856[f]
Full-time postgraduates	12,212[e]	17,836[e]	25,567[e]		33,946[f]
Part-time enrollments	15,146[e]	17,831[e]	18,077[e]		
Full-time enrollment, all higher education	122,000[g]	179,000[g]		339,000[b]	376,000[h]

*Excluding CATs.

†Estimated.

SOURCES: (a) Department of Education and Science, 1967a, pp. 50-51. (b) Department of Education and Science, *Education in 1966,* Cmnd. 3226, HMSO, London, 1967. (c) Department of Education and Science, 1968a. (d) Robbins Committee, 1963, appendix I, p. 162. (e) Department of Education and Science, 1967a, pp. 118–119, 133. (f) Material supplied by the UGC. (g) Robbins Committee, 1963, appendix I, p. 164. (h) *Times Educational Supplement,* March 6, 1970, p. 7.

TABLE 6 *Entrants in institutions of higher education in Great Britain by year and type of institution*

	1954-55	1960-61	1964-65	1966-67	1967-68
Further (advanced) education in England and Wales					
Full-time and sandwich	4,120[a]	12,000[a]	25,500[a]	42,136[b]	
Total full-time and part-time		57,290[a]	90,360[a]		
Colleges of education in England and Wales	12,410[c]	17,240	24,300[d]	33,357[e]*	
University undergraduates	22,500[f]	29,500[f]		53,692[g]	57,251[g]

*Estimated.

SOURCES: (*a*) Department of Education and Science, part II, 1967*a*, pp. 50-51. (*b*) Department of Education and Science, vol. V, 1968*b*, p. 26 (students receiving LEA full-value awards in calendar year 1967). (*c*) Robbins Committee, 1963, appendix II*a*, p. 63. Excludes overseas students, but as they constitute only about 1 percent of total enrollments, excluding them makes no significant difference to the total. (*d*) National Advisory Council on the Training and Supply of Teachers, 1965. (*e*) Department of Education and Science, 1968*a*. (*f*) Robbins Committee, 1963, appendix II*a*, p. 28. (*g*) Material supplied by the UGC.

It is the policy of neither government nor the universities for the latter to accommodate all qualified "school leavers" or to increase their proportion of all students entering full-time higher education. Studies indicate that by 1971 there will be a shortfall of about 20,000 places in universities (and in all full-time higher education) for qualified applicants from England and Wales (Layard, King, and Moser, 1969).[7] In 1967–77, the Robbins projection of qualified school leavers may be exceeded by some 40,000. Since the government did not accept the universities' enrollment projections in planning for the current quinquennium, it appears that university expansion is being determined by factors other than the demand of qualified school leavers. Among the probable consequences is increasing competitiveness for university admission that will make it correspondingly difficult to reduce specialization in upper secondary school studies. Some universities have gone through so much expansion that they are not now seeking more students, although others, which after the 1962–67 recruitment boom see no other chance for promoting staff, will push for expansion.

The number of postgraduate students (including foreign students and students in education) in British universities increased from 17,836 in 1960–61 to about 34,000 in 1967–68. The government

---

[7] The writer is indebted to the authors of this study for the opportunity to see it prior to publication.

restricted postgraduate enrollments for the current quinquennium, apparently believing that many postgraduate students might more usefully enter into employment instead of further education and fearing, too, that many science and technology students might be disposed toward careers in pure instead of applied research. In 1967, the UGC gave the following reasons for restricting postgraduate studies:

The Committee . . . think that the flow from the schools into undergraduate places should be a real priority;

The numerical proportion of the first degree output which embarks on postgraduate work already substantially exceeds the Robbins estimate;

There is uneasiness that the rise in the proportion of graduates who stay in the universities for postgraduate studies rather than moving into teaching, or the outside world, is greater than the country can afford at present;

With the slackening in the rate of growth of students there will be less need in most disciplines for recruitment to university staff *via* a higher degree, than has been the case during the past few years (University Grants Committee, 1968*a*, pp. 25–26).

Postgraduate enrollments may also increase more slowly in response to the requirement that since the beginning of the current quinquennium annual fees of £ 250 be imposed upon students from outside the United Kingdom.

Despite limits of university expansion, particularly at the graduate level, enrollments in all full-time higher education will continue to expand more rapidly than the Robbins Committee predicted. The percentage of 18-year-olds in England and Wales entering full-time higher education went up from 5.8 percent in 1954 to 8.4 percent in 1962 and 16.9 percent in 1967. The size of this age group is expected to increase from 725,000 in 1970 to about 900,000 in 1980.

Length of Study Period First-degree courses at universities in England and Wales usually take three years. In Scotland and the atypical Keele University in England, they take four years. Medical and dentistry courses usually require five to six years. The average length of courses for full-time students in England and Wales in 1965–66 was 3.44 years at the former CATs, 3.78 years in other universities, 2.89 years in colleges of education, and 3.0 years in further education (Layard et al., 1969, tables 4.5, 4.12, and 4.14).

	1955	1962	1966
First degrees and diplomas	$16,800^a$	$22,200^a$	$32,070^b$ $3,462^c$
Higher degrees	$2,700^d*$	$3,495^d$	$6,498^e$
Higher diplomas		$6,495^d$	$8,459^c$

TABLE 7
Degrees and diplomas awarded by universities in Great Britain

*Degrees only.

SOURCES: (a) Robbins Committee, 1963, appendix IV, p. 161 (home students only). (b) UGC, 1966, p. 130. (c) *Ibid.*, p. 154. (d) Robbins Committee, appendix IIa, pp. 57-58. (e) UGC, 1966, p. 142.

Relatively few students (5 to 20 percent, depending upon their subjects) in the universities take longer than the prescribed study period to complete their first-degree studies because in many cases repeating examinations is discouraged or prohibited. The Robbins Committee reported that less than 5 percent of students in colleges of education and advanced full-time further education institutions repeat a year.

Persistence A recent study of university students who should have obtained their first degrees in 1966–67 showed that the overall failure rate was declining. About 78 percent of these students obtained their first degrees in the minimum time. About 8 percent did so after one additional year. Excluding students at the former CATs, the proportion of students leaving university without obtaining their first degree was only 11 percent.

The failure rate varied from institution to institution and in different fields of study. At Cambridge, it was only 3 percent; at Scottish universities it was as high as 19 percent. From one-fifth to one-third of the students at the former CATs failed. There are fewer failures in arts and sciences than in medicine, engineering, and technology. To reduce failures still more, a research unit at the University of London is studying such ideas as providing more advance warning to students who are in academic difficulty and improving advising and counseling generally.

Wastage rates are higher for students at colleges of education than they are in the universities, but they are declining generally. Nonsuccess rates are still higher in the further education institutions. This writer was told by one authority that the nonsuccess rate of all students in full-time advanced further education was as high as 53 percent.

STAFF-
STUDENT
RATIOS The high persistence rate and short study period in British universities is generally ascribed to competitive admissions and high staff-student ratios. According to the Robbins Report, this ratio, based on full-time teachers and students, went from 1:8.4 in 1950–51 to 1:7.6 in 1961–62. It varied among disciplines, however. In 1961–62 the ratio was 1:6 in medicine and 1:8.8 in arts and technology. It also varied between universities. Oxford and Cambridge, with ratios of 1:8.9 and 1:8.4 respectively, were, in 1962, somewhat less favorable to students than others (University Grants Committee, 1968*b*). The Robbins Report calculation is slightly inflated because it includes staff members who are principally engaged in research and do little or no teaching.

The UGC estimates of staff-student ratios excludes persons who are engaged mainly in research. It also assigns weights to students on the basis of their study fields and levels. The resulting ratios are somewhat lower than those of the Robbins Committee Report. The UGC formula produced an overall staff-student ratio of 1:10.4 for 1960–61 (University Grants Committee, 1962, pp. 18–19).

In the last few years, the number of university staff members increased faster than the number of students. In 1965–66, excluding those paid wholly or partly from nonuniversity sources, there were 21,865 full-time university staff members. Including those paid from nonuniversity sources, there were 25,294. A year later, these figures increased to 23,600 and 26,540 respectively, giving staff-student ratios of 1:7.8 and 1:6.7. In its *Annual Survey* for 1966–67, the UGC indicated that it did not anticipate "any marked change" in the ratio for the current quinquennium. If this is true, enrollment projections of about 225,000 by 1972 will be accompanied by increase in staff to about 33,600. By 1968–69, the staff-student ratio had moved to 1:8.

At the beginning of this quinquennium, the UGC advised that the proportion of the total of professors, readers, and senior lecturers to total staff (excluding medicine) should be limited to 35 percent. In 1966–67 the proportion of all senior staff to total staff was about 31 percent, but more than 50 percent of total staff were lecturers. By including professors in the new limit on total senior staff, normal promotion opportunities for the current bulge of middle-level staff members are shut off.

In the colleges of education in England and Wales, the ratio of full-time teachers to full-time students was 1:11.2 in 1962 and 1:10.9 in 1965. In advanced further education in England and

Wales, the Robbins Committee calculated a ratio for CATs of 6.8 full-time equivalent students per full-time equivalent staff in 1961–62. For 77 other colleges, the Robbins Committee gave a ratio of 1:5.7.

HIGHER EDUCATION AND CIVIL GOVERNMENT The chief national agency concerned with higher education is the Department of Education and Science (DES), established in 1964 and headed by the Secretary of State for Education and Science, a cabinet minister. Under this secretary are three ministers concerned respectively with the universities and civil science, with all other education, and with the arts, museums, and galleries and the "Open University."[8] The department is divided into branches including one which deals with universities in Great Britain, and others dealing with schools, teacher training, and further education in England and Wales. A planning branch was established in December 1966.

The University Grants Committee By virtue of their royal charters, universities are autonomous but depend upon the government for some 90 percent of their income for capital expediture and for about 75 percent of their income for recurrent spending.

The University Grants Committee, a nonstatutory body, was established by the Treasury in 1919 to advise on financial needs of the universities and allocate to the institutions the funds voted by Parliament. After World War II, its functions were extended to include "the preparation and execution of such plans for the development of the universities as may from time to time be required in order to ensure that they are fully adequate to national need."

Part of the UGC's effectiveness is attributed to the fact that it is fairly small and is composed mostly of academics who have a personal knowledge of university affairs. The committee and its sub-committees visit the universities during each quinquennium. On the basis of information gathered in these visits and supplied by the universities, the committee recommends the level of public grants for recurrent and capital expenditures required by the universities for the next quinquennium. The funds voted by Parliament, in the

[8] The Open University, a university enrolling students in degrees and other courses, will operate through radio, television, correspondence, programmed instruction, and tutorials. It will, at least initially, be a direct grant institution of the DES rather than part of the UGC system. The Open University enrolls its first students in 1971.

form of block grants for recurrent expenditures and annual grants for specified capital expenditures, are subsequently allocated to the individual universities by the committee. Occasionally, the UGC provides earmarked funds for special development efforts for a a limited period. Universities are, in principle, free to spend block grants as they see fit, although because grants are calculated on the basis of plans and needs of the individual universities as approved by the UGC it is understood that the universities will not significantly depart from the approved plans without consulting the UGC. Even so, a former chairman of the committee has pointed out that the principal feature of the UGC is that "at no point are the universities in Britain in direct confrontation with the Government."[9]

The Robbins Committee further recommended that an agency like the UGC be established to serve the growing ranks of autonomous institutions other than the universities. It also recommended that the UGC be transferred from the treasury to a new Minister of Arts and Sciences.[10]

The Robbins Committee further recommended that a separate ministry be created for the nonautonomous sector of higher education, but in 1964 the Prime Minister announced that all education would be placed under a new Secretary of State for Education and Science. Separate administrative units for the universities and for all other education, with their own accounting officers, were created to give the organization "something of a federal character," but in practice there were two accounting officers for only a brief period. The UGC became an advisory board to the DES and was given direct access not only to the Secretary of State but also to the ministers in the DES concerned with universities and other education.

The conversion of CATs into universities and the establishment of seven new universities in the last decade had added to the UGC's responsibilities, and it has been enlarged from 18 to 22 members (including a full-time chairman). It has also adopted an elaborate

[9] Sir John Wolfenden, "The Government-University Relationship in Britain," speech delivered at annual meeting of the American Council on Education, October 2, 1967, Washington, D.C.

[10] The treasury was finding it increasingly difficult to act both as a guardian of the public purse and a claimant upon it on behalf of the universities. The Robbins Committee Recommendations might also have been prompted by the fact that, in 1962, the Treasury, for the first time, totally rejected some of the UGC's proposals.

subcommittee structure that involves many noncommittee members, but its procedures are less personal and more oriented to academic fields and the professions than they were in the past. The size of the UGC staff has increased fivefold since 1953.

One of the most significant recent changes in the relationship between government and the universities was the requirement, announced in July 1967, that the Comptroller and Auditor General (CAG) should have access to the books and records of the UGC and of the universities. As of the beginning of 1968, such access became a condition of grants to universities. In 1968 the CAG set up an office in the headquarters of the UGC and began sending staff members to examine the books of the universities. The fears of the universities that CAG inspection of internal records might eventually lead to more governmental intervention in university affairs are fading.

Another source of pressure for active government influence in university matters is the Committee on Estimates of the House of Commons. This committee has recommended that the UGC review its composition and methods of operation. It has urged the UGC, for instance, not just to be a buffer between universities and the government but to give "more constructive and effective guidance" to the universities in a number of fields (Estimates Committee, 1965). The Estimates Committee has also pressed the UGC for more information on university costs. As a result of this pressure, the universities were explicitly informed that for the 1967–1972 quinquennium the UGC adjusted allocations on the basis of relative costs "where there seemed . . . to be under- or over-financing of individual universities in relation to their responsibilities (University Grants Committee, 1968a, p. 35). In 1967, for the first time, the UGC issued a detailed Memorandum of General Guidance to the universities. Among other things, it urged university collaboration with industry and more interuniversity coordination and, in general, spelled out the UGC's expectations on university developments.

In principle, the universities are free to recruit the professors they want to teach the subjects they want to the students they choose to admit. In practice these freedoms are limited by the UGC's authority to set up broad salary scales, prescribe the balance for junior and senior staff members, determine formulas for unit construction costs of buildings, withhold funds for expansion, approve establishment of new universities, and "indicate" what academic specialties different universities should strengthen or abandon.

How much longer the UGC will be regarded as an effective device for balancing university autonomy with a degree of government influence over university development is uncertain. Universities are too important to national development and too expensive to permit the kind of freedom they enjoyed in the past, sheltered by the UGC system. Some critics of the UGC see its role as a buffer between the dons and government fast becoming obsolete. They see its academically oriented structure, staffing, and methods of operation as a means of perpetuating an elitist approach toward the universities in an age when this approach should be discarded (Halsey, 1969, pp. 128–148). Recognition that universities no longer constitute the main part of higher education and the rest an inconsequential fringe adds to pressures to require more national accountability of them and therefore to revise the UGC system faster than it may revise itself.

Public Higher Education

The relations between the national government and the colleges of education and further education in England and Wales are direct and continuous. DES sets standards and provides sustained guidance through regulations and circulars and the counsel of Her Majesty's Inspectorate. The Inspectorate, a branch of DES, has more than 500 inspectors for England and Wales. They visit higher education institutions and advise the college and local authorities on curriculum, teaching methods, and other matters. They also give special training programs for teachers, communicate the department's interests to the colleges' LEAs, and provide information and advice to the Secretary of State on local development and plans in all educational institutions except the universities.

Most colleges of education and institutions of further education in England and Wales are run by LEAs, elected councils of counties and country boroughs. The exceptions are colleges of education run by voluntary bodies, and specialized institutions (such as national colleges) which have their own boards. The LEAs plan and supervise the education provided in their areas subject to DES regulations and standards. Institutions under these local authorities are financed on a national basis with funds apportioned on the basis of school population figures and other internal factors and on certain cost limits set by the DES. A large proportion of LEA expenditures are met by rate-support grants from the national exchequer.

The magnitude of these grants is partly determined in negotiations between various national officials and local authorities. The DES is the agency which studies local estimates of future expenditures. The higher education institutions to which the DES makes direct grants, national colleges and colleges run by voluntary bodies, are directly accountable to the DES, and the CAG has access to their accounts.

INTERNAL GOVERNMENT OF THE UNIVERSITIES There are different systems of governance for the civic and new universities, the federal universities, and Oxford and Cambridge.

In the civic and new universities, the chief administrative officials are the vice-chancellors, who usually hold office until retirement (the chancellorship is a ceremonial position held for life); one or more pro-vice-chancellors, who are professors holding office for limited terms; the registrars, who handle academic matters; and the bursars, who are primarily concerned with university finance. The largest unit in university government is convocation, in which all graduates are eligible for membership. Its powers are usually limited to discussing and expressing an opinion on matters relating to the university, but it may nominate some of its members to decision-making bodies. Not all the new universities have a convocation.

The main decision-making bodies of the universities are the courts, councils, senates, and boards of faculties. (These are often referred to as parts of a two-tier structure, one tier being the lay bodies of the courts and councils and the other being the academic bodies of senates and faculty boards.)

The courts are the supreme governing bodies and may have several hundred members, including representatives of the convocations, academic staffs, local schools, other universities, local authorities, educational associations, and members of Parliament. They meet once or twice a year to hear reports on the state of the university, appoint a majority of the council's members, and generally endorse recommendations that come from the councils.

The councils are, de facto, the executive committees of the universities. They have about 30 members, most of whom, including the chairmen of the councils, are laymen. About two-fifths are academics, usually elected for two- or three-year periods by the senates. The chancellors and vice-chancellors are ex officio members. Local authorities also nominate some members. The council is responsible for the university's financial affairs, confirms the senate's recommendations on academic appointments in consultation with the senate, in most universities appoints the vice-chancellor, and generally approves academic regulations proposed by the senates.

The principal responsibility for academic affairs resides in the senates, which often may include all professors ex officio, additional elected academic staff members, and usually the registrars and chairmen. The vice-chancellors are ex officio chairmen and serve as links between the senates and councils. The senates' powers extend to coordinating the work of the faculty boards and making recommendations on appointments of professors, the awarding of degrees, student discipline, and teaching programs.

The boards of faculties deal primarily with academic affairs. In the smaller universities they may include all permanent members of the teaching staff. In the large universities they often include the professors and various other elected academic staff members. Faculty boards are headed by deans who are professors elected by the faculties to several-year terms. Some of the new universities have boards of studies or schools instead of boards of faculties and give their deans longer terms of office.

With the expansion of nonprofessorial staffs at the universities, their representation in various governing bodies increasingly has become a problem. At some of the new universities, special bodies that include or represent all full-time staff members have been created. They can elect representatives and submit proposals to the higher bodies.

At Federal Universities At the two federal universities of London and Wales, academic and financial matters affecting the entire university are handled by central bodies, while the constituent colleges and institutions handle all other matters.

At the University of London, the chief body controlling finance is the 17-member court. Academic affairs are handled by a senate whose 50 members include representatives of the faculties, the constituent institutes and schools, and graduates. The chief governing bodies of the institutes and schools include lay and academic members. The vice-chancellorship of the University of London is held for terms of several years only, and the principal is the top permanent official.

The University of Wales has a large court of more than 250 members, including representatives of the constituent colleges. A small council handles finances, and academic affairs are handled by an academic board. Constituent colleges have their own boards, councils, and senates and handle many academic, financial, and administrative matters which at other universities are the concern of central authorities.

At "Oxbridge" The main organs of academic government at the two ancient foundations are:

1 Congregation at Oxford and Regent House at Cambridge. These include all administrative and teaching staff members. They meet frequently during the academic year.

2 The chief executive bodies, composed of the senior members of the university. At Oxford this body is called Hebdomadal Council. At Cambridge it is called the Council of the Senate. These bodies can only recommend and cannot make final decisions on matters within their jurisdictions.

3 Bodies composed of registered senior graduates (holders of master's or doctor's degrees). The one at Oxford is known as convocation; the one at Cambridge is called the senate. They meet bimonthly and can postpone but cannot amend or reject proposals coming to them.

Financial affairs are the responsiblity of the Curators of the Chest at Oxford and the Financial Board at Cambridge, small, mainly elected bodies. At both universities, academic policy and administration are mainly in the hands of a General Board of the Faculties. The Hebdomadal Council at Oxford and the Council of the Senate at Cambridge require the agreement of the chief financial and academic bodies to advance proposals on financial and academic matters to convocation and senate, respectively. Because the colleges at both Oxford and Cambridge handle their own internal administrative, academic, and financial affairs (they depend financially on fees and endowment and do not directly receive funds from the UGC), the cohesiveness and effectiveness of university governance depend largely on the overlapping membership of heads and members of colleges with membership in the chief organs of university governance. Continuity in university administration is provided mainly by the registrars because of the short terms of office of the vice-chancellors.

Interuniversity Coordination So far, interuniversity coordination has been achieved most significantly by the allocation of funds by the UGC and research councils. For example, the UGC has provided occasional earmarked grants to encourage development of lagging specialties and, in the current quinquennium, has "indicated" to the universities which fields it will or will not give special support for expansion. In its *Annual Survey* for 1966–67, it "recommended that undergraduate teaching in Agriculture be discontinued at three universities in order to concentrate resources in fewer schools (University Grants Committee, 1968*a*, p. 28). In approving enlarged enrollments in certain fields, the UGC, in the same report, favored expansion of existing schools and courses instead of creating new ones.

The UGC favors a minumum enrollment for universities of 3,000 to 5,000 students in the interests of economy. In 1968–69, 17 universities had less than 2,000 students.

Increasingly, the main channel for university coordination is the Committee of Vice-chancellors and Principals, established in 1930. In the 1960s its membership nearly tripled, and its professional staff expanded significantly. It functions through five divisions which deal with university development and capital finance, recurrent finance, staff and student matters, academic matters, and relations with overseas universities. Standing and ad hoc committees are concerned with such subjects as the transition from secondary school to university and university admissions. The committee has undertaken special studies on distribution of staff time among graduate and undergraduate teaching and research, plant utilization, year-round operations, unit costs, and productivity.

The prospect of increasing intervention of external bodies—the UGC, DES, and now the Public Accounts Committee of Parliament —has motivated increasing interest in coordinating efforts by the universities themselves. They are coming to recognize that the high cost of research and the rapid obsolescence rate of advanced equipment require concentration of research in a few centers so that quality will not deteriorate. They are also recognizing the need to surrender some of their individual autonomy in order to strengthen the Committee of Vice-chancellors and Principals, which so far has not had any real executive power. In so doing, the universities may make it possible for the committee to make decisions in some areas which until now have fallen to the UGC. The UGC is urging this very promising development.

Colleges of Education In the past the capacity of colleges of education to govern themselves has been limited. Academic affairs have been handled by institutes of education, and administrative affairs have been directed by the national government under its power to control the training and supply of teachers and to affect the level of financing teacher training outside the universities.

In 1966 a working group was set up under the auspices of the DES to study and make recommendations for the liberalization of the system of governance in colleges of education (Department of Education and Science, 1966*b*). T. R. Weaver, a member of the department, was its chairman. The report of this group urged amendment of existing provisions according to which the LEAs or their subcommittees on education were, in fact, the governing bodies of LEA-maintained colleges of education. Creation of separate governing bodies that would consist of representatives of the LEAs, universities, principals, and academic staff members, teachers, and others was recommended. The Weaver report also noted that not all LEA-maintained colleges of education had academic boards and recommended that this deficiency be remedied. In general, the report recommended more autonomy for the colleges in administrative affairs. The Education (No. 2) Act of 1968 provided for implementation of the Weaver report. The legislation put the governing bodies of the colleges of education outside the LEA committee structure. The act gave the colleges more autonomy in academic affairs as well as more broadly representative governing bodies.

Governance of Colleges and Further Education The government requires that colleges of further education have governing bodies. Sometimes they are subcommittees of the education committees of the LEAs; however, most governing boards of these institutions include not only representatives of the LEAs but also substantial representation from local (and sometimes regional) commercial and industrial firms and trade unions. The governing boards of colleges that give advance courses frequently include representatives of local universities, secondary schools, and professional bodies. The academic councils of the colleges of further education play a limited role in academic affairs. Major decisions on curricular matters are made in coordinated deliberations of the regional advisory councils, which consider proposals for the establishment of new advanced courses, and the DES. Teaching staff members are appointed either by the governing body or by the principal with the governing body's concurrence.

The new polytechnics may have more autonomy than other further education institutions because, as of this writing, LEA representatives on their governing bodies will be limited to a maximum of one-third of the total number of members. All the polytechnics have two student representatives each on their governing bodies and two to three on their academic boards.

In June 1969, a royal commission chaired by Lord Redcliffe-Maud published its report on *Local Government Reform.* It called for wide reorganization of local government to reduce and consolidate over a thousand local government units into 58 larger units. The government accepted the main recommendations in principle and in February 1970 presented a white paper outlining plans to decrease the number of LEAs outside of London from 142 to 56. A probable by-product will be more autonomy for institutions of higher education now under the LEAs.

HIGHER EDUCATION AND ECONOMIC PLANNING

One of the explicit functions of the UGC is to help ensure that the universities "are fully adequate to national needs," and this principle in slightly different words has been confirmed by the Committee of Vice-chancellors and Principals. It has been carried out with the appointment of special committees to study and recommend on the need to expand different areas of university teaching and research and by subsequent measures to encourage and finance such expansion. Because of the difficulty of accurately predicting future manpower needs, and because university first-degree enrollments have been determined mainly by student demands, the role played in university growth by estimates of future needs of highly trained manpower has thus far been limited.

The Robbins Committee based its forecasts of enrollment on estimates of "social demand"—projections of the number of qualified persons who would seek higher education—rather than on the future needs of the economy for highly qualified manpower. But it recommended that machinery be established for "continuous statistical investigation" so that manpower needs might be taken into account in future higher education planning (Robbins Committee, 1963, appendix IV, part II, pp. 70–74). The recommendation led to the establishment of several research bureaus, including one at the London School of Economics in 1964. Known as the Higher Education Research Unit, it is under the direction of C. A. Moser, who has since become head of the Central Statistical Office. Financed by the UGC, the Department of Education and Science, the Social Science Research Council, the Ford Foundation, and other sources, the unit is conducting research on a variety of projects: the educational implications of institutional change (taking the former

CATs as a case study), the scale of higher education since the Robbins Committee Report, the costs and benefits of industrial training, the electrical engineering industry's need for qualified manpower, and, most pertinent to higher education planning, the development of a computable model of Britain's education system. The Higher Education Research Unit works closely with the new planning branch in the DES, established in 1966 to look at higher education as a whole and to advise the policy branches within DES on alternatives for possible development schemes. The planning branch also attempts to gather information pertinent to future needs for trained manpower.

Another governmental agency concerned with matters relevant to higher education was the Committee on Manpower Resources for Science and Technology, disbanded in 1968 and responsible jointly to the DES and the Minister of Technology. It has been succeeded by a new and more broadly based body concerned not only with policy relating to scientists and technologists but also to all other highly qualified manpower.

A significant element in the total planning process in Great Britain is the time-honored practice of setting up independent and usually prestigious committees to study particular areas of education and recommend on future development. Although these committees lack executive authority, and although their recommendations, even when accepted, are not always implemented, their work is important in drawing attention to problem areas and often in generating public support for the reforms and developments they recommend.

FINANCING HIGHER EDUCATION The Robbins Committee reported that public expenditures on all higher education—part-time and full-time, including capital and recurrent expenditures, loan charges, and student maintenance—increased from £63.4 million in 1954–55 to an estimated £219.0 million in 1962–63. Allowing for growth in real incomes, it estimated that public expenditures on higher education (full-time only) would go up from about £206 million in 1962–63 to £357.4 million in 1970–71 and to £742 million in 1980–81 (Robbins Committee, 1963, appendix IV, part IV). By 1965, public expenditures were approaching the Robbins Committee estimate for 1970–71 (Department of Education and Science 1967*b*, vol. V).

As a percentage of the gross national product, public expenditures on higher education increased from about 0.35 percent in

TABLE 8		*1954–55*	*1959–60*	*1965–66*
Expenditures	*Universities*			
for higher	Current expenditures	34.5[a]	57.7[a]	161.0[b]
education in	Capital expenditures	6.7[a]	21.5[a]	89.0[b]
Great Britain	TOTAL	41.2[c]	79.2[c]	250.0[c]
by type of				
institution (in	*Colleges of education*			
millions of	Recurrent expenditures	5.0[a]	8.4[a]	50.9
pounds)	Capital expenditures	1.2[a]	2.6[a]	10.9
	TOTAL	6.2[c]	11.0[c]	61.8[c]
	Advanced further education			
	Recurrent expenditures	8.2[a]	18.0[a]	
	Capital expenditures	2.2[a]	5.3[a]	
	TOTAL	10.4[c]	23.3[c]	
	All higher education			
	Recurrent expenditures	47.7[a]	84.1[a]	
	Capital expenditures	10.1[a]	29.4[a]	
	TOTAL	57.8[c]	113.5[c]	

SOURCES: Robbins Committee, appendix IV, section 2. (*b*) UGC, 1966, p. 171, 186. Recurrent expenditures exclude allocations to reserves. Capital expenditures calculated on basis that Exchequer grants were 90 percent total. (*c*) Calculated using data in this table.

1955–56 to about 1.1 percent in 1965–66. The Robbins Committee estimated that it would be about 1.9 percent in 1980–81.

Before World War II, UGC recurrent grants made up about one-third of the current income of universities. In 1965–66, they made up 74.1 percent of current income (University Grants Committee, 1966, p. 173). Since 1946–47, the proportion of university income from student fees has decreased from 23.2 to 7 percent; endowments decreased from 9.3 to 1.5 percent; and local authority grants decreased from 5.6 to 1.1 percent (University Grants Committee, 1966, p. 173; 1948, p. 89).[11]

UGC grants for current expenditures went up from about £14.2 million in 1950 to about £150 million in 1967–68. The allocation for 1971–72 is £171 million (University Grants Committee, 1968*a,* p. 24). UGC grants for capital expdenditures increased from £7.3 million in 1950 to nearly £75 million in 1967–68.[12]

Between 1954–55 and 1966–67, expenditures on teacher training

[11] Endowment income remains significant for "Oxbridge" colleges, meeting two-fifths of the expenditures of Oxford colleges in 1961, for example.

[12] Information supplied by UGC. The total for 1967–68 is the actual grant paid for building work, fees, furniture, sites, and equipment.

went up from £6 million to £72 million. Expenditures on advanced further education increased from about £10 million in 1954–55 to some £37 million in 1962 and about doubled in the first half of the present decade.

The colleges of education and further education institutions have long been almost totally dependent upon public financial support. "Voluntary" colleges of education, which receive some support from founding bodies, usually churches, are the main exceptions.

The growing dependence of the universities on public support has caused increasing concern. In 1967, the UGC assumed that "universities will do everything they can . . . to augment their income from non-UGC sources." But the government rejected a Robbins Committee recommendation that university fees be raised in order to meet at least one-fifth of current expenses. Instead, several years later, fees were increased only for students from outside the United Kingdom who are not supported by official British sources. Normal fees are between £75 and £110; for most overseas students the rate is now £250. In announcing this measure in 1966, the government indicated that it would eliminate what amounted to a concealed subsidy of £12 million in 1966–67. The universities favor increased fees despite the fact that UGC grants probably would be reduced proportionately if they were adopted and despite the fact that nearly all student fees are publicly funded under the national system for student financial support.

Over the years, several formulas for calculating annual costs per student have been used. All produce different figures while indicating continued increases in costs. One such calculation is in the *National Plan,* published in 1965. It gave a figure of about £200 per student in all types of further education in 1964–65 and about £900 per student in the universities. UGC calculations are weighted according to the student's subject of study and level. Its estimated cost per unit in 1966–67 ranged from £230 for education to £1,256 in veterinary sciences.[13] Current cost per student in teacher training was £770 in 1966–67 (Department of Education and Science, 1967*b*, p. 20).

Concerned over the rising cost of higher education and the need

---

[13] Per unit costs in the various fields were £230 in education, £252 in social studies, £287 in arts, £378 in physical sciences, £473 in engineering, £467 in other applied sciences, £512 in agriculture, £673 in preclinical medicine and dentistry, £763 and 921 in medicine and dentistry, respectively, and £1,256 in veterinary medicine.

to expand higher education in the 1970s to meet the projected doubling in enrollment by 1982, the government in September 1969 set forth 13 proposals for reducing unit costs of higher education. Among these were the introduction of two-year courses, a six-term university year, a deterioration of the staff-student ratio, an expansion of part-time courses, the development of nonresidential universities, the substitution of loans for grants for graduate students, and closer cooperation among the universities, colleges of education, and polytechnics. University reaction to the proposals was generally unfavorable. The extent to which these proposals and probable counterproposals from the Committee of Vice-chancellors and Principals will become policy will probably be indicated in a white paper on the future of higher education the government is expected to issue late in 1970. If implemented, many of the proposals will significantly change the traditional characteristics of British university education.

FINANCIAL ASSISTANCE TO STUDENTS Before 1962, public financial assistance was provided to undergraduates through a combination of state scholarships administered by the Ministry of Education, local authority awards, and university awards. In 1958–59, 83 percent of first-degree students from the United Kingdom attending British universities had public awards.

A new national scheme for student assistance was put into effect with the passage of the Education Act of 1962. It provides a minimum £50 for students with high parental incomes. All qualifying students receive a means-tested grant covering fees, maintenance, books and equipment, clothing, and travel from home, plus additional allowances for vacations and dependents. Apart from the minimum £50 the amount of the award depends on parental income in that a "parental contribution," determined after deducting allowances for dependents, mortgages, and other items from net joint parental income, is subtracted from the full award. To qualify for the awards, students must have lived in the United Kingdom at least three years, be admitted to a first-degree course at university or equivalent, and have two A levels in the General Certificate of Education examinations or equivalent qualifications.

The student assistance system applies equally to students in universities and advanced further education, and a comparable system provides full maintenance and other costs to "recognized resident" students in the colleges of education in England and Wales. "Recognized" students include virtually all students who are British subjects ordinarily resident in England or Wales.

For Oxford, Cambridge, and London, the maximum full grant for students (in residences and lodgings) is now £420; for students at other universities it is £380. The minimum parental residual income for qualification for maintenance is £900. The number of awards for first-degree and lower students in all higher education in Great Britain increased from 122,657 in 1958–59 to 291,671 in 1965–66 and to about 330,000 in 1967 (Department of Education and Science, 1968a, p. 124). By 1966–67, all public financial support to undergraduate students cost £110 million (Department of Education and Science, 1968a, p. 124). Including postgraduate awards, the cost in 1967–68 had increased to £123 million, including about £54 million for students at universities, £28 million for students at further education institutions, and £41 million for students at colleges of education. About £7 million was for postgraduate awards. More than 90 percent of all home students at British universities receive awards paying part or all of their fees and other expenses. Undergraduate students in higher education who do not receive public support are mainly students in further education who receive assistance from their employers. Despite periodic pressure to replace the grant system with loans, such a change appears unlikely.

Even undergraduates who receive maximum awards apparently have some difficulty in meeting all their expenses. A detailed study of student costs in 1967 reported that the minimum full grant necessary to cover basic expenditures during term time is £435 to £460 for university undergraduates, depending on location of the institution and student living arrangements. This was between £65 and £75 more than grant rates then.[14] A sampling of students at one of the new universities showed that 84 percent worked an average of eight weeks during vacations and earned an average of £88. A UGC survey published in 1963 found that 62 percent of undergraduate students (excluding those in dentistry, veterinary science, and medicine) worked for a median period of more than six weeks during their vacations.

Postgraduate awards are provided by the research councils and

[14] "President's Address," *Forty-fifth Annual Council Meeting, National Union of Students, Minutes and Summary of Proceedings, November 24–27, 1967,* London, 1968, p. 22.

the DES, but industry also supports some postgraduate students. Until 1965, most postgraduate students in science and technology (excluding medicine and agriculture) were financed by the Department of Scientific and Industrial Research (DSIR) set up in 1916 to promote scientific research. When the DSIR was dissolved in 1965, its function of providing postgraduate awards devolved mainly upon five research councils, chartered autonomous bodies that get their money via DES. There are councils for science, agriculture, medicine, natural environment, and social science. New postgraduate awards in science and technology increased from 805 in 1957–58 (DSIR only) to 3,673 in 1966–67, awarded by all the research councils (Department of Education and Science, 1968a, p. 93; Robbins Committee, 1963, appendix IIa, p. 231).

The DES awards state studentships to postgraduate students in the humanities. New awards in this field increased from 243 in 1957 to 751 in 1966. In 1966, 1,570 state studentships were held by postgraduates in the humanities. In 1967, students took up 881 out of 996 awards offered in the humanities (Department of Education and Science, 1968a, p. 126). The total number of postgraduate students holding awards in all fields increased from 6,664 in 1958–59 to about 16,000 in 1966–67 (Department of Education and Science, 1968a, p. 124).

In principle, postgraduate studentships and fellowships pay for all fees, provide a maintenance grant for which there is no parental means test, and include travel and other allowances. In July 1968 the Secretary of State for Education and Science announced that publicly supported research grants for postgraduate students would increase from £410 to £425 annually for students living at home and from £530 to £550 for students in halls and lodgings. Unlike grants to undergraduates, grants to postgraduates do not vary according to the institutions attended. About three-fifths of all home postgraduate students have public awards, and the total value of awards went up from £2.1 million in 1958–59 to £8.4 million in 1966–67 (Department of Education and Science, 1968a, p. 124).

STUDENT CHARACTERISTICS AND ORGANIZATIONS   The Robbins Committee noted that "the proportion of children who reach full-time higher education is about six times as great in the families of non-manual workers as in those of manual workers; the chances of children of non-manual workers reaching courses of degree level are about eight times as high. Children with fathers in professional and managerial occupations are 20 times more likely to enter full-time higher education than are those with fathers in semi- and unskilled jobs" (Robbins Committee, 1963, appendix I, p. 38). The committee also found little change in the relative chances of middle- and working-class children reaching higher education, although for both groups the proportion had risen. Because of the system of maintenance grants, family income, as such, seemed to have little to do with the likelihood of a child's entering higher education once he had acquired the necessary A levels. According to the committee's data, however, the proportion of children whose fathers were "higher professionals" constituted 45 percent of the young people born in 1940–41 who entered full-time higher education whereas "higher professionals" constituted not quite 3 percent of employed fathers in Great Britain (Robbins Committee, 1963, p. 50).

A 1966–67 sampling of 4,000 Scottish students in higher education showed that 58.5 percent were from families having an annual net income of £1,225 or less after deductions allowed under the system of maintenance grants and that 37.8 percent came from families with net incomes of £913 or less. This sampling supports the generally accepted estimate that about one-third of the students in full-time higher education in Britain are from relatively low-income families.

Student associations in Great Britain have been much less "activist" than those on the continent. Among the major reasons are the relatively short study period in full-time higher education and the close contact students have with staff members.

The chief student organization, the National Union of Students (NUS), was founded in 1922. It is a federation of student unions at some 700 colleges and universities in England, Wales, and Northern Ireland. Students at Scottish institutions of higher education have their own Scottish Union of Students. The NUS is deliberately unaligned with any political party. It has about 400,000 members: about 98 percent of the university students, 85 percent of students at colleges of education, and a growing proportion of full-time students at colleges of further education. The NUS is financed by compulsory union fees of 5 shillings paid to institutions in return for amenities. The LEAs are required to pay these fees in respect of university students and may pay them in the case of students in public sector institutions of higher education. Some student union presidents at universities are so-called sabbatical presidents, taking a year off from their studies to work for the student unions.

In its early period of development, the NUS was concerned mainly with student amenities, grants, travel, welfare, vacation employment, and other essentially nonpolitical matters. Always relatively active, the NUS has been more noticeably so since the early 1960s. At that time the massive expansion of higher education and the disarray of leftist student movements which had flourished in the aftermath of the Suez crisis and Hungarian uprising (but languished from lack of Labour Party support) brought large numbers of students, including the leftists, into NUS. Membership quadrupled between 1958 and 1968, as additional universities became affiliated.

In the last several years, the NUS has become more active in its advocacy of student interests with higher education institutions and government authorities, both at the local and national levels. It has pressed for increases in student maintenance grants and the abolition of means tests for them, for national insurance benefits for students, for expanded residential accommodations, for more liberal parietal rules, for the expansion of higher education facilities, for raising the school-leaving age, and, in particular, for student participation in decision making in higher education institutions. But it pursues its objectives through established channels rather than through organized student protests and strikes. In a disagreement on these tactics, the radical students parted company with the NUS and founded the Radical Student Alliance in February 1967 (Halsey and Marks, 1968, pp. 116–136).

The last several years have witnessed increasing numbers of demonstrations, sit-ins, and other forms of protest at universities and at some of the colleges of further education. Issues have been primarily related to such matters as examinations, curriculum, and student participation in decision-making bodies, although demonstrations on domestic and foreign policy of the national government are now more common. In general, only a fraction of the student population of universities has been involved, and demonstrations have been locally, rather than nationally or regionally, organized. Student protest in February 1970 was unusual in spreading from one to a number of universities and may mark a new tendency in student activism in Britain.[15]

[15] Students protested against the alleged practice of universities of keeping secret files on students' political activities.

CHANGES AND REFORM

The major changes in British higher education in this decade include innovations at the "new" universities, the establishment of first-degree programs in the public sector through the Council for National Academic Awards, and the creation of the polytechnics.

The New Universities

These institutions are departing from tradition in several respects. First, they are located away from major industrial cities. Second, unlike the older universities, they have been given the right to award their own degrees immediately, skipping the heretofore normal probationary status of university colleges offering external degrees. They are attempting to avoid excessive specialization and are rejecting organization on the basis of faculties in favor of boards of schools or of study with group-related subjects. Some have fourth years of supervised postgraduate study rather than the independent research more usual in British graduate work. The new universities also attempt to eliminate sharp distinctions between academic, social, and residential life by blending the physical facilities involved, by modifying collegiate structures, and by adopting measures that integrate the students living away from campus into the life at the university.

Governance Proposals

The Robbins Committee recommended that governing bodies of universities normally have a majority of lay members, that non-professorial staff members participate more fully in internal self-government, and that the administrative burden on vice-chancellors be reduced.

At Oxford and Cambridge

The Robbins Committee also urged that independent inquiries be undertaken on the problems arising from the collegiate structure at Oxford and Cambridge. A commission appointed in 1964 by the Hebdomadal Council at Oxford to examine the university's functioning was headed by Lord Franks. A somewhat similar body, the Bridges Committee, considered reform of Cambridge in its report of 1962. The Franks Commission was particularly interested in establishing a stronger central authority and shifting from the tutorial system toward more lectures.

The Franks Committee recommended that the Hebdomadal Council become the chief executive body of the university, that the powers of the convocation be restricted to electing the chancellor, that the vice-chancellor have a four-year full-time position, that a comprehensive statistical service be established, that the existing

15 faculties be combined into 5 comprehensive ones, that a council of the colleges be established, and that the committee structure and university-college relations be restructured to achieve a more unified system in which the colleges would have a less dominant role. Some of these proposals, including making the vice-chancellorship a four-year, full-time position and the development of better statistical services, have been put into effect, and others are still under consideration. But the prospects for essential changes in the relationship of the colleges to the central administration are considered to be very slim.

In the Universities of London and Wales

The Robbins Committee found anomalous the fact that the heads of the larger colleges of the University of London (some of which are larger than independent universities) lacked direct access to the UGC or membership in the Committee of Vice-chancellors and Principals. Since the Robbins Committee Report was issued, both the University of London and the University of Wales have been given several additional full voting members on the Committee.

Student Participation in University Governance

A survey published in October 1968 by the National Union of Students shows that representation of students on university committees has expanded greatly in recent years, that there tends to be more student participation in major university committees at the "new" universities than at the older ones, and that the committees having student participation most commonly are those concerned with matters directly affecting students — refectories, lodgings, libraries, athletics, and student relations. A few universities have provided for student representation in their governing bodies.[16]

In October 1968 an agreement between the Committee of Vice-chancellors and Principals and the NUS was announced. It calls for more student participation in decision making in the universities of England, Wales, and Northern Ireland, recognizing, however, that the degree of student participation should vary depending upon the subjects involved. For example, while "student views should be properly taken into account with respect to curricula and

[16] A recent NUS survey showed that in 1968–69 the number of universities in England and Wales with students represented on the council increased from six to seventeen and on the senate from six to fourteen. In late 1969 there were 29 universities with staff-student committees, whereas four years before there were none (*Time Educational Supplement,* May 15, 1970, p. 7).

university management and planning, the ultimate decision must be that of the statutorily responsible body." And although the presence of students would not be appropriate in bodies making decisions on staff appointments and promotions, students should "have opportunities to discuss the general principles involved." The agreement strongly suggested varying degrees of student participation in bodies dealing with student welfare up to and including student control of some activities. These principles were being implemented rapidly through direct negotiation at individual universities in 1968–69.

THE BALANCE SHEET The British concept that higher education should be a personalized process requiring close contact between teacher and taught and the participation of both in a shared community is historic. It survives in the remarkably low staff-student ratios and in the universities' emphasis on community life; it contributes to the high success rate of students and makes short study periods possible. On the other side of the coin, however, are high selectivity in admissions and limitations on university expansion. These are linked to the national conviction that only a fraction of the population requires or has the capacity to profit from university education, the notion of a "limited pool of ability."[17]

The flexibility of advanced further education, which is being enlarged and restructured to give ever greater numbers of students the opportunity to pursue education, is an obvious strength. It offers a second chance to "late bloomers" and "low flyers," permitting qualified young people who leave school at 15 to progress through part-time, full-time, and sandwich courses up to and through university-equivalent advanced education.

A relatively low esteem of technology is a weakness in British higher education. Historically, advanced technological training was offered in nonuniversity institutions, and only with the elevation of the CATs to university status has the provision of this training in high-level institutions become fully and officially realized. It still fails to attract students in the numbers needed by the society, however, and university training is not commonly regarded in industry as a necessary qualification for leading positions. One result is the widespread view that advanced further education,

[17] It is interesting that while the percentage of the age group entering university increased from 3 percent in 1952 to 5.5 percent in 1965, the proportion of entering students "wasted" dropped from 16.7 to 13.3 percent in that period.

even though it is frequently of university quality, is inferior to university education.

UGC, which has ensured the autonomy of public-supported universities in the past, is generally considered a special strength of the British university system. But there have been indications that its methods of operation and functions are shifting so that it is less a buffer and more an agent of governmental influence. This capacity to change is another strength of the UGC although there is some question whether it is changing enough.

THE FUTURE There will be a continued rise in the demand for, and cost of, higher education in Great Britain. Enrollment will surely increase as a result of the now tentatively planned increase in the school-leaving age to 16 and increasing demand—despite current restrictions—in postgraduate study. The recent increases in student grants notwithstanding, whether students should be financed by grants, loans, or "salaries" remains an issue.

Some current cost and productivity analyses and manpower studies currently under way may lead to more effective utilization of higher education resources, but they cannot significantly reduce costs unless accompanied by fundamental structural changes, e.g., raising staff-student ratios in universities. In fact, these studies may confirm what has often been alleged: the apparently high cost of producing first-degree recipients via the university route is a bargain, considering high success rates of university students and the fact that university-equivalent courses, wherever they are given, cost about the same unless their quality is inferior.

A major problem in the future appears to be the determination of criteria for allocating funds and supporting expansion in the two sectors of British higher education. If cost factors are set aside, the principal difference between the two sectors may be the autonomy of the universities as contrasted to the governmental control of public-sector insitutions, though this gap is narrowing. In the last analysis, the main difference may relate to the question of social responsibility. The universities are sometimes criticized for not being sufficiently responsive to the needs of society. This criticism raises the basic philosophical problem of whether the university itself can best evaluate and decide how to serve society most effectively or whether society should determine what needs the university meets, and how. This problem may be more acute in Britain than in North American universities because the chief executive officer in British universities has relatively less authority. The major role of faculty members in university governance, carried to the ultimate at Oxford and Cambridge, militates against strong central direction by the organ of governance best situated to look equally within and without the immediate academic community. There are signs, however, that the office of the vice-chancellorship has become stronger in the last several years. This tendency may continue as the issue of social responsibility of universities becomes more acute in the years ahead.

Universities in the United Kingdom

University of Aberdeen

University of Aston in Birmingham

Bath University of Technology

Queen's University of Belfast

University of Birmingham

University of Bradford

University of Bristol

Brunel University, London

University of Cambridge

The City University, London

University of Dundee

University of Durham

University of East Anglia, Norwich

University of Edinburgh

University of Essex, Colchester

University of Exeter

University of Glasgow

Heriot-Watt University, Edinburgh

University of Hull

University of Keele

University of Kent at Canterbury

University of Lancaster

University of Leeds

University of Leicester

University of Liverpool

University of London

Loughborough University of Technology

University of Manchester

University of Newcastle upon Tyne

University of Nottingham

University of Oxford

University of Reading

University of St. Andrews

University of Salford

University of Sheffield

University of Southampton

University of Stirling

University of Strathclyde, Glasgow

University of Surrey, London

University of Sussex, Brighton

New University of Ulster, Coleraine

University of Wales

    University College of Wales, Aberystwyth

    University College of North Wales, Bangor

    University College of South Wales and Monmouthshire, Cardiff

    St. David's College, Lampeter

    University College of Swansea

    Welsh National School of Medicine, Cardiff

    Welsh College of Advanced Technology, Cardiff

University of Warwick, Coventry

University of York

References

Central Office of Information: *Students from Overseas in Britain,* London, 1965.

Committee on Manpower Resources for Science and Technology: *The Brain Drain: Report of the Working Group on Migration,* Cmnd. 3417, HMSO, London, 1967.

Corbett, Anne: *Much Ado about Education,* Council for Educational Advance, London, 1968.

Department of Education and Science: *Education and Science in 1967,* Cmnd. 3564, HMSO, London, 1968a.

Department of Education and Science: *A Plan for Polytechnics and Other Colleges,* Cmnd. 3006, HMSO, London, 1966a.

Department of Education and Science: *The Government of Colleges of Education,* HMSO, London, 1966b.

Department of Education and Science: *Statistics of Education 1965,* parts II and III; *1966,* vols. II, III, and V; *1967,* vols. II and V, HMSO, London, 1967a, 1967b, 1968b.

Department of Education and Science and Ministry of Technology: *Statistics of Science and Technology,* HMSO, London, 1967c.

Estimates Committee: *Fifth Report from the Estimates Committee,* 1964–65 Session, HMSO, London, 1965.

Halsey, A. H.: "British Universities," *European Journal of Sociology,* vol. III, no. 1, 1962.

Halsey, A. H.: "The Universities and the State," *Universities Quarterly,* vol. 23, no. 1, Spring 1969.

Halsey, A. H., and Stephen Marks: "British Student Politics," *Daedalus,* vol. 97, no. 1, Winter 1968.

Layard, Richard, John King, and Claus Moser: *The Impact of Robbins: Expansion in Higher Education,* Penguin Books, London, 1969.

Lukes, J. R.: "The Binary Policy: A Critical Study," *Universities Quarterly,* vol. 21, no. 1, December 1967.

National Advisory Council on the Training and Supply of Teachers: *9th Report, Demand and Supply of Teachers 1963–86,* HMSO, London, 1965.

Report of the Working Party on Liaison between Universities and Government Research Establishment, Cmnd. 3222, HMSO, London, 1967.

Robbins Committee: *Higher Education: Report of the Committee Appointed by the Prime Minister under the Chairmanship of Lord Robbins 1961–63,* Cmnd. 2154, HMSO, London, 1963, appendixes I, IIa and b, III, IV.

University Grants Committee: *Annual Survey, Academic Year 1966–67,* Cmnd. 3510, HMSO, London, 1968a.

University Grants Committee: *Enquiry into Student Progress,* HMSO, London, 1968b.

University Grants Committee: *Returns from Universities 1955–56,* Cmnd. 211, HMSO, London, 1957.

University Grants Committee: *Returns from Universities and University Colleges, Academic Year 1960–61,* Cmnd. 1855, HMSO, 1962.

University Grants Committee: *Returns from Universities and University Colleges 1965–66,* Cmnd. 3586, HMSO, London, 1966.

University Grants Committee: *University Development from 1935 to 1948,* HMSO, London, 1948.

5. Higher Education in Canada

Canadian universities and colleges range in size from large multi-faculty institutions enrolling more than 15,000 students to small liberal arts colleges and theological schools with only a few hundred. Except in Quebec, practically all the universities are designed along British and Scottish lines; Sherbrooke, Laval, Montreal, and the new University of Quebec are modeled on the French pattern. The American tradition of land-grant colleges has made a discernible impression on universities in the western provinces, and Canada's community college movement owes much to recent American junior college developments.

Less than one-fourth of the Canadian universities were started by provincial authorities; the rest were started by religious groups or private secular bodies. But in funding and governance there is no clear distinction between public and private institutions. In Quebec, Manitoba, and the three maritime provinces, private institutions receive public support, and throughout Canada the universities established by public (mainly provincial) authorities are characteristically governed by boards made up of both public representatives and private individuals. In recent years there has been a trend toward secularization of the denominational institutions.

COMPONENTS In 1967-68, Canada's postsecondary institutions of higher education included 62 degree-conferring colleges and universities. There were also 250 institutions (most of whose degrees are granted by universities with which they are affiliated) providing instruction to the bachelor degree level or beyond. By 1969 the number of these institutions had been reduced by about one-third because so many of the classical colleges affiliated with the French universities had become absorbed into *colleges d'enseignement général et professionnel* (CEGPs) or ceased to prepare students for the *baccalauréat.*

Canada's institutions of higher education also include about 90 junior or community colleges, a score of CEGPs in Quebec, some 75 normal schools, about 170 nurses' diploma courses in hospital schools, and 3 colleges operated by the military services.

Much like the University of London, many Canadian universities have federated or affiliated colleges that may have separate governing bodies or budgets. Most of these colleges offer work in the humanities and social sciences leading to the degree of the university with which they are affiliated. They retain degree-conferring powers in theology.

Until recently, the French Canadian universities consisted of groups of professional schools, the core of which were the more than 100 classical colleges that were attached to them and formed their faculties of arts. Students who completed an eight-year classical college course successfully (following seven years of elementary school) used to be awarded the *baccalauréat ès arts,* qualifying them for admission to the other faculties of the university. But this system has changed radically. Between 1963 and 1966 a special commission under the chairmanship of Monsignor Alphonse-Marie Parent made a study of education, including higher education, in Quebec. One of the commission's key recommendations, which was mostly implemented by 1970, requires students to take their twelfth and thirteenth years of school at new CEGPs. In 1968–69, 23 of these colleges were operating, and by 1971 there will be 30 to 32. They will become the only avenues to the universities of that province. Eventually, all the classical colleges will fuse with other institutions to become CEGPs, will offer CEGP-equivalent courses as private institutions, or will reduce their offering to courses at the secondary level. The CEGPs offer two- and three-year technical and vocational programs and a two-year academic program leading to the university. In 1969, one English-language CEGP, Dawson College, in Westmount, opened. Until more English-language CEGPs are established, the English-language universities are offering the equivalent of the two CEGP years preceding their regular degree courses.

Since the late 1950s, junior or community colleges have been established in nearly every province. Alberta and British Columbia led in this development by establishing new subuniversity institutions as an alternative to expanding their universities to meet increasing demand for postsecondary education that provides access to first-degree work. In Alberta the junior colleges are affiliated with the provincial university. In British Columbia they are separate. Typically, these institutions offer both transfer and vocational-terminal courses. In early 1968, the Canadian Commission for the Community College was established to strengthen and develop junior and community college programs throughout Canada.

All teachers for secondary schools are now trained in the universities, and increasing numbers of teachers for primary schools are being trained there. In 1967, about 40 percent of Canada's teachers in training were enrolled in universities rather than in teachers colleges. Only four provinces—Nova Scotia, New Brunswick, Quebec, and Ontario—had normal schools or teachers colleges that were separate from universities. Of the 76 teachers colleges in existence in 1966 (there were 126 in 1961), 61 were in Quebec. Even there, they were tending to move under the aegis of the universities. In Ontario, present plans call for placing all elementary school teacher training under the universities by the early 1970s. Not only has the number of independent teachers colleges been decreasing, but since 1963 their enrollments have declined.

Technical colleges and institutes constitute another branch of the subuniversity higher education system. The new colleges of applied arts and technology (CAATs) in Ontario offer vocational programs only. They do not have "transfer" programs to prepare students for admission to university at an advanced level.

In some provinces, junior matriculation in secondary schools (completion of 11 or 12 years of schooling) suffices for university admission, and students who have enrolled through the senior year (completing 12 or 13 years of schooling) may require only three, instead of four, years to earn their first degrees. But these senior-year secondary school courses are not considered higher education. Variations in secondary school programs are now under review in some of the provinces.

FUNCTIONS The curricular programs of Canadian colleges and universities are more specialized and more oriented to the professions than those of American institutions of higher learning, but the Canadian institutions generally resemble those in the United States in the roles they play in research, in introducing new fields of knowledge, in providing adult education, in participating in international education and assistance programs, and, to a lesser extent, in promoting and sponsoring the arts.

Until recently, Canadian universities have received few contract research grants from industry and the federal government. In the past, the federal government has preferred to support research in its own laboratories. However, federal research grants, e.g., those of the National Research Council, the Medical Research Council, and the Defense Research Board, have been important to university research for a long time. Government expenditure for university research has been increasing, and influential agencies have urged that it increase still more.

In response to new scientific developments and to meet the need for research and teaching in new fields and in interdisciplinary studies, many of the larger universities have established centers and institutes specializing in such fields as computer technology, space research, northern studies, urban problems, and industrial relations.

Adult education programs, some of which lead to degrees, are offered by many of the universities. In the western provinces, university extension programs in agriculture and other fields function in widely scattered communities. In the more populated provinces, such as Ontario and Quebec, the universities give evening courses in teacher training, nursing, business education, the humanities, and various technical and scientific subjects. Some universities offer correspondence courses for credit.

Most of the adult education provided in Canada is in the form of classes offered by provincial and municipal government agencies. In 1965-66, these classes enrolled 125,531 in academic programs, 538,611 in vocational programs, and 146,707 in cultural, humanities, public affairs, and other informal classes, for a total enrollment of 1,568,212 (Dominion Bureau of Statistics, 1968*b*, pp. 48–50). But institutions of higher learning are also engaged in adult education, especially in academic and professional programs. Enrollments in adult education degree courses reached 148,129 in 1965–66, and enrollments in noncredit courses increased to 177,779 in the same period (Dominion Bureau of Statistics, 1968*b*, pp. 48–50).

Canadian universities are relatively active in international education. By 1967–68 there were 15,356 students from abroad attending Canadian universities and colleges. Close to one-half of them were from British Commonwealth countries; 1,100 were from Africa, 5,472 were from Asia, 2,474 were from Europe, 4,045 were from North America, 503 were from Latin America, 1,370 were from the West Indies, and 250 were from Oceania.[1] Large numbers

---

[1] Information supplied by the Dominion Bureau of Statistics.

of foreign students in Canada receive financial support from Canadian sources, including the universities and colleges. With substantial financial assistance from the Canadian International Development Agency, the Canadian University Service Overseas (CUSO), a private organization initiated partly by universities, provides volunteer assistance in a number of developing countries. Other international assistance programs include "twinning" relationships with foreign universities. In 1966, Quebec and the French government entered into an accord relating to exchange of teachers and students. The International Development Agency sponsors the teaching of school teachers and university professors abroad, particularly in French-speaking countries.

The performing and creative arts have a stronger position on university campuses than they did 10 years ago, but their place in university life, especially in curricula, is controversial and not yet secure. In a report entitled *The Current State of the Arts in the University,* prepared for a conference in connection with Canada's centennial in 1967, the director of the Canada Foundation found few examples of universities providing cultural leadership to their local communities or cooperating with adjacent towns in music, art, and drama activities. However, he saw the "impending emergence of the Arts as a force in the University" to be inevitable and noted a growing public interest in the arts and the initiative of university students in bringing cultural events to the campus. The extent of the universities' roles in cultural affairs is suggested by the fact that in 1965–66, 591,626 people attended university lectures, music and dramatic performances, art exhibits, and film showings (Herbert, 1967).

ENROLLMENT TRENDS

The number of full-time students enrolled in courses leading to a first degree or diploma in Canadian universities and colleges (comparable generally to a bachelor's degree in the United States) nearly quadrupled between 1951–52 and 1967–68, when it reached 237,020. In 1975–76, it is expected to be about 475,700. Full-time graduate enrollment increased sevenfold between 1951–52 and 1967–68, when it reached 24,187. It will be about 64,300 (or 13.5 percent of total enrollments) by 1975–76.

There are several reasons for Canada's rising enrollments in colleges and universities. The number of students in grade twelve increased from about 45,000 in 1951–52 to 176,000 in 1965–66 (Illing and Zsigmond, 1967, pp. 139–140) and is projected to be 238,000 in 1975–76. The likelihood of a primary school student's eventually going to a university increased from 1 in 12 in 1950 to 1 in 6 in 1964 (Commission on the Financing of Higher Education in Canada, 1965, p. 12). The proportion of women students in institutions of higher learning went up from less than one-fourth in 1951–52 to one-third in 1966–67 and is expected to be two-fifths in 1975–76. And the proportion of the 18- to 24-year-old age group enrolled in colleges and universities increased from 4.2 percent in 1951–52 to 10.1 percent 1965–66 and is expected to be 20.7 percent in 1975–76.

Part-time enrollments are increasingly significant. They went up from a little over 10,000 in the mid-1950s to about 73,000 in 1965–66. By 1975–76 they are expected to be about 196,000, or close to one-third of all postsecondary enrollments.

Persistence Rates

Between one-third and one-fourth of the students entering Canadian colleges and universities fail to obtain their first degrees. In some faculties, the dropout rate may be as high as 50 percent.

A 1966 study prepared for the Economic Council of Canada suggested that for the period of 1946-58, 61 percent of the entering students received university degrees in their fourth year, 21 percent completed the first year only, 11 percent completed no more than two years, and 7 percent completed no more than three years (Bertram, 1966, p. 101).

The dropout rate of first-year students at the University of British Columbia decreased from 26.1 percent in 1960 to 15.4 percent in 1965. The decrease is attributed to the establishment of community colleges as alternative institutions to the university ("The Public Financing of Universities," 1966, p. 6).

Staff-Student Ratios

In 1955–56, the Dominion Bureau of Statistics estimates indicated that the full-time teaching staff in universities and colleges, including some research personnel and junior assistants, was 6,719, giving a staff-student ratio of 1:10.8 (Dominion Bureau of Statistics, 1967, p. 368). The ratio estimated for 1967–68 was 1:12.6 and was based upon a full-time faculty of about 20,700 and an enrollment of 261,200.[2] It was estimated that at least 3,200 new teachers will be required annually to maintain the 1967–68 ratio into 1970 (OECD, 1966, p. 61).

[2] Information supplied by the Higher Education Division, Dominion Bureau of Statistics.

TABLE 9 *Enrollment in Canadian institutions of higher education by year and type of institution (regular winter session, in thousands)*

	1955–56	*1960–61*	*1965–66*	*1967–68*	*1975–76*
Colleges and universities					
Full-time undergraduates	69.3[a]	107.3[a]	188.7[a]	237.0[b]	475.7[c]
Full-time graduates	3.4[a]	6.6[a]	17.2[a]	24.2[b]	64.3[c]
TOTAL	72.7[a]	113.9[a]	205.9[a]	261.2[b]	540.0[c]
Part-time undergraduates			66.2[a]	88.0[b]	180.6[c]
Part-time graduates			7.7[a]	11.0[b]	15.7[c]
TOTAL	10.1[a]	28.9[a]	73.9[a]	99.1[b]	196.3[c]
Part-time and full-time undergraduates			254.9[a]	325.0[b]	656.3[c]
Part-time and full-time graduates			24.9[a]	35.2[b]	80.0[c]
TOTAL	82.8[a]	130.8[a]	279.8	360.2	736.3
Full-time in teachers colleges	10.7[d]	19.0[d]	20.6[d]	23.8[e]	
Full-time in postsecondary technical institutes	6.5[d]	11.7[d]	26.0[d]	42.6[e]	
Total full-time enrollment in postsecondary institutions	89.9[d]	114.6[d]	252.5[d]	357.8[e]	

SOURCES: (a) Illing and Zsigmond, 1967, p. 141. (b) Dominion Bureau of Statistics, *Daily Bulletin,* vol. 37, no. 60, March 25, 1968, Queen's Printer, Ottawa, 1968. (c) Illing and Zsigmond, 1967, p. 142. (d) *Ibid.,* p. 143. (e) Dominion Bureau of Statistics, *Advance Statistics of Education 1967–68,* Queen's Printer, Ottawa, 1967. Includes all nonuniversity postsecondary enrollment excluding nurses' diploma courses (23,800), so the total enrollment figure includes more categories of institutions than included in statistics for previous years. Hence the large increase in total enrollment for 1967–68 over 1966–67.

HIGHER EDUCATION AND CIVIL GOVERNMENT

Although the earliest Canadian universities were chartered by the Crown, the British North America Act of 1867 assigned exclusive responsibility in the field of education to the 10 provinces. In the last century, most new universities were created by provincial legislation. None were created by the federal government because it lacks the power to give degree-granting authority to higher education institutions.

Although the federal government has no constitutional authority in university affairs, it has shown increasing concern for them. Since 1951, federal financial support has increased, and since 1960 nearly one-fifth of the university's operating costs including assisted research have been met from federal funds. About 40 federal agencies have significant higher education interests. Among them are the National Research Council, established in 1916 to en-

TABLE 10
*Enrollment in
Canadian
institutions
of higher
education as a
percentage of
18- to 24-year-
olds in the
population*

	1955–56	1960–61	1965–66	1975–76
Full-time university enrollment	4.7	6.7	10.1	20.7
Full-time enrollment in all postsecondary institutions	5.7	8.6	12.4	22.6

SOURCES: Illing and Zsigmond, 1967, pp. 151-152.

courage the development of scientific and industrial research; the Defense Research Board, established in 1947; the Medical Research Council, set up in 1960 mainly to promote medical research in the universities; the Canada Council for the Encouragement of the Arts, Humanities and Social Sciences, set up in 1957; the Department of Finance, which has been involved in grants to universities; the Central Mortgage and Housing Corporation, which handles loans for student residences; the Dominion Bureau of Statistics, whose Higher Education Section compiles and publishes statistical material on higher education; the Department of Labour; the Economic Council of Canada, established in 1963 to advise the government on Canada's economic growth; the Science Council of Canada, established in 1966 to advise the government on policy for promoting research; and the Department of External Affairs and the Canadian International Development Agency, which are concerned with international education assistance.

The idea of establishing a single federal agency to coordinate federal involvements in higher education has received growing support during the 1960s. The Prime Minister appointed a special adviser on university grants attached to the Privy Council in 1963, but this adviser was not authorized to coordinate federal programs in higher education. When, after 18 months, the first adviser left this position, it was not filled. In 1966, the Department of the Se-

TABLE 11 *Degrees awarded by Canadian institutions of higher education*

	1955–56	1960–61	1965–66	1967–68	1975–76
First degree or equivalent	13,800[a]	20,200[a]	38,500[b]	50,800[c]	106,600[d]
Master's degree or equivalent	1,500[a]	2,400[a]	5,200[b]	7,400[c]	18,200[d]
Doctorate	266[a]	305[a]	697[b]	940[c]	2,500[d]

SOURCES: (a) Illing and Zsigmond, 1967, p. 145. (b) Dominion Bureau of Statistics, 1968b. (c) Dominion Bureau of Statistics, *Advance Statistics of Education 1967-68,* Queen's Printer, Ottawa, 1967. (d) Illing and Zsigmond, 1967, p. 146.

cretary of State was given responsibility relating to "the encouragement of . . . learning and cultural activities" and advising the cabinet with respect to higher education. In a sense this new role of the Secretary of State represented succession to the role of the special adviser. A special consultant was assigned to the staff of the Undersecretary of State to develop a secretariat to assist with this function. In October of the same year at a meeting of federal and provincial higher education officials the federal government made clear that responsibility for research, cultural affairs, and adult training falls within the jurisdiction of the federal government. Plans were also announced for new arrangements for federal financial support of postsecondary education. In 1967, an office in the Department of the Secretary of State was established to be an information center on federal involvements in postsecondary education, to administer payments of federal funds for it in the provinces, and to determine the extent to which the federal government was, in fact, giving financial support to postsecondary education. In the spring of 1968, this office, known as the Education Support Branch, was still primarily engaged in collecting information about federal aid to postsecondary education.

In 1966, the Standing Committee of Ministers of Education (since renamed the Council of Ministers of Education), which was loosely linked with the Canadian Education Association, a semiofficial body supported by the provinces, appointed a committee to study ways to achieve more interprovincial cooperation in educational development. Since that time, a secretariat has been established temporarily in Toronto, and several committees, including one on postsecondary education, have been appointed.

The federal role in Canadian higher education may be significantly affected by results of discussions of revision of the country's 101-year-old constitution. These discussions between the Prime Minister and the provisional governments were initiated in September 1968.

Intraprovincial Coordination
Parallel to growing federal concern for higher education, there has been rapid development of intraprovincial coordination since the early 1960s. In 1965, an independent Commission on Financing Higher Education in Canada, under the chairmanship of Vincent W. Bladen, recommended that "all provinces that have not yet established a 'Grants Commission' do so . . . to advise the government on the aggregate needs of the universities, capital and opera-

ting, and to divide among the universities the total amount in fact voted by the province." A high degree of compliance with this recommendation is evidenced by the fact that most of the provinces now have special agencies concerned with higher education.

In Nova Scotia, a University Grants Committee was set up in 1963 to advise on the development and financial support of higher education institutions in the province and to plan cooperation among them.

The Universities Commission in Alberta, created in 1966, acts as "an intermediary between Government and universities, and between the universities." Since it is made up of government appointees and has no academic representation, it is not a university grants committee in the British sense. Working with the Universities Commission is the Provincial Board of Post-secondary Education, established in 1967. If adopted, legislation introduced in early 1969 will change the board to a Provincial Colleges Commission. It advises the Department of Education on general postsecondary education needs.

In British Columbia, the Advisory Board on Finances, set up under the Universities Act of 1963, advises the Minister of Education on the allocation but not the size of the government's financial grant to universities. In addition to its chairman, the board has equal numbers of members appointed by the universities and by the Minister of Education. The Academic Board of Higher Education in British Columbia, also set up in 1963, advises on the development and standards of higher education in the province. In late 1968, the provincial government announced the establishment of an ad hoc committee to investigate the structure of higher education including the formation of a university grants commission.

In Ontario, the advisory Committee on University Affairs, set up in 1961 and reorganized in 1964 to include educators and laymen, advises on provincial support to universities. In 1964, Ontario established the first Department of University Affairs in Canada.

There has been a Council on Higher Learning in Manitoba since 1965. It advises on postsecondary education. In both Manitoba and New Brunswick, university grants commissions (called the Higher Education Commission in New Brunswick) were established in 1967. Formally, the Manitoba Commission's powers are extensive because they include the power to approve all new facilities and programs requiring Commission funding.

Prince Edward Island established a Commission on Post-secondary Education in 1969.

Newfoundland and Saskatchewan have only one university each. These institutions deal directly with their provincial governments.

The Quebec Conference of Rectors and Principals, which held its first meeting in 1963, has urged the establishment of a universities board or council of higher education. Since 1965, an advisory committee appointed by the Ministers of Finance and Education has submitted proposals on the funding of universities in the province. In late 1968, the government established a Council of Universities, which is, for all practical purposes, a university grants commission under another name.

Most of these provincial agencies are small and include political figures, civil servants in the education field, and university officials (mostly presidents or other members of governing boards) as members. A Bladen Commission recommendation that "in all such Commissions there should be strong academic representation" has been limited in its implementation. Of the existing agencies about one-half are wholly advisory. The other half combine advisory and executive functions.

In October 1966 the federal government announced a plan, developed in agreement with the provincial governments, for a transfer of taxing power to provincial governments to support postsecondary education. Within the limits of certain criteria, the provinces can use the funds as they see fit. This development heightened the concern of the universities that restraints on provincial government interference in university affairs were inadequate.

On the initiative of the Canadian Association of University Teachers (CAUT), joined by the Association of Universities and Colleges of Canada (AUCC), the Canadian Union of Students, and l'Union Générale des Étudiants du Québec, a two-man Commission on the Relations between Universities and Governments was created in 1967. The commissioners are Donald C. Rowat and René Hurtubise. Supported by a $150,000 grant from the Ford Foundation, this commission is studying the role of universities, "the need, nature and extent of: a) university autonomy and b) government and public control of universities" (Steering Committee for the Study of Relations between Universities and Governments, 1967). Its recommendations, expected in mid-1970, should significantly influence future relations among universities and provincial and federal governments.

In the traditional form of university governance in Canada (French universities provide the exception) authority in academic affairs is vested in a senate, and authority in nonacademic affairs is vested in a lay board.

The president (titled principal or vice-chancellor in many institutions) is the chief executive officer.[3] He presides over the senate and is usually an ex officio member of faculty councils and many of their subcommittees. He is also a member of, and reports to, the governing board. He is assisted by a number of administrative officials.

The governing board, known as the board of governors, trustees, or regents, appoints the president, deans, and department chairmen; decides on faculty promotions; controls the property of the institution; approves the recommendations of the senate on academic matters; and has financial responsibility for the institution. Until recently with few exceptions the boards were composed of laymen only and, except in Saskatchewan and New Brunswick, statutes of provincial universities barred academic staff from membership. Most of the members were drawn from business and the professions. Boards of denominational institutions included many church representatives. On the boards of provincial universities there are a considerable number of government officials. Most of the provincial institution board members hold their positions by virtue of governmental appointment. Typically, most of the boards' work is done through committees.

The academic senates normally include deans and some additional elected or appointed faculty representatives. Additional members are drawn from the ranks of alumni, provincial government appointees, and other outside persons with special interests in higher education. They may have as many as 200 members. Senates have jurisdiction over academic policies that include admissions, curricula, degrees, and student discipline. Like the governing boards, they function through a number of committees.

Internal concerns of individual faculties and their constituent departments are governed by faculty councils or boards, which function like a senate. But deans of the faculties are usually appointed by the institution's governing board on recommendation of the president. They are not elected by their faculties.

[3] In universities which have them, chancellors perform mainly ceremonial functions.

French universities differ from the non-French institutions of Canada in that their chief governing body, called the Conseil d'Administration in some universities, combines the functions of the governing board and the senate. The Conseil d'Administration usually includes both academic and administration members. The revision of Laval University's charter about five years ago set a precedent for including teaching staff members in the governance of French-language universities.

Reforms in University Governance

As Canada's universities have expanded, the presidents' roles as liaison between governing boards and senates has become increasingly difficult and administrative duties have become more burdensome. Senates often have been weak or inactive. Academics have enjoyed limited participation in university affairs. The incongruity of dividing too sharply jurisdiction over academic and financial affairs has become obvious.

These and related problems were studied by a special commission sponsored by the AUCC and the CAUT. It was undertaken by Sir James F. Duff and Robert O. Berdahl, who issued their report in 1966 (*University Government in Canada,* 1966).

The Duff-Berdahl report recommended more representation of elected faculty in the senates, representation of faculty members on governing boards, and representation of board members in senates. It also recommended that the membership of governing boards be made more diverse; that the size of senates be limited to 50 members; that senates be empowered to make recommendations to the governing boards on any matter of interest to the university; that new officers called rectors who would be elected by students be given a place on governing boards; that the positions of deans, department chairmen, and some of the other administrators be rotated frequently; that students be represented on senate committees; that a system of biennial or triennial grants to universities be inaugurated; that university grants committees be established in each province; and that more interuniversity coordination be developed.

Many of the recommended reforms were begun even before the Duff-Berdahl report was published (Monahan, 1967, pp. 33–41). By October 1967, 15 universities had provided seats for representatives of senates on their governing boards, and others were considering similar action. One institution had provided a student-elected rector with a seat on the board. Senates had received more authority, and senates with a majority of members who were elected by the faculty became more common. At eight universities, students were participating not just in senate committees but in the senates themselves.[4] Several have provided for student membership on their boards of governors. Only six universities had made no changes in their governance by late 1967. In 1968–69 a number of universities further reorganized their systems of governance, chiefly through arrangements for greatly enlarged student participation in decision making at all levels. Several universities were considering the establishment of a unicameral governmental structure including representatives of faculty, staff, students, alumni, senate, and board of governors.

INTERUNIVER-SITY COORDI-NATION

Within the provinces Interuniversity coordination has expanded. In 1966, the then four-year-old Committee of Presidents of Universities in Ontario acquired a formal constitution. It now has a central office and permanent executive and has been developing cooperative programs in admissions, library resources, the development of new graduate facilities, and the use of new technology, including computers and television. The committee has worked out common approaches for its 14 member institutions in dealing with the Ontario Committee on University Affairs and has begun to cooperate with the Ontario Confederation of University Faculty Associations in support of common interests.

In Alberta, where the Universities Act of 1966 converted two branches of the University of Alberta into two separate institutions, interuniversity coordination is provided by an advisory Coordinating Council. It is composed of the president, academic vice-president, two deans, and other academics from each university.

In Quebec, the Conference of Rectors and Principals of the Universities has facilitated communication and cooperation. Interuniversity coordination is also developing in other provinces having more than one university.

At the interprovincial level The Interprovincial Committee on University Rationalization (IPCUR) coordinates the development of

[4] According to *Issue* (vol. 1, February 2 and March 8, 1968), a newspaper published by the Canadian Union of Students, by the spring of 1968, 17 universities had admitted students to representation on their senates. University of Toronto students rejected an offer of seven seats in the 196-member Senate as "tokenism," and the University of Western Ontario rejected the rector representative system for the same reason.

higher education in Manitoba, Saskatchewan, Alberta, and more recently in British Columbia. Formed in 1964, the Association of Atlantic Universities facilitates consultation and cooperation among institutions in Newfoundland, Nova Scotia, New Brunswick, and Prince Edward Island. The University of the West Indies is also a member of this association.

At the national level The Association of Universities and Colleges of Canada, established in 1911 as the National Conference of Canadian Universities, helps coordinate the interests of universities, conducts research on university problems, serves as a clearing-house for information on Canadian higher education, and represents the interests of higher education institutions in negotiations with the government.

FINANCING HIGHER EDUCATION The largest share of the revenues of Canadian colleges and universities comes from provincial governments, but income is also derived from student fees, the federal government, and other sources. By 1967–68, the total operating and capital expenditures of Canadian institutions of higher education had reached $1.13 billion (all amounts are Canadian dollars). The percentage of Canada's gross national product devoted to universities and colleges rose from 0.031 in 1950–51 to 1.4 in 1966–67.[5]

Federal Support for Operations The federal government gave no direct financial support to universities until World War II. In the immediate postwar period, it provided $150 for each student supported by the Department of Veterans Affairs. When the veteran influx and its accompanying subsidies abated, the universities faced a grave financial crisis and a royal commission, the Massey Commission, was appointed to study the federal role in the arts, letters, and sciences, including higher education (*Report of the Royal Commission,* 1951). This commission recommended that the federal government inaugurate a program of annual unrestricted grants to help meet operating costs of universities. Such grants for both public and private universities were instituted in June 1951. They provided 50 cents per capita of population in each province. Allocation to institutions was based on enrollment. As the costs of higher education rose, the per capita grants increased to $1.00 in 1957, $1.50 in 1958, $2.00 in 1962, and $5.00 in 1966. By 1966–67 the total annual grant under this

[5] Information supplied by Higher Education Division, Dominion Bureau of Statistics.

program was $100 million. In practice, the system had built-in inequities favoring the more populous provinces with relatively low enrollments. For example, in 1964–65 institutions in Nova Scotia received $183 per student, and institutions in Ontario received $282 per student (Commission on the Financing of Higher Education in Canada, 1965, p. 42).

From 1952 to 1959, Quebec did not accept federal grants for fear they might bring with them federal infringement of provincial autonomy in education. In 1959, it accepted federal assistance in the form of tax abatement instead of grant. Under this system the federal government reduced the corporate income tax in Quebec and offered equalization grants, thus increasing Quebec's fiscal resources, on condition that the province accept responsibilities for financing its universities.

In 1964, the Canadian Universities Foundation, the federal government's intermediary in financing universities and the executive agency of the National Conference of Canadian Universities and Colleges, both of which have been succeeded by the Association of Universities and Colleges of Canada, appointed the commission headed by V. W. Bladen to estimate the financial needs of Canadian universities and recommend means of supplying them. In its 1964 report, the commission predicted operating costs of $924 million in 1970–71 and $1.675 billion in 1975–76. These costs were based on enrollment projections that have since proved to be too low. The commission also reported an anticipated capital expenditure that would increase to $390 million in 1970–71 and then decrease to $357 million in 1975–76. Its recommendations that the per capita federal grants be increased immediately from $2 to $5 and by $1 annually thereafter were put into effect as interim measures in 1966–67. Other recommended measures included a major increase

TABLE 12 Percent of operating income for higher education in Canada by source	Source	1950–51	1955–56	1960–61	1965–66
	Fees	35.0[a]	26.9[b]	26.0[b]	25.9[b]
	Federal government	4.0[a]	15.1[b]	18.5[b]	17.1[b]
	Provincial governments	41.0[a]	40.8[b]	43.7[b]	43.2[b]
	Other	20.0[a]	17.2[b]	11.8[b]	13.9[b]

SOURCES: (a) Edward F. Sheffield, *Financing Higher Education in Canada, No. 2, Sources of University Support,* Canadian Universities Foundation, Ottawa, 1961, kp. 8. (b) Commission on the Financing of Higher Education in Canada, 1965, *Financing Higher Education,* Vincent Bladen, chairman, University of Toronto Press, Toronto, 1965.

TABLE 13 *Expenditures and grants for colleges and universities in Canada (in millions of Canadian dollars)*

	1950–51	1955–56	1960–61	1965–66	1967–68
Operating expenditures	48.000[a]	80.427[b]	181.311[b]	432.332[c]	
Capital expenditures		16.000[b]	80.000[b]	250.502[c]	
TOTAL OPERATING AND CAPITAL		96.000[b]	261.000[b]	682.834[c]	
TOTAL OPERATING, CAPITAL, AND FINANCIAL AID TO STUDENTS				723.122[c]	1,130,000[d]
Federal grants for operating expenditures	2.000[e]	5.500[f]		73.125[g]	
Provincial grants for operating expenditures	20.000[e]			183.200[g]	451.500[h]
Federal grants for capital expenditures				6.800[g]	
Provincial grants for capital expenditures				162.700[g]	259.800[h]

SOURCES: (*a*) Edward F. Sheffield, *Financing Higher Education in Canada, No. 2, Sources of University Support,* Canadian Universities Foundation, Ottawa, 1961, p. 9. (*b*) Dominion Bureau of Statistics, *Canadian Universities, Income and Expenditure, 1964-65,* Queen's Printer, Ottawa, 1967, pp. 26-27. Includes Canadian service colleges since 1959-60. (*c*) Dominion Bureau of Statistics, *Preliminary Statistics of Education 1966-67,* 1968*b*, pp. 45-46, 48. (*d*) Dominion Bureau of Statistics, *Advance Statistics of Education 1967-68,* 1967, p. 9. (*e*) Sheffield, 1961, p. 8. (*f*) Dominion Bureau of Statistics, *Survey of Higher Education 1952-54,* Queen's Printer, Ottawa, 1955, p. 12. (*g*) Dominion Bureau of Statistics, *Preliminary Statistics of Education 1966-67,* 1968*b*, p. 48. (*h*) Dominion Bureau of Statistics, *Daily Bulletin,* 1968*a*, p. 4. Excludes funds for student aid and includes in operating grants funds for assisted research. Estimates only.

in federal financing of capital expenditures, the coordination of federal aid to higher education by a Minister of the Crown, the establishment of provincial grants commissions, substantial increases in federal research grants, the introduction of provincially defined weighted enrollment formulas for determining the distribution of federal support to universities, and doubling financial aid to students.

In March 1967 a new system of federal support for higher education was authorized. It involves a return of portions of personal and corporation income tax to provincial authorities, thus increasing their taxing power, and supplementary funds. In 1967–68, these funds were calculated either to equal $15 per capita of the population of the province or to meet one-half of the operating expenses of not only the universities but also of all postsecondary institutions (including the senior matriculation year in secondary schools), whichever was higher. The funds available through the new system can be used at the discretion of the provinces. The per capita allowance rises with national increases in postsecondary school operating expenditures and in 1969–70 was about $20.

The new arrangement increased federal support to higher education to at least as much as was proposed by the Bladen Commission report. In 1967–68, federal grants were expected to total about $345 million ("Federal Payments to the Provinces for Post-secondary Education: Fiscal Tables," 1967, p. 18) calculated on the basis of 50 percent of estimated operating costs and excluding about $353 million of equalization payments. It was estimated that about two-thirds of this amount, over twice as much as was available to them in the previous year, would go to university-level institutions (Dominion Bureau of Statistics, 1968a, p. 3). In 1968, seven provinces received federal aid on the basis of the 50 percent of operating costs formula. Newfoundland, Prince Edward Island, and New Brunswick were on the $15 per capita rate. By midyear, it was apparent that the $345 million estimate for federal grants for 1967–68 was too low (Mitchener, 1968, p. 18).

Although the new federal aid program is not intended to meet capital expenditures, there is general expectation that it will provide some help indirectly.

Some provinces have followed the Bladen Commission recommendation that a formula of weighted enrollments be used to determine the level of financial support to the universities. The weights are determined by the provinces using the formula. For example, Ontario has devised a system which assumes that the cost for doctoral candidates in their final years is about six times that of undergraduate students in liberal arts courses. Aid based on such systems is putting a premium on holding down costs per student and attracting as many students as possible in the levels where costs per student are highest. Variations in costs per student among institutions and at different levels of instruction and variations in the proportion of expenditures devoted to instruction, administration, and other items are being considered as a part of current deliberations on the federal aid question. A national study on costs of university programs, cosponsored by the AUCC, the Canadian Association of University Business Officers, and the Canadian Association of Teachers was begun in 1966–67.

Capital Expenditures   Between 1955–56 and 1965–66 nearly 60 percent of the capital expenditures of Canadian universities were financed by provincial governments, and about 8 percent were financed by the federal government. The remainder were financed from donations, endowments, and other sources. It is estimated that Canadian colleges and universities spent $700 million on building programs.

The federal government provided no funds for capital expenditures of universities until 1957, when it established the Canada Council and endowed it with two $50 million funds. One fund was to be used for a graduate fellowship program. The other, the University Capital Grants Fund, was authorized to make matching grants to universities established before 1957 for construction of buildings devoted to the humanities or social sciences.

The National Housing Act of 1960 provided for federal loans to a maximum of $50 million to provide up to 90 percent of the construction costs of student residences. The maximum was increased to $150 million in 1963. By 1967, some $137 million in loans had been used to finance housing for 27,000 students.

Gifts and Endowments

Contributions have financed some of the new construction at higher education institutions, but these sources have become decreasingly adequate to the expanding need. In the late 1950s and early 1960s corporate giving to higher education was encouraged by the Industrial Foundation on Education.[6] Of $37 million contributed to higher education by corporations between 1956 and 1959, $25 million was used for capital grants. The foundation went out of existence in the early 1960s. Virtually all universities have conducted their own fund-raising drives to meet capital expenditures. In 1965 York University launched a campaign to raise $15 million. The three public universities in British Columbia collaborated in a drive to raise $28 million for capital improvements, and in 1968 the University of Saskatchewan launched a drive for $11 million. In 1969 the three universities in Alberta were waging a joint campaign.

As a proportion of total income, income from endowments has been decreasing sharply. But it still provides one-fourth or more of the revenues of some institutions. Fortunately the total amount of endowments and investment income combined has increased, from about $3 million in 1954 to $8.1 million in 1963.

Student Fees

Average tuition fees increased from $250 in 1950 to $525 in 1970. (Fees in engineering and medicine were higher.) In the eleven years between 1954 and 1965, acutal income from fees increased from

[6] Corporate gifts for charitable causes, including higher education, are deductible for income tax purposes if they are not more than 10 percent of profits.

$14.2 million to $110.6 million, but because of the increase in federal financing of postsecondary education, the proportion of fee income to other revenues is declining.

Research In 1968–69 21 percent of all federal expenditures on research, or $109 of the $514 million total, went to universities. Among the federal agencies contributing to the support of research are the National Research Council, the Medical Research Council, the Defense Research Board, the Department of National Health and Welfare, and Department of Labour, and the Atomic Energy Control Board. The Bladen Commission recommended that the National Research Council provide $40 million for university research in 1966–67 and that this amount be increased by 20 percent each year thereafter. In the spring of 1968, a special commission, the Macdonald Study Group, began a study on federal support of research programs in the universities to find new guidelines for future federal support. In its report of 1969, the study group emphasized the importance of the research function to the university and the need to encourage the expansion of federal support in all fields of university research and recommended a reorganization of the system of research councils as a means to achieve this expansion.

HIGHER EDUCATION AND ECONOMIC PLANNING Despite the position of the Economic Council of Canada, which has urged the establishment of a single agency to coordinate and control manpower policy and has argued persuasively in behalf of education as an investment in economic growth, Canadian colleges and universities resist the idea of planning to produce graduates trained to fill manpower needs. The Bladen Commission, for example, estimated university needs mainly on the basis of future student demand.

STUDENT FINANCES In 1967–68, Canadian students spent an average of $1,800 a year for tuition and living expenses (Pike, 1967, p. 3). Three years earlier, the only period for which such statistics are available, a study of the income of undergraduates indicated that 8.6 percent came from grants-in-aid, including scholarships and bursaries; 32.93 percent from loans or gifts from friends and family (including spouses), 28.75 percent from earnings, 5.73 percent from personal savings, and the remainder from other sources (Rabinovitch, 1965). The same year, 82 percent of the undergraduates responding to another inquiry said they had worked during the previous summer (Rabinovitch, 1965, p. 28).

There were virtually no programs of financial aid to students before 1937, and relatively few were developed prior to World War II. Since the war, and particularly in the past decade, they have developed to the point where, in 1966–67, 35 percent of all post-secondary students were receiving aid in the form of government loans (Pike, 1967, p. 1) and perhaps half again as many were receiving nonrepayable financial aid.

In 1964, the Canada Student Loans Plan, which enables Canadian students to borrow up to $1,000 per year for five years, was introduced. These loans are interest-free until six months after the borrower is no longer a student. Repayment of principal and interest was at the rate of 5.75 percent until August 1968, when amending legislation changed it to a maximum of 1 percent plus a base rate set by the Minister of Finance calculated on the basis of yields of five- to ten-year Government of Canada bonds for the preceding six months. The value of student loans totaled about $65 million in 1967–68 and was expected to be $115 million in 1970–71.

Between 1964–65 and 1967–68 nonrepayable student aid increased about sixfold to about $14 million. All student aid increased from $3.3 million in 1956–57 to $53 million in 1964–65 (Commission on the Financing of Higher Education in Canada, 1965, p. 32). The Bladen Commission expressed hope that "other forms of aid will slow down the growth in the volume of federal student loans" and recommended programs offering nonrepayable aid for first-year students and half-grant half-loan aid (with some differentiation on the basis of sex) for students in later years.

The Bladen report also recommended that student aid averaging $300 for each recipient in 1965 should increase to $650 in 1970–71 and to $700 in 1975–76. Additionally, the report recommended revision in tax regulations so that more students from low-income families might be enabled to attend a university.

Student aid is inequitably available from province to province. The government of Newfoundland pays full or partial tuition fees to full-time undergraduate students at Memorial University. Students receiving this assistance must meet certain residence requirements and take the first $400 of assistance as a Canada Student Loan. This province also provides living allowances to third-, fourth-, and fifth-year full-time undergraduate students, also taking into account financial need, residence requirements, utilization of

Canada Student Loans, and whether or not the student must commute to university. The other provinces also have their separate student assistance programs which supplement aid available through the Canada Student Loans Program, private assistance, and teacher training awards.

Financial aid to graduate students has received increasing attention. In the humanities and social sciences, one of the two $50 million funds allocated to the Canada Council in 1957 (the other was for capital expenditures) was designated the Endowment Fund. It provided about $1 million a year for graduate fellowships (as well as other assistance to faculty members and cultural organizations). In 1965 the Endowment Fund received an additional grant from Parliament, making it possible to increase its expenditures by $10 million annually.

Graduate students in the sciences and engineering receive financial aid from several federal agencies. The National Research Council is foremost among them.

The Bladen Commission reported that the average amount of aid per graduate student in 1964–65 was $1,500. The commission recommended that this amount, which included money paid to teaching assistants, be increased to $2,000 per student in 1965–66, to $2,500 in 1970–71 and to $3,000 by 1975.

STUDENTS Most Canadian students enroll in institutions in their home provinces. Half of the undergraduates responding to a survey in 1964–65 lived within 25 miles of the institution in which they were enrolled, and 65 percent were within 100 miles of their homes (Rabinovitch, 1965, pp. 24, 74). Increasing numbers of students come from the less affluent sectors of society and are keeping down their costs by living at home and attending nearby institutions.

In terms of parental income, however, Canadian undergraduates are not representative of society as a whole. In 1965–66, more than half of the total population earned less than $5,000 a year, but only one-fourth of the university students came from families with this income and another one-fourth of the student population came from families earning more than $10,000 a year—a group constituting only 6.1 percent of Canadian families (Dominion Bureau of Statistics, 1959, pp. 21, 24).

Student self-governments operate at all institutions, and some of them have a large degree of independence.

Until 1969 there were two main national student unions. The

Canadian Union of Students (CUS) was made up of student associations at higher education institutions in all provinces except Quebec. The CUS had become increasingly active in seeking greater student participation in university governance. Although not affiliated with any political party, it had strong radical leanings. The Union Générale des Étudiants du Québec (UGEQ) is a relatively new student association created when students in that province broke away from the CUS. By the spring of 1969, many local student associations severed ties with CUS because of its radical leanings. The UGEQ experienced parallel difficulties.

In November 1969 the CUS disbanded as a result of the decision of the local unions at the University of Toronto, Dalhousie University, and Carleton University to withdraw from it. The resultant reduction of membership from 140,000 students at 44 universities in 1964 to 39,348 students at two campuses left the CUS too enfeebled to continue as an effective organization. In essence, as the union became more radical, it ceased to be representative of the majority of students in Canada.

Students have a growing concern for the wider community. It is reflected in their participation in Canadian University Service Overseas; in the Company of Young Canadians, established in 1966 to work on community development programs in Canada; and in other service-oriented organizations.

Disruption of Canadian universities and colleges by student protests escalated in 1968–69. In the fall of 1968, strikes, closures, and student takeovers occurred in a number of the CEGPs, where students demonstrated for the establishment of a second French-language university. Student allegations of racial discrimination against black students from the Caribbean at Sir George Williams University catalyzed student protest and demonstrations resulting in 2 million dollars' worth of property damage at that institution. Demonstrations at other universities, especially Simon Fraser, focused on student demands for more participation in university governance, for more effective teaching, and, on the part of the most radical students, for a basic transformation of society.

RECENT CHANGES The most important changes in Canadian higher education in recent years are those involving increased federal financial support and the organization of federal and provincial agencies to provide encouragement and coordination. Changes in university governance since the Duff-Berdahl report have also been significant.

A trend toward diversification has been achieved by the creation of new kinds of postsecondary schools: the junior or community colleges (primarily in the West), the CEGPs in Quebec, and the CAATs in Ontario.

Admissions policies may be changed soon. Traditionally, admission to Canadian universities has been based upon external essay examinations modeled on the British pattern. They are taken at the end of the final secondary school year. The Service for Admission to College and University (SACU), which was created in 1966 and is comparable to the College Entrance Examination Board in the United States, is now studying the use of nationwide objective admissions tests. The SACU tests were administered for the first time in 1969. In 1968–69, Ontario became the first province to use aptitude tests as the only external criterion for university admissions.

Year-round operation has been introduced at two universities (Simon Fraser in British Columbia and Guelph in Ontario) and at a number of small colleges. Year-round operation involving the alternation of work and study has existed for some time at the University of Waterloo and has been recently inaugurated at the University of Sherbrooke and Memorial University of Newfoundland.

THE BALANCE SHEET Canada's colleges and universities have shown remarkable capacities for adaptation. Despite enrollment pressures and rapid expansion, they have been able to maintain their academic standards and to resist deterioration in staff-student ratios and student persistence. They have also refrained from imposing rigid barriers to admission.

Apart from difficulties inherent in rapid expansion, the main problems in Canadian colleges and universities have been insufficient financial aid for students, lagging development of graduate studies and research, and, until very recently, the lack of coordination between institutions, between provincial governments, and between the numerous governmental agencies involved in higher education. As has been indicated, substantial progress has been made in correcting these problems. The Rowat-Hurtubise Commission is expected to provide further guidelines on the balance between university autonomy and public control of higher education institutions.

The strengths of Canada's higher education include its diversification and the relative autonomy of its institutions. The relationship between public and private institutions and the manner in which the interests of church and state are combined is an unusual feature. Affiliation or federation of small private liberal arts colleges and church-related institutions to universities, provincial and private, has distinct advantages. The smaller institutions retain administrative independence and are able to concentrate on relatively low-cost liberal arts studies without depriving their students of access to the more expensive scientific and professional courses offered by the universities with which they are affiliated. The universities gain because the students in their affiliated colleges enjoy close staff-student relations.

In contrast to the traditional higher education systems of continental Europe, protracted study periods pose no problem in Canada. The structured curricula, examinations, and attendance requirements and a system that eliminates from the student body those who do not progress according to established procedures are the main reasons.

THE FUTURE The major factor affecting the future of higher education in Canada is the federal government's decision to shift tax revenues to meet half of the operating costs of postsecondary education to the provinces — without imposing an obligation on provincial governments to support higher education with these funds. The new provision makes the universities more dependent than formerly upon provincial governments and more vulnerable to interference by them. It may make the financing of higher education more of a political issue than it has been in the past.

It is conceivable that a national system of Canadian higher education will eventually develop out of the present congeries of provincial endeavors. Certainly the establishment of an office at the federal level to coordinate federal support for higher education and research and the increased emphasis on education as an investment in national economic development all indicate a greater federal concern. The principal obstacle is the resistance of the provinces — particularly Quebec. If current recommendations of the Royal Commission on Bilingualism and Biculturalism, which aim at diminishing cultural and educational separatism in Canada, are implemented, opposition to a federal role in higher education could decline. The election of a French Canadian as the new Prime Minister in the spring of 1968 served at first to augur well for such a development. The Official Languages Act, which became effective in September 1969 and has placed French on an equal footing with English as a language to be used throughout Canada, may eventually help to reduce culture separation and facilitate the emergence of a national system of higher education. Conversely, this act may represent a necessary response to a sharpening of the separate identities of Canada's two main cultural communities—a development which may reinforce rather than diminish the differences and mutual isolation between the higher education systems of the two communities.

Canadian Universities and Colleges

Partly based on Rosemary A. Cavan (ed.), *Universities and Colleges of Canada,* The Association of Universities and Colleges of Canada, Ottawa, 1969.

I. UNIVERSITIES AND COLLEGES OF CANADA AND THEIR FEDERATED OR AFFILIATED INSTITUTIONS

Acadia University
  Maritime School of Social Work*

The University of Alberta
  Camrose Junior College†
  Collège Saint-Jean†
  St. Joseph's College†
  Red Deer Junior College†
  St. Stephen's College†

Bishop's University

Brandon University

The University of British Columbia
  The Anglican Theological College of
    British Columbia†
  Union College of British Columbia†
  Carey Hall†
  St. Andrew's Hall†
  St. Mark's College†

Brock University

The University of Calgary
  Medicine Hat Junior College†
  Mount Royal College†

Carleton University

Dalhousie University
  University of King's College*
  Nova Scotia College of Art†

University of Guelph

Lakehead University

Laurentian University of Sudbury
  Algoma College†
  Collège de Hearst†
  Huntington University‡
  Nipissing College†
  Thorneloe University‡
  University of Sudbury‡

Université Laval
  Collège de Lévis†
  Collège de Victoriaville†
  Collège des Jésuites†
  Collège Jésus-Marie†
  Collège Notre-Dame de Bellevue†
  Collège Ste-Anne†
  École Normale Notre-Dame de Foi†
  Externat Classique†
  Séminaire de Québec†
  Séminaire de St-Georges†
  Séminaire Marie-Reine du Clergé†
  St. Lawrence College†
(Faculté de Théologie:)
  Grand Séminaire de Chicoutimi
  Grand Séminaire de Rimouski
  Grand Séminaire de Trois-Rivières

*Associated school or university.
†Affiliated college.
‡Federated university or college.

Grand Séminaire d'Halifax
Scholasticat St-Jean-Eudes

The University of Manitoba
St. Andrew's College*
Collège de Saint-Boniface†
St. John's College†
St. Paul's College†

McGill University
Montreal Diocesan Theological College†
Presbyterian College of Montreal†
United Theological College of Montreal†

McMaster University
McMaster Divinity College†

Memorial University of Newfoundland
Queen's College†
St. Bride's College†

Université de Moncton
Collège Saint-Joseph†
Collège de Bathurst†
Collège Saint-Louis†
(Collèges Annexés:)
Collège Maillet
Collège Jésus-Marie

Université de Montréal
Loyola College†
Marianopolis College†
École des Hautes Études Commerciales
École d'Optométrie
École Polytechnique
Institut Pédagogique CND
L'École de Médecine Vétérinaire de la
    Province de Québec
Thomas More Institute for Adult
    Education
Collège Bourget
Collège Jean-de-Brébeuf
Externat Classique de Longueuil
Collège Mont-Saint-Louis
Collège Notre-Dame-du-Sacré-Coeur
Séminaire de Philosophie
Collège Classique de Rouyn

Séminaire de Saint-Hyacinthe
Collège Saint-Ignace
Collège de Saint-Laurent
Collège Saint-Paul
Collège Saint-Viateur
Séminaire Sainte-Croix
Collège Sainte-Marie
Séminaire des Saints-Apôtres
Collège Stanislas
Séminaire de Valleyfield
Collège Marguerite-Bourgeoys
Collège de l'Assomption
Séminaire de Joliette
Séminaire de Saint-Jean
Séminaire de Sainte-Thérèse
Institut Familial et Social
Institute Familial de Sainte-Martine
Institut Familial Bilingue des Soeurs de
    Sainte-Anne

Mount Allison University
Mount Saint Vincent University
University of New Brunswick
St. Thomas University‡
Notre Dame University of Nelson
Nova Scotia Agricultural College
Nova Scotia Technical College
Osgoode Hall Law School
Prince of Wales University
University of Ottawa
Saint Paul University‡
Collège Bruyère†
Notre Dame College†
St. Augustine's College†
St. Thomas College†
University of Prince Edward Island
Prince of Wales College
St. Dunstan's University
University of Quebec
Queen's University of Kingston
Queen's Theological College†

*Associated school or university.
†Affiliated college or école.
‡Federated university or college.

Royal Military College of Canada
  Collège Militaire Royal de Saint-Jean‡
  Royal Roads†

St. Dunstan's University

St. Francis Xavier University
  Maritime School of Social Work*
  Mount St. Bernard College†
  St. Martha's School of Nursing†

St. Mary's University
  Ignatius College†
  Regis College†

Seminary of Christ the King

University of Saskatchewan
  St. Thomas More College‡
  Campion College†
  College of Emmanuel and St. Chad†
  Luther College†
  Lutheran Theological Seminary†
  St. Andrew's College†
  St. Joseph's College†
  St Peter's College†

Université de Sherbrooke
  Séminaire de Sherbrooke†
  Externat Classique St-Raphael†
  Collège du Sacré-Coeur†
  Collège Notre-Dame-des-Servites†
  Collège du Mont Sainte-Anne†
  Externat Classique, C.P.†
  Séminaire Salésien†
  Mont Notre-Dame†
  Grand Séminaire de Nicolet†
  Grand Séminaire de Sherbrooke
  Grand Séminaire de Saint-Hyacinthe†
  Scholasticat de l'Abbaye St-Benôit-
    du-Lac†

Simon Fraser University

Sir George Williams University

University of Toronto
  University of St. Michael's College‡
  University of Trinity College‡
  Victoria University‡
  Knox College‡
  Wycliffe College‡
  Emmanuel College of Victoria
    University‡
  Massey College‡

Trent University

University of Victoria

University of Waterloo
  University of St. Jerome's College‡
  Notre Dame College‡
  Resurrection College‡
  Conrad Grebel College†
  Renison College†
  St. Paul's United College†

Waterloo Lutheran University
  Mennonite Brethren College of Arts†

University of Western Ontario
  Brescia College†
  Huron College†
  King's College†

University of Windsor
  Assumption University‡
  Canterbury College†
  Holy Redeemer College†
  Iona College†

University of Winnipeg

York University

*Associated school or university.
†Affiliated college.
‡Federated university or college.

II. COMMUNITY COLLEGE LEVEL INSTITUTIONS OF HIGHER EDUCATION

Alberta

Camrose Lutheran College

Canadian Union College

Fairview Agricultural and Vocational College

Grande Prairie College

Hillcrest Christian College

Lethbridge College

Medicine Hat College

Mount Royal College

Northern Alberta Institute of Technology

Olds Agricultural and Vocational College

Red Deer College

College St. Jean

Southern Alberta Institute of Technology

Vermillion Agricultural and Vocational College

British Columbia

British Columbia Institute of Technology

Capilano College

Malaspina College

College of New Caledonia

Okanagan Regional College

Royal Roads College

Selkirk College

Trinity College

Vancouver City College

Manitoba

Manitoba Institute of Applied Arts

Manitoba Vocational Center

Mennonite Brethren College of Arts

Northern Manitoba Vocational Center

New Brunswick

Maritime Forest Ranger School

New Brunswick Institute of Technology

University of New Brunswick in Saint John

Saint John Institute of Technology

Newfoundland

Newfoundland College of Fisheries, Navigation, Marine Engineering, and Electronics

Newfoundland College of Trades and Technology

Nova Scotia

Nova Scotia Agricultural College

Nova Scotia College of Art

Nova Scotia Eastern Institute of Technology, Sydney

Nova Scotia Institute of Technology, Halifax

Nova Scotia Land Survey Institute

Nova Scotia Marine Navigation School

Junior College of the Sacred Heart

Xavier Junior College

Ontario

Algonquin College of Applied Arts and Technology

Algonquin College, Ottawa (2), Pembroke (1)

Cambrian College of Applied Arts and Technology

Cambrian College, North Bay and Sault Ste. Marie

Centennial College of Applied Arts and Technology

Centennial College, Scarborough and Toronto

Centralia College of Agricultural Technology

Conestoga College of Applied Arts and Technology

Confederation College of Applied Arts and Technology

Durham College of Applied Arts and Technology

Fanshawe College of Applied Arts and Technology

George Brown College of Applied Arts and Technology

George Brown College, Toronto (2)

Georgian College of Applied Arts and Technology

Humber College of Applied Arts and Technology

Humber College, Toronto (2)

Kemptville College of Agricultural Technology

Lakehead University Schools

Lambton College of Applied Arts and Technology

Lambton College, Sarnia (2)

Loyalist College of Applied Arts and Technology

Mohawk College of Applied Arts and Technology

New Liskeard College of Agricultural Technology

Niagara College of Applied Arts and Technology

Niagara Parks Commission School of Horticulture

Northern College of Applied Arts and Technology

Northern College, Haileybury, Kirkland Lake, and South Porcupine

Ontario College of Art

Ridgetown College of Agricultural Technology

Ryerson Polytechnical Institute

St. Clair College

St. Clair College of Applied Arts and Technology

St. Lawrence College

St. Lawrence College of Applied Arts and Technology

Seneca College of Applied Arts and Technology

Sheridan College of Applied Arts and Technology

Sheridan College, Oakville and Port Credit

Sir Sandford Fleming Loyalist College

Sir Sandford Fleming Loyalist College of Applied Arts and Technology

Prince Edward Island

Holland College

Quebec

Collège d'Ahuntsic*

Collège de l'Assomption

Collège Bois-de-Boulogne*

Collège de Chicoutimi*

Collège Edouart-Montpetit*

Collège de la Gaspésie*

Collège de Hauterive

Collège de Hull*

Collège Jean-de-Bréfeuf

Collège Jesus-Marie de Sillery

Collège des Jésuites

Collège de Joliette*

Collège Lévis

Collège de Limoilou*

*CEGP

Collège Lionel-Groulx*

Collège de Maisonneuve*

Collège de Matane

Collège Militaire Royal de Saint Jean

Collège Notre-Dame-de-Bellevue

Collège de la Pocatière*

Collège Rigaud-de-Vaudreuil

Collège Rimouski*

Collège de Rosemont*

Collège de Rouyn-Noranda*

Collège de Sainte-Foy*

Collège de Saint-Hyacinthe*

Collège Saint-sur-Richelieu*

Collège de Saint Laurent*

Collège de Salaberry-de-Valleyfield

Collège de Shawinigan*

Collège de Sherbrooke

Collège de Trois-Rivières*

Collège de Victoriaville*

Collège du Vieux-Montréal*

Dawson College*

Institut Marguerite-Vourgeoys

Institut de Technologie Agricole

Séminaire de Philosophie

Séminaire de Saint-Georges

Séminaire de Sherbrooke

Saskatchewan

St. Peter's College

Saskatchewan Institute of Applied Arts and Sciences

Saskatchewan Technical Institute

*CEGP

References

Bertram, Gordon W.: *The Contribution of Education to Economic Growth,* Economic Council of Canada Staff Study no. 12, Queen's Printer, Ottawa, 1966.

Commission on the Financing of Higher Education in Canada: *Financing Higher Education,* Vincent W. Bladen, chairman, University of Toronto Press, Toronto, 1965.

Dominion Bureau of Statistics: *Canada Yearbook 1967,* Queen's Printer, Ottawa, 1967.

Dominion Bureau of Statistics: *Daily Bulletin,* vol. 37, March 6, 1968*a*.

Dominion Bureau of Statistics: *Preliminary Statistics of Education 1966–67,* Queen's Printer, Ottawa, 1968*b*.

Dominion Bureau of Statistics: *University Student Expenditure and Income in Canada 1956–57,* Queen's Printer, Ottawa, 1959.

Duff, Sir James F., and Robert O. Berdahl: *University Government in Canada: Report of a Commission Sponsored by the Canadian Association of University Teachers and the Association of Universities and Colleges of Canada,* University of Toronto Press, Toronto, 1966.

"Federal Payments to the Provinces for Post-secondary Education: Fiscal Tables," *CAUT Bulletin,* vol. 15, April 1967.

Herbert, Walter: *The Current State of the Arts in the University,* unpublished paper, 1967.

Illing, Wolfgang, and Zoltan E. Zsigmond: *Enrollment in Schools and Universities 1951 to 1975–76,* Economic Council of Canada Staff Study no. 20, Queen's Printer, Ottawa, 1967.

Mitchener, R. D.: "The Pattern of University-Government Relationships in Canada," *CAUT Bulletin,* vol. 17, December 1968.

Monahan, Edward J.: "The Inevitability of Gradualness: A Report on Changes in University Government in Canada in the Post-Duff-Berdahl Era," *CAUT Bulletin,* vol. 16, December 1967.

OECD: *Training of and Demand for High-level Scientific and Technical Personnel in Canada,* Paris, 1966.

Pike, Robert: *Student Finanacial Aid in Canada,* unpublished speech, 1967.

"The Public Financing of Universities: A Brief Presented to the Governments of Canada and of the Provinces by the C.A.U.T.," *CAUT Bulletin,* vol. 14, February 1966.

Rabinovitch, Robert: *An Analysis of the Canadian Post-secondary Student Population, part I: A Report on Canadian Undergraduate Students,* Canadian Union of Students, Ottawa, 1965.

Report of the Royal Commission on National Development in the Arts, Letters, and Sciences, Queen's Printer, Ottawa, 1951.

Steering Committee for the Study of Relations between Universities and Government: *Proposals for a Study of the Relations between Universities and Governments,* Ottawa, July 1967.

6. *Higher Education in Australia*

Institutions of higher tertiary education in Australia are relatively young, dating from the founding of the University of Sydney in 1850. The six original universities have been characterized by one observer as "trying to out-Oxford Oxford," although one of these institutions, the University of Western Australia, originally intended to follow something akin to the American land-grant philosophy. Universities established since World War II exhibit considerable diversity. Although all so-called tertiary education now receives federal as well as state funds, it is nearly all under state jurisdiction. The chief exceptions are the Australian National University and the Canberra College of Advanced Education. Tertiary education now includes not only the universities but also colleges of advanced education and teacher training institutions. Colleges of the three armed services are also part of tertiary education in Australia.

COMPONENTS In 1945, there were only six universities, one in each state capital, and two university colleges at Canberra and Armidale. Now, there are fifteen universities and two university colleges, and a new university college is in the planning stage at Queensland. Development of universities has been particularly rapid since the mid-1950s, when the Prime Minister appointed a committee of inquiry into their future. Headed by Sir Keith Murray (now Lord Murray of Newhaven), the Committee on Australian Universities issued its report in 1957 and drew attention to the urgent need for university expansion, greatly increased funding, and Commonwealth financial assistance on a continuing basis. In 1958, the Commonwealth government inplemented one of the principal recommendations of the Murray Committee in establishing the Australian Universities Commission (AUC) to continuously review university development and to report to the Commonwealth government on the financial needs of the universities at three-year intervals.

Australian National University (ANU), established by the federal Parliament in 1946, was an exclusively postgraduate institution until 1960, when the former Canberra University College of the University of Melbourne became ANU's school of general studies and assumed responsibility for its undergraduate program. In 1966, ANU enrolled only about one-thirtieth of Australia's undergraduates but 10 percent of its Ph.D. students.

Established as the New South Wales University of Technology in 1949, with Massachusetts Institute of Technology among its models, the University of New South Wales is currently referred to as "the beginning of Australia's first (and only?) multiversity" (Matheson, 1965, p. 207). Art courses have been added to its curriculum, and academically oriented degree courses have been substituted for practical diploma courses, but this university continues to have a technological emphasis. It offers practical and specialized subjects that include wool technology, polymer science, and industrial arts. It also has a notable offering in part-time courses in both the humanities and the sciences. The University of New England, started in 1938 as a university college affiliated with the University of Sydney, was made autonomous in 1954. Until 1970, it was the only university located in a rural area. It is primarily residential for its internal students, but external students outnumber them.

Victoria established its second university, Monash, in 1958. After special studies of university needs, Macquarie University in New South Wales and La Trobe University in Victoria were established in 1964. In the following year, the university college of the University of New South Wales in Newcastle was given full university status. In 1966, Flinders University in South Australia, which had begun in 1963 as a separate campus of the University of Adelaide, was established. In 1970, a university college of the University of Queensland at Townsville became autonomous (and is Australia's second university to be located in a rural area). Other recent expansion involves the designation of divisions of the University of New South Wales at Broken Hill and Wollongong as university colleges.

Although it is not actually an Australian university, the first university in the Territory of Papua and New Guinea, established in 1965, grew out of Australia's trusteeship in that territory. It is funded by the Commonwealth government and is largely staffed by Australians.

By 1969, university growth appeared to be slowing down. Quotas limit admissions at a number of universities, and there appears to be an understanding in government that, at least for the next few years, the proportion of secondary school graduates going to universities will not exceed the 1969 rate and that increases in the proportion of secondary school graduates going into tertiary education will be absorbed in the colleges of advanced education. Apart from the University of Queensland's university college at Mount Gravatt and either a new branch of the University of Western Australia or a second university in that state, no new universities will be built in the near future. Reinforcing the consensus that university expansion in the future will be slower than it was in the last decade is an attitude, especially in industry, that universities are excessively expensive, not sufficiently responsive to community needs, overly academic, and not always willing or able to produce the specialized and job-oriented manpower that Australia requires.

The 1960s have altered the image and role of the universities. Traditionally, students enrolled in the single university in their state. Now there is more than one university in four of the six states, and students have a wider choice—even though enrollment quotas require many to enroll in the university of their second or third choice (and may keep some of them out altogether). Innovations in the structure and programs of some of the newer universities influence student applications, and because the rising costs of universities prevent all universities from offering a full range of courses (and the Australian Universities Commission is encouraging this restraint), an inter- and intrastate system whereby students enroll in the university strongest in their field of interest may develop.

But differences in the matriculation examinations of universities, combined with a system of limits for out-of-state student enrollments, reinforce the tradition that students attend university in their home states. This tradition is further strengthened in the case of Queensland, which charges higher fees for out-of-state students. However, students pursuing studies not offered in home state universities may go to another state. Thus the school of veterinary science at the University of New England will admit students from Western and South Australia and Tasmania, where training in this field is not offered.

Between 1954 and 1964 the number of university institutions doubled, their enrollments increased 250 percent, and there was a more than fivefold increase in university expenditures. In 1964, the Committee on the Future of Tertiary Education in Australia, led by Sir Leslie Martin and appointed by the AUC, made recommendations concerning the full spectrum of Australia's institutions of higher education. While noting the need for continued expansion in the university sector, the Martin Committee recommended a large-scale development of what is called *colleges of advanced education* (CAEs), tertiary-level institutions other than universities and teachers colleges. Among these colleges would be existing advanced-level technical and other specialized institutes and more broadly based institutions yet to be developed. The Martin Committee estimated that through this and other developments the proportion of all tertiary-level students enrolled in universities would go down from 58 percent in 1963 to 50 percent in 1975.

Colleges of Advanced Education

The Martin Committee recommendation not only sought relief for universities threatened by overcrowding but also involved reform in a medley of state-dominated institutions that gave vocationally oriented training. These institutions were characterized by a preponderance of part-time students, low persistence rates, a mixture of tertiary and subtertiary programs, inadequate physical sites and facilities (including former factories or jails), and virtually no amenities for staff or students. State authorities had an important voice in setting fees, determining curricula, establishing new staff positions, appointing staff members, and financing these institutions. These schools were preparing people for needed work in the society, but the gap in funding, autonomy, and prestige separating them from the universities was vast.

The Martin Committee recommended an expansion of tertiary-level technical colleges, the introduction of liberal studies into their diploma curricula, and augmentation of their financial support. It urged the establishment of autonomous institutes of colleges in each state. The function of these institutes would be to affiliate diploma-awarding colleges of appropriate standard and to plan, coordinate, and supervise the expansion, upgrading, and development of technical and related tertiary education. The institutes were to be responsible for recommending the allocation of state and Commonwealth funds among institutions and would be represented in an expanded and revised AUC. The Martin Committee further recommended that this new Australian Tertiary Education Commission be charged with the specific responsibility of "ensuring a balanced development of all forms of tertiary education in Australia" (Committee on the Future of Tertiary Education in Australia, 1964, vol. I, p. 171).

The Commonwealth government responded favorably to the Martin Committee recommendations on nonuniversity tertiary education but emphasized that the initiative for setting up institutes of colleges rested with the states and refused to make the availability of federal funds contingent upon establishment of the institutes. It made financial grants for 1965 and 1966 (mainly for "technical training" and not to CAEs as such). Since 1967, on a triennial basis, the Commonwealth government has shared in capital and recurrent expenditures for what is now known as advanced education. In October 1965 it established the Commonwealth Advisory Committee on Advanced Education, under the chairmanship of Ian W. Wark. This committee is not part of the expanded Universities Commission recommended by the Martin Committee but is a separate body to provide information and make recommendations to the Commonwealth Minister for Science and Education on financial needs of the colleges of advanced education. Included in the committee are persons from industry, the universities, and advanced technical education. Every triennium, some members of the Wark Committee visit as many institutions as possible.

Only in New South Wales and the Australian Capital Territory have these institutions taken on the new name of colleges of advanced education. The fields in which they offer courses include technology and engineering, agriculture, postgraduate nursing, occupational therapy, pharmacy and other paramedical fields, mining, business administration and commerce, art and architecture, domestic science, and liberal studies.

In 1965 Victoria set up an Institute of Colleges to coordinate advanced education (which had been under the State Department of Education) and, in 1967, gave it more authority. That authority now includes approving new diploma and degree courses at its affiliated institutions and also at a half dozen nonaffiliated ones. Affiliated with it are 14 of the 20 tertiary nonuniversity institutions in that state. Advanced education institutions were granted substantial autonomy in curriculum determination. By 1969 Western Australia, a forerunner in developing advanced education, had affiliated all nonuniversity, non-teacher-college higher education institutions with its new Institute of Technology. This institute now even includes some teacher college students. New South Wales established a Board of Advanced Technical Education to coordinate advanced education and recommend on its funding. Under the board are institutes to coordinate colleges in different fields (such as rural studies). The other states are also establishing new coordinating bodies and colleges. The new Canberra College of Advanced Education in the Australian Capital Territory is distinctive in its concentration on nontechnical fields and applied sciences.

As the Wark Committee put it, colleges of advanced education "are not simply to become vocational cramming grounds." They emphasize full-time and sandwich courses, admit students according to factors other than academic ability,[1] and plan a varied curriculum, including English, social science, foreign languages, psychology, journalism, and library studies, to supplement the primary technological emphasis. The AUC has emphasized the importance of enabling graduates of these colleges to pursue advanced study toward research degrees at the universities. The colleges of advanced education emphasize teaching and attempt to maintain a close relationship with industry. They are trying to fill the wide gap between the elite universities and a variety of mostly specialized, low-prestige, and skimpily funded institutions that are found at the lower end of the tertiary education spectrum. In effect, they are providing studies which are offered at universities in such countries as Canada and the United States but which have not yet been judged compatible with the academic emphasis of Australian universities. It was recently decided to permit the colleges to award degrees as well as diplomas (but not to duplicate research-degree courses given at universities). They overlap universities to some extent in training people for careers in agriculture, engineering, pharmacy, and chemistry, and it now appears that their salary levels may equal those standard at universities. The main hazard in the future is that in acquiring prestige and enlarged resources the colleges of advanced education may become almost indistinguishable from universities—following the example of the former colleges of advanced technology in Britain. Cognizant of this hazard, the Wark Committee is supporting fundamental re-

[1] In 1969, the AUC recommended that colleges emphasize "practical qualities, such as are required in certain managerial positions" while universities select "students with analytical ability and a measure of imaginative power" (Commonwealth of Australia: *Fourth Report of the Australian Universities Commission,* 1969).

search to provide guidelines for the development of advanced education as well as for better policy making. It is significant that the AUC in its Fourth Report (1969) stated that "the universities have a duty to the community to avoid . . . overlapping" between universities and colleges in the provision of courses and expressed the disinclination of the AUCs to recommend financial support for new university courses that might more appropriately be offered in the colleges. Forbearance in expansion of academic programs seems to have been urged more strongly on the universities than on the colleges of advanced education.

Teacher Education

Traditionally, teachers for Australia's state primary schools are trained in teachers colleges financed and administered by the state departments of education. Secondary teachers generally study for first degrees at a university and take a one-year concurrent course in practical teacher training, partly at a university and partly at a teachers college. This concurrent course leads to a diploma in education or similar qualification.

Over three-fourths of all teacher trainees are enrolled in the teachers colleges. Falling outside the public system are teacher training institutions for private kindergarten, primary, and secondary schools, most of which are church-affiliated. The Catholic orders train many of their own teachers. Other church-affiliated schools tend to employ university graduates and to give them inservice training.

Over the last decade, the study period for primary school teacher training has lengthened from two to three years and is comparable to the study period in other advanced tertiary courses. A full four-year course is becoming generally common for secondary school teachers.

FUNCTIONS

Australian universities have long had a markedly professional orientation. Their chief function has been to provide an adequate supply of graduates, primarily for government service, teaching, law, medicine, science, agriculture, engineering, dentistry, and veterinary medicine. Even the arts faculties tend to be vocationally oriented because many of their students train to be secondary school teachers. Students specialize from the beginning of their university careers, and nonarts students have very little exposure to liberal studies. Many students, "bonded" to their future employers, are limited by them in their choice of studies. About 40 percent of all university students are part-time and external students. Many of these are employed and pursue university studies to obtain professional qualification.

Teachers colleges and advanced education institutions have begun to modify their strictly vocational orientation. With the lengthening of teacher training curricula from two to three years, more general education is being introduced. General education is also one of the objectives of advanced education.

Research Since just before World War II, scientific research has developed largely outside the universities. The Commonwealth Scientific and Industrial Research Organization (CSIRO), established after World War I as the Council for Scientific and Industrial Research and modeled on the British Department of Scientific and Industrial Research (DSIR), became so successful in many fields that it dominated Australian research efforts. Because it was able to recruit the universities' best honors graduates in science and engineering, the potential personnel resources for university research were depleted. Very little research is undertaken in either the teachers colleges or colleges of advanced education. Although the latter emphasize teaching rather than research, they undertake (and will probably expand) research in applied fields.

In recent years, the importance of university research to the national interest has gained increasing recognition. On the recommendation of the AUC, general research was funded as an element in Commonwealth and state government support to the universities for the period 1961–1966. In 1965 the Commonwealth established the Australian Research Grants Committee (ARGC) to advise on the allocation of new funds for project research primarily, but not entirely, within the universities. This allocation is separate from the triennial general research vote to support postgraduate study and research in the universities under recommendations of the AUC. For the 1967–1969 triennium, the Commonwealth government proposed that $11 million be allocated by the ARGC for project research and $6 million be allocated for a general research vote to support postgraduate training and research. The Commonwealth further proposed that one half of each fund be provided by the Commonwealth; the other half would be provided by the state governments concerned. After bitter negotiations, the states refused to put up the money for the ARGC, and the Commonwealth decided to provide $9 million for it, leaving to state governments the problem of financing general university research. Whereas the AUC had recommended $10 million for postgraduate training and research in the 1967–1969 triennium, the states contributed little more than the $5 million they would have put up under the discarded equal-sharing arrangement, and government grants for nonproject university research in the 1967–1969 triennium declined from the $6 million allocated in the 1964–1966 triennium. But even this was a substantial increase over the 1961–1963 triennium allocation of $2 million. In 1969 the AUC, recognizing the importance of general university research and of the need for the Commonwealth government to help support it, recommended that in the 1970–1972 triennium a total of $8 million be allocated to research at the state universities and that the Commonwealth government provide half of this amount.

Development of computer facilities and new technology closely related to research has occurred, for the most part, since 1960. In 1962, the Commonwealth government agreed to the establishment by CSIRO of a computer network. It has a major central facility in Canberra and satellite units in Canberra, Sydney, Adelaide, and Melbourne for the use of government departments, the universities, and CSIRO. Special capital grants recommended by the AUC in the 1961–1966 period made it possible for all universities to have some computer facilities. The size of the grants was determined by each university's requirements and experience in computers. Plans for the 1970–1972 triennium call for an expansion of university computer facilities.

Adult Education

Adult education has been a function of several Australian universities for some years and has provided special programs of a vocational, liberal arts, and refresher nature to legions of students — some 25,000 annually in the mid-1960s. In 1966, the Universities of Sydney, New England, Adelaide, Western Australia, and New South Wales and Australian National University had departments of adult education, and some of the newer universities were contemplating establishing them.

Whether or not adult education is an appropriate university function has, however, become a controversial issue. The AUC indicated in 1966 that after the 1967–1969 triennium it proposed to terminate its support for adult education failing to meet university standards on the grounds that adult education at that level should be offered by colleges of advanced education or by agencies

TABLE 14 Enrollment in tertiary education institutions in Australia by year	1950	1955	1960	1965
Universities				
Undergraduates	23,728[a]	21,539[a]	39,218[a]	77,800[b]
Graduate students	394[a]	1,094[b]	2,771[b]	5,760[b]
Part-time students	8,602[d]	8,604[d]	15,997[e]	26,385[b]
External students	2,833[d]	3,032[d]	5,132[e]	6,825[b]
Full-time students	19,195[d]	19,156[d]	32,349[e]	50,350[b]
Total enrollment	23,394[b]	30,644[b]	53,342[b]	83,560[b]
(full-time equivalent)			(41,164)[f]	(69,360)[b]

	1950	1954	1961	1966
Teacher education				
State teacher colleges only	5,200[g]	6,671[h]	12,591[h]	18,226[i]
State teachers colleges and universities		8,374[h]	18,149[h]	25,021[i]
Advanced education total (Part-time only)			23,397[f]	
Total in tertiary education		51,000[h]		152,000[k]

*Estimate.

SOURCES: (*a*) Macmillan, 1968, p. 82; includes Commonwealth Reconstruction Training Scheme students, excludes subgraduate and postgraduate diploma and certificate students. (*b*) Commonwealth of Australia, 1966, pp. 26, 38, 39, 23, 18. Undergraduate figure for 1965 includes master's qualifying and postgraduate diploma students. Graduate students figures for 1955, 1960, and 1965 exclude master's qualifying and postgraduate diploma students. (*c*) Information supplied by AUC. (*d*) Macmillan, 1968, p. 86. (*e*) Commonwealth of Australia, *Report of the Australian Universities Commission on Australian Universities 1958-1963*, Commonwealth Government Printer, Canberra, October 1960, pp. 18-19; excludes Commonwealth Reconstruction Training Scheme. (*f*) Commonwealth of Australia, *Second Report of the Australian Universities Commission, Australian Universities 1961-66*, Commonwealth Government Printer, 1963, p. 2. (*g*) L. W. Shears, "The Training of Teachers in Australia," in George Z. F. Bereday and Joseph A. Lauwerys (eds.), *Year Book of Education 1963: The Education and Training of Teachers*, Harcourt, Brace & World, Inc., New York, 1963, p. 202. (*h*) Committee on the Future of Tertiary Education in Australia, 1964. (*i*) *Report of the Proceedings of the Third Triennial Conference of the Directors and Superintendents of Teacher Education*, October 2-7, 1966, mimeograph, p. 32. (*j*) Information supplied by Commonwealth Advisory Committee on Advanced Education. (*k*) Borrie, 1968, p. 30.

of state government. The government rejected this proposal. However, in the last several years, the universities have been cutting back generally in their subuniversity courses, including those in adult extension fields. Colleges of advanced education are expected to become more active in such programs. Meanwhile, adult education is mainly offered by state agencies and by a variety of nongovernmental organizations.

Culture   Australian society has long been characterized as anti-intellectual and anticultural, with priority given to materialistic and hedonistic values rather than to aesthetic ones. However, since World War II,

1968	1969	1972
	97,252[c]	113,628[c]
	9,964[c]	13,205[c]
	32,813[c]	36,130[c]
	6,990[c]	7,670[c]
	65,796[c]	83,025[c]
	107,216[c]	126,825[c]
	(94,361)[c]	(114,405)[c]
1968		

30,000[f]*

32,506[i]

(18,941)

163,250*

and especially in the 1960s, cultural activity and appreciation of literature, art, architecture, publishing, and the performing arts have been intensified. Government and private philanthropy have markedly increased their support of Australian cultural projects, and the universities and other institutions of higher education have enlarged their contribution in a number of cultural fields. The Universities of Sydney, Adelaide, and Melbourne each have a chair or other position in Australian literature. Sydney, Adelaide, and Tasmania publish journals of literary criticism. Universities and music conservatories are encouraging a wider public appreciation of music, and in the field of drama, the least supported of the performing arts, it is significant that the University of New South Wales Drama Department incorporated the National Institute of Dramatic Art. Even so, the universities and other higher education institutions do not as yet play a major role in national cultural development (Semmler, 1968).

ENROLLMENTS IN TERTIARY EDUCATION

University enrollments more than quadrupled between 1950 and 1969, going up from 23,394 to 107,216. The proportion of the 17- to 22-year-old age group enrolled in universities went up from 3.3 percent in 1960 to 8.2 percent in 1969 and is projected by the AUC to reach 9.3 percent in 1972. The proportion of university students enrolled for higher degrees increased from 2.78 percent in 1953 to 8.7 percent in 1968 and is projected at over 10 percent in 1970. More than 70 percent of all university students are men. Overseas students constituted 8.7 percent of total full-time enrollments in 1968; some 90 percent of these students were from Asia and the Pacific, and 24.2 percent were sponsored by the Commonwealth government. Since 1950, part-time enrollments have constituted about 30 percent of total enrollments. The proportion of university students who are external students, i.e., who study by correspondence, supplemented with intensive residential sessions, usually during May and August vacations, declined from 10 percent in the 1950s to 7 percent in 1968.

Until recently, a large number of students were enrolled in nondegree courses in Australian universities. Many of these were students enrolled in undergraduate diploma and certificate courses, and some students enrolled in courses without working toward a degree. However, the pressure of rising student numbers has reduced enrollments in these "subuniversity" courses. The proportion of university students enrolled in them decreased from 23.6 percent in 1957 to 8.1 percent in 1965 and 4.4 percent in 1968 (Commonwealth of Australia, 1966, p. 48; 1969, p. 18).

The pace of university expansion has been particularly rapid in the 1960s. After doubling between 1950 and 1960, enrollments doubled again between 1960 and 1968. Whereas in its 1960 report the AUC recommended against the imposition of admission quotas as a way to keep enrollments to manageable limits, in its 1966 report it listed quotas then in force in some 80 disciplines at 11 universities. Limits on university expansion are expected to reduce the proportion of all tertiary students enrolled at universities from 60 percent in 1966 to 50 percent in 1986. (The Martin Committee set 1975 as the date when 50 percent would be in university.)

Nonuniversity tertiary education will therefore expand more rapidly than university tertiary education. Enrollments in state teachers colleges, almost all of which are full-time, quadrupled from 1954 to 1966, increasing from 6,671 to 25,021.

Enrollments in tertiary level courses in the colleges of advanced education increased from 24,342 in 1965 to 32,506 in 1968 (and an estimated 38,738 in 1969). The 1972 enrollment is expected to be twice that of 1968. Only about two-fifths of the students in colleges of advanced education are enrolled full-time, although this proportion is rising.

The Martin Committee projected an increase in enrollments in all tertiary or higher education courses from 158,900 in 1967 to 213,000 in 1971 and to 248,000 in 1975.

The proportion of 17- to 22-year-olds enrolled in all forms of tertiary education is projected at 17.7 percent in 1975 and 20 percent in 1986. This increase in the enrollment rate, combined with the projected increase in the number of persons in the 17- to 22-year-old age group from 1,170,770 in 1966 to 1,460,143 in 1976 and to 1,564,222 in 1986 (Borrie, 1968, pp. 30, 37) makes it clear that tertiary enrollments will continue to expand (Borrie, 1968, p. 29).

The teachers colleges try to expand at the rate necessary to produce the number of teachers needed to educate the pupils expected in the schools in future years. Expansion of the universities and colleges of advanced education (colleges of advanced education are taking increasing responsibility for teacher education) is projected on the basis of the proportion of the 17- to 22-year-old age group expected to seek and be qualified for higher education, excluding those in teachers colleges.

Advocates of university expansion are reluctant to see university enrollments restrained in order to divert more students into the advanced education sector. Some university officials regard advanced education as a means of enabling the universities to be yet more selective in their admissions. Supporters of advanced education naturally oppose the proposition that its students will be only those unable to qualify for university admissions while the universities become increasingly elitist. Decisions on the respective shares of the age group obtaining tertiary education in the universities and advanced education institutions must be made by the Minister for Science and Education, if not the Prime Minister, on the basis of submissions from the AUC and the Commonwealth Advisory Committee on Advanced Education. These decisions are made in association with the state governments.

Study Period and Persistence The minimum study period for a pass degree in most fields, including arts, science, commerce, and pharmacy, is, with a few exceptions, three years. An honors degree requires one more year. It normally takes six years to complete studies in medicine. The low proportion of students who graduate in minimum time and the high failure rate are continuing problems. The Murray Committee reported that only 35.1 percent of the students entering university in 1951 graduated in minimum time; only 57.7 percent were expected to graduate ultimately. A recent study by the Commonwealth Office of Education showed some improvement: 38 percent

TABLE 15
Degrees
conferred in
Australian
institutions of
tertiary
education

	1950	1955	1960	1965	1966
First degrees	4,255[a]	3,167[a]	4,184[b]	7,937[c]	9,871[d]
Higher degrees	251[a]	265[a]	412[b]	794[c]	

SOURCES: (a) Commonwealth of Australia, *Report of the Australian Universities Commission on Australian Universities 1958-1963*, 1960, p. 39. (b) Commonwealth of Australia, *Second Report of the Australian Universities Commission, Australian Universities 1961-66*, 1963, p. 21. (c) Macmillan, 1968, p. 86. (d) Borrie, 1968, p. 6.

of full-time first-degree students entering university in 1961 graduated in minimum time, 26 percent had discontinued their studies, and the remaining students were continuing or had transferred to part-time study (Commonwealth Office of Education, 1961). Less than one-fourth of students who enter part-time study graduate.

The prolonged study period and low success rate of students in Australian universities are attributed to a variety of factors: an alleged abruptness in the transition between secondary school and university; the large proportion of part-time students; the fact that until the recent imposition of enrollment quotas and increased selectivity in admissions all students matriculating from secondary school were admitted to university; the problems of student motivation (many students are now in faculties of their second or even fourth choice); deterioration in the quality of teaching and in staff-student ratios as a result of the overcrowding; overburdened curricula; and the traditional structure of degree courses in arts and sciences which requires "the student to carry several different subjects concurrently, each of them designed for the training of the specialist and taught independently of the others" (Short, 1967, p. 40). The practice in some faculties (now waning) of requiring a student to repeat a year if he fails to pass in all subjects also contributes to a high failure rate.

The imposition of quotas has made admissions more selective but has not proportionately decreased failure rates. Universities are criticized for grading students too severely and for the implication that they regard a high failure rate as proof of their quality. At least one university is contemplating the introduction of exter-

TABLE 16
Entrants to
institutions
of tertiary
education in
Australia
by year

	1950	1955	1960	1965	1968
Number	7,034[a]	8,525[a]	15,685[a]	23,436[a]	25,669[b]

SOURCES: (a) Macmillan, 1968, p. 75. (b) Commonwealth Bureau of Census and Statistics, *Social Statistics*, no. 64, *Universities (Preliminary), Students and Staff 1968 and Finance 1967*, Canberra, August 1968, p. 5.

TABLE 17
Entrants to
institutions
of tertiary
education in
Australia
by year and
sex as
percentage
of 17-year-olds

	1951	1954	1961	1965	1968*
Men	2.02	2.51	4.47	5.03	5.78
Women	1.05	1.34	2.41	2.96	3.60

*Estimated.

SOURCE: Borrie, 1968, p. 32.

nal examinations to supplement internal examinations for first degrees and, by setting up an external "check," to lessen the impact of the sometimes excessively severe grading of internal examinations. Several universities have established special research units to examine problems of teaching and student performance.

Staff-Student Ratios

Staff-student ratios have declined in the last decade because recruitment of staff could not keep pace with enrollment expansion. This was particularly true in the 1967–1969 triennium, when there were cutbacks in the funding of universities. The AUC calculated staff-student ratios according to a formula whereby full-time higher-degree students are accorded 2 units; part-time, 1 unit; external, $\frac{1}{4}$ unit (recently changed to $\frac{1}{2}$ unit); full-time bachelor's degree, postgraduate diploma, and students taking an extra year to qualify for master's studies, 1 unit; part-time undergraduates, $\frac{1}{2}$ unit. Staff-student ratios on the basis of this formula declined from 1:10.9 in 1964 to 1:11.0 in 1966. Under the new formula introduced in the AUC in 1969, in which external students count $\frac{1}{2}$ instead of $\frac{1}{4}$ unit, the staff-student ratio was calculated to be 1:11.9.

HIGHER EDUCATION AND CIVIL GOVERNMENT

Under the Australian constitution, the Commonwealth government has no responsibility for education. However, with the assent of the states, it exercises advisory and financial functions. In 1967, the Commonwealth government established the Department of Education and Science, headed by a minister to whom the AUC and the Commonwealth Advisory Committee on Advanced Education report. Also under this department is the Commonwealth Office of Education, established in 1945. The department maintains liaison with the states and advises the Commonwealth government on educational matters. It is concerned with the planning of higher education, financial assistance to students, scientific research, the administration of international exchanges and scholarships, and Australia's international cultural and educational relations.

Universities and Government

Universities are established by acts of the state parliaments (by the federal parliament in the case of the former Canberra University College and the Australian National University), and their statutes or by-laws must be submitted for final approval to a governor, governor-in-council, minister, or parliament. Once established, the universities are autonomous and self-governing. Government interests, however, are represented in university affairs because, on an average, one-third to one-fourth of the members of university councils or senates are chosen by the governor and state parliament (federal parliament in the case of the Australian National University); for some governing bodies this proportion exceeds one-half.

The Commonwealth government has had an increasing influence on universities since World War II. One of the main concerns of the Murray Committee (Committee on Australian Universities), which reported in 1957, was the lack of a national policy for university education. Its principal recommendation, that a statutory body be established by the Commonwealth government to promote "the balanced development of Australian universities," was implemented with establishment of the AUC in legislation of 1959. The AUC has a full-time chairman, eight (originally four) part-time commissioners, and a small secretariat of about 25 persons. It is required to consult with the state governments, as well as the institutions, in drawing up its recommendations for Commonwealth support of universities. Its recommendations are implemented by acts of the Commonwealth parliament. Commonwealth grants are contingent upon certain matching support from the states, thereby limiting what the Commonwealth can do in determining university development and encouraging the states to support university development along the lines that the Commonwealth is disposed to finance. Hence, the effectiveness of the AUC depends upon its ability to negotiate agreements with the states and Commonwealth government.

The system functioned successfully for the 1961–1963 and 1964–1966 trienniums. For the 1967–1969 triennium, however, the Commonwealth government did not accept the recommendations of the AUC, and the states balked at providing the matching amounts which the AUC recommended (apparently without adequate consultation with the states). The Commonwealth government entered into direct negotiations with the state governments, and funding eventually agreed to was far below what the AUC had recommended, causing considerable hardship to the universities.

The episode impaired Commonwealth-state relations and, at least temporarily, the effectiveness of the AUC.

In recent years the states have undertaken more study, coordination, and planning of university development—in part to prevent the Commonwealth government from having a disproportionate influence through its leverage on state funding via the AUC. In 1967, New South Wales established a Universities Board to coordinate university affairs, recommend on the level and distribution of state funding, and pursue general planning. Victoria also has a universities board. Other states have had their systems reviewed by special committees.

Other Tertiary Education and Government

With the exception of the few private colleges, teachers colleges are administered by state departments of education. State departments of education also regulate, to a large extent, the training of secondary school teachers at universities. They determine student selection and support as well as curricular requirements.

The Martin Committee urged the establishment of statutory boards of teacher education in each state. These boards would take over the functions of departments of education in supervising standards of teacher preparation and granting certificates and professional awards. They would also distribute to the colleges federal funds provided (on the committee's recommendation) by the Commonwealth government on a matching formula with state governments for both capital and recurrent expenditures. The Commonwealth government rejected the committee's recommendations on financing but committed itself to providing $24 million (Australian)[2] toward capital and equipment costs of the colleges on a nonmatching basis for the 1967–1969 triennium, thereby, for the first time, contributing substantially to the funding of teacher education.

New South Wales was the only state to implement the Martin Committee recommendation that a Board of Teacher Education be established, although the board it set up in 1967 was advisory rather than statutory.

Whereas most advanced education (technical and other nonuniversity tertiary education) was directly under state departments of education[3] (of technical education in New South Wales) until

[2] Australian $1 approximately equals U.S. $0.89.

[3] In all states except Queensland, however, agricultural colleges fell under departments of agriculture.

several years ago, some states now give advanced education increasing independence. In Victoria, the institutions have a large measure of autonomy under the Victoria Institute of Colleges, which itself is largely autonomous. In New South Wales, legislation was pending in early 1969 to give autonomy to an institute combining the former Institutes of Technology and of Business Studies, and a new Board of Advanced Technical Education is to be established to advise the state government on the allocation of funds to advanced education. The new colleges of advanced education being established at Bathurst and Wagga Wagga are also expected to have autonomy. Queensland plans to set up an Institute of Colleges in the 1970–1972 triennium to coordinate its advanced education; it will give its member institutions more autonomy. The Institute of Technology in Western Australia and the new Canberra College of Advanced Education are also removed from the direct authority of government, and similar developments are occurring in Tasmania and South Australia.

As with the universities, the individual institutions or coordinating agencies (or both) include representatives of state government as well as of industry and other interests concerned with advanced education in their governing bodies.

As mentioned earlier, the Commonwealth government did not implement the Martin Committee recommendation that a single body concerned with all tertiary education replace the AUC. Instead it set up the separate Wark Committee to advise it on matters in the advanced education sector. However, in at least two states, new agencies have been established to advise the state governments on the coordination of the universities and advanced education, as well as on funding and other matters. Western Australia now has a Tertiary Education Committee, and in New South Wales a new Higher Education Board in consultation with the new Universities Board and Board of Advanced Technical Education advises the government on all higher education. In the other states, coordination arrangements between the university and advanced education sectors are less formalized.

GOVERNANCE WITHIN UNIVERSITIES The main agents of university governance are the vice-chancellor (the chancellorship is mostly an honorary position), convocation, the council (or *senate,* as it is called at some universities), and the professorial board. The vice-chancellor is a permanent, salaried, full-time officer appointed by the council and responsible to it for the general administration of the university. He provides liaison between the council and the academic bodies, is a member of many of the council's committees, and has considerable influence. Except at universities where the chancellor has the responsibility, he presides over council meetings. The registrar, accountant, and other officials who handle such matters as finance, admissions, and examinations are responsible to the vice-chancellor. The senior academic assistant to the vice-chancellor is often the chairman of the professorial board. There has been a recent tendency to appoint deputy vice-chancellors to assist with the growing burden of university administration.

Convocations, primarily advisory bodies, consist of all adult graduates of a university and in some institutions may include additional members appointed by the governor-in-council of the state or by the council. They play a very limited role and cannot initiate legislation, but they may submit proposals to the councils and, within limits, amend or reject legislation submitted to them by the councils. Convocations usually meet annually. Their main influence is derived from the fact that they elect a number (four-fifths of the total at the University of Adelaide) of council members.

Membership in the councils (or senates), the chief governing bodies, varies among the universities but generally is drawn from parliaments, industry and commerce, academic staff, government departments, the professions, and students. It numbers between 19 and 40. The chancellors are ex officio chairmen of the councils. By authority vested in them by the legislation establishing the universities, the councils appoint professors, lecturers, and other officials of the university, including the vice-chancellor. At some universities, the councils also appoint deans; at others, the deans are elected by faculties. The councils have complete control of all properties and funds and are responsible for the general management of universities' affairs. On occasion, a council may dismiss members of university staffs. Generally, the councils function through committees concerned, for example, with legislation, staff and establishment, buildings and grounds, and finance. In 1968, the provision for student representation greatly increased.

The professorial board is the chief academic body and usually includes all professors, some nonprofessorial heads of departments, and certain senior officials (such as the librarian). It is responsible for considering all academic matters except those relating to finance, but it tends to approve policy initiated by departments and faculties rather than to initiate policy itself.

At the original six state universities and the universities of New England and New South Wales the chairman of the chief academic body is a professor, not the vice-chancellor. The Murray Report commented that because this situation prevents the vice-chancellor from emerging as the main representative of academic opinion, his ability to mediate between the council and professorial board is limited so that, in fact, there exists between them "almost a natural state of tension" (Report of the *Committee on Australian Universities,* 1957, p. 95). The new universities — Newcastle, Monash, Flinders, Macquarie, La Trobe, and Australian National University — avoided this anomalous situation by making their vice-chancellors chairmen of their professorial boards.

Under the professorial boards are the faculty boards of each faculty, some 10 to 12 in the larger universities, consisting of the members of the teaching staff of all departments in the faculty and perhaps some extramural members as well. Not all universities have faculty boards. Boards of study, where they exist, also fall under the professorial boards. With the growth of universities, the faculty boards and the professorial boards have in many instances grown almost too large for effective consideration of the matters with which they are charged, and the administration of academic affairs has become an increasing burden on deans of faculties. A recent trend to appoint more permanent deans of faculties (for five-year terms), instead of having them hold an honorary office which rotates frequently, has helped to give continuity and greater efficiency to faculty administration.

The Martin Committee called attention to several difficulties in university governance: the excessive administrative burden imposed on vice-chancellors, the unwieldiness of the professorial boards and faculty boards because of university expansion, and the need for more administrative staff generally. The Committee urged the strengthening of administrative procedures; a greater delegation of authority by vice-chancellors; increased staffing in the central administration for academic planning, policy making, and budget preparation; and an examination and remodeling of professorial board and faculty structures "with a view to evolving means by which many of their responsibilities could be discharged by smaller groups." Some reforms along these lines have been instituted, mainly at new universities.

Student representation in university governance was limited until the end of the 1960s. In 1968 and 1969, a majority of the universities were in the process of reviewing this matter. In January 1969 students were represented on the councils or senates of almost all universities, though in most cases with only one member. They were represented on no professorial boards but to varying degrees on council committees and faculty boards. The most notable expansion of student participation was at Australian National University. Beginning in July 1969, students and staff were equally represented on newly established education committees in each faculty. The mandate of these committees is to advise faculty on courses, teaching, examination methods, and related matters. In general, student representation at universities continues to be limited in bodies which deal with budgets, appointments, academic policy, and other matters of central concern. Students are represented to a greater degree in university committees having to do with primarily student affairs, such as sports, residence halls, discipline, and student health. Students have little or no representation in governance of the colleges of advanced education. At many colleges of education, students serve on committees, but the major decisions are made by the departments of education in each state.

Both the Murray and Martin Committees urged increased coordination in university development in order to use resources for teaching and research as effectively as possible, but coordination tends to be alien to university tradition in Australia. The state universities developed independently, and each has aimed at self-sufficiency and has tended to compete rather than cooperate.

Since the establishment of the Australian Universities Commission, interuniversity coordination has accelerated, taking place primarily through the Australian Vice-chancellors' Committee. The committee meets five times a year, supports periodic meetings of members of university administrative staffs, and since 1963 has published *The Australian University*. The 16-member committee (the vice-chancellors of Australia's 15 universities plus, as a courtesy, the vice-chancellor of the University of Papua and New Guinea) has no authority to bind the universities. It discusses policies and then presents its views to and negotiates with the Commonwealth government on such matters as staff salaries, the level of Commonwealth scholarship aid, and Commonwealth support of the universities, including university research. In the last several years, the committee also has launched a series of studies on problems of common concern to the universities: possibilities of greater utilization of university facilities through a six- instead of a five-day week and through reorganization of the academic calendar to permit year-round operation; the determination of criteria for allocating new faculties and subjects among the universities; and student admissions and persistence in the universities.

Within the states having more than one university, coordination is still limited. In New South Wales and Victoria, the vice-chancellors of the several universities meet informally several times a year. There is little sharing of staff and facilities although in New South Wales the universities coordinate the use of a joint computer center.

GOVERNANCE WITHIN TEACHERS COLLEGES

Teachers colleges do not have governing bodies and senates comparable to the universities because they are under the direct authority of the state departments of education. The colleges are headed by principals, assisted by vice-principals and wardens. All administrative and teaching staff members are appointed by state departments of education. Despite this formal control by state authorities, the colleges have some autonomy in academic matters.

Coordination among teachers colleges occurs through frequent meetings of college principals and periodic meetings of the state directors of teacher education and of state ministers of education and of technical education with respect to teacher training programs. There is some coordination, mostly informal, among university faculties of education, colleges of advanced education, and teachers colleges.

GOVERNANCE WITHIN COLLEGES OF ADVANCED EDUCATION

Before recent reforms, technical and other nonuniversity tertiary institutions had no formal autonomy; like teachers colleges, they fell under departments of education. The new colleges of advanced education have governing bodies and academic boards comparable to the universities' councils and professorial boards. Industry is strongly represented on the governing bodies and has school boards for different fields that are comparable to faculty boards in the universities. In Victoria, the Institute of Colleges has a council and board of studies as its main governing body and academic board and has school boards in each discipline. The chief executive officer is the vice-president, comparable to a university vice-chancellor. Within the limits of the controls exercised by the Victoria Institute of Colleges, the affiliated colleges are autonomous under their own councils in matters that include curriculum determination, student admissions, and staff recruitment.

Coordination in advanced education is encouraged by the Commonwealth Advisory Committee on Advanced Education to avoid wasteful duplication in programs and to develop a few national centers of excellence in certain highly specialized fields. Within each state, coordinating agencies and state authorities encourage coordination in the development and utilization of facilities and resources and in making the colleges as responsive as possible to state needs. Comparable to the committee of vice-chancellors, the national Council of Chief Executive Officers of the colleges of advanced education meets annually to consider matters of common concern. In Victoria, the Board of Principals of colleges affiliated with the Victoria Institute of Colleges plays a similar role within that state.

Increased coordination in sharing facilities among sectors of tertiary education is anticipated in the future. Common or adjacent sites are already shared by universities and teachers colleges, and there is a trend toward locating teachers colleges and colleges of advanced education on a common site to achieve economy and operational flexibility.

FINANCING HIGHER EDUCATION Expenditures for higher education increased from $10.3 million in 1947 to about $265 million in 1967 and were projected by the Martin Committee (in 1963 prices) at about $418 million in 1975. The proportion of the gross national product devoted to all higher education went up from 0.22 percent in 1947 to 1.2 percent in 1967. The largest share of the expenditures is made by universities, whose proportion increased from 52 percent of all higher education expenditures in 1947 to 68 percent in 1967. The estimated cost of assistance to both universities and colleges of advanced education during the 1970–1973 triennium is expected to be 40 percent greater than it was in 1967–1969 and will total about $910 million.

Until World War II, tertiary education received almost no financial support from the Commonwealth government. During and after the war, the Commonwealth provided funds to the universities in connection with the Commonwealth Reconstruction Training Scheme for veterans. With the passage of the States Grants (Universities) Act in December 1950, the Commonwealth government provided annual grants for recurrent expenditures. Under terms of this act, the states matched each Commonwealth dollar given in pre-specified amounts with three dollars from state grant or fee income. Under this program, Commonwealth funds available for tertiary education increased from $2.2 million in 1951 to $4.66 million in 1957" (*Report of the Committee on Australian Universities,* 1967, p. 25).

The Murray Committee found a need for substantial increases in funds to meet rising university costs resulting from expanding enrollments. In accordance with its recommendations, the States Grants (Universities) Act was revised to provide for Commonwealth grants for three-year periods beginning with 1958–1960. The Commonwealth recurrent grants were to be matched on a 1 to 1.85 basis from state grants and student fees; Commonwealth capital grants were to be matched on a 1 to 1 basis. Under the new system, Commonwealth recurrent grants to the universities increased from $10.57 million in 1958 to an average of $133.363 million per annum for the 1967–1969 triennium. Commonwealth funds as a share of total university recurrent income increased from 10.3 percent in 1950 to 41 percent in 1965. State support declined from 43 to 35 percent and student fees from 18.5 to 13 percent in the same period. Support from alumni, business, or foundations is very limited.

In addition to helping finance the capital and recurrent costs of the universities, the Commonwealth provides grants for the capital costs of the universities' halls of residence and residential colleges and for the recurrent and capital costs of teaching hospitals affiliated with the universities. These grants are subject to matching by state and other funds on the same formulas as are used for the universities. The Commonwealth contribution to the teaching and administrative costs of the halls of residence and affiliated colleges has no matching requirement. In the 1967–1969 triennium, about 5 percent of the total state and Commonwealth grants[4] of $520.-558 million went to the halls of residence, residential colleges, and teaching hospitals.

The Commonwealth provided virtually no financial assistance to teacher education until 1967, but in the period 1967 to 1969 it provided $24 million in unmatched grants meeting the capital

[4] Including both capital and recurrent expenditures and expenditures for computer development but excluding research.

costs of teacher education institutions. (Since 1955, denominational teachers colleges have been eligible for governmental financial support.) The state departments of education favor the continuance of Commonwealth funding of part of the capital costs of teacher education, but because of state responsibilities in this area, they neither expect nor want Commonwealth funding of recurrent expenditures, fearing that the Commonwealth government might supplant state governments in determining the future direction of teacher education. Expenditures on teacher education have increased nearly eightfold since 1954; more than half are devoted to student support because the overwhelming majority of students at state teachers colleges are recruited by state departments of education and attend college as salaried employees of the departments.

Exact figures on the financing of advanced education are not available for the 1950s because, until recently, most of these institutions offered courses at both the secondary and postsecondary levels and did not keep separate statistics for these levels. Since the establishment in 1965 of the Commonwealth Advisory Committee on Advanced Education, the separation of postsecondary courses into colleges of advanced education, and the infusion of Commonwealth funds into this field, the amount of money available to advanced education has increased dramatically. Since 1967, Commonwealth funds have been made available for the recurrent and capital expenditures of advanced education institutions following the same formulas as for the universities. Until this recent

TABLE 18 *Expenditures for Australian universities (in thousands of dollars)*

Expenditures	1955	1960	1965	1967	1969
Recurrent	20,368[a]	45,408[a]	114,394[b]	130,911[c]	161,350[c]
Capital	4,588[a]	18,632[a]			
TOTAL	24,954[a]	64,040[a]	149,700[b]	181,226[d]*	

*Based on total of $527.642 million expended in the 1967–69 triennium and includes universities, teaching hospitals, student residences, capital equipment, computers, and research grants from state and Commonwealth governments. Excludes private funds expended.

SOURCES: (a) A. R. Hall, "Statistical Appendix," in Edward L. Wheelwright (ed.), *Higher Education in Australia*, F. W. Cheshire Pty., Melbourne, 1965, pp. 333–334. (b) Macmillan, 1968, pp. 34–35. Although cited as income, the total approximates recurrent expenditures. (c) Estimated by increasing by 10 percent (the proportion of recurrent income derived from sources other than Commonwealth and state grants and student fees) the sum of these items for 1967 and 1969. Australian Universities Commission, *Fourth Report*, Commonwealth Government Printer, Canberra, 1969, p. 40. (d) Commonwealth Bureau of Census and Statistics, *Social Statistics*, no. 64, *Universities (Preliminary), Students and Staff 1968 and Finance 1967*, Canberra, August 1968, p. 26.

TABLE 19 Commonwealth- state grants (including fees) for recurrent expenditures (in thousands of dollars)	Period	
	1958-1960	107,945
	1961-1963	166,110
	1964-1966	277,089
	1967-1969	400,089

change, about 80 percent of the technical colleges' expenditures were met by the state governments, and less than 2 percent were met by the Commonwealth. Because student fees for advanced education courses are very low and endowment and gifts are meager, Commonwealth and state government grants meet nearly all of the funding requirements of colleges of advanced education. Total capital and recurrent expenditures for technical institutes and other advanced education were an estimated $32.925 million in 1968.

Total expenditures on all higher education in Australia was an estimated $266 million in 1967.

HIGHER EDUCATION AND ECONOMIC PLANNING The expansion of higher education facilities is mainly determined by social demand, but manpower needs influence the policies of government bodies that provide financial support. The Department of Labour and National Service prepares periodic manpower need surveys which indicate where shortages may develop in the future. The Australian Universities Commission tries to take future manpower needs into consideration in recommending on the financing of universities. The expansion of colleges of advanced education has been pushed because of a general conviction that more technologists will be needed in the future. Efforts are made to relate teacher college enrollments to future needs of trained teachers, determined mainly on the basis of population projections. However, forecasts of needs for highly trained people are not yet available in sufficient detail to guide higher education development.

FINANCIAL ASSISTANCE TO STUDENTS In 1968–69, university students needed an estimated $1,400 to $1,500 for tuition fees and living expenses. This amount varied, of course, depending on whether a student lived in a college, in lodgings, or at home.[5] The high proportion of part-time and external

---

[5] At one of the larger universities a 1968 study reported that the median weekly living costs of students were $14.70 for students living at home, $32.50 for those in colleges, $28 in hostels and comparable institutions, and $22.60 in private accommodations. University of Melbourne, *Special Report of Student Housing Board of the University of Melbourne,* August 1968, p. 42.

students (38 percent in 1968) results from the need of many students to work while pursuing their academic studies.

Financial assistance to students has expanded greatly since 1950, but because of enrollment increases, the proportion of students receiving some form of financial assistance—about half of all students at universities—is not appreciably higher than it was in the mid-1950s.

The main financial assistance to Australian students is provided under the Commonwealth Scholarship Scheme for undergraduates, the Commonwealth Postgraduate Scheme for graduate students, the teacher training awards of state government, and, since 1966, the Commonwealth Advanced Education Scholarships. The Commonwealth Scholarship Scheme, introduced in 1951, provides awards, mainly on the basis of matriculation examination results, to entering students in higher education institutions. The awards cover basic fees and tuition; they also provide a living allowance for full-time students. The amount of the living allowance is based on a means test, on whether the student is living at home or away, and marital status. Second or "later-year" Commonwealth Scholarships are available to students after one or more years of successful study, and Mature Age Scholarships are open to full-time students commencing their study between the ages of 25 and 30. The number of Commonwealth scholarships available to entering students increased from 3,000 per year in 1951 to 6,000 in 1966; later-year awards increased in this period from less than 100 to 1,530. Mature Age Scholarships, 100 annually in 1961, increased to 120 in 1964. Postgraduate Commonwealth awards increased from 100 annually when the program began in 1959 to 400 per year in the mid-1960s. They cover tuition expense and provide a stipend. About half of all graduate students receive financial aid. Commonwealth Postgraduate awards for master's degree students in 1968–69 were $2,140, and for doctoral candidates, $2,350.

The Commonwealth Scholarship Scheme for undergraduates gives priority to scholarship rather than financial need and does not substantially enlarge the proportion of low-income students having access to universities. Students obtaining high marks in matriculation examinations receive awards to cover tuition and fees regardless of need, or one-fourth of their educational expenses. Means test requirements permit making full living-expenses awards only to students from families with a maximum adjusted family income of $2,300 or less. These awards fall short of actual living cost; in 1968, they gave a maximum of $559 per annum to students living at home and $904.80 to those away from home. In 1968–69, 27.5 percent of undergraduate university students received Commonwealth Scholarships, and, of these, about 40 percent received living allowances.

The other sources of financial assistance to university students are loan funds—mainly from the universities—and scholarships, cadetships, and bursaries from a variety of sources. Loan funds assist only a minute fraction of all full-time students. Cadetships, some scholarships, and other awards constitute a *bonded* financial aid system, under which the students receiving assistance commit themselves to work for several years after graduation for the organization or firm which funds their university studies. The system of bonded students, most common in teacher education and to a lesser extent in engineering, agriculture, and veterinary training, was criticized by the Murray and Martin committees. They charged that the system required students to choose a career too early, caused difficulties for the university because of the inflexibility in the academic programs of bonded students, and, excluding teacher trainees (they are overwhelmingly full-time), perpetuated the emphasis on part-time study at universities.

Nearly all students at state teachers colleges are *departmental students,* selected and financed by the state departments of education. In 1966 less than 1 percent of students were privately supported. Departmental students are given free tuition and generous living allowances, which vary depending on a student's age, marital status, living arrangements, and year at college. In effect, the departmental student is a salaried employee of the education department and is subsidized accordingly. Teacher trainees are expected to serve in the state education system for several years—five years in New South Wales, for example—after completing their studies. Those failing to do so are normally required to reimburse the department of education for their awards.

Until 1966, almost no students in advanced education except in Victoria received financial assistance other than through cadetships and other bonded support. Following a recommendation of the Martin Committee, the Commonwealth Advanced Education Scholarship System was introduced in 1966. Under this system, 1,000 awards are available annually for part-time or full-time study "in approved tertiary courses at Institutes of Technology, Technical Colleges and other non-university institutions" (Commonwealth Advisory Committee on Advanced Education, 1966, p. 29).

Scholarships cover all compulsory fees and, for full-time students, provide a living allowance based on a means test. Scholarships are awarded mainly on the basis of results in matriculation-level examinations, except later-year scholarships, which are available to students who have completed one year of full-time advanced education and who are selected on the basis of their record in that year. Bonded students are ineligible for Commonwealth Advanced Education Scholarships.

STUDENTS University students come mainly from middle-class and upper-middle-class families. A study in 1959–60 of secondary school graduates showed that whereas the fathers of 7 percent were in professional occupations, the fathers of 29 percent of male and 38 percent of female university entrants came from this category; 27 percent of male and 28 percent of female university entrants came from families of unskilled, semiskilled, and skilled manual workers and farmers, but these categories accounted for 68 percent of the fathers of secondary school graduates. Furthermore, while only 4 percent of male school leavers whose fathers were in unskilled or semiskilled occupations went on to higher education, and only one-third of these went to universities, 44.8 percent of school leavers who were sons of professionals went on to higher education, and 80 percent of them went to universities (Committee on the Future of Tertiary Education in Australia, 1964, vol. I, pp. 43–44).

Student Organizations The chief national student organization, the National Union of Australian University Students (NUAUS) has over 97,500 members. The Australian Student Teachers Association, a much smaller organization, has had a full-time national office for only five years. Students at colleges of advanced education have separate union organizations.

The activities of the NUAUS include the operation of a student travel service; development of health and life insurance programs (only one Australian university has compulsory student health insurance); provision of services for overseas students; sponsorship of a biennial arts festival; participation in international student affairs; holding student conferences on a variety of subjects; publication of a national newspaper; organization of community development projects; and administration of, and fund-raising for, Australia's first scholarship program (ABSCHOL) to enable aborigines to attend universities (in 1968–69, there were seven aborigines pursuing university study; there had been five in 1967–68). The NUAUS has no political party affiliation but generally follows a leftist line. In national affairs, it has opposed conscription and the Vietnam war. Within the universities, it has pressed for more representation of students in decision-making bodies and for measures to improve the quality of teaching.

Student organizations at each university include the local university student union, which promotes the community life of the university and provides facilities for meetings, meals, amenities; the elected student government, commonly called the Students' Representative Council, which promotes the interests of the student body inside and outside the university (in some universities the student government directs the Student Union, while in the older universities these organizations tend to be separate); and a variety of clubs and associations. University halls of residence and affiliated colleges have their individual student organizations.

Until the end of the 1960s student activism was limited and focused mainly on issues outside the universities. Students have demonstrated to protest Australia's participation in the Vietnam war; to protest conscription under the National Service Act; and on behalf of equal treatment for the aborigines in access to public facilities, social benefits, and education. But demonstrations have mostly been held outside town halls, and few universities and colleges have been besieged or occupied. Students have so far gained increased participation in university decision making with little resort to violence.

The limited student activism in Australia might be explained by several complex factors. Nearly two-fifths of all university students are part-time and external and hence lack the time or opportunity for extracurricular activities. The short study period of three years for a bachelor's degree prevents the "perennial student" phenomenon from emerging. The vocational orientation of students, especially those who are bonded, and the pressure of academic work (students forfeit their Commonwealth Scholarships if they fail in their studies) also encourage undivided attention to studies. Many students are characterized by a mixture of resignation to the status quo, apathy, emphasis on leisure and recreation, and pleasure seeking, which are strong elements in contemporary Australian culture. Another factor is that students are not worried about finding employment after graduation; Australia's economy is rapidly expanding, and demand for highly trained manpower is growing. Still another set of factors is related to the anti-intellectual and highly utilitarian emphasis in Australia's social values. Students encounter the attitude that higher education is nonessential. Even the word student has pejorative overtones in some quarters. The latent hostility toward students which this phenomenon represents may ultimately foster a deeper sense of alienation in students of Australia than is found among students elsewhere.

The last several years of the 1960s witnessed the beginnings of a major change in the role and concern of students in university affairs. The NUAUS increased its demands for student participation in decision making, not only at the universities but also in other institutions of higher education. Although the NUAUS regarded the concessions of participation granted by the end of the decade as inadequate and even verging on tokenism, progress was significant. Most universities were either reviewing the whole question of student participation or had already made provisions to enlarge it. Student power generally was becoming a significant force.

THE BALANCE SHEET Some of the present weaknesses in Australian universities are attributable to their rapid expansion in the last two decades. Other weaknesses are of long standing, among them the problem of a high proportion of part-time students, whose academic work and participation in university life face the competing claims of outside employment; the small proportion of university students taking more than a pass degree and who are said to obtain "a degree without an education"; the low persistence and success rates of students; the bonding system and the inflexibilities it imposes on students and the institutions; the limitations on developing a full community life because, except at the University of New England, four-fifths of the students are commuters; the strong functional orientation of the universities and the overspecialization in curricular programs (particular because they follow two years of specialized work in secondary school); and, until recently, a slavish following of British patterns in university organization and teaching without regard to their relevance to conditions and needs in Australia.

On the positive side, Australian higher education has in the last two decades demonstrated an impressive capacity for growth and change. The 1960s saw a breaking away from the conventional mold set by the older universities, and the newer universities promise to make the entire system more adventurous and innovative.

The consistent and high academic standards of Australian universities is another notable strength. Balancing the weaknesses inherent in the large proportion of part-time and external students is the underlying principle that the universities serve society and provide educational opportunity to all, under conditions which permit them to take advantage of it.

The centralization of government in Australia has made possible the dramatic restructuring of the whole higher education system which gives the new colleges of advanced education a major role in broadening the opportunity for higher education and making it more responsive to national need.

Universities and other higher education institutions have emerged from relative obscurity and isolation in Australian life. The state and Commonwealth governments have greatly increased their financial support of higher education and are evolving new mechanisms for channeling funds to the institutions, while attempting to preserve or increase their autonomy.

THE FUTURE By 1975 some 18 percent of the college-age group is expected to enroll in tertiary institutions, with closer to 50 than 60 percent in the universities. State teachers colleges are expected to achieve a large degree of autonomy, and the new autonomy of colleges of advanced education will become more clearly defined. Teacher education is expected to become more flexible and, rather than being concentrated mainly in teachers colleges, will also draw more heavily on the resources and programs of the universities and colleges of advanced education. A major problem will be to clarify the respective spheres of universities and of colleges of advanced education in meeting student and national demands for higher education. Crucial to this problem is whether or not the colleges will be content to retain an identity and status distinct from, but in principle equal to, that of the universities. In any case. there will probably be an increasing emphasis on student transfer between these institutions.

By 1975, the number of institutions of higher education will further increase, mainly in the nonuniversity sectors, and universities, teachers colleges, and colleges of advanced education may often be on the same or adjacent sites (almost all urban) for optimal use of resources. At both the state and national levels, formal mechanisms for coordination within and between the different sectors of higher education are expected to gain strength through their authority to advise on funding. National planning of educational development at all levels seems likely to emerge, and a single agency may be established to replace the AUC and the Commonwealth Advisory Committee on Advanced Education. The current concern that government is encroaching on the internal affairs of the universities will undoubtedly intensify as state and Commonwealth bodies develop yet more effective means of scrutinizing higher education operations and as the growing financial requirements of the institutions and their dependence on public funds demands of them yet more accountability to government. It seems likely that the influence of the Commonwealth government will become still more predominant.

The growth of the 17- to 22-year-old age group, coupled with the increase in the proportion seeking higher education, may require decisions on whether or not access to higher education is a right for young people. If demand exceeds the number of students that can be accommodated within the universities' quotas, in the state teachers colleges (which accept very few students not holding department of education awards), and in the colleges of advanced education, which also are limited in the numbers they can accept, the right to higher education will become an important issue. Reinforcing the pressures to limit costly investment in higher education will be the growing demand on national resources of Australia's international security requirements as a major power in Asia and growing internal demands for enlarged social security provisions, an area in which Australia is beginning at last to fall behind other developed countries. Countervailing pressures for more expansion in higher education will be the widening awareness of the economic value of education and its contribution to national development and prosperity.

Australian Universities and Colleges

I. UNIVERSITIES

University of Sydney

University of Melbourne

University of Adelaide

University of Tasmania

University of Queensland

University of Western Australia

Australian National University

University of New South Wales

University of New England

Monash University

Macquarie University

La Trobe University

University of Newcastle

Flinders University

University of North Queensland

UNIVERSITY COLLEGES

Mount Gravatt (to be a university college)

Wollongong University College

Broken Hill University College

II. COLLEGES OF ADVANCED EDUCATION

New South Wales

New South Wales Institute of Business Studies

New South Wales University of Technology

Sydney Technical College

Hawkesbury Agricultural College

Wagga Agricultural College

Victoria

Ballarat School of Mines

Bendigo Technical College

Caulfield Technical College

Emily McPherson College

Footscray Technical College

Gordon Institute of Technology

Preston Technical College

Royal Melbourne Institute of Technology

Swinburne Technical College

Yallourn Technical College

College of Nursing, Australia

College of Pharmacy

Occupational Therapy School

School of Speech Therapy

Physiotherapy School

Longerenong Agricultural College

Dookie Agricultural College

Burnley Horticultural College

School of Forestry, Creswick

Queensland

Queensland Institute of Technology, Brisbane

Queensland Institute of Technology, Darling Downs

Queensland Institute of Technology, Capricornia

Queensland Agricultural College

Conservatorium

South Australia

South Australian Institute of Technology, Adelaide

South Australian Institute of Technology, Port Pirie

South Australian Institute of Technology, Whyalla

School of Art

Western Australia

Western Australian Institute of Technology

School of Mines, Kalgoorlie

School of Occupational Therapy

School of Physiotherapy

Tasmania

Tasmanian College of Advanced Education

Australian Capital Territory

Canberra College of Advanced Education

III. STATE TEACHERS COLLEGES

New South Wales

Alexander Mackie College

Armidale Teachers College

Balmain Teachers College

Bathurst Teachers College

Newcastle Teachers College

Sydney Teachers College

Wagga Wagga Teachers College

Wollongong Teachers College

Victoria

Ballarat Teachers College

Bendigo Teachers College

Burwood Teachers College

Coburg Teachers College

Frankston Teachers College

Geelong Teachers College

Melbourne Teachers College

Toorak Teachers College

Domestic Arts Teachers College

Monash Teachers College

Secondary Teachers College

Technical Teachers College

Training Centre for Teachers of the Deaf

Queensland

Kelvin Grove Teachers College

Kedron Park Teachers College

South Australia

Adelaide Teachers College

Western Teachers College

Wattle Park Teachers College

Bedford Park Teachers College

Western Australia

Claremont Teachers College

Graylands Teachers College

Tasmania

Launceston Teachers College

Hobart Teachers College

References

Borrie, W. D.: *Demographic Trends and Education in Australia, 1966–68,* background paper, National Advisory Committee for UNESCO, National Seminar on Educational Planning, Canberra, September 1968.

Committee on the Future of Tertiary Education in Australia: *Tertiary Education in Australia, Report of the Committee on the Future of Tertiary Education in Australia to the Australian Universities Commission,* L. H. Martin, chairman, vol. I, Government Printer, Melbourne, 1964.

Commonwealth Advisory Committee on Advanced Education: *Colleges of Advanced Education, 1967–69,* Canberra, 1966.

Commonwealth of Australia: *Third Report of the Australian Universities Commission, Australian Universities 1964–69,* Commonwealth Government Printer, Canberra, August 1966.

Commonwealth of Australia: *Fourth Report of the Australian Universities Commission, Australian Universities 1964-69,* Commonwealth Government Printer, Canberra, 1969.

Commonwealth Office of Education: *The 1961 Study, Second Report, The Progress in Their First Four Years of Study of Full-time Students Who Entered Australian Universities in 1961,* Canberra, 1961.

Macmillan, David S.: *Australian Universities,* Sydney University Press for the Australian Vice-chancellors' Committee, Sydney, 1968.

Matheson, J. A. L.: "Australian Multiversities?" *The Australian University,* vol. 3, no. 3, Melbourne University Press, Carleton, Victoria, December 1965.

Report of the Committee on Australian Universities, Sir Keith Murray, chairman, Commonwealth Government Printer, Canberra, 1957.

Semmler, C.: *Cultural Trends,* paper 4, Australian National Advisory Committee for UNESCO, National Seminar on Educational Planning, Canberra, 1968.

Short, L. N.: "Changes in Higher Education in Australia," *The Australian University,* vol. 1, no. 1, April 1967.

7. Higher Education in the Federal Republic of Germany

West Germany's university-level institutions have an elitist tradition that gives extended and flexible opportunities for learning to highly qualified students.

COMPONENTS   Typically, students admitted to West German universities have had four years of primary school (completed at about the age of ten) and nine years of special preparation in a *Gymnasium*. A few are able to prepare for admission by transferring into a *Gymnasium* from other secondary schools after six years. Mature young people who did not attend *Gymnasien* can qualify for admission by attending evening schools or full-time *Kollegien*. These routes lead to an *Abitur* (secondary degree leaving certificate) or its equivalent, which is required for admission to West Germany's (including Berlin) 23 universities, 9 technical universities,[1] 3 medical colleges, 3 specialized universities (for economics, agriculture, and veterinary medicine), 12 Catholic and 5 Protestant theological colleges,[2] and 54 pedagogical colleges for the training of primary, middle, and special school teachers.[3]

Among these institutions, those which have academic self-government, the right to nominate their own staff members, a close interrelationship between teaching and research, and the right to confer the *Promotion* (doctorate) and the *Habilitation* (which entitles the

---

[1] *Technical university* is used to designate the nine *technische Hochschulen* and the *technische Universität* in Berlin. The latter acquired the name *university* when it added teacher training to its program. The *technische Hochschule* at Aachen is also becoming a *technische Universität*.

[2] Theology is also taught at universities.

[3] *Gymnasium* teachers are trained at the universities. Academies that train *Gymnasium* teachers in music and fine arts require the *Abitur* for admission and are university-level institutions.

recipient to consideration for appointment as a professor) enjoy the greatest status. These criteria are met by the 38 general, technical, and specialized universities represented in the West German Conference of University Rectors. The theological and pedagogical colleges are excluded.[4]

Since 1964, seven general, technical, or specialized universities have been established. Among them are new universities at Bochum (1965), Constance (Konstanz) (1966), Regensburg (1966), and Dortmund (1968). New medical schools were established at Lübeck (1964), Hanover (1965), and Ulm (1966). In 1965, the medical school at Düsseldorf was expanded and became a general university. Present plans call for establishing new universities at Bielefeld (1970) and Bremen (1971), and a new college of economics will be established at Augsburg. A second university in the Rhineland-Palatinate will be founded near Mainz.

Most of the technical universities were established in the nineteenth century to provide research and training of a sort that was considered incompatible with the universities' emphasis on "pure" sciences and fine arts. Although they acquired university status at the beginning of this century, they concentrate on technological subjects though they increasingly offer humanities courses. They do not confer the *Promotion* or *Habilitation,* and their teaching staff members do not need to have the *Habilitation.* They also have a more structured curriculum and a more explicit attendance requirement than the general universities have.

With the exception of those in Bavaria, which are considered state institutions and are financed with public funds, the theological colleges are supported by religious bodies.

In 1967–68, more than two-thirds of the students training to be elementary, middle, and special school teachers attended the pedagogical colleges. The others enrolled in teacher training programs offered by some of the universities. But the traditional differences between institutions training teachers for elementary and for secondary education are beginning to disappear, and the distinction between pedagogical colleges and universities is being obliterated. In Hamburg, teacher training is given in a pedagogical institute that is part of the university, and in Hesse, Bavaria, and Berlin, the pedagogical colleges are closely linked with the univer-

[4] In late 1969 the rectors' conference voted to extend membership to the then 27 independent pedagogical colleges and to give them nine votes.

sities. In several *Länder* (states of the West German republic), colleges that were once separate denominational bodies are being amalgamated into single institutions so that the quality of their training can be improved and their status can be raised. The number of pedagogical colleges has gone down from 75 to 54 since 1950, and decreasing numbers of them are denominational.

Pedagogical colleges are moving toward university status, but three factors impede them: their curricula, requiring only about three years of study, is shorter than that of universities; they are not authorized to confer the *Promotion* or *Habilitation;* and they are considered less theoretically oriented than the universities. The future of the pedagogical colleges will also be influenced by the persistence of the system of training elementary and middle school teachers on one tier of institutions and *Gymnasium* teachers on another. At least one *Land* intends to give middle school teachers the opportunity to get more training so that they can qualify as *Gymnasium* teachers. The whole question of training teachers for different levels of schools has been under consideration by the Bildungsrat (Council on Education), which will issue a report in 1970 on the future planning of elementary, secondary, and further education. The anticipated development of comprehensive schools will also affect the curriculum and institutional structure of teacher training.

At the subuniversity level, the Federal Republic's institutions of higher learning include 11 academies of art, 13 academies of music, and 1 higher institute of physical education. The greatest expansion at this level, however, is enjoyed by the nearly 150 engineer schools, which enrolled 69,000 students in 1968.

Students in engineer schools are admitted without the *Abitur* and normally complete their studies at the age of 14 or 15 after ten years of schooling. The best engineer school graduates go on to a university, but even those who do not may rise to positions in their professions that are only slightly below those of engineers who entered universities as *Abiturienten.* In 1969, North Rhine–Westphalia drafted legislation to convert its engineering schools into technical universities.

FUNCTIONS Research holds a strong, almost characterizing position among the functions of German universities. In 1964, 17.2 percent of all funds spent on research and development in Germany were allocated to higher education institutions (Der Bundesminister für Wissenschaftliche Forschung, 1967, p. 214). At the present time about half of the scientific personnel engaged in German research and development are at the universities.

The main organization concerned with research policies is the Deutsche Forschungsgemeinschaft (DFG, German Research Association). It is a private association, registered under civil law, which promotes and coordinates research, provides funds for specific research projects, advises the *Länder* and federal government on research problems, and maintains contacts with research activity abroad. About 90 percent of its funds come from the *Länder* and the federal government. Its members include universities, scientific societies, and academies of science. The DFG works closely with two other organizations. One is the Max Planck Gesellschaft (MPG, Max-Planck Society for the Advancement of Science), which carries on the tradition of the Kaiser Wilhelm-Gesellschaft, founded in 1910 when it became evident that the rapid expansion of the sciences required research institutions as well as universities. The other is the Wissenschaftsrat, founded in 1957 by agreement between the *Länder* and federal government. Its members are appointed by the Bundespräsident — some on nomination by the *Länder* and federal government, others on nomination by the DFG, MPG, and WRK (Westdeutsche Rektorenkonferenz, West German University Rectors' Conference). In 1969, the general subsidy from the *Länder* and the federal government to the DFG and MPG were DM 191.25 million for the DFG and almost DM 236 million, respectively (*Education in Germany,* 1969, p. 25).

Much of the research conducted outside universities is done in close association with them. The MPG undertakes research in fields that are relatively untouched by the universities, but some of its 52 research institutes are located in university towns and collaborate with university research institutes in directing and staffing projects. Research institutes maintained by the *Länder,* the federal government, and industry also maintain close links with the universities. The probability that the federal and *Länder* governments will increase funds available to the DFG for financing university research in special fields — DM 20 million in 1969, increasing to an estimated DM 60 million in 1971 — suggests that the role of universities in research will expand rather than diminish.

In 1967, the Federal Ministry for Scientific Research set up an Advisory Committee on Research Policy. At its first meeting, this agency emphasized the need for legal reforms to permit the federal government to take a more active part in formulating a comprehensive policy for higher education and research. An important issue in the coming years will be whether or not increasing federal support for research, rising from one-half to two-thirds of combined *Länder*-federal support of the DFG in 1971, will be provided inside or outside the universities.

Adult Education

The traditional commitment of university education in Germany to train a narrow segment of the population for careers in the professions and the bureaucracy is beginning to expand. In 1966 the Wissenschaftsrat recommended that universities develop extension and other educational programs (Kontakstudien) for practicing professionals, but this activity is just beginning. Most adult education is provided under the auspices of such nonuniversity organizations as the denominational academies and institutes, the trade unions and employers' organizations, and correspondence colleges. Industrial firms and chambers of industry, commerce, and trade provide education programs for both salaried employees and skilled workers. They are more likely than the universities to set up special training programs in fields suffering from shortages of trained manpower. Industrial firms also provide most of the training for advanced management. The first German university to offer short-term, full-time courses for industrial workers is the new university of Bochum.

ENROLLMENT TRENDS

In 1968, the total number of university students reached 280,000 (*Deutsche Kulturnachrichten,* 1968, p. 1).[5] Between 1950 and 1965, enrollments at German universities increased by 232.4 percent, and enrollment at pedagogical colleges increased by 385.1 percent. There were smaller increases of 50.8 percent for the theological colleges and of 168.7 percent for music, art, and physical education colleges.

The proportion of West Germany's 20- to 24-year-olds enrolled in university-level institutions went up from 2.01 percent in 1950 to 2.8 percent in 1960 and to more than 5 percent in 1965. Enroll-

---

[5] Nearly 10 percent of the university students are from other countries. There were 23,358 foreign students in 1967–68. About half of the foreign students in 1968 came, in the order of greatest representation, from Iran, Greece, United States, Turkey, Norway, Austria, Indonesia, Syria, and France.

TABLE 20 *Number of new entrants to university-level institutions of higher education in West Germany by year*

	1950-51	*1955-56*	*1960-61*	*1965-66*	*1966-67*
Universities	24,550	29,637	43,609	41,271	55,119
Theological colleges	1,601	588	920	744	936
Pedagogical colleges	5,500	7,603	13,359	14,279	20,000*
Music, art, physical education	1,257	1,601	2,174	2,093	1,752
TOTAL	32,908	39,429	60,062	58,387	

*Estimated; from *Education in Germany*, no. 6, 1969, p. 5; assuming that at least about one-third of total enrollments were new entrants.
SOURCE: Wissenschaftsrat, 1967, p. 277.

ment at universities correlates closely with the number of students who obtain the *Abitur*, which is not only a prerequisite for university admission but traditionally carries with it the *right* to be admitted. Since 1956, about 80 percent of all *Abiturienten* (*Abitur* recipients) have enrolled in university-level institutions. In the early 1960s, no significant increases in enrollments were anticipated. Among the reasons were the low birth rate in the 1940s, the expectation that *Gymnasium* enrollments would not increase, and the apparent stabilization of the proportion of *Gymnasium* students who earn the *Abitur* at about 35 to 40 percent. In 1967, these expectations had to be abandoned. That year the Wissenschaftsrat reported that the high and low projections of university enrollment it had made in 1964 considerably underestimated future demand. According to new estimates, the proportion of the age group obtaining the *Abitur* would increase from 7.9 percent for 1962 to 1966 to 16.0 percent for 1980 to 1984 (Wissenschaftsrat, 1967, p. 273).

TABLE 21 *Enrollment in university-level institutions of higher education in West Germany by year*

	1950-51	*1955-56*	*1960-61*	*1965-66*	*1966-67*
Universities	107,935	127,403	203,404	250,859	262,630
Theological colleges	4,607	2,288	2,663	2,342	2,507
Pedagogical colleges	11,920	16,047	33,061	45,901	59,000*
Music, art, physical education	5,168	6,086	7,937	8,721	
TOTAL	129,630	151,824	247,065	307,823	

*From *Education in Germany*, no. 6, 1969, p. 5.
SOURCE: Wissenschaftsrat, 1967, p. 283.

	Year	Percent
TABLE 22 *Actual and anticipated percentage of 19- to 23-year-olds obtaining the Abitur (excluding night school)*	*1950-51*	3.8
	1955-56	4.4
	1960-61	5.2
	1965-66	8.0
	1967-68	7.7
	1970-71	8.8
	1975-76	12.9
	1980-81	16.0

SOURCE: Wissenschaftsrat, 1967, p. 273.

An increase in the size of the *Gymnasium* age group, together with an increase in the proportion of students obtaining the *Abitur,* will expand the number of *Abiturienten* from 63,757 to 155,360 during the same period (Wissenschaftsrat, 1967, p. 273). Some authorities consider even these estimates to be too conservative.

Three relatively recent trends contribute to the growth of enrollments in German universities. As mentioned previously, mature young people who have not attended *Gymnasien* may now obtain the *Abitur* by attending evening schools or full-time *Kollegien.* The number of students entering university institutions through this "second route" *(zweiter Bildungsweg)* increased from about 1,700 in 1958 to 2,900 in 1963—representing an increase from 4.9 to 6.6 percent of all entrants (Wissenschaftsrat, 1967, p. 273). An even more significant factor is a diversification of upper secondary education that is breaking down the traditional monopoly of the *Gymnasium* in producing students qualified for university admis-

	Year	Number
TABLE 23 *Actual and anticipated number of Abiturienten (excluding night school)*	*1950*	31,216
	1955	32,712
	1960	55,890
	1965	49,167
	1967	65,080
	1970	70,770
	1975	95,660
	1980	96,960

SOURCE: Wissenschaftsrat, 1967, p. 272.

sion. This diversification permits students to decide on university at the age of 14 or later instead of at the age of 11, as required by the customary route to a university. The third, somewhat controversial development is the establishment of specialized *Gymnasien* in some of the *Länder*. Graduates of these schools receive an *Abitur* qualifying them to study specific subjects at university institutions, primarily at the pedagogical colleges and technical universities. In 1966, nearly 5 percent of all *Abiturienten* had graduated from these specialized *Gymnasien*.

Proposals to Limit Enrollment Growth

Even with the expansion of university institutions during the 1960s, enrollments in 1970 are expected to exceed currently planned capacities. And unless there are fundamental reforms, enrollment at universities may reach 600,000 in 1980 — twice what it was in 1967.

In 1959, a report on behalf of the Federal Ministry of Interior asserted that many university students were deficient in intellectual ability and recommended, among other measures, imposing a temporary *numerus clausus* and making it more difficult for students to obtain the *Abitur*. Hajo Riese (1967), in a survey of future national needs for university-trained persons, concluded, with some qualifications, that not many more students than were graduating from institutions of higher education in 1967 would satisfy the economy's requirements for academically trained people up to 1980. He also asserted that the enrollment target for the 1970s calculated by the Wissenschaftsrat would produce an oversupply of highly trained persons. In contrast to Riese, others in Germany argue for a vigorous expansion of higher education in the interests of social justice and equal opportunity as well as economic growth.

Several proposals to slow down enrollment growth have been made. These include making the *Abitur* a certificate of *Gymnasium* completion but not a guarantee of admission to a university, shortening the time students spend at universities, establishing new kinds of postsecondary institutions as alternatives to universities, and imposing a *numerus clausus*.

One interesting suggestion is that an intermediate or "halfway" certificate, a new *Abitur*, be awarded to students completing six of the nine years of *Gymnasium*. This certificate would make leaving the *Gymnasien* before graduation more respectable and would possibly diminish the ranks of those entitled to enter the universities. A new certificate, the *Aditur*, would be given to students completing their *Gymnasium* studies.

In 1966, the Wissenschaftsrat proposed that university studies be reorganized so that they could be completed by most students in four years. The few highly qualified students who, after four years of study, wished to pursue research could continue into a second stage, the *Aufbaustudium,* lasting about two years and leading to a doctorate or equivalent qualification. The proposal has not yet been widely implemented, but some departments and faculties have started to modify their curricula along the lines proposed.

Another proposed reorganization, originated by Ralf Dahrendorf of the University of Constance (Konstanz), would bring engineering, teacher training, commercial studies, and possibly some new institutions under one roof with traditional research-oriented universities to make new "complex" universities. If, as hoped, most entrants enroll in the affiliated institutions, the traditional universities will be little affected by expanding enrollment in higher education.

In July, 1967, the Wissenschaftsrat made the unprecedented recommendation that a *numerus clausus* be applied to limit enrollment in universities. The WRK announced its support, as a temporary measure only, of a *numerus clausus* in January 1968, and the conference of *Länder* Ministers of Education and Culture did likewise the following April. Although long discussed, a *numerus clausus* has been criticized because it is incompatible with the tradition that the *Abitur* guarantees access to a university and because it is a violation of Article 12 of the Basic Law of the Federal Republic, which guarantees unrestricted admission to all sectors of education. As recently as 1967, the *Länder* ministers of education had reaffirmed their opposition to undermining the validity of the *Abitur* by restricting university admission to *Abiturienten* with the best grades.

It is up to individual *Länder* authorities and university facul-

TABLE 24 Number of degree recipients, West German higher education	1950-51	1955-56	1960-61	1965-66
First degree	18,269*	17,707*	18,951	24,591†
Doctoral degree	7,625*	7,306*	5,432	6,636†
Habilitation			385	544

*Excluding Saarland.

†Kiel 1964 examinations.

SOURCE: Wissenschaftsrat, 1967, pp. 304, 307, 319.

ties to determine the extent to which they apply a *numerus clausus.* As proposed by the Wissenschaftsrat, the policy should not deny but merely postpone university admission for the *Abiturienten* affected. The practical result, however, unless university facilities are substantially expanded, will be the creation of a backlog of *Abiturienten* whose ranks swell from one year to the next. In 1969, admissions restrictions existed in faculties of medicine, dentistry, and pharmacy at all universities and in the philosophical faculties in biology (17 universities), chemistry (17), psychology (13), and physics (11). A shift system of university education has been proposed to alleviate the growing shortage of places.

The time German students spend at universities is increasing. The average number of terms (two per year of 3½ months each) students took to complete their university studies increased from 9.7 in 1960 to 10.8 in 1965 (Wissenschaftsrat, 1967, p. 17). Between 1950 and 1965, the proportion of university students who were enrolled in their ninth or later semester rose from 12.4 to 30.5 percent, and the proportion in their eleventh or later semester increased nearly sevenfold, from 2.5 to 16.8 percent (Wissenschaftsrat, 1967, p. 19). Because this increasing study period aggravates enrollment problems, departments at some universities now require students to take examinations after four semesters and science departments are introducing a structured curriculum that encourages students to progress systematically through their studies. In 1966, some universities required students who had been enrolled for extended periods with little evidence of success to leave. The Wissenschaftsrat, the Conference of Ministers of Education, and the WRK have all urged that study time be shortened.

Some proposals for university reform aim not only at reducing study time but also at raising persistence rates. The Robbins Report estimated wastage rates of between 45 and 50 percent for Germany (Robbins Committee, 1963, appendix V, p. 87). But German students traditionally have moved from one university to another, and it is difficult to calculate persistence and dropout rates reliably.

Staff-Student Ratios In some fields, long study periods and relatively low student persistence are attributed, in part, to low staff-student ratios. In 1967, the Wissenschaftsrat reported an improvement in the average ratio of from 1:13.3 in 1960 to 1:8.4 in 1966 (Wissenschaftsrat, 1967, p. 23). But the ratio varies widely among faculties. In 1966, for example, it ranged from 1:26.3 in the social sciences and economics to 1:1.8 in agricultural technology and brewing. One must also take into account the fact that the reported ratios are based on figures for places for total "scientific personnel"—31,831 in 1966 (Wissenschaftsrat, 1967, p. 21)—which includes not only teaching staff but also certain administrative positions, library personnel, *Kustoden* (who are charged with responsibility for scientific collections and equipment), staff members in university clinics, and others who have limited teaching duties. One must also remember that the ratios relate to *places* for staff members rather than actual *numbers* of staff members. In 1966, 733 professorships, 1,199 middle-level positions and 1,044 senior assistantships and assistantships were not filled (Der Bundesminister für Wissenschaftliche Forschung, 1967, pp. 222–223). The teaching loads—5 to 6 hours weekly for assistants and about 12 to 16 for *akademische räte,* a relatively new category of permanent staff who do not have the *Habilitation,* the traditional requirement for tenure—should also be considered. In comparing chances for student-faculty contacts, it is also important to note that the academic year in Germany lasts only <u>seven months.</u> *(мu - мu)*

Faculty Status and Qualifications

Too few *Habilitationen* are awarded to keep pace with the need for an expanded permanent teaching staff. A 1969 report of the WRK indicated that the only fields in which more persons obtain the *Habilitation* than are needed by the teaching professions are classical philology, clinical medicine, dental medicine, physics, biology, and agricultural sciences. Although 81 percent of the full professors held the *Habilitation* in 1960 (Wissenschaftsrat, 1967, p. 54), the proportion has since been declining. Among the reasons are an insufficient supply of candidates; the readiness of institutions to appoint persons with experience in industry, education and international affairs to professorships even though they do not have the *Habilitation;* and the practice of filling middle teaching positions by a growing number of *Studienräte in Hochschuldienst*—teachers who do not have the *Habilitation* are recruited from *Gymnasium* teaching and other fields outside the universities. In 1966, assistants filled nearly two-thirds of all academic positions. A new system in which some teachers are primarily concerned with the traditional combination of research with teaching while others devote their time primarily to teaching may be emerging. If it does, it will be a <u>radical departure</u> from the German tradition that holds that research and teaching should be closely integrated.

Proposals to simplify and even eliminate the *Habilitation* itself eventually may affect the status and composition of the teaching staffs. Traditionally, students who have earned the *Promotion* or *Doctorat* and seek the *Habilitation* must complete a second major thesis (which takes about five years to prepare), must defend it in a colloquium before a faculty board, and deliver a test lecture.

Persons working for the *Habilitation* frequently hold assistant-ships at the same time, and the average age of persons receiving it is about 34. To cut down on the time required to earn the *Habilitation*, several proposals have been advanced. They involve making the preparation of a thesis less onerous, accepting research work performed outside the university (in government institutes, for example) as part of the requirement, ending the dependence of the candidate upon his sponsoring professors, improving the objectivity of all requirements for the *Habilitation*, and providing more financial assistance to candidates. In March 1968 academic assistants formed a new national organization, the Federal University Assistants Conference (BAK, Bundesassistentenkonferenz), in order to press these and other interests more effectively. The recent trend toward giving tenure to teaching staff who have the *Doctorat* but not the *Habilitation* may reduce pressure to modify *Habilitation* requirements.

HIGHER EDUCATION AND CIVIL GOVERNMENT

The 1949 Constitution of the Federal Republic gave jurisdiction over education and culture to the 11 *Länder.* There, responsibility rests with the parliaments, prime ministries, and the ministries of education and cultural affairs (or, in the three city states, the senators of education and culture). In 1948, the *Länder* established the Permanent Conference of Ministers of Education and Cultural Affairs, which is concerned with expansion and reform in higher education and with coordinating higher education legislation. It meets every six to eight weeks. Decisions of the conference must be unanimous and bind individual *Länder* governments only if they agree to them. In internal university affairs, decisions of the conference are binding only if the appropriate university bodies agree to implement them.

The *Länder* governments influence university affairs through their approval of university statutes, appointment of permanent teaching staff (from among nominees of the faculties), approval of examination regulations, and provision of financial support. In some *Länder,* the governments appoint "curators" or chancellors at individual universities. These officers are responsible for the financial administration of the institution. In other institutions, financial matters are handled by a *Kuratorium* composed of representatives of the university and government. In most universities in southern Germany, the handling of financial affairs has been transferred to university agencies such as the rector, senate, or special commissions.

The federal government influences internal university affairs either through direct financial support or indirect support through government-assisted research organizations which finance university research. Because permanent teaching staff are federal civil servants, some of the legislation pertaining to their status is under federal jurisdiction.

The federal government retains "competitive legislative competence" in the field of research. This permits it to handle matters that are not susceptible to uniform regulation without federal action. The Federal Ministry for Education and Science is responsible for the promotion of science and research and for handling the federal contribution to the capital costs of existing universities and certain national research organizations. This ministry, the first federal organ of government to have the word "education" in its title, was established in 1969 after the election in that year that brought the Social Democratic Party into power. This ministry replaced the former Ministry of Scientific Research. The Federal Ministry for Internal Affairs administers the federal contribution to student financial aid.

The Wissenschaftsrat, established by the *Länder* and the federal government in 1957, is an advisory body. It has two main committees: the Science Committee, whose members are prominent scientists or persons from public life appointed by the federal president, and the Administrative Committee of federal and *Länder* representatives. The latter are usually ministers of education. Although the Wissenschaftsrat's recommendations are only advisory, they represent a consensus on the part of the main government bodies involved in higher education and carry considerable weight.

Although it is principally concerned only with education through the secondary and further education levels, the Bildungsrat (Council on Education), created by the *Länder* and federal government in 1965, has an impact on higher education as well. For example, it is concerned with some aspects of teacher training, and its decisions affect the proportion of the university-age group who obtain the *Abitur*.

The Bildungsrat and the Wissenschaftsrat consult and cooperate through a joint coordinating committee. They are both associated with the Cabinet Committee for Scientific Research, Education, and Educational Grants, set up in 1965, and with interministerial committees under the Federal Minister for Education and Science and the Federal Minister for Internal Affairs which are concerned, respectively, with higher education and research and with education and educational grants.

INTERNAL GOVERNMENT OF INSTITUTIONS All university-level institutions in Germany except the pedagogical and theological colleges are public corporate bodies. They operate under acts passed by *Länder* authorities and in accordance with their own constitutions or charters. These documents set forth the structure of universities, their powers to confer degrees, their relationships to the *Länder* administration, and their rights of independent self-government and autonomy in matters such as curricula, research, teaching methods, and internal structure.

The main agencies of internal university government are the rector and pro-rector, large and small senates, plenary assemblies, and faculties.

The rector is elected from and by the full professors. Traditionally, he holds a one-year term although this is frequently extended to two years by reelection. The rector in many universities becomes the next pro-rector. Two *Länder* are moving toward having a long-term rector, or president, who might not necessarily have to be selected from among university professors. At the new University of Constance (Konstanz) the rector can serve until he reaches the age of 65. The powers of the rector are limited. He is the chief representative of the university for ceremonial and official purposes, is *primus inter pares* in relation to full professors, and convokes and presides over senate meetings. His main responsibilities relate to the direction and supervision of the nonacademic administration of the university.

Most universities have a large senate and a small senate. The large senate meets about twice a year and includes all full professors and representatives of other teaching staffs. In southern Germany, the large senate is superior to the small senate and has considerable competence. In other universities, its competence is mainly limited to the election of the rector. Members of the small senate include the rector and the pro-rector, the rector-elect, deans of faculties, professors elected as representatives of the different faculties, and, to an increasing extent, representatives of students and of nonacademic staff members. The senate's authority extends over all matters relating to the university as a whole but normally excludes teaching and research, which are the concern of the faculties. The senate is also in charge of relations with other university institutions, is consulted on academic appointments, and assists in budget preparation.

Plenary assemblies, where they exist, include all academic staff members and are advisory only.

At some universities, students participate in senate meetings when the matters under discussion directly affect them.

The large universities have as many as seven faculties. These bodies, somewhat similar to the colleges in American universities, have responsibility for teaching and research policy. Units of governance within the faculty include the dean, normally elected for one year from among full professors by the faculty council; the plenary faculty, including all members of the teaching staff; and the faculty council. The dean presides over the council and handles the administrative business of the faculty. The council decides matters of discipline and makes recommendations on the creation of new professorships and the appointment of permanent academic staff members. The council includes all full professors and representatives of other teaching staff members. At many universities, faculty councils also include student representatives.

In July 1969 West Berlin instituted reforms designed to break down traditional hierarchical powers of the faculties, place universities under strong executive administration, and give students a voice in all levels of university decision making. The new chief executive of Berlin's two universities will be presidents, elected to seven-year terms with responsibilities similar to those of university presidents in the United States. Legislative authority within institutions is given to university councils empowered to elect the presidents and generally determine university policy. Students will have one-third of the votes in these new agencies. Existing faculties will be reorganized into departments. Although the law affects only two institutions, the Free University and the Technical University in West Berlin, it could set a precedent for similar legislation elsewhere in Germany.

Some faculties, particularly those at the technical and new universities, are divided into departments. Where they have been set up at new universities (Regensburg and Bochum, for example), departmentwide and interdepartmental research is encouraged. This is a departure from the traditional system under which a professor, as the permanent head, has exclusive direction over a research institute and its staff.

INTERUNIVER-
SITY COORDI-
NATION In April 1949 the WRK was established to promote consultation and cooperation between universities. All university-level institutions authorized to confer the *Promotion* and *Habilitation* are members. It plays an increasingly active role in preparing studies and recommendations regarding university reform.

In January 1968 the WRK issued a major declaration regarding university reform, urging greater participation in decision making by all sectors of the university community, including students and assistants. In this same declaration, the conference also stressed the autonomy of the universities. In February 1968 the conference issued recommendations to improve the status of assistants, and in March, it endorsed imposition of a *numerus clausus* to restrict university admissions. Despite its lack of formal authority, the WRK, through its studies and recommendations, is playing an important part in the current debate on higher education reform.

COORDINA-
TION WITHIN
THE LÄNDER The *Länder* conferences of university rectors exist primarily for the purpose of mutual consultation. Although the Wissenschaftsrat has urged that universities collaborate and share their resources, little coordination has developed, even between neighboring institutions. An example of the difficulty is provided by proposals that library resources be shared. Before that happens, greater sharing of libraries within universities would be necessary. And that can be achieved only by a radical change from the traditional system under which each professor, institute, and department has its own library —to which access is restricted.

The need for formal arrangements for interuniversity transfer is slight. Students traditionally have migrated from one university to another and can enroll in courses at neighboring institutions simply by obtaining permission from the professor.

The principal instrument of such coordination as now exists is the recommendation of the Wissenschaftsrat for allocation of financial resources among different categories of institutions, fields of knowledge, and levels of teaching. In 1969, for example, it recommended that teaching and research in agriculture be concentrated in four universities only and that agricultural faculties elsewhere cease to exist. But this recommendation met strong resistance.

German university-level institutions are financed almost entirely by public funds. In 1964, 69 percent of all higher education expenditures were paid by the *Länder* governments, slightly more than 13 percent were paid out of income from fees and contributions (about three-fourths of these were collected by clinics), slightly less than 13 percent were met by the federal government, and about 5 percent were paid out of miscellaneous sources (Freund, 1966).

Student fees (about DM 200 per student each term) met 14 percent of the total expenses in 1950 but meet only 3 or 4 percent today. Hesse has abolished student fees for its own residents.

Nearly all the expenditures of the teachers colleges are paid by the *Länder*. This was also true for universities until the early 1950s, but since that time the federal government has contributed increasing amounts for university support.

Total expenditures on universities (excluding pedagogical colleges but including university clinics) went up from DM 1.025 billion in 1960 to an estimated DM 3.662 billion in 1966 (Wissenschaftsrat, 1967, p. 373). In the same period, recurrent expenditures rose from about DM 0.733 billion to DM 2.293 billion, and capital expenditures rose from about DM 0.293 billion to DM 1.369 billion (Wissenschaftsrat, 1967, p. 373). Total direct expenditures on the universities is expected to be about DM 4.57 billion in 1970, and nearly DM 20 billion will be required for capital expenditures alone between 1966 and 1975 (Deutscher Bundestag, 1967, pp. 279, 281).

The inequality in resources among the *Länder* makes it difficult for some of them to meet all of the construction costs of new universities. Consequently they agreed in 1964 to pool funds. The *Länder* and federal government also agreed to share equally capital costs of existing universities. Under 1964 agreements, three-fourths of the capital costs of new universities were to be shared by the *Länder* and the federal government, with the remainder paid by the *Land* in which the new university is located. In these negotiations, the *Länder* agreed to provide DM 3.075 billion for the common fund for 1966–1975. Under 1969 legislation, the *Länder* and federal government agreed to share, on a fifty-fifty basis, capital costs of expanding existing universities and of establishing new ones.

		1950	1955	1959	1965	1967
TABLE 25 Public expenditures on higher education institutions and university clinics in the Federal Republic of Germany* (in thousands of deutschemarks)	*Universities*					
	Recurrent	157,300	304,600	358,544	793,478	1,034,721
	Capital	50,700	118,300	126,410	666,851	604,408
	TOTAL	208,000	422,900	484,954	1,460,329	1,639,129
	Technical universities					
	Recurrent			154,546	425,760	469,067
	Capital			83,370	269,978	222,518
	TOTAL			237,916	695,738	691,585
	Other university-level institutions of higher education					
	Recurrent				49,473	62,058
	Capital				40,831	74,403
	TOTAL				90,304	136,461
	Teacher training institutions					
	Recurrent				126,731	178,790
	Capital				83,296	73,472
	TOTAL				210,027	252,262
	Other higher education institutions including art. music†					
	Recurrent			71,339	41,361	57,400
	Capital			23,466	11,633	10,569
	TOTAL			94,805	52,994	67,969
	General expenditures for higher education institutions‡					
	Recurrent				141,714	180,466
	Capital				13,793	40,695
	TOTAL				155,507	221,161
	Total higher education institutions					
	Current	157,300	304,600	584,429	1,578,517	1,982,502
	Capital	50,700	118,300	233,246	1,086,382	1,026,065
	TOTAL	208,000	422,900	817,675	2,664,899	3,008,567
	University clinics					
	Recurrent	91,308	187,720	309,352	692,625	919,473
	Capital	24,914	55,285	80,571	209,871	265,528
	TOTAL	116,222	243,005	389,923	902,496	1,185,001
	Total expenditures					
	Recurrent	248,608	492,320	893,781	2,271,142	2,901,975
	Capital	75,614	173,585	313,817	1,296,253	1,291,593
	TOTAL	324,222	665,905	1,207,598	3,567,395	4,193,568

*These statistics include West Germany and West Berlin.

†Generally data under this heading include schools of art, music, and sports. For 1959 they also included the pedagogical colleges, theological institutions, and other higher educations not accounted for under universities and technical universities.

‡Funds under this heading are mainly for direct and indirect promotion of higher education including student financial assistance under Honnef-Modell that do not fall under other categories. Excluded from this category are general expenditures on personnel and equipment spent by state ministries of education and cultural affairs.

SOURCE: Information supplied by the Statistisches Bundesamt, Wiesbaden.

Unless the *Länder* receive a larger share of tax revenues in the future, it will be difficult for them to increase their support of universities. Apart from new flexibility it has for funding research, it is also hard for the federal government to expand its role.

HIGHER EDUCATION AND ECONOMIC PLANNING

Cultural federalism has thus far prevented significant educational planning by the federal government except in matters involving science and research. As a result, planning has required parallel and coordinated action by the *Länder.* The principal national agency for higher education, the Wissenschaftsrat, has been asked to develop on overall plan for science (meaning higher education, research, and scholarship) on the basis of individual plans prepared by the *Bund* and the *Länder;* to coordinate plans; to establish an annual priority program; and to recommend the allocation of funds budgeted for science by the *Länder* and the federal government. Although the role of the Wissenschaftsrat would appear to be limited by the requirement that it take as its starting point the plans and budgetary allocations of the *Bund* and *Länder,* in fact, the *Länder* and the federal government tend to follow the Wissenschaftsrat's recommendations and treat them almost as though they were directives.

In 1968 the chairman of the Conference of Ministers of Education and Culture proposed the establishment of a single joint federal-*Länder* government commission for educational planning. The Christian Democratic Union Party conference held in November 1968 recommended the establishment of a federal ministry of education and increased power for the federal government in education. In a major government statement made on October 28, 1969, the new chancellor, Willy Brandt, called for joint federal-*Länder* planning of education, the drafting of a national education budget, and a "skeleton law for higher education" at the federal level to create a comprehensive university system covering all tertiary education, along with rapid expansion of the university sector. A detailed report on educational and scientific policy to be made by the federal government in 1970 is expected to produce guidelines for the future.

Within the Länder

There have been greater efforts in the past few years to plan higher education development within the *Länder.* In 1965 the ministers of education agreed to set up statistical units to aid that endeavor. Some *Länder* established advisory planning committees to make recommendations on future university expansion, and at least one

Land, North Rhine–Westphalia, established a planning department in its Ministry of Education and Cultural Affairs. A special group set up by the Conference of Ministers in 1963 has prepared a number of surveys on future needs in education.

Federal Planning The federal government is increasingly concerned with long-range planning for higher education and research. The Ministry of Scientific Research has urged that the *Länder* and the federal government agree to a three- to five-year financial plan for the expansion of existing universities and that a coordinated research system, including nonuniversity as well as university research, be created.

A report on educational planning that the Federal Chancellor presented to the *Bundestag* on October 13, 1967, was a joint effort of the *Länder* and the federal government and the first of its kind.

The Wissenschaftsrat has cooperated with the Federal Labor Office in projecting future demands in various professions and has recommended special efforts to expand science and engineering training to meet shortages in these fields; has urged more guidance and counseling at universities to help direct students into shortage fields; and has recommended against wholesale expansion of university capacity in such fields as the social sciences merely because they are popular.

But educational planning in the Federal Republic is likely to remain oriented primarily toward the demands of students rather than the needs of the economy. Basing university expansion more on the latter would be incompatible with the universities' own interpretation of their mission and with constitutional guarantees of the freedom of teaching and research and of access to education. Besides, forecasting techniques are not sufficiently developed to permit the planning of university capacity to meet the specific needs of the economy some years hence. But if it were desired, educational planning directed toward labor market forecasts should be easier in Germany, where traditionally there has been a connection between courses of study and selection of a profession, than in some other countries where higher education is less "vocational." If the Wissenschaftsrat's recommendations of 1966 for reorganizing higher education to provide "graduated courses of study leading to different academic qualifications" is implemented, more concentration and specialization presumably would be introduced into higher education. This would make it easier to estimate future graduates in different fields and to orient university capacity in those fields to labor market needs.

A by-product of the increased attention given to higher education in the last decade has been the expansion of available information on higher education. Such data have been gathered by the Federal Statistical Office, by the *Länder* statistical units in ministries of education, and by the Wissenschaftsrat, the Conference of Ministers of Education, and other organizations. Also contributing to the intensified study and analysis are the universities and other centers of research on education. Foremost among these is the MPG Institute for Educational Research in Berlin, founded in 1964, which conducts interdisciplinary studies, mainly empirical, on economic, sociological, and other aspects of the total education system. The German Institute for International Educational Research in Frankfurt, set up in the early 1950s, is similarly engaged in primarily empirical research on education.

FINANCIAL ASSISTANCE TO STUDENTS University education in Germany is not yet widely regarded as an avenue for upward social mobility. In 1965 only about 6 percent of all German university students came from working class families (which comprise about 50 percent of the total population), and only 3 to 4 percent came from farm families. In 1967, for the first time, the children of clerks outnumbered the children of civil servants (31.1 percent in comparison to 29.4 percent).[6]

In 1966, the Deutsches Studentenwerk, an organization concerned with student welfare, estimated that students in institutions of higher education in Germany needed an average of DM 400 a month (excluding DM 25 a month for fees) to meet expenses. Between 1963 and 1967, the proportion of students requiring more than DM 350 a month increased from 8.7 to 37.6 percent.[7]

Since 1957, student assistance has been available through the Honnef-Modell, a government program supported on a fifty-fifty basis by *Länder* and the federal government. In 1965, about 46,000 students received DM 290 a month through this program (Wissenschaftsrat, 1967, p. 31). Students qualify on the basis of need (parental income) and ability as determined by the institution at which the student is enrolled, and according to guidelines set by the

[6] Information supplied by Deutsches Studentenwerk.

[7] Information supplied by Deutsches Studentenwerk.

Federal Ministry of Interior and ministries of education in the *Länder*. Qualifying students receive a monthly grant for their first three terms at a university. Thereafter, they receive mixed loan and grant assistance for two terms more than the minimum (eight semesters) study time and are also exempted from study fees. About 19.1 percent of all university students were aided by the Honnef-Modell in 1965 (Wissenschaftsrat, 1967, p. 31). Between 1963 and 1967 the proportion of students receiving financial aid, public and private, who are assisted by Honnef-Modell increased from 52 to 62 percent.[8] A similar program, paid for wholly by the *Länder*, assists students at art, music, and pedagogical institutions.

Some students receive benefits from the federally supported *Kategorialforderung*, which compensates victims of World War II, refugees, and expellees, but expenditures from this fund declined from DM 20 million in 1962 to an estimated DM 10.2 million in 1967 (Der Bundesminister für Wissenschaftliche Forschung, 1967, p: 171). Scholarships for students of special ability are given by various semipublic foundations, church organizations, and other groups. In 1966 about 3,500 students received assistance from these sources. Since 1965, students from families with more than one child have received a monthly education allowance of DM 40 until they become twenty-seven years old.

In 1966, direct federal aid to university students totaled DM 139,311,000 of which DM 66,390 was for the Honnef-Modell; direct aid from the *Länder* to university students was about DM 86,000,000 with an additional DM 30,800 to students at pedagogical colleges.

During the last 10 years the proportion of students whose studies are financed completely or with considerable help by their parents has been constant at around 66 percent. One-fourth of all students are supported at least partly by public funds, and of these slightly over half, or 13.6 percent, are able to cover 80 percent or more of their expenses from such benefits. The proportion of students who depend partly or totally on their own earnings declined from one-fifth in 1963 to one-sixth in 1967. The trend is for students to work more during the academic year than during vacations; one out of every four earns money during the academic year. Some 45 percent

[8] Information supplied by Deutsches Studentenwerk.

do work during vactions—one-half or more in jobs not at all or only seldom connected with their major field of study.[9]

German students received indirect benefits in low-cost meals and housing and reduced travel costs subsidized out of public funds. In addition, the Deutsche Studentenwerk supports student restaurants and residence and other facilities, the costs of which are met by compulsory student fees, public funds, and revenue. It has branches at all universities.

The Deutsche Studentenwerk and the Verband Deutscher Studentenschaften (VDS, German National Union of Students) have pressed for student housing to accommodate close to one-third of all students. Despite the doubling of available student housing from 20,000 places in 1960 to 40,000 in 1966, only about 10 percent of the student population can be accommodated in them. This proportion has remained unchanged since 1959. When residences for an additional 20,950 students (in the planning or construction stage in early 1966) are finished, total capacity will be for 61,000 students.

STUDENT OR-GANIZATIONS There are three basic categories of student organization:

1 Local societies, interest groups, and corporations

2 Student political associations affiliated with national political parties or interests

3 Student government organizations at individual institutions and their national federation, the VDS

Among the local societies, the traditional *Korporationen,* national fraternities with a predominantly conservative outlook, have had an unexpected revival since World War II. Membership in them is lifelong and traditionally assures one of social status and connections considered useful in professional life. However, these corporations are also changing. Specifically, the practice of compulsory dueling has become a major issue in the national associations.

At each institution of higher education, students are members of student unions whose governing bodies are elected by the students and whose financial support comes mainly from student fees. The local General Commission of the student association organizes a

[9] Information supplied by Deutsches Studentenwerk.

variety of social and cultural activities.[10] The VDS coordinates the member associations, maintains relations with foreign student groups, and represents the interests of German students to governmental and other authorities. Although not affiliated with any political party, the VDS has in recent years encouraged and organized political action on the part of its members, issuing statements and calling for strikes and demonstrations aimed not only at university reform but also at issues of domestic and foreign politics. It has pressed for more student participation in university decision making, more student financial aid, and reforms in university teaching methods. At its twenty-first Congress in March 1969 the majority of delegates voted to establish a 10-member body of "project area" representatives who would encourage student activism in 10 fields, including foreign affairs, law, technology, and medicine. This and other structural changes were intended to give more authority to the local chapters, apparently because they are more radical than the central governing body. These changes caused some conservative delegates, representing 70,000 of the 300,000 VDS members, to withdraw from the organization. Shortly after the session, the federal government ceased providing its annual subsidy of about DM 800,000 for the education programs of VDS. In late 1969 a new "umbrella" student organization was set up, the combined German Students Associations (ADS, Arbeitsgemeinschaft Deutscher Studentenschaften), to serve as a student-wide body, affliliated to no political party, and in opposition to the more radical VDS.

Only a small minority of German students are active members of political student associations. The association that has mobilized student revolt in the Federal Republic since the early 1960s is the Sozialistische Deutsche Studentenbund (SDS). It has only about 2,500 members but has been able to draw on student discontent with the universities and with the existing conditions in the country, organizing massive student protests which have resulted in violent clashes between students and authorities. Student discontent on the part of the hard-core activists—a mixture of Marxists, anarchists, Maoists, pacifists, and others—is aimed at what they consider inadequate efforts to reform the universities, nonrepresentation of students in university decision making, and the "techno-

[10] Membership in such organizations is now undergoing change, however. A new law in West Berlin dissolved the General Commission there.

cratic" orientation of the universities and society. The most radically leftist student political groups see no possibility of reforming universities or society through established procedures and look to an eventual revolution to topple the present system. Accusing higher education leaders of excessive authoritarianism, the radical students have alienated liberals by adopting their own authoritarian style. Whether or not protest by the less radical majority of students can be stemmed will depend in large part on the willingness of the authories to effect needed reforms in the universities and to take firm measures to restrain activist leaders. As of early 1969, it appeared that the universities were inclined to take firmer measures to cope with student disturbances — including closing their doors and trying to mobilize the less radical majority of students against the radicals.

The federal government was considering legislation that would deny student stipends to those working against the "democratic order." In March 1969 *Länder* authorities reached agreement that activist leaders might be expelled from universities for as many as three years.

REFORM AND CHANGE   Although student disturbances are resisted, work is also under way on the reforms that students, among others, have been calling for. Such reform is taking place in the areas of curricula, development of student counseling and guidance, shortening study periods, introducing new intermediate examination requirements, adding liberal arts faculties to technical universities, encouraging joint research projects to break down the domination of institutes by individual professors, abolishing the *Kolleggeld* system under which professors are paid in proportion to the number of students in their lectures, extending the terms of office for rectors and deans, whittling down requirements for the *Habilitation,* and offering assistants and students greater participation in decision making.

Institutional autonomy makes implementation of reform by the *Länder* and the federal governments difficult, but there is a growing willingness to consider reform proposals at these levels. As of mid-1969, major university reforms were under study by the governments of at least six *Länder,* and a special group representing the *Länder* and federal government had been established by the Federal Chancellor to consider university problems and recommend a unified system for the universities. The Federal Chancellor himself was chairman of this group.

In late 1968 and early 1969, the trends of proposals on university government changed. The Wissenschaftsrat strongly urged that universities have a new chief executive (a president); that university departments be established; that university authority with regard to staffing, budget, and administration be increased; and that academic and *Länder* administration of universities form a unified system. The WRK opposed the concept of a strong president and rejected the idea of replacing the faculty system with departments, but the Conference of Ministers of Education and Culture recommended university reform along the lines proposed by the Wissenschaftsrat. The prime ministers of the *Länder* agreed on a treaty with provisions that would strengthen university administration by establishing a university presidency; enlarging representation of various groups, including students, in decision-making bodies; filling vacant chairs through advertisement; amalgamating chairs to form a departmental system; and giving universities more responsibilities in staffing and financial matters.

A treaty drafted in March 1969 for the purpose of strengthening *Länder* powers with respect to university discipline encountered resistance but appeared likely to receive ratification by some *Länder* parliaments.

Another major step was the enactment of legislative amendments that made the *Länder* and federal government jointly responsible for planning university extension and new universities. Such planning was previously under the sole jurisdiction of the *Länder*. Constitutional changes had been proposed to give general powers in university affairs and educational planning to the federal government.

THE BALANCE SHEET

The current problems of German higher education are essentially the result of massive and rapid expansion in enrollments accompanied by overcrowding of facilities, deterioration of staff-student ratios, prolongation of study periods, low persistence rates, inadequate student guidance, and mounting administrative burdens. Other problems include cumbersome academic decision-making machinery, inadequate terms of office and lack of authority for key administrative officials, and the obstacles to reforms inherent in the traditional autonomy of professors. These problems have made apparent even more fundamental weaknesses in German higher education: the absence of adequate authority or machinery to undertake needed reforms and the fact that the universities are geared to educating only a small elite of the population. What is, in effect, a lack of democractic access to university-level education occurs because the universities, with an average enrollment of about 9,700 students each in 1966, find it difficult to provide the same quality of education they did formerly. Even with expansion of facilities, students with moderate ability and ambition are not given an opportunity for higher education. Disparities in educational opportunity between urban and rural areas, early decision requirements, limited financial aid for university students, and the demanding nature of university education are restricting university education to a minority of the 20- to 24-year-old age group. The absolute and relative increase in the cohort seeking university education is clearly putting pressure on the system, is calling into question its basic orientation, and is severely testing its flexibility and resources.

The "ideology" of traditional university education in Germany remains a model for advanced postsecondary work. According to this ideology, mature and highly competent students whose critical abilities and general education have been cultivated to a high level pursue knowledge in fields of their choice on a flexible and independent basis, working with outstanding academics in a professional, specialized, and research-oriented environment as long and as deeply as their interests and abilities extend. In doing so, they acquire the methodology, background, and philosophy which equip them to be scholars of the highest order.

Needs for reform in German higher education make the present period a watershed. If new subuniversity or nonuniversity institutions are established to absorb the flood of young people seeking postsecondary education, and if the accelerated effort in scientific research, especially in the newer fields of knowledge, takes place outside the universities, reforms may be held at bay — but the role of the universities in the transmission and pursuit of knowledge will decline. A more likely development would involve reforms strengthening the machinery for coordinated planning and support of higher education and permitting the federal government to play a larger role. But such reforms need to be reconciled with the constitutional principle of cultural federalism.

Because student rebellion makes reform in the universities imperative, it may actually be an instrument of survival for the German system of higher education.

Universities and Specialized Institutions in the Federal Republic of Germany and West Berlin

UNIVERSITIES

Berlin (Free University)

Bonn

Erlangen-Nuremberg

Bochum

Constance (Konstanz)

Dortmund

Düsseldorf

Frankfurt

Freiburg

Giessen

Göttingen

Hamburg

Heidelberg

Kiel

Cologne (Köln)

Mainz

Marburg

Munich

Münster

Regensburg

Saarbrücken

Tübingen

Würzburg

TECHNICAL UNIVERSITIES

Aachen

Berlin

Brunswick (Braunschweig)

Clausthal

Darmstadt

Hanover

Karlsruhe

Munich

Stuttgart

SPECIALIZED INSTITUTIONS

Hanover Medical College

Lubeck Medical College

Ulm Medical College

Hanover Veterinary College

Hohenheim Agricultural College

Mannheim College of Economics

NEW UNIVERSITIES PLANNED

University, Bielefeld

College of Economics, Augsburg

University, Bremen

References

Der Bundesminister für Wissenschaftliche Forschung: *Bundesbericht Forschung II,* Bonn, 1967.

Deutsche Kulturnachrichten, vol. XI, no. 1, January 1968, in G. Kloss, "University Reform in West Germany," *Minerva,* vol. VI, no. 3, Spring 1968.

Deutscher Bundestag: *Bildungsplanungsbericht 1967: Bericht über den Stand der Massnahmen auf dem Gebiet der Bildungsplanung,* V. 2166, Bonn, 1967.

Education in Germany, no. 1, Inter Nationes, Bad Godesberg, 1969.

Freund, Elmer: "Offentliche Ausgaben für Bildung und Wissenschaft," *Wirtschaft und Statistik,* no. 6, June 1966.

Robbins Committee: *Higher Education: Report of the Committee Appointed by the Prime Minister under the Chairmanship of Lord Robbins 1961–63,* appendix V, Cmnd. 2154, HMSO, London, 1963.

Riese, H.: *Die Entwicklung des Bedarfs an Hochschulabsolventen in der Bundesrepublik Deutschland,* Steiner, Wiesbaden, 1967.

Wissenschaftsrat: *Empfehlungen des Wissenschaftsrates zum Ausbau der Wissenschaftlichen Hochschulen bis 1970,* Bundesdruckerei, Bonn, 1967.

8. Higher Education in Sweden

Sweden's people have developed a highly respected educational system, and their University of Uppsala, with origins that date to 1477, is among the oldest in Europe. Today, postsecondary education, which is begun after 12 to 13 years of elementary school, middle school, and *gymnasium,* is offered at both university- and subuniversity-level institutions.

University-level institutions may have several faculties or may be single-faculty or specialized universities or colleges (*fackhögskolor*). Multifaculty universities are located at Stockholm, Lund, Göteborg, Uppsala, and Umeå. Together, they include faculties of law, theology, natural science and mathematics, social sciences, humanities, medicine and pharmacy, dentistry, and technology. Three of the specialized, or single-faculty, universities provide training in technology. Training in agriculture is provided by two, in forestry by one, in veterinary medicine by one, in economics by two, in social work by four, in physical education by one, and in medicine and dentistry by one (the Royal Caroline Medico-Surgical Institute in Stockholm). The six teacher training colleges located in Stockholm, Göteborg, Uppsala, Malmö, Umeå, and Linkoping are university-level institutions. Umeå has offered university-level courses in teacher training since 1967–68, and Linköping has offered them since 1968-69. University-level technical teacher training is offered by Linköping, Örebro, Uppsala, and the Stockholm Institute of Technology.

The second level of Swedish higher education is composed of subuniversity institutions which offer specialized and professionally oriented training in journalism, agriculture, education, commerce and business, fine arts and music, medical sciences, and certain service professions. In addition, government agencies main-

197

tain postsecondary institutions that give training for the civil and military services. The essential distinction between the two higher education levels is that students entering university-level institutions must have either the general or technical secondary school leaving certificate (formerly the *studentexamen*). At the other postsecondary institutions, although varying proportions of entering students have this qualification, it is not required.

Nearly all postsecondary education in Sweden is public or state sponsored. Even the exception, the Stockholm School of Economics, has considerable public support (40 percent of its annual budget) and is similar in other respects to public institutions. Most postsecondary education institutions are under the Ministry of Education, but the specialized agricultural, forestry, and veterinary universities are under the Ministry of Agriculture; military schools fall under the Ministry of Defense; and the schools for training civil service workers in the postal service, railways, customs, and other fields are under other state agencies.

Between 1950 and 1968 the multifaculty universities increased from four to five with the addition in 1964 of a liberal arts faculty to the medical and dental faculties at Umeå. The total number of university faculties increased from 23 (UNESCO, 1955) to 46 during this period (OECD, 1967, pp. 180–181). In 1964–65 Institutes for Social Work and Public Administration, which were at the subuniversity level, acquired university status. In 1967–68 four new affiliated universities or university branches began functioning as parts of the universities of Stockholm, Uppsala, Göteborg, and Lund. Located at Linköping, Örebro, Karlstad, and Växjö, they are from 100 to 125 miles from their parent universities. The four teachers colleges mentioned earlier were all established after 1950.

FUNCTIONS Traditionally, the Swedish universities and specialized colleges have had as their principal function training for the professions of law, theology, medicine, and teaching. Training for teaching has been offered primarily in the faculty of philosophy, which was divided into faculties of arts and sciences in 1946. The faculty of arts was again divided into social sciences and humanities in 1964. As specialized institutions in technology, agriculture, and other fields were established and acquired university status, the functions of university institutions came to include training in these specialties. Although the philosophical faculties prepare students for an increasing diversity of occupations, the professional goal of the majority of their students is still teaching. Of students both enrolled in these faculties in 1956–57 and receiving their first degree in them in 1961–62, 63 percent intended to become teachers (National Central Bureau of Statistics, 1959, p. 34; 1964, p. 51). The professional orientation of education in the philosophical faculties was reinforced with the introduction of fixed curricula in 1969.

Professors spend a large share of their time in research, and training in research methods is an important part of study for the licentiate (comparable to the American doctorate) and doctorate.

Swedish universities and colleges offer an increasing number of adult education programs. Special programs are offered in medicine, technology, and other subjects so that practicing professionals can study recent developments in their fields. University courses are given at a number of centers throughout Sweden so that teachers can gain additional professional qualifications. But most adult education in Sweden is provided outside the universities under the auspices of such organizations as the People's High Schools, Education Associations, correspondence schools, the Labor Market Board and National Board of Education, industry, and unions, including the Swedish Central Organization of Salaried Employees (TCO) and the Swedish Professional Association (SACO).

Much of the teacher training in Sweden falls outside the universities. There are about 20 colleges with two- to four-year programs for training students for teaching in the first six years of the comprehensive schools. Teacher training in such fields as physical education, domestic science, and art is given in specialized nonuniversity training colleges. By contrast, most teachers of theoretical subjects in the upper three years of comprehensive school and in the *gymnasiums* and *fackhögskolor* obtain a university degree, most commonly the *filosofie kandidat.* After obtaining their degrees, they have about a year or more of pedagogical and practical training at one of the specialized colleges of education located in Stockholm, Malmö, Göteborg, or Uppsala. These colleges also train teachers for the first six years of comprehensive school and undertake research on education.

ENROLLMENT TRENDS Total full-time enrollment in university-level institutions increased from about 17,000 students in 1950 to nearly 104,000 in 1968–69,

TABLE 26 *Percentage of members of relevant age groups enrolled in secondary and higher education in Sweden and receiving degrees*

	1950-51	1955-56	1960-61	1965-66	1967-68
Percent of 16-year-olds in gymnasiums first year[a]	10.7	13.6	17.8	30.2	32.0
Percent of 20-year-olds who passed gymnasium leaving examination[b]	6.5	9.0	12.0	18.5	23.2*
Percent of 26-year-olds who receive first degrees[c]	2.5	3.2	4.6	5.7	
Percent of 19- to 24-year-olds in all higher education[d]†	5.0 (1940)		11.0	11.0 (1964)	
Percent of 20- to 24-year-olds in university-level institutions of higher education[e]	3.7	5.3	7.9	11.1	

*Preliminary figure.

†This includes all categories of postsecondary education: university and nonuniversity institutions, military and civil services, etc.

SOURCES: (*a*) National Central Bureau of Statistics, 1968*a*, p. 21. (*b*) Sweden, Ministry of Education, 1967. (*c*) *Ibid.*, p. 27. (*d*) OECD, 1967, p. 42. (*e*) UNESCO: *Comparative Statistical Data on Access to Higher Education in Europe*, Conference of Ministers of Education of European Member States on Access to Higher Education, MINEUROP/3, Paris, November 20-25, 1967, p. 40.

exceeding by nearly 20,000 Parliament's 1965 estimate for 1970. Between 1950 and 1967 the number of net new entrants per year to these institutions (excluding foreign students and those previously registered in another faculty) rose from about 3,700 to about 26,000. The proportion of 19- to 24-year-olds enrolled went up from about 2 percent in 1945 to over 10 percent in the mid-1960s. This expansion in higher education is partly due to an increase in the size of the university age group (from about 450,000 in 1955 to about 600,000 in 1965) and also to the increased population of 16-year-olds entering *gymnasiums* (from 10.7 percent in 1950 to 32 percent in 1967), of *gymnasium* students who pass their leaving exam, or *studentexamen* (from 6.5 percent in 1950 to about 23 percent in 1967), and of *gymnasium* graduates who enter university (from about 75 percent in 1957 to 85 percent in recent years). The increase in university enrollments is likely to increase still further because of reform of presecondary schooling, with the establishment by Parliament in 1962 of a nine-year comprehensive or common school to replace the previous system of a variety of presecondary schools. The new system permits the postponement of decisions on specialization until the age of about 16, thus encouraging more students to continue their education after the nine-year period of compulsory common schooling. Limitations in resources and other factors will prevent *gymnasiums* from expanding to accommodate much more than about 30 percent of the age group until after 1970.

In the past, statistics have not distinguished between part-time and full-time students, and only limited statistics are available on students enrolled for advanced degrees at university institutions. Many students have continued their studies after obtaining the number of grade points necessary for the first degree in order to have a more extensive university education without necessarily planning to work toward a postgraduate award. The number of persons enrolled as active students working toward postgraduate degrees increased from about 3,100 in 1960–61 to about 5,700 in 1965–66. Postgraduate degrees awarded, an index of expanding enrollments, increased from 360 in 1950–51 to about 801 in 1966–67. The number of first degrees awarded increased from 326 in 1950–51 to 6,454 in 1965–66 and is expected to be 20,000 by 1975. The proportion of 26-year-olds with first degrees went up from 2.5 percent in 1950 to 5.7 percent in 1965–66. By 1980 the number of first-degree recipients is expected to be about six or seven times the 1950 total.

Enrollments in nonuniversity higher education also have expanded greatly since World War II. The Robbins Committee Report indicated an increase in nonuniversity enrollments, excluding teacher training colleges, from 17,000 in 1959–60 to about 20,000 in 1962 (Robbins Committee, 1963, appendix V, pp. 2–11). Increases in nonuniversity enrollments since then have been substantial, but precise statistics are not available. Plans in 1965 called for major expansion in this sector in order to accommodate the growing demand for postsecondary education. It is estimated that by 1970 the demand for new university places will exceed the number that can be accommodated by more than 8,000, thus increasing the pressure for expansion of nonuniversity institutions.

Closed and Free Faculties   A distinctive feature of Swedish university-level education is that certain faculties are *closed*. In these faculties (medicine, dentistry, pharmacy, technology and engineering, agriculture, forestry, and veterinary medicine), new enrollments are limited by a *numerus clausus*. Other faculties, known as *free* faculties of law, theology, social sciences, economics (excluding the Stockholm School of Economics), humanities, and natural sciences and mathematics, have no such restrictions on admissions in principle. In practice, however, because of limited laboratory space and teaching staff, restrictions exist in certain of the natural sciences. University expansion programs authorized by Parliament in the 1960s have resulted in the establishment of the new university at Umeå, of the four new affiliated universities, and of new faculties at existing universities. The capacities of all faculties have been increased. Even with this expansion, however, the free faculties have had to absorb a disproportionate number of entering students. Net new enrollments in these faculties increased from 5,840 in 1960-61 to about 22,000 in 1967–68,[1] whereas the number of places in closed faculties increased from 2,621 in 1960–61 to 5,835 in 1967–68 and will be about 7,300 in 1979–80 according to plans adopted in the mid-1960s (National Central Bureau of Statistics, 1968*a*, pp. 40, 32). In 1970 it is anticipated that two-thirds of all university students will be enrolled in the free faculties.

The enrollment imbalance between free and closed faculties has been a matter of increasing concern. This is partly because of the much lower persistence rate of students in the free faculties, especially in the *philosophical* faculties of social science, humanities, and mathematics and natural sciences, and because students who

TABLE 27 *Numbers of new entrants and students enrolled in institutions of higher education in Sweden*

	1950-51	1955-56	1960-61	1965-66	1968-69
Total postsecondary enrollment		27,229[a]	39,981[a]	77,616[a]	
In university-level higher education	16,549[a]	22,298†[a]	35,505†[a]	70,591†[a]	104,000†[a]
Postgraduate enrollment			3,091[b]	5,612[b]	
New entrants to university-level institutions	3,358[a]	4,548[a]	7,402[a]	16,737‡[a]	26,249[c]*

*Estimated.

†Not included are postgraduate students at the colleges of agriculture, forestry, and veterinary medicine; in 1961 they totaled 96, or about 3 percent of all postgraduate students in that year. Doctoral students constitute normally something over one-third of all postgraduate students registered as "active" students in that year.

‡Does not include entrants in technical teacher training courses.

SOURCES: (a) Figures supplied by the OECD Directorate for Scientific Affairs. (b) Office of the Chancellor of the Swedish Universities: *Högre Utbildning och Forskning: Universitetskanslersämbetets Förslag till Anslagsaskanden för Budgetäret 1968-69*, Stockholm, 1967, p. 17. (c) National Central Bureau of Statistics: *Forecasting Information*, no. 1, Stockholm, April 4, 1968, p. 30.

[1] For demographic and other reasons they are expected to decrease to about 16,000 by 1979–80.

TABLE 28 *Number of degrees awarded at institutions of higher education in Sweden*

	1950-51	1955-56	1960-61	1965-66	1967-68
Graduates from gymnasiums		8,155[a]	13,343[a]	26,845[a]	32,262[a]
First degrees	2,326[b]	2,819[b]	4,267[b]	6,454[b]	7,690[b]
Postgraduate degrees	360[c]	394[c]	521[c]	748[c]	

SOURCES: (a) National Central Bureau of Statistics: *Forecasting Information,* no. 1, April 4, 1968, pp. 22-24. (b) Information supplied by the OECD. (c) Sweden, Ministry of Education, 1967, p. 27.

remain in free faculties take relatively longer to obtain their degrees. It is also the opinion in some quarters that the free faculties may produce more graduates, especially in the social sciences, than can find employment opportunities in the economy. A 1955 survey of students registered seven or more years earlier showed that less than half of those enrolled in the free faculties of arts (which then included social sciences) and sciences obtained their degree while 80 to 90 percent of those in the closed faculties had done so (OECD, 1967, p. 192). A more recent survey showed that by the fall term of 1963, of students first registered in 1956–57 only 50.4 percent of those in humanities and 63 percent of those in mathematics and natural sciences had obtained a degree, and 41 percent and 28.7 percent, respectively, had left university without a degree. By contrast, 77.4, 81.2, and 96.0 percent, respectively, of students enrolled in faculties of technology, economics, and dentistry had obtained their degrees, and the proportions of students in these faculties who left without the degree were 10.7, 18.4, and 1.8 percent, respectively. While only 49.1 percent of students enrolled in medical faculties in 1954-55 had obtained their degrees by the fall of 1963, only 4.4 percent had left (Office of the Chancellor of the Swedish Universities, 1966).[2]

The theoretically "normal" or minimum number of years required to obtain a first degree varies among faculties from 3½ to 4 years in the humanities to 5 in engineering and law and around 8 years in medicine. Students have tended to take longer than the normal period, especially in the free faculties, because the tradition of academic freedom has permitted them to defer taking examinations until they chose, to repeat examinations and courses with few

---

[2] In evaluating these figures one must take into account the fact that large numbers of students have enrolled in the free faculties with no intention of earning degrees in these faculties, planning instead to qualify for admission to the closed faculties.

restrictions, and to delay decisions on their area or areas of concentration. In the closed faculties, requirements and sequences of courses are such that most students complete their first degree in not much more than the normal period, following courses and taking examinations in accordance with a structured curriculum determined by their field of concentration.

The Committee on University Pedagogy, established in 1965, has made studies of ways to maximize university resources by reducing study periods and dropout rates and by increased student guidance and counseling.

Staff-Student Ratios

Even with the fivefold increase in enrollments in university level institutions since 1950, the overall staff-student ratio has not only been maintained but has somewhat improved, going from 1:14 in 1956 to 1:12 in 1965 (OECD, 1967, p. 198). Ratios vary widely among faculties. In the fall of 1966, for example, they ranged from 1:45 in law and 1:35 in social science and economics to 1:6 in medicine and 1:4 in odontology. The greatest increase in teaching staff has been at the level of assistants; including them, the ratio in 1963 was 1:13 while excluding them it was 1:32 (OECD, 1967, p. 197). Teaching staff members in the assistant category include teaching and research assistants and amanuenses recruited from among students working for their licentiates and doctorates and in some cases the first degree. In 1965–66, of the 5,330 teaching staff members in faculties under the Ministry of Education (an additional 280 were in faculties under the Ministry of Agriculture), 17 percent were professors and 48 percent were assistants (OECD, 1967, p. 199).

A heavy reliance upon the lower-level staff for teaching is also indicated by the different annual teaching loads of different categories of instructional personnel in university institutions. Full professors and associate professors teach about 130 hours per year (excluding tutorial sessions) — the associate professor level includes certain tenured staff members known as *laborators* in the natural science faculties, *observators* in astronomy, *preceptors* in law and humanities faculties, and *prosektors* in certain theoretical subjects in medicine. The docents teach about 75 hours per year and include persons who obtained the doctorate with honors and who may normally teach a maximum of six years at a given university and from among whom professors are usually selected. University lecturers teach 396 hours annually and are a new tenured instructional category established in 1958, including persons who obtained the doctorate but without honors. Assistants teach about 500 hours per year, and adjunct assistants, a recent new category, 683 hours. The latter do not have tenure and are not required to have the doctorate or licentiate but may have the latter. In view of the Swedish practice of having very few professors, the estimated additional university teachers needed between 1965 and 1970, some 3,000, may result in an even greater share of undergraduate teaching being handled by subprofessorial staff members. Beginning in 1969–70 more than 100 new research appointments were authorized, and the period of appointment for assistant professors was extended beyond the previous limit of six to seven years.

In May 1969, Parliament adopted a bill to reform the training and appointments of researchers. In the period July 1, 1969 to July 1, 1971, the traditional doctoral and licentiate degrees were being abandoned. In their stead is being established a new doctorate which can be obtained in four (instead of six to nine) years after the first degree. The new legislation will enable many more students to qualify for teaching positions in the universities and will also increase substantially the number of appointments as junior researcher and assistant professor. The titles of *laborators, preceptors,* and *prosektors* have accordingly been abandoned, and all three are called associate professors. Docents are of two categories, docents and research docents.

HIGHER EDUCATION AND CIVIL GOVERNMENT Responsibility for university-level (and most other) higher education lies with the Ministry of Education and Ecclesiastical Affairs. The agriculture, veterinary, and forestry colleges are exceptions and are under the Ministry of Agriculture. In accordance with long-standing political and administrative practice, the Ministry of Education does not exercise direct control over institutions of higher education. This falls to the Chancellor of Universities, the heirship of the medieval Archbishop of Sweden, who was Chancellor of the University of Uppsala. The Ministry shares with the Chancellor responsibility for financial and other planning for the universities. It submits annual requests to Parliament based on requests, mainly from the Office of the Chancellor of the Swedish Universities. Since the reorganization of all government ministries in July 1965, a special planning and budgetary secretariat, established out of an earlier planning unit in the Ministry, has had major responsibility for the long-range planning of higher education.

The Ministry's role must be seen in the context of the Swedish system of using special committees to study and recommend on problems and reforms. These committees are usually established on the initiative of the Parliament or Ministry, and the latter prepares the terms of reference. Depending on the importance and scope of the committee's mandate, its members may be appointed from within the Ministry, other government agencies, the Parliament, and various interest groups in the public sector. On university affairs, representatives of the national student organization may be included on the committee. A committee concerned with a major issue may take up to several years to complete its work, sometimes reporting the results by stages. Committee reports are sent for review and comment to all organizations and sectors of society likely to have an interest. If this procedure reveals fundamental criticism of the committee's recommendations, the committee may rewrite its report. In the case of particularly adverse reactions, the Ministry may postpone or even decide not to seek parliamentary implementation of the recommendations. Because recommendations ultimately submitted to Parliament are likely to reflect a consensus among the principal interest groups involved, including often the major political parties, they are likely to receive favorable parliamentary action. With respect to higher education, as with other fields, it is evident that the committees are important in the planning process. Their effectiveness can be attributed in large part to the continuous close communication, informal as well as formal, between the people and organizations involved with higher education. This communication is possible because of Sweden's relatively small population (8 million) and unique political traditions.

In 1969, a number of special committees were engaged in studies of higher education. Foremost among them was the 1968 Education Committee, which was making the first attempt in Sweden to review systematically and comprehensively all postsecondary education: goals, functions, structure and organization, size, and location of institutions. Other special committees were studying higher technical education, the financing of adult education, the rationalization of higher education operations, and access to higher education.

The Office of the Chancellor of the Swedish Universities is an independent central body which works closely with, but is not directly under the authority of, the Ministry of Education. This office is the supreme governing body for the university institutions with the exceptions of the agricultural, forestry, and veterinary colleges and the Stockholm School of Economics. Reforms in 1964 reorganized and enlarged the functions and powers of this office, integrating into the universities under it certain previously separate specialized colleges and incorporating into the functions of the revised office those previously exercised by the former National Board of the Institutes of Technology and the Board of the Pharmaceutical Institute. Before 1964 the Chancellor was elected by the various faculties and institutions; since then he has been appointed by the King-in-Council for a six-year term. The chancellorship did not become a salaried position until 1937. A major responsibility of the Chancellor is to intermediate between the universities and the government.

The Office of the Chancellor of the Swedish Universities (UKÄ) has a governing board which includes representatives of Swedish public life and the chairman, the university chancellor, and, since September 1969, one representative of the National Student Union. The office comprises five departments concerned, respectively, with planning, training, administration, organization and management, and, since fall 1969, university training. There are also five faculty councils, each representing one or more disciplines and ten educational councils which advise on educational development in various fields, principally science and technology, and which help ensure close collaboration between industry and the university institutions in curricular development. University teachers are not represented in the UKÄ governing board but are represented in the faculty councils and the educational councils.

The Chancellor's Office influences curricular development through its authority to approve and make recommendations on proposals from the faculties on curricular changes and on certain teaching appointments. It is also responsible for ensuring that national legislation on higher education is implemented. Special planning units in the Chancellor's Office are concerned with university development and with maximizing the utilization of resources and the productivity of higher education. With respect to university finance, the Chancellor's Office receives and reviews requests from the faculties and submits its own recommendations on them to the Ministry of Education. Since 1966 the budgetary requests of the universities have been submitted to the Chancellor's Office by individual faculties rather than university institutions so that the financial needs and plans in different fields can be more effectively assessed and coordinated. The faculty councils study and make recommendations on these requests to the Chancellor's Office. Under the new system, competition for funds occurs more often between faculties of the same kind at different university institutions than between the institutions themselves. In 1968 a special committee was in the process of studying the possibility of adopting program budgeting for the entire public administration system, and it seemed not unlikely that the current system of financing higher education through "global" grants for different categories of expenditures such as wages and materials might be replaced with a system of grants for subject fields. Such a system might enable the costs and relative productivity of activities in different fields to be assessed more effectively and at the same time might give to the universities a greater degree of financial autonomy.

The Council for Education advises on the total educational system. It was set up in the mid-1960s and includes representatives of the Ministry of Education, the Chancellor's Office, the National Board of Education, the labor market, employers' and employees' organizations, and the Central Bureau of Statistics. Also contributing to educational planning are the Forecasting Institute within the Central Bureau of Statistics under the Ministry of Finance, which endeavors to calculate future educational and manpower needs and prospects, and the Educational Statistics Division, which collects and analyzes statistical and other information necessary for the planning process.

The Swedish Scientific Advisory Council, established in 1962, serves as a forum for discussions of scientific policy and advises on priorities in government support of research in the universities and other sectors of society; 13 of its 18 members are academicians. The Prime Minister presides over the Council and over its seven-member working group. The Council's role is consultative only.

Supporting research by higher education institutions and other bodies are 12 publicly financed research councils established since 1942. Attached to various ministries, these councils have about 9 to 12 members nominated partly by university faculties and partly by government. As research in Sweden is more university-centered than in most other countries, the universities are correspondingly research-oriented, and the research councils, through the projects they choose to support, have a significant influence on higher education.

INTERNAL GOVERNMENT OF UNIVERSITIES

The expansion and increased centralization of the university system under the Office of the Chancellor of the Swedish Universities has prompted a reciprocal strengthening of university governance at the individual institutions. Internal governing units include the rector, university council, faculty councils, and departmental or institute bodies.

Until after World War II the position of rector was to a considerable extent ceremonial and representational. With the growth of university institutions and the evolution of more complex relations between them and government, the rector has come to play an increasingly important role as a negotiator for his institution vis-à-vis the government and as a mediator between the faculties, in addition to handling expanding administrative responsibilities of his office. Although the rector's formal authority with respect to budget preparation (except for the overall budget shared by faculties), curricular development, staff recruitment, and student affairs is limited, his position has become more influential in the last decade because he is the official channel of communication between the faculties and the Chancellor's Office. The rector is elected by the University Council from among professors who have held this status for at least three years. He has a four-year term and may be reelected. *Primus inter pares,* the rector is chairman of the University Council, the supreme governing body. Assisting in the university administration are the vice-rector and a growing number of full-time administrative staff members.

The University Council *(Konsistoriet)* includes the rector and vice-rector, deans of faculties and sections, and, on occasion, the chief librarian. It deals mainly with matters of internal administration and not directly with educational and research questions. It may, however, comment on the budgetary requests of faculties to the faculty boards of the Chancellor's Office and submit its own grant requests for certain universitywide expenditures such as local administration.

Each faculty is governed by a dean and vice-dean and consists of the professors and lecturers. The faculties decide certain major matters, e.g., budget requests, and propose the establishment of new positions and professorial appointments. Each faculty has a standing education committee consisting of the head of the faculty, three representatives from the teaching staff, one representative of the assistants, and since 1957, three representatives of the students, chosen by the local student union. This committee decides on matters concerning curricula, the content of study courses, and methods of instruction.

At the institute or departmental level, all teaching staff members participate in boards which are advisory to the director. Since 1964 two representatives of the students, chosen by the local student union, have been members of these advisory boards. The boards make recommendations on teaching methods, textbooks to be used in particular courses, and other matters of institute concern. Also in 1964, student-teacher councils, first introduced in 1953, were strengthened. Renamed Education Committees and composed of equal numbers of students and teachers, these bodies, rather than faculties, have had formal authority, since July 1, 1969, for decisions on educational matters including the content of courses and organization of teaching.

In July 1968, the government authorized the Chancellor of the Swedish Universities to launch experiments in new kinds of cooperation between teachers, other staff, and students in the department or institute level. Experiments conducted during 1969–70 and possibly for an additional year or two are to be the basis for recommendations for permanent reforms in student participation in university governance. Experiments are following four models, ranging from giving institutional councils authority only in education-related matters to giving full decision-making power in all institute matters to the governing body. In general, teachers and students have equal representation in institute bodies, and administrative and technical staff are represented as well. New nine-member Cooperative Councils composed of three representatives nominated, respectively, by the University Council, by personnel organizations (excluding teachers), and by the student union assist with the new experiments in each university or, if the University Council wishes, direct them. A key element in the new experimentation is the provision for continuing evaluation of it.

FINANCING HIGHER EDUCATION Postsecondary education is financed almost entirely by public funds. The chief source of private funds, the Wallenberg Foundation, grants about SKr 5 million annually to the universities. Since 1960 there has been only one private university-level institution in Sweden, the Stockholm School of Economics, and it receives about 40 percent of its income from the state (SKr 1.5 million in 1968–69). The Universities of Göteborg and Stockholm were nationalized in 1954 and 1960, respectively, but well before their status changed, the state began to contribute to their operating costs. The two oldest universities, Uppsala and Lund, receive some income from their landholdings and other endowments. Although this income has shrunk in relation to their total income, amounting to 5 percent or less, it is useful in meeting unforeseen contingencies and supporting activities for which state funds might not be available. The University of Stockholm has accumulated a private endowment of some SKr 20 million.

Total public expenditures on all higher education increased from about SKr 50 million in 1951 to about SKr 470 million in 1965 (the latter figure includes current expenditures on all higher education and research, excluding student financial aid but including certain capital costs, expenditures of the central administration, and nonuniversity as well as university institutions), and were estimated at SKr 650.8 million in 1967–68 (National Central Bureau of Statistics, 1967*b*). Current expenditures for university institutions only were expected to increase from SKr 245.5 million in 1965–66 to 443.2 million in 1967–68 and to 535 million in 1972 (National Central Bureau of Statistics, 1967*b*). Per student cost in universities in 1963 prices went up from SKr 4,860 in 1957-58 to an estimated SKr 5,630 in 1965–66 (OECD, 1967, p. 326). In 1966–67, the average recurrent cost per year per student ranged from SKr 1,300 in the faculty of social sciences and 1,600 in law, to 9,600 in the institutes of technology and 18,400 in the dental colleges (Sweden, Ministry of Education, 1967, p. 37).

About one-third of the higher education budget of the Ministry of Education is devoted to scientific research. Research and development in the universities is also financed by the research councils and other bodies, such as the Bank of Sweden Tercentenary Fund, which in its first two years of operation since 1965 gave about SKr 33 million to research. Over half of that amount went to the social sciences. About one-fifth of all research and development in Sweden is carried out at higher education institutions. The magnitude of this activity is illustrated by the increase in total government grants to research, including the universities, special funds, etc., from SKr 411 million in 1963–64 to 547 million in 1965–66 (OECD, 1967, p. 215). Government grants for research at universities and through the Research Councils increased from SKr 68.5 million in 1964–65 to SKr 89.9 million in 1966–67 (OECD, 1967, p. 324).

HIGHER EDUCATION AND ECONOMIC PLANNING

Since the 1930s, forecasts of the need for university graduates have been made. They were prompted initially by concern that there might be an oversupply of graduates and by the desire, in the past decade, to achieve an optimal use of educational resources in rela-

TABLE 29
Expenditures for all higher education in Sweden (in millions of Swedish kroner at current prices)

	1950	1955	1960	1965
Public expenditures, capital and recurrent[a]	934.0		3,086.7	6,620.0
Recurrent public expenditures[a]	43.0		211.3	480.0
Total expenditures on higher education as percentage of total public expenditure on all education[b]			8.0	
Public expenditures as a percent of the gross national product[c]	3.5	4.4	5.1	

SOURCES: (*a*) UNESCO Questionnaires on Statistics of Education Finance and Expenditure. (*b*) OECD, 1967, p. 330. (*c*) *UNESCO Statistical Yearbook, 1963,* Paris, 1965.

tion to labor market needs. Legislation in the 1960s, which authorized the expansion of higher education, was based in part on forecasts of manpower needs as well as on the future supply of university graduates. However, because of methodological difficulties in forecasting future manpower demand and because education is viewed primarily as a consumer good, forecasts of these manpower requirements is only one of various factors determining

TABLE 30
Expenditures for Swedish higher education (in thousands of Swedish kroner)

	1963-64[a]	1967-68[a]*
Chancellor of Universities	1,513	5,313
General, specialized, and affiliated universities under Ministry of Education—operating costs, materials, books	194,682	443,275
Other higher education institutions under Ministry of Education—fine arts, social work, journalism, School of Economics in Stockholm	62,265	23,059
Expenditures shared by universities and other higher education institutions under the Ministry of Education, and special equipment costs	3,093	33,505
Research grants by Ministry of Education to certain research councils, expenditures on international projects	54,594	99,173
Ministry of Agriculture expenditures on specialized universities and research council		61,418
Ministry of Finance expenditures on technical research council		22,428
Total under Ministry of Education	343,612	650,825[b]

*Estimated.

SOURCES: (*a*) Central Bureau of Statistics, 1967*b*. (*b*) Sweden, Ministry of Education, 1967, p. 32.

	1964-65	1966-67*	1967-68*
Central administration under the Chancellor's Office	3.1	4.0	4.5
Universities, general and specialized	304.2	432.3	485.3
Institutes of social work and public administration	3.6	6.0	9.8
Teacher training colleges	113.3	179.1	194.3
Institutes of journalism	0.7	0.8	1.0
Fine arts institutions	7.5	10.4	11.0
Total expenditures on higher education under Ministry of Education	432.4	632.6	705.9
Total expenditures on higher education under Ministry of Agriculture	37.8	62.0	
Total expenditures on higher education under both ministries	470.2	694.6	
Capital expenditures Buildings Equipment	35.0	170.0 60.0	
Total for all higher education and research†		1,585.0	1,777.0

TABLE 31 Current expenditures on Swedish higher education (in millions of Swedish kroner)

*Estimated.

† Figures cited for "all higher education and research" include higher education (including agricultural universities) and research at the general and specialized universities and research which is assisted by grants from the research councils or is conducted at subsidiary research institutes. Also included are teacher training and direct student aid. Building and equipment costs are included as part of university expenditures.

SOURCE: OECD, 1967, pp. 323, 334–335.

educational planning. So that manpower need forecasts can more effectively guide future planning, Swedish authorities are working to develop more reliable forecasting methods which will take into account such problems as the possibilities of substitution between different categories of trained manpower, the role of salaries in determining the demand and supply of university graduates, and the influence of various economic, social, and political measures, including vocational guidance, on demand and supply.

The 1968 Education Committee is also concerned with planning. Among studies being undertaken by its expert groups is an analysis of the consequences of quantitative expansion of university enrollments based on social demand for the labor market, an analysis of the labor market situation in 1980, studies of mechanisms of adaptation within the educational system and on the labor market, and cost benefit analysis.

Swedish higher education institutions charge no tuition fees although students are required to pay annual fees of SKr 50 to 100 per term to their local student unions and to the national union of students. Historically, it has been customary for Swedish students to finance their studies by contracting debts. Parliamentary legislation in 1950 broadened the system of loans and grants to enable more students from low-income groups to attend institutions of higher education. Grants covering board and lodging for three years and interest-free loans repayable starting two years after graduation were made available on increasingly broader terms to students with ability and low parental income. State-guaranteed and bank loans were available at 5 and 6 percent interest, respectively. Awards by private foundations and loans through student associations supplied still other financial assistance. In 1962–63 nearly half of the new entrants to university institutions received government grants, and over two-thirds had loans authorized through the State Scholarship Grant Board.

A 1962 survey showed that about 40 percent of all students supplemented their income through some form of work. As of 1961 the government wrote off one-fourth of students' debts under government loans.

In 1964, a new scheme of State Study Assistance was introduced to limit the heavy burden of study debts on students and to enable more students from low-income families to enroll in higher education. Under the new system, students in all levels of higher education (not just universities as formerly) receive study funds comprising a study allowance or outright grant of SKr 175 per month, or SKr 1,750 per year, and study means (loans) of up to a base of SKr 5,700 per year. The entitlement is related to student, not parental, means, and may be reduced (in the same proportion for the grant as for the loan) by two-thirds of the student's own income over SKr 7,270 per year, by one-third of the spouse's income exceeding SKr 14,840 per year, and by one-fifth of the couple's net assets over SKr 34,200. Students are also entitled to SKr 1,325 per year allowance for each dependent child under sixteen years old. Although eligibility for study means does not depend on secondary school leaving examination records or aptitude tests, the Central Study Assistance Committee, which administers the program through committees at the five university towns, demands satisfactory work and completion of studies in a reasonable time as prerequisites for continuation of a student's funds.

Repayment of the loan part of the study funds begins three years after graduation and is interest-free. However, the amount repayable (normally in 20 annual installments) is based not on the amount borrowed by the student but on that amount adjusted to current prices so that the student repays not what he borrowed as a student but on the basis of the amount contemporary students borrow at the time his repayments are due. Repayment may be postponed in accordance with criteria of ability to pay or waived altogether in the case of permanent inability to repay through illness or other cause. The beneficiary's death cancels his indebtedness. During 1968–69 it was estimated that SKr 168 million would be paid as grants to students in higher education and an estimated SKr 556 million would be paid in loans (Swedish Institute, 1966, p. 12).

Graduate students tend to be supported by grants and fellowships from their institutions, from the research councils, or from comparable sources. In 1967–68 some SKr 8.12 million was the estimated appropriation for research fellowships for postgraduate students in science (Swedish Institute, 1966, p. 12). Scholarships for graduate students were increased by SKr 50 to 1,000 annually beginning in 1969–70, and study assistance was raised to a maximum of SKr 18,870 annually. The loan portion of that amount is SKr 6,370. Students in higher education also receive indirect benefits including health care at state subsidized health services, low-cost housing for the approximately 30 percent of university students accommodated in student housing facilities, reduced transportation costs, low-cost meals at government-subsidized student restaurants, and low-cost merchandise at shopping centers run by student unions.

Broadening the opportunity for higher education among lower-income groups depends not only on financial aid but also upon admission of a larger proportion of students from low-income families to *gymnasiums.* The fathers of only 23 percent of the entrants to *gymnasiums* in 1960 were classified as industrial workers although this occupational category included 51 percent of the active male population in Sweden. In the same year, 35 percent of newly registered students at universities had fathers classified as teachers, managers, university graduates, and military officers— occupations constituting only 5 percent of the active male population (OECD, 1967, pp. 154, 213). There is some doubt whether the 1964 aid system significantly encourages students from low-income families to seek higher education because of their reluctance to incur debts on the one hand and because the funds available do not cover the monthly estimated cost of SKr 900 to 950 for attending higher education institutions on the other. In any case, the new system is alleged not to have greatly changed student aid because of the increasing generosity of terms for loans and grants in the late 1950s.

A recent survey of 3,000 students showed that while the primary source of student incomes is loans, about one-fourth of the students surveyed use their own capital to finance part or all of their studies and one-fifth receive cash contributions from their parents or guardians. The generous loan system does not appear to be broadening appreciably the representation of lower-income groups. Of the 3,000 students surveyed, some 63 percent came from the upper and upper middle classes, 16 percent from the middle class, and only 8 percent from the working class (Burke, 1969).

STUDENTS
Student unrest has been relatively limited in Sweden and has focused more on issues related to peace and authoritarianism abroad than on internal university matters. This relative tranquility is attributed to the high degree of student participation in university policy making, to the well-developed student-administered welfare system, to the fact that university authorities exercise a minimum of parietal authority over student life and behavior, to the relative maturity of Swedish students, and to the effectiveness of the National Union of Students (SFS) in pursuing the interests of students inside rather than outside of the establishment. Since the events of May 1968 in France, student unrest in Sweden has grown. Students have demonstrated much more concern with the internal affairs of universities and have pressed for greater participation in decision making.

Although student participation in decision making in the universities was relatively limited before the launching of the period of experimentation with student democracy in 1969–70, the SFS has considerable influence with governmental bodies concerned with higher education and has maintained good relations with them. It is represented on many of the special committees set up to study particular problems and, in accordance with Swedish practice, is consulted on all government proposals for change affecting student interests. Membership in the SFS is compulsory, and its annual income from student fees is about SKr 16.5 million. Not only does it articulate and press for student interests at the national and local levels, but it and its local unions also operate such welfare activities as health services, student stores and housing, restaurants, physical education programs, and student travel at the institutions. The sudden new interest of students in general has been accompanied by increasing criticism of the bureaucracy in the student unions on the part of radical students. The critics accuse the unions of having been tools of the Establishment, working for their own ends rather than for the interests of the entire student population.

In addition to belonging to the local union students belong to student *nations,* organizations based on different regions which support various ancient traditions together with social and cultural events. In recent years, student political associations, including a range of left-wing groups, have emerged, and although in principle the student union is not identified with any political party, student union elections are increasingly based on a system of political parties. In view of the increasing politization of student life, together with growing student opposition to the new plan to limit curricular choices and study time at the philosophical faculties, the possibility of increased student unrest cannot be discounted.

RECENT REFORMS IN UNIVERSITY EDUCATION By royal commission, the 1955 Committee on University Development was appointed to study and make recommendations on the future of university-level education in Sweden. On the basis of its report and those of other committees appointed later, including a special committee (the U-63 Committee) appointed in 1963, a series of legislative measures were adopted in 1958 and later years authorizing university reforms and enrollment expansion of up to 86,000 students by 1970. The reforms have been directed toward the following broad objectives:

1 Structural reorganization to facilitate more integrated administration and more effective long-range planning

2 Expansion of teaching and research staff

3 Reduction in the extended period taken by students, especially in the philosophical faculties, to obtain their first degrees

4 Improvement in instructional methods and in the productivity of higher education

Planning and Administration More centralized and integrated administration has been made possible through the reorganization and strengthening of the Office of the Chancellor of the Swedish Universities, through the intensified efforts of planning units in the Ministry of Education and the Chancellor's Office, and through the work of the Forecasting Unit. To coordinate planning in the expansion and utilization of plant and equipment, special building and equipment program committees, known as LUP Committees, have been established in most university towns. They estimate future requirements and prepare programs for facilities development which serve as the basis for construction plans prepared by the National Board of Building, the central authority responsible for all nondefense governmental construction activities.

Planning and reform in education, including higher education, has become continuous and is often referred to as *rolling reform.* Efforts are made to accommodate shifts in the social and economic demands for higher education gradually and as a matter of routine rather than suddenly or on a crisis basis.

Expansion in Teaching and Research Staffs

Enrollment increases have required a parallel expansion in teaching and research staffs. This has been accomplished through some increase in the number of professorships; by the establishment of a new category of tenured staff, university lecturers; by the creation of another new academic position, research assistantships; and by an increase in the number of research docentships, positions involving mainly research which are available to persons who have held a docentship for a maxium period of six years.

Because the relatively low persistence rate of students in the free faculties (especially the philosophical faculties of humanities, social sciences, and natural science and mathematics) was attributed in part to the failure of staff recruitment to keep pace with increasing enrollments in the late 1950s, legislation was passed in 1958 which automatically allocated increased funds for the recruitment of teaching staff (excluding professors) in the philosophical faculties. Increases are based on annual forecasts of enrollments, an average class size of about 30 students, and other factors. In mid-1968, a committee proposed certain changes in this system in view of its high cost and the difficulties in accurately predicting enrollment increases.

Another recent measure to increase the size of the teaching staff is recruitment of adjunct assistants for teaching at the new affiliated universities. A special committee, appointed in 1963 to investigate postgraduate study and related matters, proposed the establishment of a new postgraduate degree, the *aspiranta,* somewhat comparable to the doctorate but with more limited requirements and involving a structured program designed to shorten to about four years the total training period required for the doctorate. Before the enactment of legislation in May 1969, which reformed doctoral degree requirements, the doctoral candidate theoretically could expect to spend at least three to four years working for the doctoral degree after at least three years on the licentiate. In practice, the period required was longer for most students. Of 328 students obtaining the licentiate in 1960–61, 76 percent were registered as candidates for the degree for longer than three years, with more than half requiring over five years. Counting only the terms during which the students were actively working for the degree, only 38 percent took no more than three years. Of 191 students receiving the doctorate in 1960–61, only 38 obtained it in three years and only 67, or 35 percent, after three years of "active" work towards the degree (National Central Bureau of Statistics, 1964). Under the May 1969 legislation the new doctoral degree requires only four years of study after the first degree.

Reduction in Study Period   The fact that many students enrolled in the philosophical faculties take much more than the normal period of three to four years to complete their first-degree work and nearly half leave university without completing their studies has been a source of growing concern in recent years. Although the student aid system introduced in 1964 encourages students to complete their first-degree work in the normal time, in practice it has not substantially shortened their study period. So that students are not delayed in taking certain basic courses, recent reforms result in offering these courses more than once a year. The examination system has also been tightened up so that a student may be refused permission to take a final examination in any one subject more than four times except in unusual circumstances.

The Parliament adopted legislation on March 19, 1969, designed to limit the students' freedom to determine their courses and study period for the first degree in the philosophical faculties. University students in the faculties of science, arts, and social sciences, beginning with 1969–70, may choose in their first year from about 17 subjects and in their second year from about 50. In their third year they will have no restrictions but will be given recommendations on appropriate courses of study. The reforms have replaced the traditional system of units (six required for a first degree) with credits,

40 to be earned each year. Most students are expected to complete their first degree in three years, although the reforms permit some to continue at university, earning up to a maximum of 60 credits beyond the 120 for the first degree. Two-thirds of all students must now obtain 40 credits each year.

These reforms do not, in fact, constitute a major change because the new system of course combinations is the same as what some 90 percent of students took in the former system. Limits on total study period also are not new. But the reforms are significant because they offer the opportunity for a major revision of university courses in the faculties involved.

Quality and Productivity of Teaching

In 1965, the Chancellor's Office established a Committee for University Training Methods. It recommended the establishment of a special department for research and development in training methods in the Chancellor's Office and similar units at individual institutions to advise teaching staff in instructional techniques. The committee is itself sponsoring research projects on teaching methods.

In the last few years, emphasis in teaching has been shifting from lectures to classroom discussion. To provide more advice to students on their academic programs, guidance and counseling services are expanding. A staff member at the Office of the Chancellor of the Swedish Universities is responsible for the development and coordination of guidance facilities, and all university departments and institutes are encouraged to have a guidance specialist on their staffs. Plans called for establishing 60 new positions as education adviser or guidance specialists at the departmental level in 1969–70.

In connection with more effective utilization of teaching resources, year-round operations and double-shift use of laboratories and other facilities are under study. The trend toward departmentalization within faculties is bringing together into single unified departments professors and other teaching staff who had been in independent institutes or departments. This reduces the administrative burden on individual professors and permits a more efficient utilization of manpower and more coordination in related research projects.

The U-63 Committee urged a greater use of new technology, not so much to reduce the total teaching staff required but rather so they would be used more efficiently. As part of its mandate, the

Committttee on University Training investigated the possibilities for greater utilization of technical aids. Experiments in television teaching were initiated in the fall of 1966 at Uppsala University and the Stockholm Institute of Technology. Increased use of closed-circuit television teaching is anticipated elsewhere. Several universities and teachers colleges have been conducting experimental studies on programmed instruction and on the use of computers in different branches of research. Beginning in 1964–65, university courses have been broadcast by the Radio University, sponsored jointly by the Swedish Broadcasting Corporation, Stockholm University, and certain popular education bodies. Formally enrolled students are able to complete course requirements in their university programs through this medium. A committee for Education Television and Radio (TRU), established by government decree in 1967, has been investigating the use of these media in education and in 1968–69 produced over 750 experimental television and radio programs.

Increasing coordination in the use of teaching facilities and staff by more than one faculty within a given university or between neighboring university institutions is permitting more efficient utilization of total resources. The Chancellor of the Universities encourages such coordination.

THE BALANCE SHEET The principal strengths of Swedish higher education include the readiness with which reform is undertaken, the consensual process involved in decision making, the relatively high degree of student freedom and of student influence on higher education policy determination, the broad system of student financial aid freed from parental means tests, the large share of research carried on in university institutions, and the success of the country in rapidly extending access to postsecondary education to an increasing proportion of the age group with relatively little friction or strain.

The problems and difficulties confronting higher education in Sweden are largely a result of the rapid expansion in enrollments. They relate to the pressure of student numbers on educational resources and measures taken or contemplated to meet this pressure. Sweden seems to be moving to some extent toward a two-tier university system under which research and teaching are divorced both in the new branch universities, because they are mainly teaching rather than research and teaching institutions, and in the university institutions themselves, because of the large and increasing share of undergraduate teaching carried out by staff whose teaching loads or other involvements leave little time for research or who are relatively inexperienced.

The new principle of *successive choice* to be introduced in the philosophical faculties is expected to shorten study time and hence to maximize educational resources. However, this reform will at the same time restrict the traditional flexibility and breadth of education offered by these faculties. Another difficulty, also related to the need to maximize resources, may be an increasing unwieldiness in university administration resulting from the high degree of centralization in the Office of the Chancellor of the Swedish Universities. The problem is one of balancing the need for common standards and efficient administration and planning with the opportunity for local initiative and diversity among institutions. A final difficulty is the inherent conflict in basing planning on both social and economic demand because of the possible incompatibility between the two approaches. With refinements in forecasting methodology and a strengthening of the nascent counseling and guidance system, Swedish higher education may eventually reconcile these two approaches, encouraging students to concentrate in fields where manpower forecasts show a future need.

University-level Institutions
of Higher Education in Sweden, 1967

UNIVERSITIES

UNIVERSITIES	FACULTY
University of Uppsala Branch: Örebro	Theology, law, medicine, liberal arts, natural sciences (including some technical training), social sciences, pharmacy, economics
University of Lund Branch: Växjö	Theology, law, medicine, dentistry, liberal arts, natural sciences, social sciences (including economics), technology
University of Stockholm Branch: Linköping	Law, liberal arts, natural sciences, social sciences, economics
University of Gothenburg Branch: Karlstad	Medicine, dentistry, liberal arts, natural sciences, social sciences
University of Umeå	Medicine, dentistry, arts and science (including economics); the arts and science faculty is not yet fully organized

SPECIALIZED UNIVERSITIES

Stockholm

Stockholm	Faculty
Royal Caroline Medico-Surgical Institute	Medicine, dentistry
Institute of Technology	Technology*
Stockholm School of Economics	Economics and business administration
Royal Veterinary College	Veterinary medicine
Royal College of Forestry	Forestry
Stockholm Institute of Gymnastics and Sports	Physical training
Stockholm School of Social Work and Public Administration	Social work and public administration
Stockholm School of Education	Teacher training
Stockholm School of Journalism	Journalism

Göteborg

Chalmers Institute of Technology	Technology†
Göteborg School of Economics	Economics and business administration

Göteborg School of Social Work and Public Administration	Social work and public administration
Göteborg School of Education	Teacher training
Göteborg School of Journalism	Journalism

Uppsala

Royal Agricultural College, Ultuna	Agriculture
Uppsala School of Education	Teacher training

Lund

Lund School of Social Work and Public Administration	Social work and public administration

Umeå

Umeå School of Social Work and Public Administration	Social work and public administration

Örebro

Örebro Institute of Gymnastics and Sports	Physical training
Örebro School of Social Work and Public Administration	Social work and public administration

*Divided into nine sections: technical physics, mechanical engineering, aeronautics and shipbuilding, electrotechnics, civil engineering, chemistry, mining and metallurgy, architecture, land surveying.

†Divided into seven sections: technical physics, mechanical engineering, shipbuilding, electrotechnics, civil engineering, chemistry, architecture.

References

Burke, P. E.: "Still Socially Lopsided," *The Times Educational Supplement,* no. 2827, July 25, 1969, p. 12.

National Central Bureau of Statistics: *Forecasting Information,* no. 1, Stockholm, April 10, 1968*a*.

National Central Bureau of Statistics: *SOS Hogre Studier,* Stockholm, 1967*a*.

National Central Bureau of Statistics: *Statistical Abstract of Sweden,* Stockholm, 1967*b*.

National Central Bureau of Statistics: *Statistical Reports 1968,* Stockholm, February 13, 1968*b*.

National Central Bureau of Statistics: *Högre Studier,* Stockholm, 1964.

National Central Bureau of Statistics: *Högre Studier,* Stockholm, 1959.

OECD: *Educational Policy and Planning, Sweden,* UNESCO, Paris, 1967.

Office of the Chancellor of the Swedish Universities: *Universitetspedagogiska Utredningen (UPU) II, Studieresultat för en Inskrivningsargang vid Universitet och Högskolor,* Stockholm, 1966.

Robbins Committee: *Higher Education: Report of the Committee Appointed by the Prime Minister under the Chairmanship of Lord Robbins, 1961–63,* Cmnd. 2154, HMSO, London, 1963, appendix V.

Sweden, Ministry of Education: *Hogre Utbildning och Forskning i Sverige,* Stockholm, 1967.

Swedish Institute: *State Study Assistance in Sweden,* Stockholm, 1966.

UNESCO: *World Survey of Education,* vols. I–IV, Paris, 1955, 1958, 1961, 1966.

9. Higher Education in Japan

Before World War II, higher education in Japan was offered in a variety of institutions—technical schools, normal schools, colleges, and, at the apex of the system, 45 universities. Of the universities, nine Imperial universities were preeminent. They were patterned after nineteenth-century German models and emphasized research and specialization.

COMPONENTS Reforms introduced by the United States Occupation government attempted to transform Japan's elitist system of higher education into one more akin to the American. Professional training, teacher education, and general education were combined in single institutions, and the universities' functions were broadened to include civic and humanistic education for an enlarging proportion of the nation's young people. A large number of *old-system* institutions of higher learning were converted by the Occupation into four-year *new-system* universities, which were often combinations of prewar universities and various nonuniversity institutions of higher education. Although the Occupation may have catalyzed the postwar reforms, much of the impetus for them came from local communities and from the nonuniversity institutions. Excluding old-system institutions, converted or otherwise eliminated by the mid-1950s, the number of higher educational institutions increased from 350 in 1950 (Japan, Ministry of Education, 1965*b*) to 822 in 1968; the number of universities increased from 201 to 377; junior colleges increased from 149 to 468; and higher technical schools, first set up in 1962, increased to 60. In addition, there were 17 institutes for training teachers for special and industrial arts schools.

Universities Japanese universities are of four kinds: national (*kan,* or state), prefectural and municipal (both *ko,* or public), and private (*shi*).

In 1968, 75 universities were national, 35 were public, and 267 were private.[1] The number of private higher education institutions has increased fourfold since 1950.

Most universities have two or more faculties, although quite a few are single-faculty institutions, specializing for example in medicine, teacher training, liberal arts, dentistry, or pharmacy. Some of the universities have affiliated elementary and secondary schools and junior colleges. In 1966, 50 national, 18 public, and 81 private universities (a total of 149) had graduate schools. Sixteen years earlier, there were only four graduate schools (Shimbori, 1967, vol. II, p. 26). About one-third of all universities are concentrated in the Tokyo area. The prefecture and municipal universities are easier to enter and have more limited staff, facilities, and curricula than national ones. As a result, they have less prestige.

Although post-World War II reforms sought to establish a homogeneous network of universities, including at least one national university for each of the 46 prefectures, the pre-Occupation hierarchy of institutions has persisted. Highest in prestige are the seven former Imperial universities, especially Tokyo University, some of the national universities, and several of the long-established private universities, including Waseda, Chuo, Keio, and Doshisha. Today nearly all the private universities suffer because of inadequately trained staffs, overcrowded facilities, insufficient funds, and low academic standards. Universities and faculties of universities that developed out of prewar normal schools, terminal technical schools, and various specialized colleges are less esteemed than those which had university status before the postwar reforms. In fact, there is some concern that all postwar universities may have lower standards than they did before the war, partly because although the normal university study period was increased from 3 to 4 years, preuniversity education was reduced from the 14 years required for admission to the old-system universities to 12 years for new-system institutions. The number of years of education required for a university first degree has been reduced from 17 to 16 years. Prewar universities are generally considered comparable to the graduate schools of new-system universities.

A new feature of postwar universities was the introduction of general education requirements for the first two years of the undergraduate courses. This was a reaction to what the First United

[1]Information from the Ministry of Education.

States Education Mission to Japan considered to be an excessively narrow specialization in prewar universities. The mission failed to take into account the fact that students admitted to old-system universities had completed three years of general education and liberal arts studies in preparatory schools where they normally enrolled after eleven years of elementary and middle school. Postwar legislation instituted a system — which, with modifications, persists — of required credits and courses distributed among major fields of knowledge. Because courses are mostly for only 2 to 4 units each and students are required to obtain about 36 or more units in general education, in the view of many Japanese educators the general education requirement "is only an accumulation of fragmentary knowledge," is not effective in character building, and "is mostly a repetition of high school education" (Japan, Ministry of Education, 1965*b*, p. 34). The general education program is not considered effective in preparing students for subsequent specialized and professional training either and, as a matter of fact, limits the time available for specialization. Because many students are not challenged by general education studies, they become bored or develop negative attitudes and often turn to student protest movements for stimulation and a sense of purpose.

At many universities, general education is given by former higher and university preparatory schools which became part of the new system universities but often do not share the same site; hence general education tends to be physically segregated from upper-division programs. The staff teaching it are often separate from the upper-division staff. At the University of Tokyo, students admitted to the general education faculty are not automatically admitted to an upper-division professional faculty. Under the process of selection used by the university, most students go on to professional faculties but others complete their first-degree work in the general education faculty. (These are sometimes better-qualified students.)

Before postwar reforms, elementary school teacher training was given in professional normal schools. The reforms converted many of these institutions into teacher training universities or into faculties of universities which combine liberal arts with teacher training. However, faculties of education at major universities are not primarily teacher training units but instead give courses mainly in the behavioral sciences, with some teaching of educational administration. The prefectural universities provide most of the training for elementary school teachers. Secondary school teachers qualify for their professions by obtaining a university degree in their field of specialization. In the early 1960s, as a temporary measure, nine institutes to train secondary school teachers of industrial arts were attached to the engineering faculties of nine universities. Eight institutes trained teachers for other special schools. The training of kindergarten teachers and teachers of nursing is provided mainly by the junior colleges.

Junior Colleges   Junior colleges did not exist in Japan before World War II. In 1947, the government authorized the establishment of junior colleges on a temporary basis. This category of two- or three-year higher education institutions could accommodate many old-system universities and other units (mainly schools that lacked the necessary facilities to gain recognition as four-year institutions) which remained outside the network of the new system universities. Supporting the establishment of junior colleges were a number of industrialists who wanted to include in the new higher education system industrial training schools similar to the specialized technical institutes that existed before postwar reforms. Some 148 junior colleges were granted interim approval. Fearful that the junior colleges might be absorbed by the new higher technical schools launched in 1961, their advocates finally mustered enough support to secure official legal recognition for them through the revision, in 1964, of the School Education Law.

According to the revised law, junior colleges have the purpose of "providing general and professional education for secondary school graduates and developing their intellectual and practical abilities required for their future career and practical life." In 1968, about 90 percent of junior college students were enrolled in the private colleges, and 402 out of a total of 468 junior colleges were private. National and public junior colleges numbered 23 and 43, respectively. About half of the junior colleges are affiliated with secondary schools, and one-fourth are independent. Twenty-three national junior colleges, scarcely 5 percent of the junior colleges in 1968, are affiliated with national universities and constitute their evening faculties in semiprofessional subjects.

Junior colleges are organized in departments rather than faculties. Departments with the largest enrollments are home economics, nursing, and literature. The programs of junior colleges are mainly terminal and, as of several years ago, only 8.4 percent of graduates transferred to universities (usually private) (Vroman, 1966, p. 62).

One of the main functions of the junior colleges, especially those in the private sector, is to offer opportunities for postsecondary education to young women. Since 1950, according to the Minister of Education, the proportion of women in the total enrollments has gone up from 40 percent to 82 percent. In the private junior colleges it is close to 85 percent. Well over half of the junior colleges are for women only. At the national junior colleges, where men constitute nearly 90 percent of the student body, and at the public colleges, where they constitute about 30 percent, the largest enrollments are in fields such as science, agriculture, engineering, and commerce.

Higher Technical Schools
As a result of an increasing demand for technicians, legislation was adopted in 1961 to establish a new type of higher education institution, the higher technical school. From 19, in 1962, they increased to 60 in 1968. The higher technical schools are only partially higher education institutions because they offer three years of upper secondary and two years of postsecondary education in a unified curriculum combining general education and technical studies. They are thus similar to the prewar five-year technical colleges. Their establishment has been given strong support by the national government, and in 1968, 49 of the higher technical schools were national. The others were private and public. The possibility of extending the curriculum of the schools into non-technical fields was under study in 1968.

Evening and Correspondence Courses
Correspondence and evening courses offered by Japanese universities and colleges are almost entirely for degree programs. Cultural enrichment, vocational and professional updating, and general education are not their objectives. The chief aim is to give working youth who cannot attend universities by day an opportunity to obtain a university education. University correspondence courses were first introduced in 1950, but evening programs existed before World War II.

In 1966, 57 universities (43 private) had evening divisions and 9 (all private) had correspondence divisions. Close to 100 junior colleges also offer evening or correspondence study or both. Evening and correspondence courses are virtually identical to daytime degree courses. In principle, they require the same study period as full-time day programs. In 1966, out of a total enrollment of 1,239, 293 students in universities and junior colleges, 154,784 were in evening programs; about 135,500 of these were in private institutions (Government of Japan, 1968, pp. 54–55).

Students in correspondence programs pursue courses combining correspondence work and radio and television sessions and are required to spend about a month each year in classes on the campus of their university. About one-fourth of their total credits must be obtained through on-campus study. In 1966 correspondence enrollment included 80,826 correspondence students at nine universities and 11,448 correspondence students at five junior colleges. This was a substantial increase over 1962, when these enrollments were 50,575 and 5,540, respectively (Japan, Ministry of Education, 1967, 70 and 1965a, p. 52).

Postsecondary Education outside the Formal System

An unusual feature of Japanese postsecondary education is the large number of institutions outside the public system of accredited colleges and universities which provide intensive training courses to senior students and graduates of secondary schools. Their objective is to prepare students, especially the *ronin* (unsuccessful applicants to universities, named after the wandering masterless *samurai* of the Tokugawa period), to pass the admission examinations of colleges and universities. As the students in these preparatory schools, known as *yobiko,* are mostly high school graduates, the schools are essentially postsecondary. At the same time, they are secondary in level in that they enroll some high school students and supplement the training given in the recognized high schools. The preparatory schools fill an important role because the entrance examinations of universities and colleges often have little connection with secondary school curricula. However, the programs of these schools are designed mainly to cram facts into students and drill them on likely entrance examination questions rather than to prepare them for independent study or encourage their critical abilities. These institutions are financed by student fees, and are staffed by full-time former secondary school teachers and part-time secondary school teachers and university professors. In 1960, 264 private preparatory schools enrolled about 83,000 students.

FUNCTIONS

The extent to which Japanese higher education serves the usual functions of providing trained manpower and advanced research for the nation or serving as a resource for change, cultural advancement, international service, or continuing education is restricted

by several conditions. Among these are the enormous competition
to enter universities for reasons having to do more with social status
than with professional aptitudes and interests; the fact that the
majority of students are in the private institutions which, for financial reasons, concentrate on humanities and social science rather
than science and technology; the relative emphasis placed on higher
education per se and on graduation from the higher-prestige institutions rather than on the particular courses of study pursued
(Okochi, 1968);[2] the difficulty in introducing new subjects because
of the structural rigidities in the universities; the tradition that the
aim of postgraduate study is to produce academics rather than the
highly trained manpower needed in nonacademic fields; and the
lack of facilities at most of the universities for advanced scientific
research. Despite these conditions, the functions of the universities
are changing. In particular, the growing demand for persons with
advanced training in middle-level occupations is bringing a new
flexibility to higher education and is influencing public attitudes
toward it.

The tradition that the national universities, especially Tokyo
University, trained for top positions in government and that the
leading private institutions concentrated more on training people
for the liberal professions and the private sector persists. Today
many graduates from the national universities find positions in
the bureaucracy and in government research institutes while the
private institutions train large numbers of students in the humanities, social sciences, and education.

University education in Japan trains persons for careers from
which they are extremely unlikely to move during their professional
life. This situation exists not so much because of the specialization
in higher education as because of the tradition that a successful
person stays with the firm or agency with which he first works
throughout his working life, and, in fact, "employers want those
who have no previous experience in working" (Japan, Ministry of
Education, 1965*b,* p. 50). Connections and relationships formed
through his professional affiliation, the clique, or *batsu,* surround

[2]Because of the "permanent advantages" university graduates have over high
school graduates, "almost everyone tries to go to university, and rather than
take up employment on completing either middle or high school, they will enter
any university at all, with no special preference as to a course of study, but regarding it only as a stepping stone to a good job." See Okochi, 1968.

and support the individual and are the object of his loyalty for life.[3] And job immobility is reinforced by the dependence of the employee on his employer for social security. The firm or agency with which the graduate gets his first job is determined to a large extent by the prestige of the higher education institution from which he graduates. Competition is keen for elite positions in government, such as in the diplomatic service, and for positions with the leading industrial firms. During their senior year at a university, students take numerous examinations, applying for jobs and lowering their career aspirations with each successive failure. Students who specialize in science, technology, law, and political science are in greater demand than those in humanities, education, and domestic science.

Universities have responsibility for the general education necessary to citizenship, the specialized education necessary to the professions, the advanced vocational training necessary to intermediate positions in the society, and training in the arts. The postwar higher education system has found it difficult to fulfill all these functions adequately, particularly because the concept of the university as an institution only for the elite is far from dead.

The Central Council for Education has expressed the view that higher education institutions should be differentiated and specialized, with some concentrating on research and postgraduate study, others on training for the professions, still others—the higher technical schools and to a lesser degree the junior colleges—on specialized vocational training, and a final group on training for the arts. This position appears to be prompted by the need for the universities to give a more specialized preparation to students, especially in the sciences and technology. This might be done by lengthening first-degree courses, shortening the general education study period, or expanding graduate study.

Adult Education

That universities should provide continuing or adult education (whether cultural or vocational) that does not lead to a degree is still an alien concept in Japan. About 150 universities and colleges

---

[3] See Herbert Passin, *Society and Education in Japan,* Teachers College Press, Columbia University, New York, 1965, pp. 125ff. However, the traditional distaste for job changing may be giving way to the more existential values of the new generation. A recent survey cited a job turnover rate of 30 percent per year for men workers under twenty years. (*The New York Times,* December 1, 1968).

provide school extension courses, which are held primarily in the evening or during weekends and summer vacation. But most of the evening and correspondence courses of the universities and colleges involve the same academic programs as those taken by regular daytime degree students and hence cannot be considered adult education. Most adult vocational and technical training is given by business enterprises.

International Programs
The universities participate in international programs by training students from abroad and through international exchanges of researchers, especially with the United States. However, because of language difficulties and other factors, these programs are small-scale. The number of overseas students at Japanese institutions of higher education increased from about 3,800 in 1954 to about 9,300 in 1966; this excludes large numbers of foreign students, especially Koreans and Chinese, who are resident in Japan and enroll in the Japanese universities. Japanese students in foreign institutions totaled about 1,500 in 1966. A number of foreign students in Japan (about 100 in 1961) are supported by scholarships of the Japanese government. Despite the language problem, foreign students from other countries, particularly Southeast Asia, are increasingly interested in enrolling at Japanese universities. One Japanese university, International Christian University, deliberately enrolls large numbers of overseas students, who make up about 10 percent of its total enrollment. Several universities have special Japanese programs for foreign students.

Each year a number of scholars from Japanese universities study (and some teach) abroad. The purpose is to widen the research experience of the Japanese researchers and to extend Japan's participation in the international exchange of scientific information. The Ministry of Education supports those from the national universities. In 1967 there were 359 of them. Of these, 195 went to the United States. Study abroad for researchers from the private universities is supported by the Foundation for In-service Training and Welfare of the Private School Personnel Association, set up in 1953 for the mutual aid of teaching personnel of private institutions. In 1967 this foundation sponsored study abroad for 119 researchers, of whom 18 went to the United States, from private universities.

A government program established in 1965 sends teams of volunteers aged 20 to 35 (two years of university study are required) to African and Asian countries to participate in social and economic development projects in medicine, farming, fishing, education, and other fields.

Research The major responsibility for basic research in Japan rests with the universities, while applied research is carried out mainly by industry. Industry has also become more active in basic research in recent years. About two-thirds of all university research is conducted at the national universities, where it tends to be a function of research institutes. There are about a dozen joint research centers which serve several universities in research fields of national importance involving expensive equipment and scarce resources. In 1964, the total of 117,600 researchers included 59,000 in private industry, 19,500 with research organizations, and 39,100 in the universities. Of the ¥381.7 billion expended on research that year, ¥243.8 billion was spent by private industry, ¥60.6 billion by research institutes, and ¥77.3 billion by universities. The share of total expenditures used for university research declined from 29 percent in 1953 to 19 percent in 1963 (OECD, 1967, pp. 182, 184). In 1966 of a total expenditure of ¥577.6 billion on research, some 50 percent was spent by private industry (Fourth United States–Japan Conference on Cultural and Educational Exchange, 1968*a*).

Scientific research in the universities is limited by various factors. Only about 5 percent of the universities' research funds is from government contracts; only about 1 percent comes from contracts with industry. There are virtually no funds available to the private universities for research. In 1968, for the first time, staff members in private universities received some government funds for their research. Capital expenditures per researcher in the universities is only two-fifths of that in private industry.

The isolation of university research institutes from faculties and departments limits the role of research in regular teaching programs. There is little formal cooperation between researchers in the research institutes of government, universities, and private industry, although it exists informally and is increasing.

Because academic research is not held in high regard, it has not received generous support from the national legislature. The five-year goal urged by the Council for Science and Technology, an advisory body to the prime minister, of raising the share of the national income spent on science support from 1.7 percent in 1967 to 2.5 percent has not been accepted. Also not accepted was the Council's 1960 proposal of a fundamental law for science and technology which would constitute a bill of rights for researchers and would improve their status.

There are signs, however, that greater public support for academic research may be available in the future. One of the dramatic new efforts is the establishment of a government-planned academic city, Tsukuba, some 37 miles northeast of Tokyo. In 10 years, Tsukuba is supposed to have a population of 160,000 and to bring 36 government research institutes and universities together into a new science-centered city. Construction started in 1965, but by early 1969 progress was still very slow. Like university teachers and students, staff members of research institutes are loath to move out of Tokyo and accept lower incomes and less satisfactory facilities elsewhere. Other developments which may strengthen university research include the increasing proportion of university graduates who enroll in postgraduate studies, a greater emphasis on technology with the establishment of the higher schools of technology, the growing demands from industry to increase the proportion of university students enrolled in science and technology, and the increasing interest on the part of education authorities in expanding university research and in encouraging more cooperative research between universities and between them and the research institutes of government and industry. Current studies by the Central Council for Education have, as a major concern, science education and research in the universities. They may produce new plans and generate more public support. But major increases in funds for university research and radical changes in attitudes toward postgraduate study are needed to make any significant progress possible.

ENROLLMENT TRENDS   Japan has mass higher education. Total enrollments increased from 402,234 in 1950 to 1,539,250 in 1968.[4] The proportion of the age group (mainly 18-year-olds) entering institutions of higher education increased from about 10 percent in 1955 to close to 20 percent in 1968 (25 percent of males and 11 percent of females). The proportion of 18- to 22-year-olds enrolled went up from 4.1 percent in 1950 to 14.6 percent in 1965. Major factors in the increase are the expansion in the 18- to 22-year-old age group and the growth of the proportion of them who enroll in and complete upper secondary

[4] This figure includes total enrollments in universities, junior colleges, and special teacher training institutes but only students in the two postsecondary years of higher technical schools.

school studies (from about one-fourth in 1951 to close to three-fourths in 1967). Enrollments in upper schools went up from 2.7 million in 1956 to 4.9 million in 1967 (Fourth United States–Japan Conference on Cultural and Educational Exchange, 1968b). Thus, even though the proportion of upper secondary school graduates going on to full-time higher education institutions has remained at around 25 percent since 1950, in absolute numbers they have increased dramatically, from about 172,000 in 1951 to about 367,000 in 1967. The proportion of the age group graduating from upper secondary school and going on to higher education is expected to increase by as much as 10 percent by the mid-1970s (Okochi, 1968).

The 1965 white paper of the Japanese Ministry of Education estimated that new high school graduates applying for entrance to university would go up from 295,000 in 1963 to 508,000 in 1968 and then decline because of a drop in the 18- to 22-year-old age group. Whereas the 15- to 19-year-old age group in 1966 was 11.4 million, 10- to 14-year olds totaled only 8.7 million. In 1968 the government predicted that because of the declining birth rate the 15- to 19-year age group would decline to 9.09 million in 1970 and 7.78 million in 1975 (Japan, Bureau of Statistics, 1967; *The New York Times,* November 10, 1968).

TABLE 32 *Enrollment in Japan's institutions of higher education by year*

	1955-56	1960-61	1965-66	1968-69
Universities				
Total enrollment	523,355[a]	626,421[a]	937,556[b]	1,270,189[c]
Postgraduate enrollment	10,174[a]	15,734[a]	28,000[d]	37,661[c]
Junior colleges				
Total enrollment	77,885[a]	83,457[a]	147,563[b]	255,262[c]
Postgraduate enrollment	31,117[a]	32,893[a]	55,728[c]	
Higher technical schools (in last two years of matriculation only)			2,000*[b]	12,486*[c]
Special teacher training institutions				838[c]
Technical teacher training institutions				475[c]
Total enrollment in higher education	593,384[a]	709,878[e]	1,087,119[e]	1,539,250[e]

*Estimated.
SOURCES: (a) Japan, Ministry of Education, 1965b. Old-system universities included 3,059 students in university preparatory schools in 1950 and 659 in 1955. (b) Japan, Ministry of Education, *Education in Japan,* Annual Report of the Ministry of Education for the Year Ending March 31, 1966, Tokyo, 1967. (c) Information supplied by the Ministry of Education. (d) Shimbori, 1967. (e) Information supplied by the Ministry of Education; includes top two classes only of higher technical schools.

TABLE 33
Number of new entrants to universities and junior colleges in Japan by year

	1955-56	1960-61	1965-66	1968-69
Universities	174,000[a]	205,000[b]	254,524[c]	331,503[a]
Junior colleges	37,544[d]	42,318[d]	80,563[c]	127,365[d]

SOURCES: (a) Japan, Ministry of Education, 1965b. Old-system universities included 3,059 students in university preparatory schools in 1950 and 659 in 1955. (b) Japan, Ministry of Education, 1965a. (c) Japan, Ministry of Education, *Education in Japan*, Annual Report of the Ministry of Education for the Year Ending March 31, 1966, Tokyo, 1967. (d) Information supplied by the Ministry of Education.

Although the number of higher education institutions has more than doubled since World War II, applicants for admission have substantially exceeded entrance quotas. The difference between the number of applicants and spaces available increased from about 150,000 in 1960 to an estimated 270,000 in 1966. The number of applicants went up from about 360,000 to 617,000 in this period and, in 1968, was expected to be close to 800,000 (Japan, Ministry of Education, 1965a). The Ministry of Education reports that the proportion of new high school graduates applying to university and junior colleges who were admitted declined from 82.3 and 95 percent, respectively, in 1960 to 71.8 and 87.8 percent in 1966.

The large excess of applicants over available places is mainly caused by the fact that candidates may take entrance examinations as often as they wish. Some of the candidates repeat these examinations for several years, attending cram schools in between. In the early 1960s, these repeaters, or *ronin,* constituted about two-fifths of the annual applicants. Their number increased from 117,000 in 1960 to an estimated 136,000 in 1966 (Japan, Ministry of Education, 1965a, p. 144). In 1967, out of a total of about 729,000 applicants, 174,000 were *ronin.* The rate of increase of *ronin* is now approaching a plateau, because the size of the secondary school age group has decreased, but competition for admission has not appreciably lessened.

Competition for admission is greatest at the longer-established and higher-prestige universities, which may have 10 to 20 times

TABLE 34
New entrants to institutions of higher education in Japan, by year

	1955-56	1960-61	1965-66	1968-69
Number	181,265[a]	277,301[a]	337,087[b]	465,778[c]
As percentage of 19-year-olds	9.49[c]	10.35[c]	18.7[a]	

SOURCES: (a) Japan, Ministry of Education, 1965a. (b) Information supplied by the Ministry of Education; includes top two classes only of higher technical schools. (c) Information supplied by the Ministry of Education.

as many applicants as places. In some of these universities, *ronin* constitute more than 70 percent of the freshmen. The crux of the problem lies in the tradition that "social position and salary are linked to one's educational career" (Japan, Ministry of Education, 1965*b*, p. 119) and graduation from the prestige universities virtually guarantees entry into the higher levels of government, business, or finance.

Each university and junior college gives its own admissions examinations, prepared and administered within the framework of regulations laid down by the University Entrance Examination Council, a body organized by the Ministry of Education in 1953. Some private universities and junior colleges admit students who graduate from their own high schools without examination, thus putting a premium on admission to these high schools. To make admissions requirements more objective and to lessen the emphasis on cramming for examinations, efforts were made in the early 1950s to introduce aptitude tests. Neither the institutions nor the students were satisfied with the results, and these tests were abandoned in 1955. In 1963 the Educational Test Research Institute (ETRI) was established by the Ministry of Education to improve the entrance examination system and to devise and administer scholastic achievement and aptitude tests. However, while some institutions use the test results in selection of students, they are only one of various criteria used and so far have had little impact on the system as a whole. In fact, they have been strongly resisted by students, their parents, and the universities. The importance of fees from entrance examinations as a significant source of revenue to the universities, particularly for the private institutions, makes it extremely difficult to effect fundamental changes in the admissions system.

Another problem is that of multiple applications. In 1968 there were 1,902,221 applications for 331,503 first-year places at universities, 21,950 for 10,975 postgraduate places, 260,630 for 127,365 places at junior colleges, and 35,754 for 9,363 places at higher technical schools. The ratio of applications per university entrant increased from 2.4 in 1950 to 5.9 in 1967. For the junior colleges this ratio went up from 1.4 in 1950 to 2.2.[5]

Because examinations take several days, it is small wonder that the formidable pressure on applicants (and their anxious families)

[5] Information supplied by the Ministry of Education.

is commonly referred to as "examination hell" (*shiken jikoku*). The examinations are the culmination of many arduous years of study, and it is common practice for parents to arrange for their children to have supplementary tutoring during their school career in order to enhance their chances of scoring well. A major cause for this practice is the lack of close contact between secondary schools and higher education institutions with respect to entrance examinations. The examinations often include questions on subjects that are not covered in secondary school curricula.

Of university students enrolled in 1968, 82 percent were men. In the junior colleges, 82 percent of students were women. Higher technical schools had only 610 women (1.6 percent of their enrollment) in 1968. About 75 percent of all students are in private institutions of higher education. About one-half of all students are in the Tokyo area. And the proportion of postgraduate students out of total enrollments, although it has substantially expanded in the postwar period, remains extremely low—scarcely 3 percent in 1968. Postgraduate study has not been easily accepted, in large part because it is still regarded as being useful mainly for training future university faculty and there is little incentive for persons seeking careers in other fields to pursue postgraduate courses. Doctorates were not awarded by new-system universities until 1958.

Study Period Since the postwar reforms the normal study period for a bachelor's degree from a university is four years. An additional two years is commonly required for the master's, and another three or more years are needed to obtain the doctorate. First degrees in medicine and dentistry require six years; the doctorate in medicine, a postgraduate degree, requires four more years. Junior college curricula vary from two to three years.

Student Persistence Some 85 to 90 percent of university and junior college students complete their first-degree work in minimum time. In 1968 the percentage of university undergraduates enrolled for a fifth year and of junior college students enrolled for a third year was less than 2 percent of total enrollments. Of students entering university in April 1961 and junior college in April 1963 the proportions successfully completing their course of study were 90.4 and 90.7 percent, respectively (Japan, Ministry of Education, 1967, p. 73). The success rate of students enrolled in the evening and correspondence programs of universities and junior colleges is appreciably lower because of the difficulty in completing the work in the same period as daytime students. Only about one-half of the students in correspondence programs complete their studies in the normal period (Japan, Ministry of Education, 1965*b*, p. 52).

Different sources give different figures for staff-student ratios at the universities. According to information supplied by the Ministry of Education, the ratio changed from 1:15.4 in 1964 to 1:17.7 in 1968. For purposes of this calculation, staff included presidents and assistants but excluded part-time staff. According to *Educational Standards in Japan,* the 1964 ratio was 1:21.8, the same as the ratio in 1951. The ratio in junior colleges in 1968 was 1:17.2, down from 1:15.4 in 1964. These ratios must be interpreted cautiously because many full-time teaching staff members teach in more than one institution. In addition to full-time staff members there are a number of part-time staff members; in May 1966, they constituted about one-fifth of the total staff at national and public universities and close to one-half of the staff at the private universities. At the junior colleges, part-time staff outnumber those who are full-time.

The ratios in private institutions are higher than those in the national and public ones. For example, in 1963 the ratios in national and public universities were 1:7.21 and 1:6.55, respectively, while in the private universities the ratio was 1:27.7 (Japan, Ministry of Education, 1965*b*, p. 25). As stated in a publication of the OECD (1967), "In 1963, national universities with 52 percent of the teachers in higher education, had only 23 percent of the students." For public and private universities the corresponding figures were 10 and 38 percent of the teachers and 4 and 73 percent of the students, respectively. Teaching loads of staff members at the private universities (16 hours weekly) are also much higher than at the national universities (typically 8 to 10 hours a week). Inferences regarding staff-student relationships must also take into account the fact that many staff members at the national universities are primarily or entirely engaged in research while few staff members at the private institutions find it possible to pursue research. Furthermore the great majority of teaching staff members, even at the higher-paying national universities, engage in "moonlighting," holding another job outside their home institution, and thus limiting their time available to it. Finally, in keeping with Japanese tradition, there is almost no horizontal mobility of teaching staff among universities.

The most important relations between higher education institutions and governments are with the national government. The interest of the United States after World War II in decentralizing higher education through the provision of a major university of comparable status in each of the 46 prefectures was not feasible in the absence of strong prefectural governments. More successful were the Occupation reforms to diminish the extensive prewar powers of the national government with respect to private as well as public higher education. And the Fundamental Law of Education and the School Education Law of 1947 set forth basic principles for higher (and other) education that concerned equal educational opportunities, respect for human rights, and academic freedom.

The extent of government supervision and influence varies according to whether institutions are national, prefectural, municipal, or private. Ministry of Education approval is required for the establishment and dissolution of all new institutions and of their branches and campuses. In practice, on the establishment of new institutions the Ministry follows the recommendations of an advisory body, the University Chartering Council, whose members include government, university, and lay persons appointed by the Ministry. Almost one-half of these members are recommended by the University Accreditation Association, a voluntary organization of the institutions which sets standards for accreditation but has little authority to enforce them. All universities are, in principle, bound by standards laid down by the Ministry on such matters as the content and duration of professional training in different fields of graduate studies and the awarding of degrees. At the national universities, over which the Ministry of Education has more direct control because it finances them, the government influences enrollments by providing funds for a specific number of students and by prescribing ratios between graduate and undergraduate students.

National universities, junior colleges, and higher technical schools are administered directly by the Minister of Education. It approves appointments of presidents, deans, and teaching staff— all of whom are national civil servants. The Ministry sets conditions for staff qualifications, approves promotions, determines salary levels, and in general handles major issues of personnel administration. In practice, the recommendations of various university bodies on appointments and promotions are normally followed by the Ministry. For the national institutions, the Ministry can also determine staff-student ratios, the establishment of new faculties, departments and research units, the level of student fees, and budgets. To establish new courses, the national universities must get prior approval from the Ministries of Education and Finance. Meeting this requirement may take as long as five years and causes rigidity in institutional administration and in curricular programs. Also, at each national university the *jimukyokucho,* a major administrative official in charge of business, financial, and, to some extent, student affairs, is a Ministry of Education appointee. Although he serves under the president of the university, he is at the same time responsible to the Ministry. He holds office for three to five years and sometimes even longer. The position resembles that of curator in some of the German universities that were models for the Imperial universities.

— Prefectural and municipal universities are administered under the jurisdiction of the prefectural governors and mayors of municipalities and their associated local bodies, which, while bound by national standards for higher education, determine the financing, staffing, academic and other policies of these universities. Staff members at the prefectural and municipal universities are prefectural or municipal civil servants. Although it appears on the surface that the universities, especially in the national and public sectors, have little autonomy, in practice they have had great independence. They are very sensitive about their autonomy, and a crucial issue in 1969 was whether the national government, in the interest of minimizing the crisis caused by increasing student disruption, might at least exercise its formal authority over these universities. The national government alleged that the universities had already lost their autonomy in bowing to the pressure of student violence. The universities, of course, disagreed.

Since 1918, the private universities formally have had only limited autonomy. The powers of the national government include approval of the establishment of new universities, branches, and campuses; authority to reprimand the private universities for "suspension of normal classes, deficiency of buildings or equipment, excess enrollment and other hindrances to education," (Japan, Ministry of Education, 1965*b,* p. 79); and the right to dissolve them in cases of violation of the law. Added to these powers are the existence of standards set by the national government and the obligation of private universities receiving subsidies from the national government to submit financial reports on the use of those funds. The Private School Law of 1949 requires, however, that on important issues, the government consult the Private University Council, an advisory body mainly made up of representatives from the private establishments, before interfering with these establishments.

On balance, the government's formal authority over private institutions is substantial. As the Ministry of Education White Paper of 1964 (1965*a*) put it, "private schools are, in many respects, under public control." However, to a greater extent than with the national universities, the actual control by government over private universities is minimal in day-to-day affairs. For example, they enroll many students in excess of their quotas in order to maximize their income. While the prestige of the national universities ensures a high degree of autonomy to them, the fact that government contributes so little to the financing of the private institutions (less than 2 percent of their income) even though they enroll three-quarters of all students, restricts the leverage of the national government in directing their affairs. As with the national universities, in 1969 the continued autonomy of the private universities was an issue because with both it was a major obstacle to urgently needed reform. And this autonomy, taken together with the decentralization of authority within the universities, effectively hampers efforts both by government and the institutions themselves to institute major internal changes.

In carrying out its responsibilities in higher education the Ministry of Education is advised by various bodies in addition to those already mentioned. Foremost among them is the Central Council for Education, a body of 20 members appointed by the Minister with cabinet approval. This council studies and advises on matters referred to it by the Ministry and, in effect, formulates national policy on higher education. In 1967 it launched a major three-year study on the educational development of Japan in the last 100 years, especially since World War II. The object was to make proposals on the future demand for education, including higher education, the appropriate distribution of costs of financing it, and major reforms needed in its long-range development.

Another body advisory to the Ministry of Education on matters relating to higher education is the Science Encouragement Council. Its recommendations deal with the support of research, science information, and materials. The Science Council of Japan, an organ of the Office of the Prime Minister, also advises with respect to science in the universities: the encouragement of science, the training and status of researchers, the administration of the national universities, and related subjects. From time to time the Ministry of Education appoints special committees to study particular problems in higher education. For example, in 1968, one such committee was engaged in a study of the financing of private universities.

Since the mid-1950s, the national government has appeared more inclined to attempt to influence university affairs. The power of the Ministry of Education to set standards for all higher education, its direct responsibility for the prestigious national universities, and its role in supporting university research give the Ministry substantial authority over the universities. The growing recognition of the importance to national development of increasing the universities' output of scientists and technologists is creating further pressure for enlarging the role of the national government. So too is the perilous financial situation of the private universities and the escalating expenditures of all higher education institutions. Still another factor likely to bring an expansion of government influence in higher education is the mounting disruption not only to the universities but also to the national order caused by increasing student activism.

In 1969 relations between government and the universities seemed on the verge of major change. For the first time in history the government intervened in what is traditionally regarded as the internal jurisdiction of universities by ordering the cancellation of entrance examinations at the prestigious University of Tokyo, a measure which met with strong but futile protest from university authorities. The government also set up several new bodies to study and recommend on university reform. These include the Education Reform Council, attached to the Prime Minister's Office, and the Education Research Committee, attached to the Secretariat of the Cabinet. Eventual recommendations of these various bodies promise to bring drastic change into the universities and in their relationship to government.

INTERNAL GOVERNMENT OF UNIVERSITIES The main agencies of governance in the national universities are the presidents, boards of councillors, councils, deans of faculties, and faculty conferences.

The presidents normally serve for a four-year term and may be reelected once. They are nominated by the councils or faculty councils and are appointed by the Ministry of Education. The

Ministry has never vetoed a nomination. In 1969, however, the Ministry of Education vetoed the election of a professor as Acting President at Kyushu University by failing to act on his nomination. The professor had publicly stated that the "police are our enemy." The faculty eventually withdrew the nomination. The presidents are responsible for the administration of all university affairs, preside over the boards of councillors, and are required to consult it on all important matters. The top executive officials assisting a president are appointed by him from among full professors and hold office only during his tenure. There is virtually no semipermanent high-level administrative staff. In practice, much of the administrative work of the universities is handled by faculties, and the presidents' authority is very much restricted. They cannot veto faculty recommendations on staff appointments and have no formal power to determine major policies. Presidents function mainly on the basis of "democratic leadership," and implement decisions reached jointly by the faculties.

The boards of councillors are made up of the presidents and their chief executive officials, deans and several full professors from each faculty, and directors of the large research institutes. The boards of councillors enact university regulations, recommend on the creation and dissolution of faculties and departments, co-ordinate faculties and institutes, set forth personnel standards, and are concerned with staff discipline and the size of the student bodies. The boards also recommend and pass on the university budgets.

Membership on the council includes the board of councillors, the university librarians, and the heads of the university hospitals. The functions of the councils are to set standards for the selection of presidents, librarians, and directors of research institutes, to determine the term of office of presidents and deans, to consider the discipline of the presidents, and to nominate the presidents. Despite the extensive functions of the boards of councillors and councils, they exercise little important decision-making authority on universitywide affairs. Faculty deans and other officials cannot be committed to decisions without the full support of all the full professors in their faculties or institutes. They have virtually no independent authority.

Faculty domination of university affairs is modeled on the nineteenth-century German university, which had the faculty as its principal unit. Faculties in Japanese universities are headed by deans, elected usually for two-year terms by and from full professors in each faculty, approved by their president, and appointed by the Minister of Education.

Each faculty has a faculty conference made up of full professors and in some cases associate professors and possibly other staff members as well. The faculty conferences often consult all teaching staff before making recommendations on important matters. Students are not represented in faculty conferences but often are consulted informally on matters relating to student affairs. Faculty conferences recommend on the creation and elimination of departments and chairs and on courses of instruction. They are also concerned with the admission and graduation of students enrolled in the faculty. The faculty conferences make recommendations for the selection of staff to the faculty which are submitted to their respective presidents before going to the Ministry for final action. The Ministry rarely fails to concur in the recommendation of a faculty conference. In universities having only one faculty, the faculty conferences function as boards of councillors. Because of the autonomy and power of the full professors, faculty conferences seldom function through subcommittees, and their operations are therefore time-consuming and cumbersome.

Teaching and research staff members in the more prestigious Japanese universities are usually attached to chairs, and funds are allocated on the basis of chairs. In higher education faculties which developed out of the old-system higher schools or colleges *(semmongakko)* and in faculties which prepare students for an occupation (teaching, for instance), the chair system is modified, but professors have less authority and smaller financial awards than in faculties adhering to the traditional chair system. Appointments to chairs are held until the incumbents resign, die, or retire, thus blocking opportunities for subordinate staff members to advance. Consequently, the chair system determines, in large measure, the staffing of universities, what subjects are taught, and the fields in which research is pursued. Titular professors holding chairs are assisted by and direct all other staff associated with the chair. The most junior staff members, known as assistants, function more as personal aides to their full professor than as independent teachers. There are no graduate student teaching assistants in Japanese universities. The system is rigid, hierarchical, and self-perpetuating, and the entrenched power of the senior professors tends to obstruct the introduction of new subjects in the curriculum and the organization of interdisciplinary teaching and research. Postgraduate studies and research are also affected because students must be accepted by a titular professor to pursue their postgraduate work in a particular field and their thesis research must fit into the research conducted by the chair.

Public and private universities are organized along much the same lines as the national universities except that, with respect to the public universities, prefectural and municipal authorities make final appointments and pass on major decisions. At the private universities the pertinent authorities are the juridical bodies or boards of trustees. In some universities, trustees are selected from within the university community. The efforts of Occupation authorities to provide for a majority of lay members on directing boards was not successful, and similar efforts to provide an equal representation of lay and official members on the Private University Council resulted in only one-third lay membership. There is a concern that lay participation in university governance might result in political control, lower academic standards, and less academic freedom.

Students rarely participate in university decision making, but, increasingly, they are demanding participation. At some private universities they participate indirectly or in the preliminary stages in the selection of presidents. Some important breakthroughs have occurred, however. Students now vote for deans in several facilities of Nagoya University, Hokkaido University, and Osaka University of Medicine. A significantly enlarged role for students seems likely before the crisis in the Japanese universities ends. A subcommittee of the Central Council for Education, in its interim report of March 1969, recommended against student participation in "organs which are *de facto* final decision-making organs of universities," and while supporting student participation in decisions on such matters as extracurricular activities and health and welfare services, urged against their participation in decisions on staff appointments, finance, and "the rating of academic achievement."

FINANCING HIGHER EDUCATION Annual expenditures on higher education increased nearly fifteenfold, from about ¥20 billion to ¥290 billion between 1950 and 1965. This enormous increase resulted from the tripling of enrollments, the need to reconstruct and expand facilities destroyed or extensively damaged during World War II, the multiplication of institutions, and rising costs per student. According to the

Ministry of Education, the average recurrent expenditure per student in all higher education went up from ¥61,978 in 1950 to ¥142,959 in 1965. Total expenditures per student rose from ¥91,193 to ¥261,298. Per capita income in this period increased from ¥73,970 to ¥255,068. The proportion of the gross national product devoted to higher education increased from 0.39 percent in 1950 to 0.7 percent in 1960 to 1.1 percent in 1964,[6] a remarkably low percentage considering the proportion of the age group enrolled.

The most critical problem in the financing of higher education in Japan is the inadequate resources of the private institutions. In 1965 they received only 49.7 percent of total funds expended on higher education although they enrolled some three-fourths of the students; national universities received 44.6 percent, public, 5.7 percent. Much of the difficulty of the private institutions stems from their dependence on student entrance-examination, admission, and tuition fees—the source of 45 percent of their income in 1965 (and in 1966) and of only 2.2 percent of the income of the public and national institutions in that year. Student fees at the national universities are uniform throughout the country. They are relatively low at both the national and public institutions. In 1968–69, undergraduate examination and admission fees were ¥3,000 and ¥4,000, respectively, at the national universities, and annual undergraduate and graduate tuition fees were ¥12,000 and ¥18,000 (about $33.50 and $50.00) respectively. By contrast, fees vary considerably among the private institutions and, on the average, are about five times higher. At some private institutions they are as much as 10 or even 20 times higher than at the national universities. The private universities have been reluctant to raise their fees despite their urgent need for more income lest an increase provoke student disturbances.

In 1965, 80.9 percent of the income of the national institutions came from the national government. By contrast, only 1.6 percent of the income of private universities came from the government in 1966 and 1.7 percent in 1967. The private institutions do not receive funds for recurrent expenditures from government. One

---

[6] Information supplied by the Ministry of Education and the *United Nations Yearbook of National Account Statistics.* The 1960 figure was cited in UNESCO, *World Survey of Education,* vol. IV, Paris, 1966, p. 69.

reason is the fear that this practice might cause the government to exercise supervision of their operations, e.g., in the setting of fees and staff salaries, enforcing enrollment quotas, and determining the size of teaching staffs. The private institutions receive loans and subsidies from the national government for buildings and science equipment. However, because Article 89 of the Constitution prohibits the appropriation of public funds for educational operations not under public control, public funds are usually channeled to the universities and colleges indirectly through the Private School Promotion Association. This body, established in 1952, is under government jurisdiction, is funded by government, and is authorized to make loans to the private institutions. The Constitution is not violated because the Public School Law of 1949 authorized government authorities to advise private institutions on budgeting matters and to obtain financial information from them, thus establishing at least a degree of public control. However, because the government does not participate in decisions of the Private School Promotion Association on loans to the private institutions, their independence is, in principle, preserved.

The other sources of income of the private universities and colleges in 1965 were: gifts (6.8 percent), interest from assets (6.1 percent), profits from moneymaking enterprises (11.6 percent), and borrowing (28.8 percent) (Fourth United States–Japan Conference on Cultural and Educational Interchange, 1968*a*). In 1966 income from endowments made up only 1 percent of the income of private universities. Because their costs have risen and their income from fees, gifts and other sources has not kept pace, private institutions have had to borrow increasing amounts. Borrowing nearly doubled between 1960 and 1965. The mounting costs of debt service is a growing burden, coming to about 18 percent of the total expenditures of the private universities in 1964–65 (Government of Japan, 1968, pp. 88–89). The financial plight of the private institutions is reflected in their overcrowded facilities, high staff-student ratios, preponderance of enrollments in the humanities and

TABLE 35 **Total** **expenditures** **on higher** **education in** **Japan (in** **millions of yen)**	*1950*	*1955*	*1960*	*1965*
At current prices	19,813.794	51,604.448	97,873.224	289,342.0
At 1965 prices	36,061.0	69,666.0	122,342.0	289,340.0

SOURCES: Information supplied by the Ministry of Education.

TABLE 36
Expenditures
on higher
education in
Japan by type
of institution*
(in millions
of yen)

	1950	1955	1960	1965
National universities		25,196.0[a]	41,518.0[a]	129,054.0[a]
Prefectural and municipal universities		4,396.0[a]	8,240.0[a]	16,465.0[a]
Private universities	5,149.0[b]	22,010.0[a]	48,054.0[a]	143,821.0[a]
All universities	23,223.7[c]	49,101.6[c]	91.432.8[c]	
Junior colleges	569.0[c]	2,734.6[c]	5,096.9[c]	

*Since data were taken from different sources, total expenditures do not fully correlate with figures for expenditures in the different subcategories.

SOURCES: (*a*) Fourth United States–Japan Conference on Cultural and Educational Interchange, 1968*a*. (*b*) Japan, Ministry of Education, 1965*b*. (*c*) Japan, Ministry of Education, 1965*a*.

social sciences relative to science and technology,[7] and low income expenditure per student relative to the national and public universities. In 1962, the average recurrent expenditure per student in private institutions was ¥77,384 while in the national institutions it was ¥277,707 (Japan, Ministry of Education, 1965*b*, p. 89).

Recommendations made in late 1968 by a special committee appointed by the government to study the financial problems of private higher education institutions called for a major increase in state aid to private institutions and offer the most effective means for helping these institutions. The rising cost of debt service limits the usefulness of loans as a solution. Student fees have already tripled since the mid-1950s, and further increases are likely to provoke more student revolts. Substantially increased revenue from beneficiaries is unlikely without liberalization of legislation affecting tax deductions for philanthropic purposes, and the moneymaking

TABLE 37 *Total recurrent and capital expenditures on higher education in Japan (in millions of yen)*

	1950	1955	1960	1962	1964
Recurrent expenditures	19,446.0[a]	38,012.0[a]	64,434.0[a]	99,572.0[a]	190,931.0[b]
Capital expenditures	2,949.0[a]	4,926.0[a]	17,185.0[a]	30,597.0[a]	74,695.0[b]

SOURCES: (*a*) Japan, Ministry of Education, 1965*b*. (*b*) Japan, Ministry of Education, *Education in Japan,* Annual Report of the Ministry of Education for the Year Ending March 31, 1966, Tokyo, 1967.

[7] In 1965, 60 percent of all students in the private institutions were in humanities and social sciences and only 23 percent were in science and technology. In the national and public institutions combined, the corresponding figures were 48 and 29 percent, respectively.

enterprises of the private institutions show little prospect of expansion. Increased government support, especially by means of expanded government funding of the research expenses of teaching staff and increased student aid, appears essential in the 1970s to avoid further deterioration of standards in the private universities and eventually to avert their becoming bankrupt.

HIGHER EDUCATION PLANNING AND ECONOMIC DEVELOPMENT Planning related to higher education and overall national development is undertaken by the Ministry of Education and bodies affiliated with it; the Economic Planning Agency; and the Council for Science and Technology. Among these, the Ministry of Education has a major role because of its authority with respect to the expansion of enrollments and the establishment and expansion of faculties and departments.

Since 1954, the ministry has prepared periodic projections of the future production of graduates from secondary schools and institutions of higher education and of manpower needs for persons trained in various fields. The most recent projections were made in 1963 and 1968. According to the 1963 projections, without an expansion of higher education capacity there would be an overall shortage of 350,000 graduates from higher education institutions for the period 1963–1970 (Japan, Ministry of Education, 1965*b*, p. 183). However, if the institutions expanded to meet projected enrollment increases based on student demand, there would, in 1970, be an excess of about 290,000 higher education graduates in law, literature, and economics, about 32,000 in education, about 28,000 in agriculture and about 63,000 in homemaking and related fields. There would be a shortage of 167,070 in engineering, of 3,860 in natural science, and of about 51,120 in medical science and pharmaceutics (Fourth United States–Japan Conference and Educational Interchange, 1968*a*). These anticipated shortages have been the basis for steps taken by the Ministry of Education to increase enrollments in science and engineering in the universities including postgraduate studies and to establish the higher technical schools. In determining the higher education policy in relation to national development, the Ministry is assisted by its Central Council for Education. Since July 1967 this body has been engaged in studies of the future social demands for higher education and the kinds of education appropriate to persons of different ages and aptitudes.

The Economic Planning Agency (EPA), one of a small number of organs in the Office of the Prime Minister, periodically prepares long-range economic plans which set forth recommended guidelines on future developments and indicate probable trends. In response to the EPA's Economic Plan of 1957, the Ministry of Education expanded enrollments in science and engineering by 8,000 students in the period 1957-1960. In response to the EPA's Plan of 1960, the Double-income Plan, which called for doubling the national income by 1970, increasing expenditure on research to 2 percent of the national income, and expanding the output of persons trained in science and technology, the Ministry of Education established a plan to enroll an additional 20,000 students in science and technology, agriculture, and pharmacy in the period 1961-1964. This goal was exceeded, and an additional 23,990 students enrolled in these fields in 1964–1967. The EPA's Medium-term Economic Plan for 1964-68 placed greater emphasis on the role of research and education in national development than previous plans, urging further expansion in the number of scientists and engineers trained, expansion of university-affiliated national research establishments, and more cooperative research between universities and the private sector research institutes. Although the plans prepared by the EPA are more in the nature of recommendations than a blueprint for action, they have had an important influence on higher education expansion.

Since 1960, long-range planning in the development of science and technology, including university research, has been a function of the Council for Science and Technology, an advisory body in the Office of the Prime Minister. Like the EPA, it predicts further developments and makes recommendations. In its first report, published in 1960, the council set forth a number of objectives for national science policy. In the higher education sector it urged that the status of university teachers and researchers be improved and that the universities' output of scientists and engineers be increased. The council's recommendations on national investment in research have been used by the EPA in preparing long-range economic plans. In 1966, the Council for Science and Technology submitted a new five-year plan, which, among other things, proposed an expansion in the number of academic fields in which public funds support research and an increase of 2.5 percent by 1970 of the share of the national income devoted to research. Although the goals of the 1966 five-year plan were not fully accepted by the government, they represent general aims for the distant future.

In the last decade, the government has become increasingly concerned with the relationship between higher education, research, and national development; it now gathers statistics and other information relevant to the long-range planning of higher education and the economy. However, Japan does not claim to have a comprehensive planning system under which the functioning and development of the universities and colleges are directed by estimates of future needs for research and trained manpower.

Apart from the difficulties of forecasting manpower needs, a national plan making future manpower needs the chief determinant in higher education development seems improbable. Among the various obstacles are the autonomy of the universities in directing their own affairs, the prospect of increased student disturbance as a reaction to making higher education more overtly an instrument of government policy, the high cost of enrolling a substantially greater proportion of students in the more expensive fields of priority interest to the economy, and the basic principle that access to higher education is determined by the interests and abilities of young people rather than national need.

STUDENT FINANCES The vast majority of students in the universities and colleges rely on their families and their own earnings to meet their higher education costs. The situation is most difficult for students in private institutions. Whereas the share of total higher education costs borne by parents is less than 10 percent in the national universities, in the private universities in 1965 it was more than 40 percent. In 1967 about 222,000 students, 15 percent of the enrollment in higher education, received government supported financial assistance (*Report of the Japan Scholarship Foundation,* 1968, p. 7). Between 1955 and 1967, the proportion aided declined and the absolute number aided increased by almost one-half. There was a marked increase in aid to graduate students in this period.

About four-fifths of all financial aid to college and university students is provided by the Japan Scholarship Foundation, which was set up in 1943 as a public corporation aided by the Ministry of Education. Aid is given on the basis of economic need and the student's ability and consists of interest-free loans repayable on completion of studies in annual installments over a 20-year period. There are two categories of loans: special loan scholarships of some ¥8,000 per month given to students of outstanding ability who cannot otherwise attend university and ordinary loan scholarships which provide a monthly stipend of ¥3,000 to undergraduates, ¥13,000 to master's degree candidates, and ¥18,000 to doctoral candidates. Students in correspondence programs may receive scholarship loans of ¥13,000 to help meet the costs of their required on-campus studies. Since tuition fees for correspondence courses are relatively low, financial assistance is not provided to pay for them. Graduates who teach in elementary, secondary schools, and certain other educational institutions for a specified period after graduation may be exempt from repayment of loans. Beginning in 1967, some students in private institutions (about 4,600, or less than one-tenth of scholarship recipients in these institutions) received loans 50 percent larger than those of other recipients because of the much greater cost of enrolling in the private universities and colleges.

Apart from the Japan Scholarship Foundation, financial assistance, largely through loans, is provided by about a thousand private and public organizations. In 1960 it was estimated that these organizations offered scholarships to about 73,000 students and bursarships to about 9,900 (Hidaka, 1965, p. 202). Some of these recipients were in secondary rather than higher education. In 1968 about one-fifth of all financial aid available to students came from private and public organizations other than the Japan Scholarship Foundation.

Even students receiving financial assistance find difficulty in paying the costs of their higher education. In 1966, the average annual expense for tuition, fees, books, and other educational items was ¥43,492 for students enrolled in national universities and ¥100,352 for those at private universities. The average living expenses were ¥70,414 for students living at home, ¥122,566 for students living in dormitories, and ¥164,328 for students in lodgings (Japan, Ministry of Education, 1965a, p. 105). In early 1969, the average undergraduate student living away from home required about ¥20,000 to ¥25,000 monthly, several times the loan stipend received by the minority of students qualifying for aid, for his living expenses. Under the circumstances, it is not surprising that an estimated 50 percent of the income of undergraduates comes from their families (some of whom devote as much as one-half of their income to supporting their children at university) and that nearly all students supplement their income with outside work, referred to as *arubaito,* chiefly the tutoring of high school students. At the graduate level some three-tenths of master's degree candidates and two-fifths of doctoral students work in order to meet their educational and living expenses (Shimbori, 1967, p. 72).

The loan basis of student aid in Japan does not give the lowest income groups an equal opportunity to attend higher education institutions. In the early 1960s the proportion of upper secondary students from families with an income of under ¥180,000 who enrolled in higher education institutions was only 4.2 percent whereas for all upper secondary students the rate was about 16 percent. For students from families with an annual income of over ¥900,000 the rate was 26.6 percent (Hidaka, 1965, pp. 261–263). Toward the end of the last decade about 70 percent of university students were from upper- and middle-income groups, and only about one-fourth were from lower-income groups. The rising cost of higher education in the 1960s has further decreased the representation of the less affluent sector of society in higher education. During the 1950s the failure of many students to repay loans granted to them by the Japan Scholarship Foundation threatened to undermine the revolving-fund character of this financial aid system. In 1960 the proportion of students failing to repay loans was about 46 percent. Since then, the repayment rate has shot up, and in 1967 it was about 90 percent. The main reasons for the higher repayment rate are intensified moral pressure applied to graduates, a simplification in repayment procedures, and more frequent resort to legal action against delinquents. Repayment of loans increased from ¥4.61 million in 1958 to ¥33.2 million in 1967. In 1968 loans repaid covered 20 percent of student loans made by the Foundation in that year (*Report of the Japan Scholarship Foundation 1968–69,* 1968, pp. 4, 11).

STUDENTS   In 1968–69, student disputes were either disrupting or had paralyzed close to 50 universities and colleges. In October 1968 Japan's leading university, Tokyo University, became completely inoperative as a result of student disruption, and its president resigned. The unprecedented action of the government in intervening in university affairs by postponing for one year the entrance examinations to the University of Tokyo prevented it from enrolling new first-year students in 1969 and exacerbated the long-standing problem of having too many university applicants for the available places. Three thousand students, five times the number arrested in 1967–68, were arrested in the first ten months of 1968. Student violence reached such a point by 1969 that the governing Liberal Democratic

Party was said to be considering invoking against student organizations the Subversive Activities Prevention Law of 1952. This law has been invoked rarely—but notably in the Shinjuku incident in 1968, when students disrupted train service in an effort to halt shipment of jet fuel to the U.S. Air Force. It empowers the government to dissolve organizations advocating violence and subversion. The government was concerned that the universities were not disciplining students, and in 1968-69 the educational affairs council of the Liberal Democratic Party, prompted in large part by persistent campus disputes, conducted a major review of the universities and colleges.

Since the end of the Occupation, Japanese university and college students have been increasingly activist. In 1948 the student governments of 260 universities and colleges, representing 300,000 students, about two-thirds of the total higher education enrollment at the time, jointly established the Zengakuren, or National Federation of Students' Self-governing Associations (Zen Nihon Gakusei Jichikai no Rengo). In 1968 it was said to have the nominal support of close to half a million students. Since its establishment, the Zengakuren has alternated between campus and off-campus issues. The mainstream group (now Minsei) has emphasized issues focusing on student concerns such as tuition. The antimainstream group concentrated on political issues of national and international scope, broadening and blowing up purely local university disputes into massive demonstrations, strikes, and boycotts. Student agitation was particularly widespread and violent in 1960 in opposition to the United States–Japan Mutual Security Treaty. It forced the resignation of the Premier and the cancellation of the planned visit of the President of the United States to Japan. Persistent targets of student demonstrations have been the presence of United States bases in Japan; the continuing occupation of Okinawa and the other Ryukyu Islands by the United States; the Vietnam war; measures regarded as leading to a return to prewar authoritarianism, militarism, or imperialism; threats to academic freedom; increases in university fees; and, most recently, the lack of student participation in university administration and management. Opposition to United States foreign policy is a factor in many demonstrations.

Almost since its inception, Zengakuren has been composed of different ideological factions, some allied to political parties.[8] In-

[8] See Usami Sho, "Zengakuren," *Japan Quarterly,* vol. XVI, no. 2, April–June 1968, for a full discussion and chart of the genealogy of the Zengakuren and its factions.

ternally, the organization has been rent by dissension on whether its basic objectives should relate to the campus or to the national political situation. Support for the latter has usually prevailed. The Zengakuren actually consists of three separate organizations. The Zengakuren of the Japanese Communist party, known as the Minsei (Japanese Democratic Youth League), which follows non-violent strategy, is said to be supported by the majority of students, and concerns itself primarily with the internal problems of higher education institutions. The Sampa Zengakuren, or Three-faction League, composed of three anarchistlike or leftist (new left) factions which broke away from the Communist Party and often clash violently between themselves, has been responsible for much of the student violence in recent years. It has the support of a large number of students and is the group usually meant in references to Zengakuren. The Kakumaru of Revolutionary Marxist Zengakuren, the third Zengakuren branch, pursues militant strategy and has been in conflict with the Sampa Zengakuren. The main clashes between student groups, however, have been between Sampa and Minsei. Recently the Kakumaru has tended to join with the Sampa grouping.

The most radical organizations reject any possibility of negotiation with the authorities and oppose the present order but have no clear concept of what should replace it (or refuse to articulate it) and compete with each other for supporters by staging noisy and violent demonstrations. Although most students are not active members of the leftist group and the radicals constitute only a minority of all students, the radicals are able to mobilize up to 50 percent of all students for their demonstrations. In early 1969, many educationists feared that the ostensibly more moderate Minsei might attempt to take over the universities in 1970 on the grounds that this faction is better organized than the Sampa and has evinced more willingness to negotiate with university authorities, for example at the University of Tokyo, than the more radical-seeming groups.

Numerous factors are cited as among the causes of student unrest in Japan. Some of these have little to do with universities: a deep malaise and sense of the dehumanization of life, the rigidities of Japanese society, and the deep division in Japanese politics, particularly on Japan's relations with the United States. After finally succeeding in gaining admission to universities, students are freed from an enormous pressure and often are neither challenged nor absorbed by their initial two years of general education at university. In fact, a majority of participants in demonstrations are lower-division students. The availability of time, and relaxation from the fiercely competitive admissions situation, turns them to other pursuits. The fact that they are not subject to compulsory military service gives them a freedom not found in most other developed countries. The paucity of extracurricular activities; the inadequacy of guidance and counseling which might give students a greater sense of purpose in their academic work; uncertainty about their future and concern for the future direction of the country; and the influence of the Marxist outlook of many of the teaching staff members in universities — these are contributing factors. The concentration of half of the total student population in and around Tokyo facilitates student interchange, makes possible the rapid mobilization of large numbers of students for demonstrations, and reinforces student discontent.

With the massification of higher education, particularly at the private institutions, students are increasingly resentful of university conditions: overcrowded facilities; insufficient and often inadequately qualified staff; lack of student housing for all but a fraction of students; rising fees and limited public funding for the private institutions which many students interpret as evidence of an antidemocratic policy on the part of the government, limiting the opportunity for higher education to the affluent; and the lack of student participation in almost all phases of university governance. One further factor is that students have a sense of mission to play the part of revolutionaries. This is influenced by the long tradition of student activism in Japan and exacerbated, perhaps, by the many problems arising out of Japan's rapid economic growth, such as the sudden expansion of cities, imbalance in income distribution, and the like. Students feel that the country is neither looking for a change nor to students as agents of change.[9]

Contrary to some predictions, 1968-69 saw no appreciable decline in demonstrations. However, numbers of parents of students, concerned that disruption of the universities would prevent their children from graduating and securing good jobs, began organizing protests. Employers also were beginning to apply more pressure to end student disruption, in some instances indicating they would

---

[9] For a recent analysis of the Japanese student movement see Michiya Shimbori, "The Sociology of a Student Movement: A Japanese Case Study," *Daedalus*, vol. 97, no. 1, Winter, 1968.

not hire students who had participated in disturbances even though the students had passed the necessary employment examinations. Pressure from the government was also apparent in its refusal to provide to at least one private university, Nihon, subsidies due under university assistance legislation. The reason: Nihon was closed. Disruption was climaxed by the closing of Tokyo University and the Tokyo School of Education; at these institutions no students were to be graduated in 1969 and no new students admitted in the spring of that year. All examinations were canceled in December 1968. A growing source of anxiety was the prospect for greatly intensified student disruption in 1970, when the United States-Japan Mutual Security Treaty would be subject to review and could be revoked by either party on one year's notice.

In August 1969 during an unprecedented extension of the regular session of the Diet, the government obtained approval of a bill to enable it to cope with student disputes. It strengthened the powers of the Minister of Education to intervene in both private and public universities involved in prolonged student disputes. The Bill for Temporary Measures Concerning University Administration[10] authorized the Minister of Education to designate a university as "a university in conflict" if it was unable to resolve a student disorder one month after its eruption. The action can be taken only at the request of the institution and after consultation with a "university normalization committee," a neutral advisory organ to the Ministry. If this action is taken, a temporary executive committee is assigned the powers normally resting with the board of trustees and faculties. If, after six months, the committee is still unable to resolve the conflict, the Minister can order the institution closed. If the conflict is still not settled after one year, the Ministry can abolish particular faculties or the entire institution.

The new legislation met with widespread opposition from students and university staff because it transferred sweeping powers of control to the government without touching the causes of student dissent. However, the new legislation was resorted to within one month of its adoption by universities having serious student disruption. Between August 17, when it was promulgated, and the end of 1969 officials at 41 universities where student difficulties had

---

[10] Law no. 70, August 7, 1969; the writer is indebted to Ray A. Moore, Amherst College, for his translation of the law.

impeded normal functioning sought police assistance. In December 1969 only 23 universities were disrupted by student disputes, down from 77 in October 1968. Although violence among student groups increased after adoption of the new law, in late 1969 it appeared that the new legislation would not after all provoke more student violence than it quelled.

THE BALANCE SHEET Current problems in Japanese higher education can be attributed to the enormous growth in enrollment and to its failure to keep pace with the increasing number of secondary school graduates seeking admission. Since World War II admission to the university has replaced admission to upper secondary school as a prime goal of young people. Concomitant problems include the emphasis on a university education per se rather than on education suited to the individual's aptitudes and interests; the consequent lack of coincidence between the student's choice of specialization and the demands of society; the financial burden on parents and the waste in time and money for society as a whole inherent in the common practice of having supplementary private tutoring for children during the school years and for the *ronin* after high school graduation; and discrimination against the poorer segments of society because of the inadequacy of financial aid for university students and the high cost of the supplementary study many students need to pass university entrance examinations.

Other current problems in higher education resulting from the enrollments expansion are the overcrowding of facilities; the paucity of personal and intellectual contact between students and teachers; the excessive teaching load required of staff; the oftentimes low quality of instruction; inadequacies in residential, counseling, and extracurricular facilities; the inflated enrollments in the less costly fields of humanities and social sciences, especially at the private institutions; and the fact that the majority of students who are enrolled in private institutions are required to pay about five times as much as the minority of students who gain admission to the higher-quality national and public institutions for an often inferior education. Still another problem is the fact that continuing education for professionals or for leadership elites has not so far become a significant function of the higher education system.

A more fundamental weakness in the university system, in the view of many critics, is confusion about the aims of university education. It is alleged that the standards of university education have declined since the prewar period, when universities concentrated on training for the professions and on research-oriented advanced studies, leaving general education, vocational training, and teacher education to other institutions. Now, as a result of postwar reforms, they are expected to handle all these tasks and are unable to do so adequately. On the practical basis, the lower-division general education program is frequently not related to subsequent upper-division specialized study and may leave insufficient time for it. Because only a fraction of university graduates continue into postgraduate study (and of these about 90 percent continue at the same university) (Shimbori, 1967, pp. 7–72) few ever remedy the alleged inadequacies of their undergraduate programs through further formal study. In sum, many people inside and outside the universities have yet to become reconciled to the basic concept of the new-system university, and hence its several functions have not been sufficiently integrated.

Another critical problem in Japanese higher education is the inadequate financial resources of the private institutions. The government's reluctance to provide public funds for them and the reluctance of private institutions to risk losing autonomy if they accept public funds force them to rely mainly on student fees, including fees for admission examinations. As long as this situation persists, there is little hope for reforming the fiercely competitive admissions system with its multiple applications, lack of interuniversity coordination, and persistent backlog of *ronin* attending cram schools to better their chances. Even with their fee income, the financial situation of the private institutions is precarious, and the low level of salaries of university staff generally and their failure to benefit from the postwar prosperity have tended to embitter many of them.

The lack of public financial support to institutions of higher education, reflected in the higher and rising fees of the private institutions, is not compensated for in publicly supported schemes of student financial aid. The inadequacy of present student aid provision would appear to be a weakness in the total picture of Japanese higher education. While the mutual support characteristic of extended family units in Japanese society makes it possible for many young people from the less affluent segments of society to attend university, it is nevertheless true that they are less represented in higher education institutions than the more affluent segments.

A final problem is the structural rigidity of higher education institutions. The weakness of central administrations, the dominance of chairs and faculties, the lack of interchange with industry and other segments of society or with each other stand in the way of reform, innovation, and responsiveness to changing national needs. They also make it difficult to institute effective measures for coping with student disturbances. The fact that 68 percent of all university staff members teach at the university from which they graduated (about 90 percent of staff at Tokyo and Kyoto Universities) and that there is virtually no faculty mobility between universities reinforces the rigidities and inbred character of the universities.

Japanese higher education also has important strengths. The proportion of the college-age group in full-time study at Japan's universities and colleges has risen significantly in the postwar period and, next to the United States, is the highest in the world. Once a restricted system primarily for the elite, higher education has become largely democratized. The better-quality institutions offer an education of the highest level. Although university research does not receive generous public support, it, too, is of the highest quality, especially in the basic research field. Another notable strength of Japanese higher education is the high success rate of students. However, this success rate is somewhat artificial because of a tradition that university students do not "flunk out." It therefore intensifies pressures for admission and is also a factor in student disturbances because the lack of pressure once in university permits students to engage in extracurricular pursuits including student demonstrations.

Perhaps the chief strength (which is also at times a weakness) of Japanese higher education has been the fact that it has been so highly regarded, though this is now changing. Professors used to be among the most highly respected members of society. A university education guarantees its recipient a good situation for life. Families of all socioeconomic levels dedicate a large share of their resources to enabling their children to attend university. And because of the vertical mobility in Japanese society, even in the absence of lateral mobility, the children of families of modest incomes have an opportunity to attend elite universities. In this sense, the democratization of access to higher education is probably surpassed by no other country. The common attitude toward education pertinent today was expressed by Yukichi Fukuzawa, a great educator at the beginning of the Meiji period, in his saying that "learning is capital for success in life."

A final significant strength of the higher education system, a development since World War II, is the liberalization of thought in the universities. "Moral guidance" in the sense of indoctrination in a particular set of values has been eliminated. In its place, there is complete freedom of expression and teaching, carried at some universities even to the point where students can study economics from an avowed Marxist professor or from a professor who supports traditional capitalist beliefs. The freedom to teach and to learn are practiced with few restrictions. This new development fits with and reinforces the antiauthoritarianism of Japanese youth today.

THE FUTURE Barring major domestic or international developments radically changing the circumstances affecting higher education, the 1970s may see significant modifications in Japan's higher education system. One possible change would elevate some or all of the old Imperial universities to the status of primarily graduate institutions. This would both help meet the rising demand for postgraduate education and preserve the values of the more established institutions in the face of massification and student radicalism.

Other changes in the allocation of functions among institutions are unlikely. Prefectural and local authorities have too strong an interest in maintaining their institutions as full-fledged universities and would resist measures to reconvert them to single-function institutions in the prewar tradition.

Support is also growing for reforms in the internal structure of the universities. Suggestions involve strengthening central administrations and reducing the power of faculties and chairs in order to facilitate curricular change, to permit firmer disciplinary measures against students, to allow wider participation in academic self-governance by subprofessorial teaching staff, and to achieve more effective university administration generally.

Because of the decline in the size of the relevant age group, no major expansion in universities and colleges seems likely between 1970 and 1975 unless, of course, there is a substantial rise in the proportion of the age group entering these institutions. For example, an increase from the 1967 entry rate of nearly 20 percent to a rate of 25 percent by 1975 would bring little net increase in enrollments. However, an increase of the proportion of the college-age group enrolled to one-third would result in enrollment increases in higher education, including the higher technical schools, from close to 1.5 million in 1967 to over 2 million in 1975.

The greatest increases in enrollment seem likely in the higher technical schools and in female and postgraduate enrollments. Since their establishment in 1962 the higher technical schools have grown rapidly. Government support for them, the interest of business and industry in recruiting young people who have had advanced technical training, the lower costs of the schools compared to universities, and lower fees (most of them are national) enhance the appeal of these schools.

The number of women enrolling in higher education has increased since World War II from less than one-tenth of total enrollments to close to one-fourth. Most of the increase has taken place at the junior colleges. In contrast to other developed countries, it does not seem likely that the increased enrollment of women in higher education institutions in Japan will appreciably change the structure and functions of these institutions. It is unusual for women to work in Japan after they are married, usually at age 24. Hence the higher education system is not as yet called upon to provide postsecondary training for women other than that which prepares them for their domestic roles or for short-term occupations in the mainly nonprofessional positions they hold before marriage.

Enrollment in postgraduate studies, which lagged in the 1950s, increased at an accelerating rate in the 1960s, and this trend seems certain to continue. The proportion of university graduates enrolling in postgraduate study is under 5 percent. In government and the private sector, the value of postgraduate study for large numbers of students, particularly in science and engineering, is gradually replacing the prewar view that postgraduate study is needed only for future academics. The more generous provision of financial assistance to postgraduate than undergraduate students is also encouraging postgraduate enrollments.

As enrollment increases begin to taper off, admissions competition should decline and an increased proportion of new high school graduates and *ronin* applicants be admitted to the universities. This development could have far-reaching repercussions, ranging from stimulating reforms in the admissions process, to cutting down on the income of the private universities from admission examination fees, to cutting down on the income earned by university students through tutoring *ronin* to prepare them for admission examinations and through grading admission examinations, to decreasing the number of *ronin* and thereby moving young people more rapidly to employment (a result which, in the face of increasing labor shortages, would be welcomed by industry). Such developments would reinforce the patent need to increase the funds available to private universities, the financial aid available to students, and the salaries of university teachers. It seems likely that all three needs will receive increased attention in the coming decade.

The year 1970 was regarded as a deadline for higher education reform because greatly intensified student violence was expected to accompany review of the United States–Japan Mutual Security Treaty. Irrespective of this event, the tensions and problems arising from the financial plight of the private universities, from the competitiveness of the admissions process, and from the impotence of the universities in the face of violent student protests are reaching a point where basic reforms are necessary and cannot long be postponed. Parents, employers, government, university administrators and teachers, and the majority of students appear increasingly impatient for reform so that the orderly process of higher education may be resumed. The current studies on higher education of the Liberal Democractic Party and the Central Council on Education may indicate the shape these reforms will take. Likely victims of these reforms are the authoritarianism, initiative, and cumbersome decision-making procedures of higher education institutions.

Japanese Colleges and Universities

Aichi Gakuin University

Aichi Institute of Technology

Aichi Prefectural Women's College

Aichi University

Aichi University of Liberal Arts

Akita College of Economics

Akita University

Aoyama Gakuin University

Ashiya College

Asia College

Azabu Veterinary College

Baika Women's College

Beppu University

Bukkyo College

Bunka Women's College

Chiba Commercial College

Chiba Engineering College

Chiba University

Chubu Institute of Technology

Chukyo University

Chukyo Women's College

Chuo University

Daido Technical College

Daiichi College of Pharmacy

Dairy Agriculture, College of

Daito Bunka University

Doho College

Dokkyo University

Doshisha University

Doshisha Women's College

Ehime University

Eichi College

Electrocommunications, University of

Elisabeth University of Music

Fine Arts, Women's College of

Fuji Women's College

Fukui University

Fukuoka Dempa Gakuen Institute of Technology

Fukuoka University

Fukuoka University of Liberal Arts

Fukuoka Women's University

Fukushima Prefectural Medical College

Fukushima University

Gakushuin University

Gifu College of Pharmacy

Gifu University

Gumma University

Hanazono College

Himeji Institute of Technology

Hirosaki University

Hiroshima Commercial College

Hiroshima Institute of Technology

Hiroshima Jogakuin College

Hiroshima University

Hitotsubashi University

Hokkai Gakuen College

Hokkaido University

Hokkaido University of Liberal Arts

Hokusei Gakuen College

Hosei University

Hoshi Pharmaceutical College

Hyogo University of Agriculture

Ibaraki University

International Christian University

Iwate Medical College

Iwate University

Japan College of Social Work

Japan Lutheran Theological College

Japan Women's University

Jikei University of Medicine

Jissen Women's College

Juntendo University

Kagawa Nutrition College

Kagawa University

Kagoshima College of Economics

Kagoshima University

Kanagawa Dental College

Kanagawa University

Kanazawa College of Fine and Industrial Arts

Kanazawa University

Kansei Medical School

Kansei University

Kanto Gakuin University

Keihin Women's College

Keio University

Kinjo Gakuin University

Kinki University

Kitakyushu University

Kitasato University

Kobe Commercial College

Kobe (Jogakuin) College

Kobe Municipal College of Foreign Studies

Kobe University

Kobe University of Mercantile Marine

Kobe Women's College of Pharmacy

Kochi University

Kochi Women's University

Kogakuin University

Kogakukan College

Koka Women's College

Kokugakuin University

Kokushikan University

Komazawa University

Konan University

Konan Women's College

Koyasan College

Kumamoto Commercial College

Kumamoto University

Kumamoto Women's College

Kunatachi Music College

Kurume University

Kansei Gakuin University

Kyoritsu College of Pharmacy

Kyoritsu Women's University

Kyoto City College of Fine Arts

Kyoto College of Pharmacy

Kyoto Prefectural University

Kyoto Prefectural University of Medicine

Kyoto University

Kyoto University of Foreign Studies

Kyoto University of Industrial Arts and Textile Fibers

Kyoto University of Liberal Arts

Kyoto Women's University

Kyushu Dental College

Kyushu Institute of Technology

Kyushu University

Kyushu University of Industry

Kyushu Women's College

Matsuyama Commercial University

Meiji Gakuin University

Meiji Pharmaceutical College

Meiji University

Meijo University

Meisei University

Mie Prefectural University

Mie University

Mishima Gakuen Women's College

Miyagi Gakuin Women's College

Miyazaki University

Mukogawa Women's University

Muroran University of Technology

Musashi Institute of Technology

Musashi University

Musashino Art University

Musashino College of Music

Nagasaki University

Nagoya Commercial University

Nagoya Gakuin College

Nagoya Institute of Technology

Nagoya Municipal University

Nagoya University

Nagoya Women's College

Naniwa College of Arts

Nanzan University

Nara Gakugei University

Nara Prefectural Medical College

Nara Women's University

Nihon College of Physical Education

Nihon College of Social Welfare

Nihon University

Niigata University

Nippon Dental College

Nippon Medical College

Nippon Veterinary and Zootechnical College

Nishogakusha College

North Japan College

Notre Dame Seishin University

Notre Dame Women's College

Obihiro College of Stock-raising

Ochanomizu University

Oita University

Okayama College of Science

Okayama University

Osaka City University

Osaka College of Commerce

Osaka College of Economics

Osaka College of Music

Osaka College of Pharmacy

Osaka Dental College

Osaka Electrical Engineering College

Osaka Gakuin College

Osaka Institute of Technology

Osaka Medical College

Osaka Prefecture, University of

Osaka Shoin Women's College

Osaka University

Osaka University of Foreign Studies

Osaka University of the Liberal Arts and Education

Osaka Women's College

Otani College

Otaru Commercial College

Otsuma Woman's College

Reitaku College

Rikkyo University

Rissho University

Ritsumeikan University

Ryukoku University

Saga University

Sagami Institute of Technology

Sagami Women's College

Saitama University

Sapporo Medical College

Seijo University

Seikei University

Seinan Gakuin University

Seisen Women's College

Seiwa Women's College

Senshu University

Shibaura Institute of Technology

Shiga University

Shikoku Christian College

Shimane Agricultural College

Shimane University

Shimonoseki City College

Shinshu University

Shizuoka University

Showa Pharmaceutical College

Showa University

Showa Women's University

Shuchiin College

Soai Women's College

Sophia University

St. Andrew's University

St. Luke's College of Nursing

Sugino Women's College

Sugiyama Women's College

Sugiyama Women's Senior College

Taisho University

Takachiho Commercial College

Takasaki City College of Economics

Takushoku University

Tama University of Fine Arts

Tamagawa University

Tenri University

Tezukayama University

Toho Gakuen School of Music

Toho University

Tohoku Institute of Technology

Tohoku Pharmaceutical College

Tohoku Social Welfare College

Tohoku University

Tokai University

Tokushima University

Tokyo, University of

Tokyo College of Economics

Tokyo College of Pharmacy

Tokyo College of Science

Tokyo Dental College

Tokyo Electrical Engineering University

Tokyo Gakugei University

Tokyo Institute of Technology

Tokyo Kasei Gakuin College

Tokyo Medical College

Tokyo Medical and Dental University

Tokyo Metropolitan University

Tokyo Union Theological Seminary

Tokyo University of Agriculture

Tokyo University of Agriculture and Technology

Tokyo University of Arts

Tokyo University of Education

Tokyo University of Fisheries

Tokyo University of Foreign Studies

Tokyo University of Mercantile Marine

Tokyo University of the Sacred Heart

Tokyo Woman's Christian College

Tokyo Women's College of Domestic Science

Tokyo Women's Medical College

Tokyo Women's Physical Education College

Tottori University

Toyama University

Toyo College of Music

Toyo University

Tsuda College

Tsuru College of Literature

Tsurumi Women's College

Ueno Gakuen College

Utsunomiya University

Wakayama Prefectural Medical College

Wakayama University

Waseda University

Wayo Women's College

Yamagata University

Yamaguchi University

Yamanashi Gakuin University

Yawata College

Yokohama Municipal University

Yokohama National University

References

Fourth United States–Japan Conference on Cultural and Educational Interchange: *Future Problems,* paper 7.2, Washington, D.C., April 1968*a*.

Fourth United States–Japan Conference on Cultural and Educational Interchange: *Japanese Background Paper,* no. 7.3, Washington, D.C., April 1968*b*.

Government of Japan: *Education in 1966, Japan,* Annual Report of the Ministry of Education, Tokyo, July 1968.

Hidaka, Daishiro: "Japan," *Access to Higher Education,* sec. V, vol. II, *National Studies,* UNESCO and the International Association of Universities, Paris, 1965.

Japan, Bureau of Statistics, Office of the Prime Minister: *Statistical Handbook of Japan, 1967,* Tokyo, 1967.

Japan, Ministry of Education: *Education in Japan: A Graphic Presentation,* Tokyo, 1967.

Japan, Ministry of Education: *Educational Standards in Japan,* The Ministry's 1964 White Paper on Education, Tokyo, 1965*a*.

Japan, Ministry of Education: *Higher Education in Postwar Japan,* John E. Blewett, S. J. (ed. and trans.), Sophia University Press, Tokyo, 1965*b*.

The New York Times, November 10, 1968, and December 1, 1968.

OECD: *Reviews of National Science Policy, Japan,* Paris, 1967.

Okochi, Kazuo: "Japanese University Problems," *Japan Quarterly,* vol. XIV, no. 1, October-December, 1967, Asahi Shimbum Publishing Company, 1968.

Report of the Japanese Scholarship Foundation 1968–69, Tokyo, 1968.

Shimbori, Michiya: "Graduate Schools in Japan," *Education in Japan Journal for Overseas,* vol. II, The International Educational Research Institute, Hiroshima University, 1967.

Vroman, Clyde: *Japan: A Study of the Educational System of Japan and Guide to the Academic Placement of Students from Japan in United States Educational Institutions,* American Association of Collegiate Registrars and Admissions Officers, World Education Series, Washington, D.C., 1966.

10. Higher Education in the Soviet Union

GENERAL ORGANIZATION

All higher education institutions in the Soviet Union are public state institutions, operated, financed, and administered by the state. The regular system of higher education is made up of universities, polytechnical institutes, and a variety of specialized institutes. The term *VUZ, vysshee uchebnoe zavedenie,* "higher education institutions" (plural-*VUZy*) is used to refer to all types of institutions.[1] In addition, there are a number of separate establishments run by the military services, security police, and the Communist Party, which provide the equivalent of higher education for persons appointed to these institutions. Foremost among the institutions of advanced education operated by the Communist Party is the CPSU Central Committee's Academy of Social Sciences, which accepts only persons who have been Party members for at least three years, have a higher education, and can give evidence of active Party involvement. The three-year instructional program offers specialization in economics, philosophy, scientific communism, Soviet history, and related fields.

As a result of consolidation and a decrease in the number of teacher training and fine arts colleges, the number of higher education institutions excluding military and Communist Party institutions decreased from 880 in 1950 to 767 in 1966. Since then, they have increased. Eight new institutions were launched in 1968, and

---

[1] The relationship between specialized secondary schools, or *tekhnicums,* and higher education institutions is difficult to define. Most of the specialized secondary schools accept students after eight years of schooling and give them two years of secondary-level study, plus about 1½ years of postsecondary training. About one-third of the *tekhnicums* accept 10-year school graduates. Although these schools, therefore, appear to fall partly in the postsecondary category and are comparable to institutions preparing semiprofessionals in technical fields in other countries, in practice, they generally are not so considered.

in 1969 four new universities accepted their first students. Nearly three-fifths of the institutions are concentrated in the Russian Soviet Federated Socialist Republic (RSFSR). Including affiliates and branches of *VUZy*, close to one-tenth of the institutions are located in Moscow. The geographic distribution of higher education institutions has broadened with the establishment of many more institutions in the central and far eastern regions of the Soviet Union, but the development of higher education institutions still lags in some of the Soviet republics, such as the Kazakh, Moldavian, Kirghiz, Tadzhiz, and Turkmen Soviet Socialist Republics.[2]

The universities, the oldest category of higher education institution, concentrate mainly on training teachers and researchers in the physical sciences, social sciences, and humanities. There are almost 50 universities, with at least one in each republic, enrolling about 10 percent of all students in higher education. Foremost among them is Moscow University, founded in 1755, which has over 25,000 undergraduate students, more than 220 departments, and 13 faculties.

In 1966–67, there were, in addition to the universities, about 222 specialized engineering institutes; 200 teacher training institutes; 98 agricultural institutes; 86 medical and pharmaceutical schools; close to 50 institutes of art, architecture, music, and drama; over 30 polytechnical institutes; 24 institutes of economics; and 16 institutes of physical culture. A number of *VUZy* have branches and other affiliated units. Polytechnical institutes train students in a number of engineering fields, and some have as many as 15 faculties. Other institutes focus on a single field, such as medicine, education, mining, metallurgy, music, and other arts.

Students normally enter a higher education institution after 10 years of primary-secondary schooling. (This period was 11 years after reforms initiated by Khrushchev in 1958 to make upper secondary education polytechnical. These reforms added one year of practical work until this system was abandoned in 1964.) The intensive program involved in the 10 years is said to be the equivalent of the 12-year preuniversity program in the United States. Soviet higher education institutions award diplomas, not academic de-

---

[2] Whereas the number of students in higher education institutions per 10,000 population averaged 144 nationwide in 1963–64, in the above-mentioned republics, it was, respectively: 98, 89, 101, 101, and 94. For the RSFSR, it was 161 (Nozhko, et al., *Planification de l'Education en URSS,* 1967).

grees. The study period for full-time students varies from 4 to 5½ years, depending upon the field. Graduates from full-time programs are required to work for three years in positions determined by the state. They do not receive their diplomas until after one year in their assigned positions. Failure to work the full three years may result in revocation of the offender's diploma.

A major characteristic of Soviet higher education is the high degree of specialization in curricula. There is no equivalent to the general or liberal arts education commonly provided in lower division work of United States colleges and universities. Students are expected to decide what field they will specialize in before they are admitted. All fields of study are categorized in 22 major groupings, each having a number of specialties totaling over 300 in 1965 (Korol, 1965, pp. 109–111). For each specialty, there is a detailed standardized curriculum specifying the number of hours to be devoted to different subjects. Common to all curricula are study of a foreign language and compulsory courses in Marxist-Leninist political economy, and dialectical and historical materialism.

Graduate training is offered at a number of *VUZy*—360 of the 856 institutions and branches in 1960 (Rosen, 1963, p. 124). Graduate programs, known as *aspirantura,* involve a maximum of three years. The students, or *aspiranty,* are engaged mainly in research under the supervision and guidance of specialists. A large proportion of *aspiranty* pursue their advanced-degree studies at research institutes rather than at *VUZy*—about 37,000 out of the total of 90,000 *aspiranty* in 1965 (*Narodnoe Khoziaistvo SSR v1965g,* 1966, p. 716) and almost 40 percent of postgraduates in 1968. The only advanced degree for which *aspiranty* formally enroll is "candidate" (*kandidat nauk*), which is generally comparable to the American Ph. D. degree. The candidate degree is certified by the Supreme Attestation Commission (*Vysshaia Attestatsionnaia Komissia, VAK*), a special body attached to the USSR Ministry of Higher and Secondary Specialized Education. Some *kandidat* awards are made not on the basis of enrollment in formal programs followed by defense of a thesis but on individual merit for persons who have not undertaken the *aspirantura.* The second advanced degree of "doctor" (*doktor nauk),* comparable to the French *doctorate d'état* degree, is awarded exclusively by the *VAK,* not on the basis of a formal training program but in recognition of advanced original work or as a result of a defense of a dissertation or both. The average age of obtaining the doctorate is 40 to 50 years.

An unusual feature of Soviet higher education is the emphasis given to evening and correspondence study. In 1965, 29 independent institutions and over 1,000 faculties and sections of regular *VUZy* offered this form of higher education, (Nozhko, et al., p. 81). In 1968 about half of the first-year enrollment in higher education institutions were in evening and correspondence programs. This, in fact, represents a decline. Several years ago full-time day study had less priority than it does today. Students in evening programs have about 12 hours of instruction weekly. Those in correspondence programs supplement correspondence work with short residential courses, periodic consultation with tutors, and, to a limited extent, study through television and radio courses. Evening and correspondence courses require one year more than day programs to complete, the study period theoretically being about six years, but many students require a longer period.

With education reforms in 1958, a new type of higher education institution was established, the factory higher technical education institution, known as *Zavod VTUZ*. Organized as divisions of regular higher education institutions and maintained at the factories, *Zavod VTUZy* train technical staff inside major industrial establishments in programs involving theory and practical work. In 1961, there were five *Zavod VTUZy*. However, their experimental role in higher education remains limited.

FUNCTIONS In essence, higher education in the Soviet Union is entirely professional. It trains selected persons in the quantities and fields dictated by the national plan. Since the mid-1950s, higher education institutions have been expected to undertake an increasing share of teacher training, scientific research, and the development of new technology. The universities and higher institutes have the additional functions of producing textbooks and other educational materials, training the increasing number of overseas students and participating in international development projects, contributing to the solution of national problems, and teaching the doctrines of Marx and Lenin so as to strengthen the ideological foundations of the society.

Research The Soviet government has repeatedly stated that higher education institutions should increase their research activities and that academic staff should expand their contribution to the identification, study, and solution of national problems. Particularly since 1950, the government has increased support for research and has made special efforts to encourage the research activities of the *VUZy.* At 25 selected *VUZy,* additional teaching faculty have been hired to reduce teaching loads so more time can be spent on research. Extra funds for capital expenses for research are being provided. Between 1956 and 1960, the number of scientists at *VUZy* (in all fields and full-time equivalent) who were conducting research increased from 6,000 to 22,000 (Korol, 1965, p. 86). A government decree of 1964 called for closer links between higher education institutions and enterprises. Researches at *VUZy* can expand their income by 50 percent by serving as consultants to enterprises or by other part-time research or teaching.

In the last decade, a number of "science cities" (*academgorad*), where higher education institutions, research institutes, and enterprises collaborate in research and development, have been established in different parts of the country (*The New York Times,* October 16, 1967, p. 26). The science city of Novosibirsk, established in 1959, is a leading example. In this new setting, there is close cooperation between research institutes and higher education institutions.

In general, however, there is institutional separation of undergraduate professional education and research.

On the postgraduate level, many students pursue their research not at *VUZy* but at research institutes, and many scientists at *VUZy* divide their time between *VUZy* and research institutes. In the last several years, the government has increasingly urged that specialists from research institutes and enterprises work with *VUZy* on temporary full-time assignments or on a part-time basis. Since 1962, links between research institutes and *VUZy* have been further strengthened by the assignment of undergraduates (500 in 1963) to work in specially created supporting positions at institutes of the USSR Academy of Sciences in order to enable them to gain research experience (Korol, 1965, p. 173).

Development of New Fields

Special emphasis has been given in the current decade to the development of new technology, especially electronics and computer science. The number of students enrolled in electronics and automation increased from about 14,200 in 1950–51 to 281,000 in 1965–66 (*Narodnoe Khoziaistvo SSR v1965g,* 1966, p. 689). Although computer technology in the Soviet Union is said to be about five to ten years behind that of the United States (*The New York*

Times, October 16, 1967, p. 26), intensified efforts are being made in this field, and institutions of higher education are playing a major role in its development. Other efforts of high priority include the training of specialists in automated control systems and the design and production of electronic computer apparatus.

The need for economists and for engineers trained in economics has expanded sharply in the 1960s. Consequently, institutions of higher education are enlarging their economics departments, providing extension training in economics to thousands of management personnel from industrial enterprises, and directing a greater proportion of their research toward higher mathematics, statistics, productivity and cost analysis, and related fields. Related to this expansion in economics teaching is the growing interest in increasing higher education facilities offering training in management, from 4 institutions in 1970 to as many as 150 by 1980 (*The New York Times,* April 12, 1970, p. 11).

In the last few years, empirical research and basic theoretical analysis on the economics of education have begun to play an important part in educational planning. In 1964, a special laboratory, the Scientific Research Laboratory on Economics and Public Education, was established at the Lenin Pedagogical Institute in Moscow to conduct research on the socioeconomic problems of education and to integrate this research with manpower planning. In recent years, several major conferences have been held which have stimulated research on aspects of the economics of education, and new research groups have been established at higher educational institutions to pursue research in this field. Various academic administrators, including the rector of Leningrad State University, have come out in favor of applying economic accountability in the operation of higher education institutions, in part to give the institutions greater freedom in determining resource allocations and in part to maximize their productivity.

Adult Education With the 1958 education reforms, institutions of higher education for the first time began offering noncredit courses in cultural and other fields to meet popular demand for adult education not provided for by the existing system of evening and correspondence diploma programs. However, noncredit educational programs are offered mainly by the People's Universities of Culture, institutions which developed rapidly in the late 1950s and which provide courses—an increasing number by radio—in cultural fields and in a variety of skills, mainly nonprofessional. Staff from higher education institutions contribute to the People's Universities, both by teaching and by assisting in organizing courses. Institutions of higher education have been called upon to provide increasing numbers of courses of a refresher nature in vocational and professional subjects. Since 1967, major industrial and agricultural enterprises and research institutes also have been providing special training courses, both part-time and full-time, for teachers of specialized disciplines at higher education institutions.

International Education Assistance The role of higher education institutions in international education has expanded significantly since the 1950s. Foreign students enrolled at *VUZy* went up from about 13,000 in 1958–59 to more than 21,000 in 1964–65 (Rosen, 1966, p. 833). In 1969 more than 7,000 new foreign students enrolled in higher education institutions. Although foreign students constituted only 0.5 percent of total enrollments in Soviet institutions of higher learning in 1964, they accounted for 13.68 percent of all foreign students enrolled in higher education institutions in Europe (UNESCO, 1967, p. 368). More than half were from other Communist countries, nearly all the others coming from Africa, Asia, and Latin America. Foreign students enroll in *VUZy* either on an individual basis or under cultural and economic cooperation agreements between the Soviet Union and other countries. As with all students in higher education, foreign students pay no tuition. The largest foreign student enrollments are at Moscow University—an estimated 3,000 in 1965 (Rosen, 1966, p. 835)—and at Patrice Lumumba People's Friendship University—an estimated 3,800 students in 1965.

Friendship University was founded in 1960 by the Soviet government jointly with the Soviet Afro-Asian Solidarity Committee, the Union of Soviet Societies for Friendship and Cultural Relations with Foreign Countries, and the All-union Central Council of Trade Unions, in order to assist newly developing nations by providing opportunities for advanced training to their nationals. Friendship University has a special preparatory faculty in which new students enroll for intensive Russian language study before pursuing advanced work in other subjects. Graduates of the university receive a special diploma, the *magister,* rather than the diploma issued to Russian students on completion of their undergraduate work. Friendship University graduated its first students in 1965—approximately half of the 600 students entering in 1960–61, indicating a 50 percent success rate. Its enrollment in 1965–66 was almost 4,000.

In addition to providing higher education to increasing numbers of foreign students, the *VUZy* assist in international education and development by sending professors and teachers abroad, particularly to socialist countries, to teach in higher education institutions.

ENROLLMENT TRENDS

Enrollments in higher education increased from 1.2 million in 1950 to 4.5 million in 1968 (Yelyutin, 1969), graduate student enrollment going up from 22,000 to over 100,000 in this period (*Izvestia,* November 26, 1967). The largest increases have been in evening enrollments (twentyfold) and in correspondence enrollments (fourfold). Full-time day-student enrollments went up little more than twofold. It is almost certain that estimates in the early 1960s that total enrollments would reach 4.6 million by 1970 and 8 million by 1980 will be exceeded (Nozhko, et al., 1964, p. 5). A major factor in the large enrollments has been the high proportion of women, although the ratio of women to total enrollments has been declining: from 52 percent in 1955–56 (Rosen, 1963, p. 102) to 43 percent in 1965 (UNESCO, 1967, p. 367).

Figures on the proportion of an age group enrolled in higher education are somewhat misleading because of the sharp drop in the relevant age group enrolled in the latter part of the 1950s. As a result of World War II losses, the number of 18-year-olds enrolled declined from 4.7 million in 1956 to 3.7 million in 1960 to 1.8 million in 1962, after which it increased to 3.1 million in 1965

TABLE 38 *Entrants in higher education in the Soviet Union*

	1950-51	1955-56	1960-61	1965-66	1966	1967
Full-time day	228,400[a]	257,200[a]	257,900[a]	378,400[b]	427,100[c]	436,900[c]
Evening	9,100[a]	28,400[a]	77,000[a]	125,200[b]	134,500[c]	135,000[c]
Correspondence	111,600[a]	175,800[a]	258,200[a]	350,100[b]	335,900[c]	316,200[c]
TOTAL	349,100[a]	461,400[a]	593,100[a]	853,700[b]	897,500[d]	888,100[c]
University[a]	27,100	36,700	65,600			

SOURCES: (a) Rosen, 1963, pp. 103, 105. (b) *Narodnoe Khoziaistvo SSR v1965g: Statisticheskii Yezhegodnik,* 1966. (c) *Narodnoe Khoziaistvo SSR v1967,* Moscow, 1968. (d) UNESCO, *Factual Background Document on Access to Higher Education,* Conference of Ministers of Education of European Member States on Access to Higher Education, vol. III, MINEUROP/3, Paris, November 20-25, 1967, p. 302.

TABLE 39 *Enrollment in higher education in the Soviet Union*

	1950-51	1955-56	1960-61	1965-66	1966-67
Full-time day	817,900[a]	1,147,000[a]	1,155,500[a]	1,584,000[b]	1,823,000[c]
Evening	27,200[a]	80,900[a]	244,400[a]	569,000[b]	600,000[c]
Correspondence	402,300[a]	639,100[a]	995,100[d]	1,708,000[b]	1,700,000[c]
TOTAL	1,247,400[a]	1,867,000[a]	2,395,500[a]	3,861,000[b]	4,123,000[d]
Universities	109,737[a]	166,256[a]	248,962[a]	279,400[b]	

SOURCES: (a) Rosen, 1963, pp. 100, 105. (b) *Narodnoe Khoziaistvo SSR v1967, Statisticheskii Yezhegodnik,* Moscow, 1968. (c) UNESCO, 1967, vol. III, p. 298. (d) UNESCO, *Factual Background Document on Access to Higher Education,* Conference of Ministers of Education of European Member States on Access to Higher Education, vol. III, MINEUROP/3, Paris, November 20-25, 1967, p. 308.

and 3.5 million in 1966. Projections for 1970 and 1975 are, respectively, 4.5 and 4.7 million (Brackett and DePaux, 1966, pp. 662, 668).

A further consideration with respect to the proportion of the age group enrolled is the cohort involved. Reforms instituted in 1958 which extended secondary schooling from 10 to 11 years and which required most secondary school graduates to spend two years in productive work before they could be admitted to higher education and required males to spend two to four years in military service caused the age group at *VUZy* to shift from approximately 17- through 20-year-olds to 20- through 24-year-olds. By 1966, the work requirement had mostly been abandoned, schooling had been reduced to 10 years, and the cohort reverted to the 17- through 20-year-old age group. These developments account for the tripling

TABLE 40 *First degrees by enrollment by institutions of higher education in the Soviet Union*

	1950-51	1955-56	1960-61	1965-66	1966-67	1967-68
Full-time day	145,900[a]	179,200[a]	227,400[a]	224,800[c]	229,300[c]	249,900[c]
Evening	2,000[a]	4,600[a]	15,500[a]	43,500[c]	56,000[c]	65,700[c]
Correspondence	29,000[a]	62,000[a]	99,200[a]	135,600[c]	146,500[c]	163,900[c]
TOTAL	176,900[a]	245,800[d]	342,100[a]	403,900[c]	431,800[c]	479,500[c]
Universities	15,600[d]	22,800[d]	38,300[d]			

SOURCES: (a) Korol, 1965, p. 272. (b) *Narodnoe Khoziaistvo SSR v1966: Statisticheskii Yezhegodnik,* Moscow, 1967. (c) *Narodnoe Khoziaistvo SSR v1967: Statisticheskii Yezhegodnik,* Moscow, 1968. (d) Rosen, 1963, p. 105.

TABLE 41 *Postgraduate enrollments in the Soviet Union*

	1950-51	1955-56	1960-61	1965-66	1966-67
Postgraduate enrollments at VUZy					
Extension and correspondence[a]	1,288	3,562	6,943	20,068	20,517
Full-time[a]	11,199	13,212	13,463	33,344	34,509
TOTAL[a]	12,487	16,774	20,406	53,412	55,026
Aspiranta graduates VUZy[a]	2,461	4,752	3,020	11,845	13,156
TOTAL[a]	4,093	7,607	5,517	19,240	21,820
Doctorate degrees awarded[b]		621	722		

SOURCES: (a) C. Freeman, and A. Young, *The Research and Development Effort in Western Europe, North America and the Soviet Union,* Paris, 1965, p. 149. (b) Rosen, 1966, pp. 844-845.

of the proportion of 20- to 24-year-olds enrolled in higher education between 1955 and 1965—from 10.6 percent in 1955, to 11.8 percent in 1960 (Unesco, 1967, p. 310), to about 30 percent in 1965–66 (Brackett and DePaux, 1966, p. 615). In 1967, when the cohort included 17- to 24-year-olds, only 22 percent of the age group were enrolled in higher education. If the age group had remained at 20- to 24-year-olds, the proportion enrolled would have been about 32 to 33 percent. The difference between these two cohorts in 1967 was substantial, 17- to 21-year-olds totaling 17.4 million, whereas 20- to 24-year-olds totaled 11.9 million (Brackett and DePaux, 1966, pp. 617–619).

The proportion of 18-year-olds entering *VUZy* went up from 12 percent in 1958–59 to 30 percent in 1960–61 and is estimated to be about 20 percent in 1970 and 40 percent in 1980.[3] Graduates of *VUZy* have increased as a proportion of the age group from 3 percent in 1950 to 8 percent in 1963 and are projected at 12 to 13 percent in 1970 and 19 to 20 percent in 1980 (Nozhko, et al., p. 317).

The main requirement for admission to higher education is the certificate of completion of secondary schooling or its equivalent, i.e., *technicum.* The maximum age for admission to full-time day *VUZy* is 35; there is no age limit for evening and correspondence students. Eligible candidates compete for admission on the basis of oral and written entrance examinations given by each institution

[3] For 1970 estimate, see Yanowitch and Dodge, 1968, p. 263. For other figures, see Great Britain, *Higher Education: Report of the Committee Appointed by the Prime Minister under the Chairmanship of Lord Robbins, 1961–63,* Cmnd. 2154, HMSO, London, 1963, appendix V, pp. 9, 197.

under the supervision of the USSR Ministry of Higher and Secondary Specialized Education. Preference is given to applicants with references from the Communist Party, trade union, and Komsomol and to veterans.

Competition for admission to *VUZy* has increased and is expected to intensify in the future. The number of eligible secondary school graduates has risen faster than places for full-time students. Sixty to ninety percent of these graduates aspire to higher education, but less than one-third make it. Less than one-fourth of the young people who complete secondary school are able to enroll in the higher schools; this proportion is not expected to increase during the current decade (Yanowitch and Dodge, 1968, p. 258). Added to the growing numbers of general secondary school graduates are graduates from specialized secondary schools, the top 5 percent of whom are eligible for admission to higher education. These students were formerly accepted automatically at *VUZy,* but because of the growing competition, their admission is no longer automatic.

In principle, all students from general secondary schools have an equal opportunity for higher education, having followed a common program of studies in secondary school. This principle has been reinforced by the "search for talent" policy pursued in the Soviet Union since the late 1950s. Four very selective upper secondary schools have been established in association with universities in Moscow, Leningrad, Novosibirsk, and Kiev. They offer students chosen for outstanding ability the last three years of secondary schooling and provide special training in mathematics, science, and computer technology. As graduates of these schools have an advantage in gaining admission to mathematics faculties of higher education institutions, the establishment of these schools has aroused some controversy. In general, however, they have strengthened the principle of access based on student ability.

The emphasis given to work experience as a qualification for admission has varied. Reforms initiated in 1958 established two years of full-time employment as a criterion for preferential entry to higher education. The official aim of this and the related reform of expanding part-time enrollments (students who combine employment with part-time study) was to obliterate the distinction between mental and physical labor, between study and work, and to "link school with life," by making higher education and productive enterprise more closely related. As a result of these reforms, the proportion of entrants to full-time higher education with a record of employment increased from 28 percent in 1958 to 57 percent in 1960 (Kitzitzev, 1965, p. 415).

In the early 1960s, it became increasingly apparent that these reforms were causing a deterioration in academic standards in higher education, a higher rate of student failure, and a drain on enterprises—as their productivity suffered, rather than gained, from the student influx. Consequently, the government decided in 1965 to change the policy of selection of applicants with work experience so that applicants who worked or served in the armed forces after completing their secondary studies—and hence often do less well on entrance examinations than those fresh from secondary school—had an equal chance at admission. They compete separately, and the numbers accepted from each group are proportionate to the number of applicants in each group.

Increasing the proportion of students from peasant and worker families in Soviet institutions of higher education has been an objective of the government since the Bolshevik Revolution in 1917. In the early years of the new regime, higher preferences were given to these students than to students from bourgeois families, and, in 1931, 58 percent of students came from peasant and worker families. However, by the early 1950s, these students constituted only an estimated 10 percent of total enrollments, about 50 percent coming from various elite groups, such as the bureaucracy, the armed forces, and Party officialdom (Korol, 1957, pp. 189-190). It is explicitly recognized that the socioeconomic background of Soviet youth significantly affects their educational opportunitites and future careers. Moreover, there is also a growing debate on whether social need requires admission to *VUZy* to be based on equality of access or student ability. The official policy, explicitly based on the admission of "best qualified" students, appears nevertheless to support preferential entry of young people from worker and peasant families. To increase the representation of workers and peasants in higher education enrollments and to raise the numbers of persons with advanced education in the enterprises or with collective or state farms and other agricultural organizations, preference in admissions to full-time study is given to young persons sent by the industrial and agricultural organizations that employ them. Special efforts are also made to strengthen the preparation of workers and agricultural youth for the entrance examinations for higher education institutions.

A large proportion of students are enrolled in higher education on a part-time basis. This proportion increased greatly when the 1958 reforms went into effect—from 34 percent in 1950-51, to 46 percent in 1958-89, to 59 percent in 1965-66 (Goodman and Feshbach, 1967, p. 9). However, since the combination of employment and part-time study brought a lowering of standards and student success, in 1966 the government indicated that henceforth priority would be given to the development of full-time study programs.

At both the undergraduate and graduate levels, enrollments in the different subject specialties and in full-time and part-time programs are determined by a quota system. Quotas are arrived at on the basis of projections of graduates needed in different fields, and the quotas for different specialties are assigned to *VUZy* on the basis of their faculties and enrollment capacities. Since well before World War II, there has been a major emphasis on technology and science. In the period 1926-1960, of the total of 4.5 million graduates, nearly 60 percent were trained in engineering, medicine, science, and agriculture (DeWitt, 1963, p. 141). The distribution by field of students enrolled in 1965-66 presented a strong emphasis on technology and almost 60 percent of all graduates in 1966 were in engineering and the sciences.

Study Period   The normal study period required to obtain a diploma varies in different fields. Before the 1958 reforms, the period was 4 years at pedagogical institutes, 5 years at universities, 5½ at most engineering institutes, and 6 years at medical schools. Part-time students then, as now, required an additional year. The 1958 reforms added an average of one semester to study periods because of the new requirement that most students engage in productive work, raising the average study period to 5½ years. With the subsequent deemphasis on employment in 1964-65, study periods have been reduced by six months to one year. At the present time, therefore, higher education study lasts four to six years. Study for the candidate degree requires three to four years.

Persistence   The 1958 reforms, by increasing the number of part-time students and giving more priority to work experience relative to scholastic record caused a decrease in graduation rates among both full-time and part-time students. It has been estimated that the proportion of full-time students graduating in 1951-52 was 84 percent, whereas for correspondence students for the same period, the rate was 46.6

percent, making an average of about 78 percent (Korol, 1957, pp. 192-199). In the period 1955–59, 76.4 percent of full-time students and 56.3 percent of part-time students graduated in normal time, with an average rate for all graduates of 69.6 percent (DeWitt, 1961, p. 651). In the 1950s, the proportion of all postgraduate students completing the *aspirantura* who subsequently successfully defended a dissertation on time appears to have been only about 20 percent (Korol, 1957, pp. 91-92). In 1965, for full-time postgraduate students only, the rate was 47.5 percent (Eliutin, 1967, p. 15).

Studies at the University of Urals indicated that factors in the high dropout rate were deterioration of preparation during the interval between secondary school and entering a higher education institution, the lower level of knowledge required for the admission of "production" workers and persons sent by various enterprises, poor living conditions, inadequate educational facilities, and the difficulties evening and correspondence students had in combining work and study (Rutkevich, 1966, pp. 13-22).

Staff-Student Ratio In general, total professional staff in institutions of higher learning have more than doubled since 1950, but as the increase has not paralleled enrollment expansion, the staff-student ratio has gone down. Total professional staff increased from 86,542 in 1950 (Noah, 1966, p. 40), to 110,100 in 1955 (Meyer, 1959, p. 38), to 158,400 in 1963 (UNESCO, 1966, vol. IV, p. 1142), to about 220,000 in 1965 (Eliutin, 1967, p. 15). The staff-student ratio for full-time and part-time enrollments went down from 1:14 in 1950, to 1:16 in 1960,[4] to 1:18 in 1965.[5] The staff-student ratio is appreciably lower for part-time students than for full-time; at the beginning of the 1960s, the ratio for full-time students was 1:7.9, whereas, for total enrollments, it was 1:16.3, indicating a ratio for part-time students at least half that for full-time (Poignant, 1965, p. 232). The staff-student ratio varies widely among institutions, being highest probably at Moscow University. Accompanying the problems of dropping staff-student ratios has been a decline in the pro-

[4] Noah, 1966, p. 40; see also DeWitt, 1961, p. 370, which gives 1:14.4 and 1:16.5 as the ratios for total enrollments in 1950 and 1959, respectively. For full-time students, the ratios were 1:9.5 and 1:8.4, respectively, for these years, but if full-time staff only are included for 1950, the ratio was 1:10.3

[5] Computed by dividing total enrollment by total staff.

portion of teachers at higher education institutions who have graduate degrees (Stanis, 1968, p. 35).

HIGHER EDUCATION AND CIVIL GOVERNMENT

All higher education is under state jurisdiction, and state control is virtually total. The Praesidium of the Central Committee of the Party determines all policy matters, and within the Central Committee the Department for Science and Establishments of Higher Education is the policy-initiating body for higher education. The Central Committee sets objectives for higher education development, which are then approved at periodic Party congresses.

Although higher education administration is centralized and hierarchical, the system of control is highly complex. Implementing Party decisions at each level, down to the *VUZy* and departments within them, are party units. Control is exercised by a number of national agencies, including the State Planning Committee (Gosplan), the State Committee for Science and Technology, the USSR Ministry of Finance, and the USSR Academy of Sciences. Union and Republic Ministries and agencies exercise controls on the basis of regions and fields of interest. Supplementing the pyramidal Party organization are independent bodies, and leading ones of which are the Communist League of Youth (Komsomol) and the Committee on Popular Control. The latter has regional and republic branches, and assists in putting into effect the directives of the Party. The great majority of students belong to Komsomol. This organization, along with Republican and Regional Party Committees, participates in the supervision of *VUZy* activities at the regional and local level. Among other organizations which help in implementing the goals of the Party is the trade union of *VUZy* workers, which includes staff and students.

Decisions of the Party Central Committee go to the Council of Ministers of the Soviet Union, in principle the top governmental body, for approval. Represented on the Council of Ministers is the USSR Ministry of Higher and Secondary Specialized Education, which since mid-1959 has had primary responsibility for implementing higher education policy. Within the Council of Ministers, power is concentrated in its Praesidium, which includes its chairman and 11 vice-chairmen.

The chief functions of the USSR Ministry of Higher and Secondary Specialized Education relating to higher education are to coordinate the activities of the republic ministries and committees of higher and specialized secondary education; to review their budget requests; to participate with the Gosplan, the State Planning Committee, in higher education planning; to determine admissions policy and enrollment quotas; to approve curricula and the establishment or elimination of institutions and their branches, faculties, and departments; to determine norms for staff salaries, per student costs, student stipends, unit costs for maintenance and operations, and staff-student ratios used by individual institutions in their budget preparation; to coordinate research at *VUZy*; to approve textbooks and other teaching materials; and to handle international education affairs.

The national ministry is also charged with inspecting all institutions of higher education. An important unit in the ministry is the *VAK* (Supreme Attestation Commission) which has responsibility for awarding (and revoking) advanced degrees; determining at which *VUZy* and in what fields study for the *kandidat* may be pursued; approving academic and administrative appointments, including rectors, deans, and department heads; and ratifying appointments of junior staff members. Within the ministry, major decisions are taken by the Collegium, which includes the minister, deputy ministers, and department heads. All actions of the ministry are subject to criticism and review by the primary Party unit in the ministry. The research activities of all institutions of higher education are planned and coordinated by the Scientific-Technical Council, a ministerial agency created in 1956.

Since 1966 about 30 *VUZy* have fallen directly under the Union Ministry of Higher and Secondary Specialized Education. About the same number fall under other ministries. The remaining *VUZy*, more than nine-tenths of the total, are under the ministries or committees of higher and specialized secondary education in the Republic or under such other Republic ministries as health, culture, communications education, and trade. These Republic ministries are responsible for the supervision, coordination, financing and planning of *VUZy* under their jurisdiction—subject to the overall control by the national Ministry. The institutions taken over by the national Ministry in 1966 are the focus of experimentation and curricular change which the republic ministries are encouraged to imitate in institutions under their jurisdiction.

INTERNAL GOVERNMENT OF INSTITUTIONS At the head of each institution is a rector appointed for an indefinite period by the national Ministry of Higher and Specialized Secondary Education, with the approval of the Party Central Committee and the *VAK*. The possiblity of electing rather than appointing rectors has been under study. Assisting the rector are several pro-rectors, who supervise teaching, research, and business affairs. Academic administrators tend to have little independent authority because of the detailed planning conducted by the state.

The chief governing body is the learned, or academic, council *(soviet),* presided over by the rector and including pro-rectors; deans of faculties; heads of chairs; representatives of other teaching staff; the head librarian; and trade union, Party, and Komsomol representatives. Academic councils at technical *VUZy* frequently include representatives from enterprises operating in the same field. The academic council is concerned with the development of teaching and research and the implementation of government policies and plans. In few areas is the council itself a policy-formulating body. Decisions on the content and number of lectures in courses are made by the academic council within the limits of detailed directives and guidelines laid down by the ministry. The council makes recommendations to the rector on staff appointments, on the basis of a secret-ballot vote on candidates submitting applications for positions. All appointments to teaching positions are for a maximum of five years. The council also recommends on the appointment of departments, deans, and other senior administrative staff, and these appointments are made by the *VAK*.

Faculties are headed by deans, who are elected for three-year terms by secret ballot from the academic senior staff and whose appointment must also receive *VAK* approval. Faculty boards consider matters relating to the work of the faculty, including appointment of junior staff and assistants. Teaching and research are organized on the basis of chairs held by full professors, who direct the work of staff and research units associated with the chair. However, the subjects taught, number of lectures per course, course content, textbooks used, numbers of students admitted and graduated, allocation of funds, and research progams undertaken are mostly determined by government authorities. Consequently, relatively few matters fall under the jurisdiction of the faculties or chairs. The independence of academic staff consists mainly in determining the emphasis given to different subjects in the courses they teach.

The entire system of governance is penetrated by the Party and its related organizations, the Komsomol and trade unions. Each faculty and department has a primary Party unit composed of both students and faculty, and each *VUZy* has its Party committee, which reports via a regional committee to the Party Central Committee. Komsomol representatives have an important influence with respect to admissions and allocation of student stipends.

The foregoing discussion suggests a high degree of centralization in higher education affairs. But coordination occurs on a vertical rather than a horizontal basis. So far there is relatively little direct contact or coordination among Soviet institutions of higher education.

FINANCING HIGHER EDUCATION

Expenditures under the national budget for higher education increased from 7.2 billion old rubles in 1950 to 1.594 billion new rubles in 1965 (15.94 billion old rubles; the 1961 devaluation made one new ruble the equivalent of ten old rubles).[6] It is unusual that while enrollments more than tripled during this period, expenditures went up only twofold. Assuming that public expenditures on higher education in 1969 accounted for 1.5 percent of the national budget, as they did in 1965, they were approximately 2.4 billion rubles out of the budget of 133.8 billion rubles approved for that year (*The New York Times,* December 11, 1968, p. 2). In 1964 higher education expenditures constituted approximately 0.66 percent of the gross national product.

Annual expenditures per student in higher education went down from 5,774 rubles in 1950 to 4,925 in 1960 (DeWitt, 1963, p. 145). The decrease occurred because of the increasing proportion of part-time students in total enrollments and the much lower per student cost for part-time students. Annual expenditures per full-time student went up from 8,801 old rubles in 1950 to 10,298 rubles in 1960 (DeWitt, 1963, p. 145). In 1965, the cost per student, full-time and part-time, was 419 new rubles.[7] Recurrent per student costs declined from 424 new rubles in 1962 to 361 in 1965.[8]

According to information available, 1959 expenditures for higher education were distributed as follows: salaries, 44.2 percent; student stipends, 30.8 percent; equipment, construction, and other capital expenditures, 12.6 percent; related expenditures, including certain research and library acquisitions, 5.5 percent (Nozhko, et al., 1961, p. 201).

[6] Pre-1961 figures are given in old rubles; figures since devaluation in 1961 are given in new rubles. In 1968, the official exchange rate was 1 ruble = US $1.11.

[7] Computed by dividing total expenditure by total enrollments.

[8] Material supplied by Unesco.

TABLE 42 *Expenditures on higher education in the Soviet Union (in millions of new rubles)*

	1950	1955	1960	1965
Total state budget on higher education	721.0[a]	1,020.5[a]	1,167.0[b]	1,593.8[b]
Union budget	485.3[a]	612.1[a]	56.1[b]	235.2[b]
Union republic budgets	235.7[a]	408.4[a]	1,110.9[b]	1,358.6[b]
Capital expenditures	85.4[c](11.8%)	1,020.1[c](10%)		

SOURCES: (*a*) International Arts and Sciences Press, *Soviet Education,* no. 10, August 1967, pp. 49-50. (*b*) Helgard Wienert, "The Organisation and Planning of Research in the Higher Educational Establishments," in OECD, *Science Policy in the U.S.S.R.,* Paris, 1969, p. 363. (*c*) DeWitt, 1961, p. 364.

Nearly all higher education expenditures are financed by public funds. Whereas before the 1959 decentralization, the proportion of total public expenditures derived from the national budget exceeded funds from budgets of the republics, since 1959 the overwhelming proportion of *VUZy* funding is carried on by the republic budgets. Apart from state funds, higher education receives some funding from fees for research done on contract for industrial and other organizations. The amount of contract research tripled between 1957 and 1960 and multiplied another 2½ times between 1960 and 1965. Higher education also receives supplementary financial support indirectly through private costs of student maintenance paid by parents. In 1960 this was estimated to be as much as 15 percent of total public funds for both higher and secondary specialized education.

HIGHER EDUCATION AND ECONOMIC PLANNING Through centralized planning, the Soviet Union attempts to relate the functioning and development of its higher education system to future needs for trained manpower. Two basic approaches are used to calculate these needs. Under the first approach, the numbers of specialists required for each type of position in the full range of enterprises in the economy are aggregated into a national total. The second approach calculates the need for trained manpower on the basis of the proportion of specialists to the total working force, broken down on the basis of regions and occupations. These two approaches are combined, and allowances are made for anticipated changes in technology and productivity to obtain final estimates.

Integral to the planning system is the detailed classification of all occupations into major and subcategories. In 1965 over 330 subcategories required higher education qualifications. The State Planning Committee, or Gosplan, using forecasting approaches outlined above and with the collaboration of various national and regional bodies, arrives at estimates of numbers of graduates in all fields requiring higher education in a particular planning period. These estimates are used to determine the number of students who may be admitted in different fields and at all higher education institutions, taking into account such factors as study periods required and probable dropout rates. The enrollment quotas thus arrived at — together with formulas for staff-student ratios, teaching loads, class sizes, space and equipment needs and policy decisions on the relative emphasis to be accorded to full-time, evening, and correspondence study — largely determine the magnitude and direction of higher education development in the planning period. The USSR Ministry of Higher and Secondary Specialized Education has overall responsibility for putting into effect the measures needed to reach the agreed upon targets. Implementation involves coordination with agencies at the national, regional, and local levels.

Closely linked with higher education planning is the placement of graduates. Each year, the Division of Specialized Personnel of Gosplan and the Division of Placement of the USSR Ministry of Higher and Specialized Secondary Education prepare for every institution of higher education a *placement schedule* for its imminent graduates. These schedules are based on decisions made by enterprises more than a year before the students involved graduate. Students are required to decide still earlier what specialty they are training for. In principle, all new graduates take up jobs in their field of specialization.

Although a greater effort is made to plan higher education in the Soviet Union than elsewhere, persistent difficulties in the methodology for forecasting needs of highly trained manpower result in miscalculations and inadequate synchronization of supply and demand.

As DeWitt has noted, Khrushchev himself admitted in July 1959 — and the situation has not changed significantly since then — that the Soviet Union lacked scientifically reliable methods for forecasting needs for specialists in different fields, the future demand for different kinds of specialists, and when such demand would emerge (DeWitt, 1967, p. 230).

Perhaps the most serious problem in educational planning is the neglect until very recently of cost and return factors of education for training specialists and allocating them within the economy and of the economics of allocating resources to education in comparison with other activities.

Once the lists of positions requiring *VUZy* graduates for the period of the plan have been arrived at by the national office of Gosplan and by the Council of Ministers, the national Ministry of Higher and Secondary Specialized Education implements the result in decisions on overall admissions to higher education institutions; numbers of students to be accepted in evening, correspondence, and full-time study, and in different fields; expansion or freezing of teaching staff and facilities for different faculties; and levels of stipends for various specialties. More detailed decisions for higher education within economic regions and individual republics are made by councils of ministers and other government organs of the republics, subject to the concurrence of the Gosplan.

Although methods of forecasting future needs for highly trained manpower have been developed more in the Soviet Union than elsewhere, persistent difficulties in methodology result in miscalculations and inadequate synchronization of supply and demand. This difficulty is a particular problem in the Soviet Union because the specialization in its higher education allows little occupational mobility for graduates of *VUZy* and places a premium on maximum accuracy of forecasts. But some graduates are unable to find employment in their specialties; e.g., in 1965-66 over 6,000 graduates were unsuccessful in obtaining jobs with enterprises that had requested specialists. A relatively new factor is the greater flexibility of enterprises in recruiting staff made possible by the Statute of Socialist State Enterprises of 1966; this may result in less detailed planning for the output of specialists from the higher education system.

STUDENT FINANCES In 1956, all tuition fees for higher education were abolished. Students obtain their textbooks and other study materials free of charge. All students receive free medical care. Sanitoriums and summer vacation resorts, operated by student trade unions, are available to students at nominal rates.

About 75 percent of all full-time undergraduate students and all postgraduates receive state scholarships, or stipends, which are financed from the national education budget. Although awarded on the basis of financial need and academic record, the state stipends are actually more comparable to wages paid apprentices than to student aid found in most other countries. Like other workers, the students are compensated for doing work to which, in effect, they are assigned and the nature of which is determined by the national plan. As with wages, stipends vary with time in service, the importance of the work to the national interests, and performance. For example, in 1958–59, first-year students received from 275 to 434 old rubles per month, fifth-year students 362 to 600 (Prokofiev, Chilikin, and Tulpanov, 1961). In 1967, the average monthly stipend for undergraduates was 30 to 40 rubles (*The New York Times,* October 5, 1967, p. 18). In 1969 it was probably 40 to 60 new rubles, roughly equivalent to the minimum wage. Students receiving excellent grades receive a 25 percent bonus. Students in mathematics, engineering, and medicine receive larger stipends than students in the social sciences and other low-priority fields. Stipends for postgraduates are about twice as high as those for undergraduates.

Students assigned to *VUZy* by enterprises receive stipends 15 percent higher than those of other students. About 20 to 25 percent of the students do not receive stipends. Some 10 to 15 percent do not receive stipends because they are disqualified by the means test (parental income). About 8 to 12 percent do not receive stipends because they have at least one "fail" grade.

Since stipends are not continued for students who fail their examinations, the aid system thus encourages student effort. Stipends are awarded by faculty commissions in each institution, made up of the dean and other staff of the faculty concerned, as well as student representatives, including the Komsomol. Commission decisions are subject to confirmation by the rector.

Students in evening and correspondence programs do not receive stipends but are given paid leave by their employers for up to 30 days each year for laboratory work, consultation, and preparation for examinations and other projects at the institution where they are enrolled. They also travel at reduced rates.

Apart from the state stipends, there are a number of scholarships awarded, without regard to financial need, to students having satisfactory grades who are blind or deaf and dumb, "Heroes of the Soviet Union," "Heroes of Socialist Labor," or former residents of children's homes or colonies. Rectors of institutions also have at their disposal funds which they may grant to individual students on the basis of emergency aid.

Although the great majority of students have stipends, many students need additional funds to cover their maintenance costs.

STUDENTS Political factors play a strong part in the nature of student organizations. A variety of student organizations exist, including trade unions and various cultural associations. The only official political organizations are the Komsomol and Communist Party. About

10 to 15 percent of the students are Communist Party members. Komsomol members are drawn from the 15- to 28-year-old group —young people in senior secondary schools and in higher education, as well as in the armed forces, industry, government, commerce, and agriculture. There is at least one Komsomol branch in each faculty of higher education institution. The basic aims of the organization—aims of the Communist Party—are to provide training for new recruits to the Party; to instill the values of the Party in young people; to mobilize young people for socially useful work, such as assisting in construction projects and harvests at agricultural enterprises; and to "stimulate young people to learn so that the personnel necessary to run a modern industrial society will be available" (Cornell, 1968).

The Komsomol is said to have only mixed success in achieving these objectives. Many students exhibit indifference and resistance to Party demands. However, their resistance is mostly passive: rather than taking the form of protest movements and demonstrations, although there have been some of these, it is manifested in attitudes of skepticism, in hooliganism, and in the reading of prohibited publications. In 1965, some 7,000 students were said to have been expelled from higher education institutions in Leningrad for reasons of "ideology, immaturity, moral uncleanliness, and unsatisfactory performance" ("Recent Events in World Education," 1966, pp. 516-517). Resistance also takes the form of refusal of *VUZy* graduates to fulfill their postgraduate work assignments, and of undergraduates "openly admitting that they cram Marxism in order to pass while privately harboring views opposed to official ideology" ("Recent Events in World Education," 1966, pp. 516-517).

Apart from fulfilling certain Party aims, student organizations at higher education institutions organize a range of cultural and sports activities. Student clubs and hostels, some organized by the Komsomol and others by student trade union associations, support a wide range of activities: drama, literature, sports competitions, and vacation resorts.

THE BALANCE SHEET The problems of the Soviet higher education system stem partly from its being highly centralized and planned and from its overwhelmingly professional orientation. However, the system shares with higher education systems elsewhere problems inherent in rapid expansion: the problem of achieving a reasonable equilibrium between the output of secondary school graduates aspiring to higher education and the capacity of higher education institutions to absorb them; the problem of ensuring equal access to higher education to young people from all sectors of society; and the problem of raising the quality of higher education, specifically of teaching. In connection with this last item, special institutes have been functioning since 1966 at the universities of Moscow, Leningrad, and Kiev to strengthen the teaching qualifications of young teachers at other institutions of higher learning.

One problem of the Soviet system is the allocation of graduates of higher education institutions to jobs which utilize their specialties. Substantial misallocation and resultant waste of trained manpower is said to take place. A number of graduates resist or evade efforts to assign them to work in their specialties in areas which may be remote from the major urban centers.

In the 1960s, the high level of specialization in higher education was subjected to increasing criticism because of the resultant lack of professional flexibility, creativity, and even productivity of specialists. As a result of decisions made by the government in 1963, there is a greater stress on broad training in higher education, so that students at *VUZy* acquire more general education and have more interchangeability in employment.

No immediate solutions are in sight for the problem of access to higher education of qualified secondary school graduates or of young people from sectors of society underrepresented in higher education. Recent studies suggest that some 60 to 70 percent of secondary school graduates aspire to higher education. However, under present plans, only about one-fifth of the age group are expected to be admitted to *VUZy*. The wide disparity between applicants and students admitted remains an unsolved problem in Soviet higher education and can give rise to increasing frustration on the part of young people.[9] A related problem is the relatively low representation in higher education enrollments of children from worker and peasant families and from rural areas in comparison to children from specialist and urban families. Although equity of access to higher education for all sectors of society has been an important goal of the Soviet government since 1917, satisfactory methods of implementing it have not yet been found.

A final problem is the failure of the higher education system to achieve its aim of developing student commitment to the Party

[9] See Yanowitch and Dodge, 1968, for a fuller discussion of this problem.

ideology and objectives. Here again the Soviet system shares to some extent a problem faced in a number of countries, where one of the functions of organized education is to transmit certain values of the society to the new generation—with mixed success in this effort.

From the student point of view, the Soviet higher education system has special strengths in the guidance provided to students; in the extensive financial aid system, coupled with free tuition and low costs for housing and many other items; and in the fact that · students are guaranteed a job by the state upon completion of their studies. Still another strength of the system may be the relatively early entry age of students into higher education institutions (around age 18) and the fact that they complete their studies according to a sequential program which minimizes the number of repeaters and dropouts and prevents a protracted study period.

THE FUTURE   Some tendencies and problems common to the Soviet and Western systems of higher education have been emerging in the last decade. This trend seems likely to persist in the future. As countries in the West, spurred in part by rising costs, are moving in the direction of more long-range planning of higher education, in the Soviet Union difficulties in traditional planning methodology still defy solution, and economic considerations are beginning to receive attention. In the West, there is a tendency to increase specialization in postsecondary education at the expense of general or liberal education, while in the Soviet Union there is an opposite tendency, although higher education there remains more specialized than elsewhere. In the last decade in the West, science and technology have gained in enrollments and financial support relative to the social sciences and humanities; in the same period in the Soviet Union, the social sciences have expanded more rapidly than in the past, particularly in economics, where enrollments went up from 5 percent of total enrollments in 1950 to 10 percent in 1965.

However, enrollments in the Soviet Union are still 65 percent in scientific fields. Both the Soviet and Western systems are more and more confronting common problems in their higher education: coping with mounting student alienation and unrest; meeting the escalating demand for higher education; more effectively democratizing access to higher education; finding the appropriate balance of centralization and decentralization in higher education control; and identifying and maximizing the return to society of investment in higher education.

Institutions of Higher Education in the Soviet Union

UNIVERSITIES

Azerbaijan S.M. Kirov State

Bashkir State

Byelorussia V.I. Lenin State

Cheboksary State

Chernovtsy State

Daghestan V.I. Lenin State

Dnepropetrovsk State

Donetsk State

Far Eastern State

Gorkey N.I. Lobachevsky State

Irkutsk A.A. Zhdanov State

Kabardino-Balkar State

Kazakh S.M. Kirov State

Kazan V.I. Lenin State

Kharkov A.M. Gorky State

Kiev T.G. Shevchenko State

Kirghiz State

Latvian P. Stuchka State

Leningrad A.A. Zhdanov State

Lvov Ivan Franko State

Mordovian State

Moscow M.V. Lomonosov State

Novosibirsk State

Odessa I.I. Mechnikov State

Ordzhonikidze State

Patrice Lumumba People's Friendship

Perm A.M. Gorky State

Petrozavodsk O.V. Kuusinen State

Rostov State

Samarkand Alisher Navoi State

Saratov State

Tajik V.I. Lenin State

Tartu State

Tashkent V.I. Lenin State

Tbilisi State

Tomsk V.V. Kuibyshev State

Turkmen A.M. Gorky State

University of Urals

Uzhgorod State

V. Kapsukas State University of Vilnius

Voronezh State

Yakutsk State

Yerevan State

TECHNICAL EDUCATION

Aeronautical Engineering

Kazakh Institute of Aviation

Kharkov Institute of Aviation

Kuibyshev Institute of Aviation

Leningrad Institute of Aeronautical Instrument Construction

Moscow Institute of Aviation

Moscow Institute of Aviation Technology

Ufa Institute of Aviation

Automobile Engineering

Moscow Institute of Automobile Engineering

Technology and Chemical Technology

Byelorussia Institute of Technology

Bryansk Institute of Technology

Dnepropetrovsk Institute of Chemical Technology

East Siberian Institute of Technology

Ivanovo Institute of Chemical Technology

Kazakh Institute of Chemical Technology

Kazan Institute of Chemical Technology

Kostroma Institute of Technology

Leningrad Institute of Paper Technology

Leningrad Institute of Technology

Moscow Institute of Chemical Technology

Moscow Institute of Precision Chemical Technology

Siberian Institute of Technology

Tambov Institute of Technology

Voronezh Institute of Technology

Yaroslavl Institute of Technology

Cinematographical Engineering

Leningrad Institute of Cinematographic Technology

Civil Aviation

Kiev Institute of Civil Aviation

Leningrad Institute of Civil Aviation

Riga Institute of Civil Aviation

Civil Engineering

Byelorussia Institute of Civil Engineering

Dnepropetrovsk Institute of Civil Engineering

Gorky Institute of Civil Engineering

Kazakh Institute of Civil Engineering

Kazan Institute of Civil Engineering

Kharkov Institute of Civil Engineering

Kiev Institute of Civil Engineering

Kuibyshev Institute of Civil Engineering

Leningrad Institute of Civil Engineering

Moscow Institute of Civil Engineering

Moscow Correspondence Institute of Civil Engineering

Novosibirsk Institute of Civil Engineering

Odessa Institute of Civil Engineering

Penza Institute of Civil Engineering

Poltava Institute of Civil Engineering

Rostov Institute of Civil Engineering

Tomsk Institute of Civil Engineering

Tselinograd Institute of Civil Engineering

Voronezh Institute of Civil Engineering

Electrical Engineering

Leningrad Institute

Novosibirsk Institute

Power

Ivanovo Institute

Moscow Institute

Moscow Correspondence Institute

Engineering Schools Attached to Factories

Dneprodzerzhinsk Metallurgy Factory Institute

Kazakh Metallurgy Factory Institute

Leningrad Metallurgy Factory Institute

Moscow Automobile Factory Institute

Penza Factory Institute

Rostov Agricultural Machine Factory Institute

Fish Industry

Astrkhan Institute

Kaliningrad Institute

Vladivostok Institute

Food and Refrigeration Technology

Leningrad Institute of Refrigeration Engineering

Moscow Institute of the Meat and Dairy Industry

Odessa Institute of Food and Refrigeration Technology

Food Technology

Kiev Institute

Moscow Institute

Moscow Correspondence Institute

Odessa Institute

Geology and Prospecting

Moscow Institute

Light Industrial and Textile Technology

Byelorussia Institute of Light Industrial Technology

Ivanovo Institute of Textile Technology

Kiev Institute of Light Industrial Technology

Leningrad Institute of Textile and Light Technology

Moscow Correspondence Institute of Textile and Light Technology

Moscow Institute of Light Industrial Technology

Moscow Institute of Textile Technology

Tashkent Institute of Textile Technology

Machine Engineering

Kurgan Institute of Machine Construction

Lugansk Evening Institute

Mogilev Institute

Moscow Correspondence Institute

Moscow Institute of Electronic Engineering

Rostov Institute of Agricultural Engineering

Zaporozhe Institute

Marine Engineering

Leningrad Institute

Nikolaev Institute

Mechanical Engineering

Izhevsk Institute

Leningrad Institute

Leningrad Institute of Precision and Optical Engineering

Moscow Institute

Moscow Institute of Precision Engineering

Russian Evening Institute of Technology

Sevastopol Institute of Precision Engineering

Metallurgy

Dnepropetrovsk Institute

Moscow Institute

Moscow Institute of Steel and Alloys Technology

Siberian Institute

Zhdanov Institute

Meteorology and Hydrology

Leningrad Institute

Odessa Institute

Mining

Dnepropetrovsk Institute

Kharkov Institute

Kommunarsk Institute of Ore Mining and Metallurgy

Krivoi Rog Ore Mining Institute

Leningrad Institute

Magnitogorsk Institute of Mining and Metallurgy

North Caucasian Institute of Mining and Metallurgy

Sverdlovsk Institute

Navigation

Leningrad College

Murmansk College

Odessa College

Vladivostok College

Nonferrous Metals

Krasnoyarsk Institute

Oil Technology

Baku Institute of Oil Technology and Chemistry

Grozny Institute

Moscow Institute of Oil and Gas Technology

Ufa Institute

Physiotechnology

Moscow Institute of Physics and Engineering

Polytechnical Institutes

Baku

Barnaul

Chelyabinsk

Donetsk

Dushanbe

Frunze

Gorky

Irkutsk

Kalinin

Kaunas

Kazakh (Alma-Ata)

Kemerovo

Khabarovsk

Kharkov

Kharkov Correspondence

Kiev

Kirov

Kishinev

Komsomolsk Evening

Krasnodar

Krasnoyarsk

Kuibyshev

Kursk

Leningrad

Leningrad Correspondence

Lvov

Minsk

Moscow

Novocherkassk

Odessa

Omsk

Penza

Perm

Riga

Saratov

Sverdlovsk

Tallinn

Tashkent

Tbilisi

Tomsk

Tula

Turkmen (Ashkhabad)

Ulyanovsk

Vladimir

Vladivostok

Volgograd

Voronezh

Yerevan

Industrial Institutes

Kramatorsk Evening

Norilsk

Pavlodar

Tyumen

Printing Technology

Lvov Institute

Moscow Institute

Radioelectronics

Minsk Institute

Moscow Institute of Radioelectronics and Mining Electrical Engineering

Ryazan Institute

Taganrog Institute

Tomsk Institute of Radioelectronics and Electronic Technology

Surveying

Moscow Institute of Surveying, Aerial Photography, and Cartography

Novosibirsk Institute of Surveying, Aerial Photography, and Cartography

Telecommunications

Kuibyshev Institute

Leningrad Institute

Moscow Correspondence Institute

Novosibirsk Institute

Odessa Institute

Tashkent Institute

Town Planning

Kharkov Institute

Transport

Byelorussia Institute of Railway Engineering

Bryansk Institute of Transport Technology

Dnepropetrovsk Institute of Railway Engineering

Gorky Institute of River Transport Engineering

Khabarovsk Institute of Railway Engineering

Kharkov Institute of Automobile Transport

Kharkov Institute of Railway Engineering

Kiev Institute of Automobile Transport

Leningrad Institute of Railway Engineering

Leningrad Institute of River and Maritime Transport

Moscow Institute of Automobile and Road Construction

Moscow Institute of Railway Engineering

Moscow Correspondence Institute of Railway Engineering

Novosibirsk Institute of Railway Engineering

Novosibirsk Institute of River Transport Engineering

Odessa Institute of Maritime Transport Engineering

Omsk Institute of Automobile Transport

Omsk Institute of Railway Engineering

Rostov Institute of Railway Engineering

Sverdlovsk Institute of Electromechanical and Railway Engineering

Tashkent Institute of Railway Engineering

PROFESSIONAL EDUCATION

Agricultural Institutes

Altai (Barnaul)

Belaya Tserkov

Byelorussia Academy of Agriculture

Blagoveshchensk

Cheboksary

Dnepropetrovsk

Dushanbe

Frunze

Gorky

Grodno

Irkutsk

Izhevsk

Kaunas

Kazakh (Alma-Ata)

Kazan

Kelasuri Institute of Subtropical
Agriculture

Kharkov

Kherson

Kiev Academy of Agriculture

Kinel

Kirov

Kirovabad

Kishinev

Kostroma

Krasnodar

Krasnoyarsk

Kurgan

Kursk

Leningrad

Lugansk

Lvov

Makhachkala

Moscow

Moscow Correspondence

Novosibirsk

Odessa

Omsk

Ordzhonikidze

Orenburg

Penza

Perm

Poltava

Ryazan

Rostov

Samarkand

Saratov

Simferopol

Stavropol

Tartu

Tashkent

Tbilisi

Tselinograd

Tyumen

Turkmen (Ashkhabad)

Ufa

Ulan-Ude

Ulyanovsk

Uman

Uralsk

Ussuriysk

Velikie Luki

Volgograd

Voronezh

Yelgava

Yerevan

Architectural Institutes

Moscow

Archives

Moscow

Commerce

Donetsk

Leningrad

Lvov

Moscow

Moscow Correspondence

Moscow Institute of Cooperative Commerce

Novosibirsk Institute of Cooperative Commerce

Samarkand Institute of Cooperative Commerce

Economics

Alma-Ata

Kharkov Institute of Industrial Organization and Economics

Kiev

Kuibyshev Institute of Planning

Leningrad Institute of Industrial Organization and Economics

Minsk

Moscow Institute of Economic Statistics

Moscow Institute of Industrial Organization and Economics

Rostov Institute of Finance and Economics

Saratov

Tashkent

Finance

Irkutsk Institute of Finance and Economics

Kazan Institute of Finance and Economics

Leningrad Institute of Finance and Economics

Moscow Correspondence Institute of Finance and Economics

Moscow Institute of Finance

Odessa Institute of Finance and Economics

Forestry and Wood Technology Institutes

Arkhangelsk

Ioshkar-Ola

Leningrad Academy

Lvov

Moscow

Sverdlovsk

Voronezh

Horticulture

Michurinsk Institute

Irrigation and Rural Planning Institutes

Dzhambul Institute of Water Utilization

Moscow Institute of Water Utilization

Moscow Institute of Rural Production

Moscow Institute of Rural Planning

Novocherkassk Institute of Water and Land Utilization

Rovno Institute of Water and Land Utilization

Tashkent Institute of Irrigation and Mechanization of Agriculture

Law

Kharkov Institute

Moscow Correspondence Institute

Saratov Institute

Sverdlovsk Institute

State Institutes of Library Science

Kharkov Institute

Leningrad

Moscow

Ulan-Ude (Eastern Siberian State Institute of Culture)

Literature

Moscow Correspondence Institute

Mechanization and Electrification of Agriculture Institutes

Chelyabinsk

Kharkov

Melitopol Institute of Mechanization of Agriculture

Minsk

Saratov

Azov–Black Sea Institute (Zernograd)

Medical Institutes

Aktyubinsk

Alma-Ata State

Andizhan

Arkhangelsk

Ashkhabad State

Astrakhan

Baku State

Barnaul

Blagoveshchensk

Chelyabinsk

Chernovtsy

Chita

Dnepropetrovsk

Donetsk

Dushanbe State

Frunze State

Gorky

Grodno State

Irkutsk State

Ivano-Frankovo

Ivanovo State

Izhevsk

Kalinin

Karaganda

Kaunas State

Kemerovo

Khabarovsk

Kharkov

Kiev

Kishinev State

Krasnodar

Krasnoyarsk

Kuibyshev State

Kursk

Leningrad

Leningrad Institute of Hygiene

Leningrad Institute of Pediatrics

Lugansk State

Lvov

Makhachkala

Minsk State

Moscow

Novosibirsk

Odessa State

Omsk State

Ordzhonikidze

Orenburg

Perm State

Riga

Ryazan

Rostov State

Samarkand State

Saratov State

Semipalatinsk State

Simferopol State

Smolensk State

Stavropol

Sverdlovsk State

Tashkent

Tbilisi State

Ternopol State

Tselinograd

Tyumen

Ufa

Vinnitsa

Vitebsk State

Vladivostok

Volgograd State

Voronezh State

Yaroslavl

Yerevan

Dentistry

Kharkov Institute

Moscow Institute

Institutes of Pharmacy

Kharkov

Leningrad

Perm

Pyatigorsk

Tashkent

Zaporozhe

Veterinary Science, Animal Husbandry, and Milk Production

Alma-Ata Institute of Veterinary Science and Animal Husbandry

Kaunas Academy of Veterinary Science

Kazan Institute of Veterinary Science

Kharkov Institute of Veterinary Science and Animal Husbandry

Leningrad Institute of Veterinary Science

Lvov Institute of Veterinary Science and Animal Husbandry

Moscow Academy of Veterinary Science

Omsk Institute of Veterinary Science

Saratov Institute of Veterinary Science and Animal Husbandry

Semipalatinsk Institute of Veterinary Science and Animal Husbandry

Tbilisi Institute of Veterinary Science and Animal Husbandry

Troitsk Institute of Veterinary Science

Vitebsk Institute of Veterinary Science

Vologda Institute of Milk Technology

Yerevan Institute of Veterinary Science and Animal Husbandry

References

Brackett, James W., and John W. DePaux: "Population Policy and Demographic Trends in the Soviet Union," in U.S. Congress, Joint Economic Committee, 89th Cong., 2d Sess., *New Directions in the Soviet Economy*, part III, *The Human Resources*, Washington, D.C., 1966.

Cornell, Richard: "Students and Politics in the Communist Countries of Eastern Europe," *Daedalus*, vol. 97, no. 1, Winter 1968.

DeWitt, Nicholas: *Education and Professional Employment in the USSR*, National Science Foundation, Washington, D.C., 1961.

DeWitt, Nicholas: "Educational and Manpower Planning in the Soviet Union," in Mark Blaugh (ed.), *The World Year Book of Education 1967: Educational Planning*, Harcourt, Brace & World, Inc., New York, 1967.

DeWitt, Nicholas: "Soviet and American Higher Education: Magnitude, Resources, and Costs," in Seymour Harris (ed.), *Economic Aspects of Higher Education*, OECD, Paris, 1963.

Eliutin, V. P.: "Higher and Secondary Education," *Soviet Education*, vol. 6, no. 1, November 1967.

Goodman, Ann S., and Murray Feshbach: "Estimates *and* Projections *of* Educational Attainment *in the USSR 1950–1985,*" in U.S. Department of Commerce, Bureau of the Census, *International Populations Reports*, ser. p-91, no. 16, Washington, D.C., 1967.

Izvestia, November 26, 1967, p. 2; also p. 26 in *Current Digest of the Soviet Press*, vol. XIX, no. 47, December 13, 1967.

Kitzitzev, V. A.: "Union of Soviet Socialist Republics," in Unesco and International Association of Universities, *Access to Higher Education*, vol. I, sec. 9, Paris, 1965.

Korol, Alexander: *Soviet Education for Science and Technology*, The Technology Press of The Massachusetts Institute of Technology and John Wiley & Sons, Inc., New York, 1957.

Korol, Alexander: *Soviet Research and Development: Its Organization, Personnel, and Funds*, a study sponsored by the National Science Foundation, Office of Economic and Manpower Studies, M.I.T. Press, Cambridge, Mass., 1965.

Meyer, Klaus: *Das Wissenschaftliche Leben in der UdSSR*, Free University of Berlin, East European Institute, Berlin, 1959.

Narodonoe Khoziaistvo SSR v1965g: Statisticheskii Yezhegodnik [The National Economy of the Soviet Union in 1965: A Statistical Yearbook], Moscow, 1966.

The New York Times, October 5 and 16, 1967; December 11, 1968; April 12, 1970.

Noah, Harold J.: *Financing Soviet Schools,* Teachers College Press, Columbia University, New York, 1966.

Nozhko, K. G., et al.: *Planification de l'Éducation en URSS,* UNESCO, International Institute for Educational Planning, Paris, 1967.

Nozhko, K. G.: "Methods of Estimating the Demand for Specialists and of Planning Specialized Training within the USSR," *UNESCO Statistical Reports and Studies, 1964,* ST/S/9, Paris, 1964.

Poignant, Raymond: *L'Enseignement dans les Pays du Marché Commun,* Institut Pedagogique National, Paris, 1965.

Prokofiev, M. A., M. G. Chilikin, and S. I. Tulpanov: *The Soviet Higher School,* Educational Studies and Documents, no. 39, UNESCO, Paris, 1961.

"Recent Events in World Education," *Comparative Education Review,* vol. 10, no. 3, October 1966.

Robbins Committee: *Higher Education: Report of the Committee Appointed by the Prime Minister under the Chairmanship of Lord Robbins, 1961–63,* Cmnd. 2154, HMSO, London, 1963, appendix V.

Rosen, Seymour: "Changing Guideposts in Soviet Education," in U.S. Congress, Joint Economic Committee, 89th Cong. 2d Sess., *New Directions in the Soviet Economy,* Washington, D.C., 1966.

Rosen, Seymour: *Higher Education in the USSR: Curriculum, Schools, and Statistics,* U.S. Department of Health, Education, and Welfare, Office of Education, (OE-14088), Bulletin 1963, no. 16, 1963.

Rudman, Herbert C.: *Structure and Decision-making in Soviet Education,* U.S. Department of Health, Education, and Welfare, Office of Education, (OE-14094), Bulletin 1964, no. 2, 1964.

Rutkevich, M. N.: "Why a Student Does Not Arrive at the 'Finish,'" *The Soviet Review,* vol. 7, no. 1, pp. 13–22, Spring, 1966.

Stanis, V.: "Graduate Student, Candidate, Doctor," *Pravda,* February 17, 1968, p. 3; also pp. 35–56 in *Current Digest of the Soviet Press,* vol. XX, no. 7, March 6, 1968.

UNESCO: *Factual Background Document on Access to Higher Education,* Conference of Ministers of Education and European Member States on Access to Higher Education, vol. III, MINEUROP/3, Paris, 1967.

UNESCO: *World Survey of Education,* vol. IV, Paris, 1966.

Yanowitch, Murray, and Norton Dodge: "Social Class and Education: Soviet Findings and Reactions," *Comparative Education Review,* vol. 12, no. 3, October 1968.

Yelyutin, V.: "Competition, the Student and Occupation," *Pravda,* July 19, 1969, p. 3; also p. 35 in *Current Digest of the Soviet Press,* vol. XXI, no. 29 August 13, 1969.

Zaleski, Eugene, Joseph P. Kozlowski, Helgard Wienert, R. Amann, M. J. Berry, and R. W. Davies: *Science Policy in the USSR,* OECD, Paris, 1969.

11. Higher Education in India

by Philip G. Altbach

This essay describes a large and complex higher educational system set in a society very different from the Western nations in which modern universities first developed and faced with massive problems of economic, social, and educational advancement. India today ranks third, following the United States and the Soviet Union, in number of students enrolled in universities. In 1965–1966 there were about 1.7 million students in Indian colleges and universities (*University Development in India,* 1966, p. 3).

The problems of universities in a developing area like India differ sharply from those of advanced industrial countries described in other chapters of this book. The educational heritage of colonialism, for example, is crucial in many developing countries. Educational institutions, including universities, were established by colonial powers in their dependencies for various reasons—to provide trained civil servants, to convert "natives" to Christianity, and others. These new institutions were usually modeled on metropolitan universities and generally did not reflect the historical or educational conditions of the colonial area. During the colonial period, education was controlled largely by the metropolitan power, and policy was made to meet colonial needs (Ashby, 1966, pp. 19–36). In some cases, educational development was consciously inhibited by the colonial authorities for political or other reasons.

The postindependence challenges to higher education in the developing areas are also somewhat different. In many nations, India among them, education has been seen as one of the key factors in economic and social advancement—indeed, as the door to "modernization." As a result, educational systems have been expanded very rapidly, and large amounts of money have been spent on them. Universities assumed a key political role as well, since the proportion of politically articulate individuals in societies marked by widespread illiteracy (70 percent in India) and traditional patterns of social organization is small. The university community constitutes perhaps the largest reservoir of articulate "modern-oriented" individuals in many of the developing nations.

Some developing countries have tried to preserve the elitist nature of the university and have maintained high standards of academic quality. Others have sought to provide university education to large numbers of people, and institutions of higher education have expanded rapidly. India is an example of this latter trend. Since independence in 1947, the growth of the university system has been by about 10 percent a year, and collegiate education is now available not only in the major cities but also in many provincial centers which until recently had virtually no provision for education. Higher education is now within reach of young people from diverse social class and caste backgrounds, although the majority are probably still from the urban middle and upper classes.[1]

It is perhaps a general rule that in developing countries it is easier to expand education and to "modernize" this segment of society than it is to build infrastructures in other areas of the economy. Thus, education tends to be overdeveloped, at least on some levels, in that it may temporarily produce too many skilled individuals for the positions available in the economy. This phenomenon leads to what has become known as the brain drain, to political instability, and to other social dislocations. The fact that the universities were developed to serve foreign needs and follow foreign organizational patterns has also made it difficult for the institutions to change to meet new needs and serve new political elites. While India is by no means typical of developing societies, many of the problems which face Indian higher education are common to other nations.

HISTORICAL FACTORS The Indian university is a creation of the British. Traditional (pre-British) higher education, focused largely on religious themes, either collapsed or receded into the background as British rule established itself on the Indian subcontinent in the eighteenth century. The few colleges which were founded prior to 1857 were

---

[1] In fact, college education for students from the formerly untouchable castes and some tribal groups is now entirely free, and a proportion of seats in the universities are reserved for such students—a kind of reverse discrimination which is only now being considered in a number of otherwise advanced nations.

established by Christian missionaries or by the government, with growing pressure and initiative from the rising Indian urban middle class.

Indians increasingly demanded English style higher education because it provided prestigious jobs in the British bureaucracy or in the growing commercial sector of the economy. The British themselves found that they needed a class of educated Indians to man secondary-level posts in the government and to act as intermediaries between the Raj and the Indian population. It is important to note that higher education was not fostered as a means for development of national consciousness in India (this in fact was an unwanted result of the growth of universities) for the intellectual uplift of the people but for rather specific and narrow British interests (McCully, 1940). Several elements in India had an interest in expanding higher education in the early nineteenth century. As the educational system grew (there were 27 colleges in existence in 1857), British authorities felt the need for some standardization and a means of maintaining quality in these colleges. As a result, three universities were established in 1857 at the provincial capitals of Calcutta, Bombay, and Madras.

Rather than developing a new organizational framework for the university system in India, the British simply adopted the model

TABLE 43
Development of higher education in India

Year	Number of universities	Number of colleges	Student enrollment
1857	3	27	2,000*
1882	3	72	
1901	4	191	23,009
1921-22	11	207	66,258
1936-37	16	446	126,228
1946-47	18	933	225,000
1950-51	29		263,000
1956-57	38	1,171	769,468
1960-61	46	2,360	1,034,934
1965-66	64	2,572	1,728,773
1966-67	70	2,749	1,949,012

*Approximate figure.
SOURCES: Compiled from a number of historical studies. Due to discrepancies in figures, most statistics are not exact.

of the University of London, which was then coming into its own as a major university in England. Thus, the early universities were not so much teaching institutions as administrative agencies, responsible for maintaining standards and giving examinations to students in colleges spread over a vast area of India. The concept of the *affiliating university* has remained the key organizational pattern in India's higher education. The early Indian university was not an academic institution in the Western sense of the term and fostered no scholarly community. It did, however, manage to provide a sense of uniformity to widely scattered colleges with different orientations. The establishment of universities marked a turning point of rapid expansion. The number of colleges grew from 72 in 1882 to 191 in 1901-02. The number of students was 23,000 in 1901, a tenfold increase in 50 years.[2]

Not only has the traditional organizational structure of the Indian university maintained its hold, but a number of other factors are still a part of the university system in India. The curriculum of the early Indian universities and colleges was very strongly influenced by British practices at the time. Major emphasis was placed on the classics and humanities, and there was very little stress on science or on the more practical subjects of engineering and other applied technical fields. Law and medicine were the traditional professions and had most impact in India. Thus, the curriculum of higher education had little relation to the needs of a developing area, and in fact did not even serve most effectively the needs of the British bureaucracy. These traditional curricular notions, however, are still important in Indian higher education.

The social class basis of collegiate education developed during the British period also influences postindependence higher education. The university was a preserve of the upper classes and castes and was basically limited to the urban areas; while about 80 percent of India's population is now rural, the proportion was even higher prior to independence. Thus, most Indians were completely cut off from the universities. A university degree became a means for social mobility, but this mobility was largely limited to the urban

---

[2] One of the problems in discussing Indian higher education, and for that matter in making policy for the universities, is the fact that accurate statistics in many areas do not exist. Even where statistics do exist, there are often contradictions and difficulties in interpretations. The recent work of the University Grants Commission in providing a factual basis for discussion has been most valuable.

upper castes and classes. The ecological pattern of higher education was also well established during the British period and has only slowly changed. As has been noted, universities and most colleges were located in the cities. Even within cities, the colleges were generally located in upper-class areas, and the whole subculture of higher education reflected this Western upper-caste bias. Recent trends, particularly the expansion of the university system and the establishment of colleges in smaller towns, has meant that poorer segments of the population for the first time have access to a college degree.

THE INSTITUTIONS The large majority of colleges in India are private colleges in that they were founded and financed, to some extent at least, by private groups of various kinds. Caste associations, regional groups, philanthropic or social service societies, and other interests are typical founders of colleges in India. In recent years, a number of colleges have been founded by groups interested in making a profit from the operation of an institution of higher education. Missionary higher education, founded and operated largely by Protestant and Roman Catholic missionaries, is technically private but is usually considered in a special category because of its long historical tradition and often high academic standards. Colleges financed directly by state governments are also able to maintain generally high standards because of their more adequate financing and longer academic traditions. The newer *university colleges* are similar to undergraduate divisions of American universities, in that they are located on a central campus with the other elements of the university. These colleges, although fairly new, are often quite good because of their contact with the rest of the academic community and more adequate financial recources.

In 1964-65, there were 1,686 private colleges, 527 government colleges, and 147 university colleges in India; 85 percent of the students and 83 percent of the staff were located in private affiliated colleges. College size varies substantially, but the average college has between 100 and 500 students, although some of the larger colleges have as many as 2,500 (*Report of the Education Commission,* 1966, p. 302). India's University Grants Commission (UGC) is concerned about the 15 percent of the colleges which have fewer than 100 students and has stated that such institutions are uneconomical and cannot offer quality education.

Graduate Departments and Professional Schools

While the colleges are the most important aspect of the university system numerically, the graduate departments and professional schools also constitute a powerful element. Teachers in the graduate departments (called postgraduate in India) generally have higher status, more security, and higher salaries. In many universities, graduate departments have a key role in the setting of university examinations and designing syllabi. Such bodies as the Academic Council usually have strong representation from graduate departments as well. Because virtually no research is carried on at the college level, the responsibility for training students for higher degrees and for university-sponsored research is left to the graduate departments. A substantial proportion of the research conducted in India, particularly in the natural sciences, is done outside the universities in government-sponsored research institutes or laboratories. This is particularly true of applied research.

Graduate departments are organized in the traditional British pattern, with a single professor who also acts as head of the department. The head has almost complete control over the department and over the other tenured members of the staff. Junior faculty and research workers are particularly subject to this academic hierarchy. Vacant positions are generally advertised publicly and open to competition, although in fact many positions are filled from within the department. Lecturers and readers on the graduate level have a fair degree of job security, and in general conditions, both for teaching and research, are much more favorable than in the colleges. The Ph.D. degree in India is a research degree for which little or no course work is required. The major qualification for the Ph.D. is the submission of a dissertation of acceptable quality. The Indian M.A. (and generally the M.Sc.) is, however, a degree awarded on the basis of examinations covering a specified series of courses in each subject.

Professional education in India falls between graduate and collegiate education. Fairly large numbers of students enroll in professional courses in commerce, law, and, more recently, engineering, education, and other technological areas. While the status of professional degrees in law and commerce have declined substantially in recent years and students in these areas now find considerable difficulty in locating remunerative jobs, these programs still have substantial popularity, in part because it is easy to gain admittance to them. Engineering, business management, and other more technologically oriented professional programs have become important on the Indian academic scene only in the past two decades due largely to the demand for these skills and their high market value. Admission standards tend to be high in the fields which attract large numbers of applicants. For example, a student must have attained a significantly higher score on his matriculation (high school) examination to gain entrance to a science course than to an arts course in the same college. This is also true on the graduate level, where a first-class degree is often required for admission to an engineering or science graduate program, while a high second class is often sufficient for arts subjects.

RELATIONS WITH GOVERNMENT Higher education, according to the Indian constitution, is a responsibility of India's 16 states. It is also, however, a *concurrent subject,* which means that the central government has certain limited roles in the area of higher education. The central government administers several universities directly and has other indirect powers through the UGC and the Ministry of Education. For all practical purposes, however, major decisions concerning the universities are generally made at the state level. All universities in India are state universities — all institutions must be chartered by the state, and most receive a large proportion of their funding from the state.

The central government–state mix in higher education requires careful analysis, since the constitution divides responsibility and a number of complicated practices have grown up since independence. As has been noted, technical power lies with the states, but the center, particularly through the UGC, has taken an increasingly important role in recent reforms.[3] Various high-level commissions have concerned themselves with the universities, and these reports have some impact on the institutions. The fact that the UGC provides funds to universities for innovations, buildings, libraries, and other facilities and that these funds are allocated on a selective basis is another area of central government participation in higher education.

[3] The UGC is an independent statutory agency created by the Indian government in 1953 to act as a buffer between the government and the universities. It is patterned closely after the British University Grants Committee, although its effective links to the government, and particularly to the Ministry of Education, are stronger. The UGC provides funds to universities for improvements and innovations and attempts to maintain standards. Although the UGC has substantial statutory power to effect change, it has thus far not used its powers, according to a report of the Estimates Committee of the Lok Sabha (parliament).

UNIVERSITY
AND COLLEGE
GOVERNANCE

The college remains the cornerstone of the higher educational system. There are more than 2,500 colleges in India, which are affiliated to the 70 universities. The colleges have a substantial measure of autonomy in some areas but are circumscribed by university policy in others (Airan, 1967). For example, university authorities, with the participation of the colleges, decide on syllabi for the courses which are offered in the colleges and administer examinations for these courses. The individual teacher has relatively little direct control of his students, with the result that both student and teacher are more concerned with the syllabus and the examination than with what actually occurs in the classroom. While the colleges are regularly inspected by university authorities, there has been little effort to enforce standards on individual colleges. University authorities do have power to enforce regulations concerning such aspects of academic life as proper teacher-student ratio, the maximum number of students allowed in any college, prescribed expenditures which must be made for library facilities, and other matters. The universities have felt that they should maintain at least a minimum standard of education, and control over the newer and often less adequate colleges is a potential means of standardizing higher education. University officials can use various methods of enforcing their regulations, including withholding funds from the college or even disaffiliating an institution, but in fact this is almost never done and does not constitute a very effective sanction.

While some innovations have been made in the university structure since 1857, the basic organizational pattern for most of India's universities remains very similar to the original conception of the affiliating university. Several of the newer institutions are *unitary* in the sense that all their colleges are located on the campus. Such universities resemble the typical American university in the arrangement of the campus, although the administrative structure remains Indian. The geographic limits of many of the affiliating universities have been circumscribed, but an institution like the University of Calcutta still has 146,500 students in 162 affiliated colleges, some of which are located more than 100 miles from the university's main campus. The aim of the newer unitary universities is to create an academic community and to promote innovation and quality through interaction between the various parts of the university. All the universities, regardless of their mode of organization, now have graduate faculties and departments on their main campus, and many have created research institutes as well. But the

Indian university remains an examining and inspecting body first and an academic entity afterward (Gaudino, 1965).

Patterns of internal government at institutions are fairly uniform through the country. The legislative powers of most universities are divided into three parts—the senate, the syndicate, and the academic council. The senate, which is technically the highest decision-making body, is in fact relatively inactive. Meeting only once or twice a year and with a very large membership—often running to 200 representatives of various groups in the population such as labor, university alumni, government, and parts of the academic community itself—the senate deals only with the broadest issues and seldom has a vital role in university policy making. Of more importance is the syndicate, which meets approximately once a month and which has a much smaller membership. The syndicate makes the day-to-day policy decisions which are crucial to a university and makes broader recommendations to the senate as well. It has substantial power over the functioning of the university and its constituent colleges. It decides, for example, on examination policies, on hiring of new staff, on details of new construction, and other matters. The syndicate consists of representatives of various groups in the university. Some, such as the vice-chancellor or state director of education, are members ex officio; others are elected by constituencies or by the senate from among its members. The colleges are represented, as are graduate departments, and there are some public members as well. Elections for both the syndicate and the senate are often marked by political, regional, or caste considerations, and in institutions where there are political disputes or factional problems, such elections can be heated.

The body most directly concerned with the educational life of the university is the academic council. It consists of the various segments of the academic community and has representatives from college teachers, principals of colleges, professors in the university graduate departments, and others. The council meets only several times a year but recommends and in some cases acts on policies relating to examinations, new courses, qualifications of teachers, research policy and practices, and similar topics. The academic council acts according to the guidelines set down by the senate and syndicate but within these often general restrictions has substantial power to regulate and also to innovate.

Decision making on all levels in Indian higher education tends to be hierarchical and is generally vested either in senior individuals with high positions in the university structure or in senior public figures such as retired judges and the like. Because of the complicated and often slow process of decision making, university policies tend to evolve slowly and often only through the process of compromise and accommodation with all the various elements represented on the various legislative bodies. It is certainly true that the legislative structure of the Indian university does not make for streamlined decision making, nor in general does it facilitate serious educational discussion and debate.

The principal is a key personality in any college, and is, in fact, perhaps the most important element in determining the orientation and quality of the institution. The principal is, of course, subject to the constraints of university policy regarding curriculum, payment of staff, and other matters, but within his institution he is otherwise supreme. Traditional respect for a senior teacher combined with the lack of a national academic community contributes to the stature and power of the college principal. It is generally true that college teachers have little power over the governing of their institutions. In the lower ranks (and a substantial proportion of the staff are junior lecturers) there is virtually no security of tenure, and thus individual teachers are subject directly to the principal, who can fire staff members for cause. An imaginative principal can have a major impact on the quality of his institution, the morale of the teachers, and the examination results of the students. An authoritarian or simply incompetent principal, however, can have negative effects. The principal is subject to the wishes of his managing committee (similar to boards of trustees in American colleges), and in the private colleges managing committees occasionally interfere directly in the operation of the institution.

The executive functions of the university are related to the legislative but also have a good deal of autonomy. The titular head of the university is the chancellor, usually the governor of the state in which the university is located, but the effective executive officer of the university is the vice-chancellor, who is usually aided by a registrar and sometimes a rector. The vice-chancellor has the right to inspect all parts of the institution and its affiliated colleges; he acts as the chairman of many of the university's committees and agencies, and is generally the institution's spokesman to the government. The vice-chancellor is sometimes the only individual in the university who is aware of all its activities and who is able to coordinate the various decision-making bodies. This in itself is an important lever for power. The vice-chancellor, and occasionally the registrar, are also key political figures, not only because of their prestige in the community but because they can influence university policy on the broader level and such mundane but vitally important matters as hiring of teachers and administrative personnel and promotions.

The role of the vice-chancellor cannot be overemphasized. Despite the fact that many Indian vice-chancellors complain that they are constrained by a multitude of committees and outside influences, the post is a vitally important one. A vice-chancellor with educational vision can exercise substantial influence on his institution, succeed in maintaining or even raising educational standards, obtain funds from the central government for new programs, and otherwise stimulate innovation. It must be said that few vice-chancellors have played this constructive role. Most have been content to keep the institution functioning normally—itself a difficult task in some cases—without making many innovations. While vice-chancellors are often selected from among the ranks of distinguished educators, they are sometimes men with little or no educational experience. This practice has added to the ineffectiveness of the office in some institutions, since the vice-chancellorship is a complex position which requires an intimate knowledge of the university and of the political and other relationships which exist in it.

SOME ECOLOGICAL FACTORS There are a number of ecological factors, not quite organizational in the proper sense of the term but aspects of the university system which are important in gaining an understanding of Indian higher education. In India, the undergraduate degree consists generally of a three-year course, preceded by a year of *preuniversity study,* usually at a college but, in several states, in a senior high school. Students are often younger than in the United States or Europe. In recent years, a number of universities have passed legislation placing a minimum age requirement on entrance to the university. In most cases this age minimum is 15 or 16 years. While the age of the Indian student is gradually rising, many students enter college at 15 or 16 years of age. Most of the colleges are fairly small and often isolated institutions, with little physical or intellectual contact with the university subculture or with the main university campus. The average undergraduate student's education is limited to this institution and the rather meager facilities it offers. Colleges are typically housed in a single building, resembling an American high school in many architectural respects. Libraries tend to be very small, and a collection of 10,000 to 15,000 volumes is considered quite respectable. Classes tend to be large, and, what is more important, there is little or no opportunity for person-to-person interaction with the teacher. Despite the relatively small size of many colleges, they are typically highly bureaucratized, with regulations and forms in abundance. Staff members as well as students are circumscribed by a multitude of regulations.

Relatively few students in India live away from home. About 19 percent of the student population lives in approved student hostels, with an additional small percentage living independently. The typical Indian student, however, lives with his family and is subject to the traditional influences of the family environment. While the proportion of women in Indian higher education has risen dramatically in recent years, only 19 percent of the student population consists of women, and women are overrepresented in education (34 percent) and the liberal arts (29 percent).

While the structure of Indian higher education has remained basically static for a century, a number of changes are taking place in the university. The growth of "mass" higher education has necessarily involved expansion of the university and some changes in its orientation, curriculum, and administration. The university has become an important political institution in India. It contains large numbers of politically articulate individuals — both students and faculty — and it is a force to be reckoned with in many parts of the country. The university is a large-scale employer and thus is in a key position in a society marked by great problems in securing employment. Since universities spend large amounts of money for various purposes, they are economic powers in their regions. Perhaps most important is the fact that universities provide academic degrees, a key to social mobility and economic success in a stratified yet economically developing society (Altbach, 1969).

Universities and Politics

Universities have played a direct political role on a number of occasions. In the 1967 general elections, students were crucial in defeating the Congress Party in several states, and many politicians have supporters in the universities who provide intellectual substance to campaign oratory and other help (Singh, 1969). The university community, through militant demonstrations, has had a role in the language question, one of the controversial issues in Indian politics.

Indian universities are subject to external political pressure from state governments, local interests of various kinds, and occasionally from the central authorities. Indian authorities have also been thrown into crises due to internal political fighting, and in two well-known cases, at Banaras Hindu University and Aligarh Muslim University, authorities had to close the institutions when internal disputes stimulated student violence. Indian universities have been shaken by factional problems to a much greater extent that their Western counterparts.

Strong traditions of academic freedom and university autonomy never developed in India. There is no clear separation between government and the university—the universities are technically arms of the state government, which must charter them and which supply substantial sums of money for academic programs.

Political leaders have found it difficult to maintain a neutral attitude toward higher education, particularly when resources are scarce and the universities offer an especially vulnerable target for influence.

GROWTH   Postindependence higher education in India has been marked by rapid growth—in the opinion of many educators—much too rapid. The number of universities has increased from 20 in 1947 to 70 in 1968 (Table 43). Between 1950 and 1966, the annual increase in numbers of students averaged 10 percent, and the number of students grew from 263,000 to 1.9 million. The Education Commission (1964–1966)[4] has recommended that the rate of growth for undergraduate education be cut to 5.3 percent per year for the period 1967–1985 and has estimated that graduate education will maintain a rate of growth of about 11 percent (*Report of the Education Commission,* 1966, p. 302). Continued expansion of higher education will continue almost unabated, and due to the inability of various planning agencies to predict future trends accurately, it is likely that the rate of increase will be higher than the estimates of the Education Commission.

Almost all observers agree that while the quantitative growth has been impressive, maintenance of standards has been very difficult. Although it has not been stated in any official documents concern-

---

[4] The Education Commission was set up by the Government of India in a resolution passed in July 1964. Its purpose was to "advise the Government on the national pattern of education and on the general principles and policies for the development of education at all stages and in all aspects." The Commission included 17 members, including several foreign experts.

ing higher education, it is probably true that in India it is possible to choose between rapid numerical expansion of the system on the one hand and maintenance or improvement of quality on the other—but not to do both at the same time. The reason for this observation is a simple one. The resources available for higher education—both human and financial—are inadequate to provide for improvement on both the quantitative and qualitative scales. The choice in India has clearly been for quantity, and it is not surprising that standards on a number of levels have declined in recent years.

RECENT CHANGES While political pressure and inertia have made change slow, Indian higher education has been able to make some changes in recent years. The institution of the uniform three-year degree course throughout the country came largely with the prodding of the UGC. Language policy has also changed in the universities, due in large part to growing pressure from the society to shift the medium of instruction from English to the regional languages. Various commissions on such matters as examination reform, language, and university organization have submitted lengthy reports which have been only partly implemented. Given all the constraints on the university—both internal and external—reform has been a slow and difficult process.

It is also true that there are a number of bright spots in Indian higher education which provide some hope for the future and some models for overall improvement. A number of the traditionally prestigious colleges in India have managed, against substantial odds, to maintain standards or to improve them. Many of these institutions are missionary colleges, although a few, such as Elphinstone College in Bombay and Presidency College in Calcutta, are relatively well financed government colleges. While these institutions have not been very innovative in terms of new methods of teaching or organizational restructuring, they have continued to provide a solid academic preparation for their students, a large proportion of whom continue to come from upper socioeconomic classes in the urban population. The establishment of a number of new technological institutions and research facilities, such as the five Indian institutes of technology (established with foreign collaboration), the Indian Institute of Management at Ahmedabad and Calcutta, the Tata Institute of Fundamental Research, the Indian Institute of Science at Bangalore, and a few others, have provided islands of high-quality graduate training for students which are on a par with similar institutions in the industrially advanced nations.

Despite the recommendations of the Education Commission and the work of the UGC, substantial improvement of overall standards of higher education in India seems unlikely. There are massive political pressures for continued expansion, and politicians in India's parliamentary system must be responsive to these demands. Popular pressure also favors continued dilution of quality in higher education so that more people can obtain the B.A. degree. While it is clear that the economic value of a B.A. is relatively low and probably diminishing, it is a key to social mobility and certainly provides one of the main avenues for advancement. Thus, individuals are willing to risk becoming one of the army of educated unemployed in order to have a chance, however slim statistically, to break out of traditional occupational and social roles.

While statistics (Table 45) indicate that the largest proportion of students are in the arts faculties (40.9 percent in 1966, down slightly from 1965), science enrollment is growing slowly in size, with 32.7 percent of students in 1966; it is clearly much more prestigious and provides a more useful avenue for jobs and high-status positions in society. Next to arts and science, commerce is the most popular course, enrolling 9.6 percent of the students. Education and agriculture are surprisingly underrepresented in a largely agricultural nation which has undergone substantial expansion of its

TABLE 44 University development in India, basic facts and figures		1963-64	1964-65	1965-66
	Universities	55	62	63
	Teaching departments	1,102	1,160	1,327
	University colleges	128	147	163
	Affiliated colleges	1,983	2,213	2,409
	University enrollment	1,384,697	1,528,227	1,728,773
	Women students	230,513	267,776	318,996
	(Percentage of women)	(19.5)	(20.3)	(21.4)
	Staff including tutors/ demonstrators	68,634	77,120	84,676
	(Staff-student ratio)	(17.3)	(17.1)	(17.6)
	Residents in hostels	219,263	250,113	268,330
	(Percentage of student population)	(18.5)	(19.0)	(18.0)

SOURCE: *University Development in India, 1965-66,* 1966, p. 3.

Faculty	Total enrollment	Percentage	
		1965-66	*1964-65*
Arts	706,641	40.9	42.0
Science	565,254	32.7	31.3
Commerce	165,283	9.6	9.7
Education	33,546	1.9	1.9
Engineering and technology	85,555	4.9	5.1
Medicine	70,088	4.0	4.0
Agriculture	51,190	3.0	2.9
Veterinary science	6,257	0.4	0.4
Law	37,318	2.2	2.1
Others	7,641	0.4	0.6
TOTAL	1,728,773	100.0	100.0

SOURCE: *University Development in India, 1965-66,* 1966, p. 39.

schools. Students enrolled in education programs account for 1.9 percent of the total, while agriculture accounts for 4 percent. Engineering, one of the most prestigious courses, enrolls 4.9 percent. It should be noted that some of the professional degrees require a longer period of time than a degree in the arts and sciences, and some are semigraduate programs. This may account for the somewhat lower enrollment proportions in them. Law, traditionally the key to a political career and many other occupations, has lost much of its status and usefulness; 2.2 percent of the student population is enrolled in law school.

While the total number of students enrolled in universities in India is high, the proportion of the age group engaged in higher education is low by international standards and the rate of failure (or *wastage* as it is called in India) is quite high. The percentage of the age group entering college in India is around 3 percent, while the proportion of the total age group which obtains a first degree is slightly over 1 percent. This compares to slightly over 10 percent entering in Great Britain and more than 35 percent in the United States. Only the United States comes close to matching India in the volume of wastage in higher education, and the American rate is considerably lower than the Indian. In addition, there are significant regional differences in enrollments in higher education in India. The economically more advanced parts of the country—generally those areas with a significant proportion of the population in urban areas — provide college education for more people than the more backward areas do. For example, national statistics indicate that there are about 3,000 students attending college or university for every million of the population. The figure for Delhi, an urban area in which the national capital is located, is more than 9,000, while the figures for Rajasthan and Orissa, two of the less developed states, are under 2,000 students per million population.

One of the most significant patterns of higher educational development in the postindependence period has been the *deurbanization* of the colleges and universities. Many of the 49 universities founded since 1947 are located outside the major cities, as are a large proportion of the newer colleges. Many of these newer institutions are less adequate academically than the older, urban-oriented universities. While there are no national statistics as yet, it seems clear that a growing proportion of the student population now comes from smaller towns and even villages which never before had access to higher education.

STAFF-STUDENT RATIOS Relatively less is known about the 84,676 teachers who staff the universities and colleges of India. The increase of faculty has been similar to the growth in student enrollments, or about 10 percent per year. It is significant that the staff-student ratio has become slightly more favorable in recent years. In 1965–66, the overall staff-student ratio was 1:17.6, while it was 1:17.1 for the previous year. There is considerable difference between faculties with regard to teacher-student ratio. Arts and science colleges have a ratio of about 1:18.5, commerce 1:37.8, and law 1:32.2. Medicine, on the other hand, is 1:8.8. Ratios in the graduate departments and the university colleges are more favorable than those in the affiliated colleges. Teaching requirements in the university graduate departments are also much lower than in the colleges, with many university staff teaching about 6 hours of classes per week, in addition to the substantial responsibility of guiding doctoral research. College teachers generally teach 15 or more hours of classes per week. There are also substantial differences in salary. Arts and commerce college teachers earned an average of Rs 4,000 per year, while university teachers earned an average annual salary of Rs 6,500 per year, although senior teachers earned much more (Table 46). Recent suggested salary scales for college teachers, for example, start at Rs 300 per month and go up to Rs 800 per month, a substantial improvement over current practices in many institutions. There is sub-

TABLE 46 *Average annual salaries of teachers in higher education (1950-51 to 1965-66) (in rupees)*

Type of institution	Average annual salary of teachers (at current prices)				Average annual salary in 1965-66 (at 1950-51 prices)
	1950-51	*1955-56*	*1960-61*	*1965-66*	
University departments	3,759	5,456	5,475	6,500	3,939
	(100)	(145)	(146)	(173)	(105)
Colleges of arts and sciences	2,696	3,059	3,659	4,000	2,424
	(100)	(114)	(136)	(148)	(90)
Professional colleges	3,948	3,861	4,237	6,410	3,885
	(100)	(98)	(107)	(162)	(98)

SOURCE: Sir John Sargent, *Society, Schools, and Progress in India*, Pergamon Press, Oxford, 1968, p. 214A.

stantial regional variation in the payment of college and university teachers. Salaries are higher in Delhi than in Bombay and higher in West Bengal than in Madras. Urban institutions also often provide more benefits than rural schools. Top salaries for university professors under the new scales are Rs 1,600 to 1,800 per month, substantially higher than the highest paid college teachers.[5] The fact remains, however, that the academic community in India is not well paid, and it is increasingly difficult to lure the brightest students into academic work when they can make several times as much money in business or government service. Many college teachers must hold outside jobs in order to make enough money, and the situation for teachers in the rural and new institutions is particularly precarious.

FINANCING Financing has been one of the most serious problems of higher education in India and one of the main obstacles to improvement. India, unlike some developing countries, does not spend a very large proportion of its gross national product on education, the amount being estimated at around 3 percent. The rate of growth of educational expenditure, however, increased at about 10 percent per year, while the gross national product increased at a 2.5 percent level. The per capita expenditure on education remains quite low at a rate of Rs 12 (around $2) per year in 1965–66. Some 32 percent of India's total educational expenditure is spent on higher education, a figure substantially higher than that for most industrially advanced nations. A high proportion of educational funding comes from

[5] The current exchange rate is Rs 7.50 per $1. This, however, is slightly misleading since the general cost of living is fairly low in India.

government sources, some 53.1 percent, with an additional 34.7 percent from student fees.

By international standards, the cost per student in colleges and universities in India is extremely low. In arts and commerce colleges, for example, the annual per student cost is Rs 328. Science and vocational education on the undergraduate level is more expensive, costing Rs 1,167. In most colleges, a substantial proportion of the cost of education is met by the student through fees.

Most government support for higher education comes from the states, with central government aid coming largely through the UGC for special projects aimed at improving quality of education or making innovations. While the UGC has had a substantial impact on the universities through its grants to specific institutions for various purposes, its total share of the educational budget is not very significant. The colleges, as has been mentioned previously, are largely self-financing through fees and some donations from private sources. Many universities undertake to meet the rather frequent deficits in college budgets, but the institutions are technically responsible for their own financing. The exception to this rule is, of course, the government colleges, which receive financial support directly from state governments and therefore are generally in better financial condition than the private affiliated colleges.

The low per student expenditure and the general scarcity of resources for higher education in India mean that facilities are often minimal and that funds for libraries, new classrooms, and such amenities as common rooms or offices for professors are scarce and that many—perhaps most—colleges do without some facilities considered standard in most countries. The university graduate departments are in much better financial condition than the colleges, due largely to the fact that because the university directly finances much of their work, state government funds are

TABLE 47
Total direct expenditure on universities and colleges by sources, 1960-61

Source	Expenditure, %
Government funds (central and state)	53.1
Local board funds	0.4
Fees	34.7
Endowments	3.9
Other	7.9

SOURCE: *Education in India, 1960-1,* vol. 1, Ministry of Education, New Delhi, 1966, p. 176.

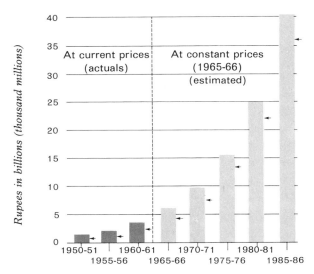

Indian expenditure on education, 1950-1985

NOTE: (1) The portion below the arrow represents expenditure met from government funds and that above it from other sources. (2) The lighter bars represent estimated expenditure at constant prices of 1965-66.

SOURCE: *Report of the Education Commission, 1964-66: Education and National Development,* 1966, p. 475.

readily available. There is little private philanthropy in higher education except for the private support of some colleges. This support is generally from religious or caste communities and is restricted to institutions reflecting their own traditions.

STUDENT ACTIVISM

Indian student activism has been analyzed elsewhere (Altbach, 1968, pp. 17–73) and can be mentioned only briefly here. Student activism, or *indiscipline* as it is called in India, has been a subject of discussion and concern for almost 50 years. Students took a very active role in the independence struggle in the 1920s and 1930s and constituted a strong left wing of the nationalist movement. In the postindependence period, however, activism has changed from a self-conscious, articulate, and unified movement into a more spontaneous series of usually locally oriented campaigns. The mass student movements of the nationalist period have disappeared, and in their place ad hoc committees have sprung up in all but a few localities, such as Calcutta, where ideological politics is still viable. Most student activism since 1947 has been oriented around local, usually nonpolitical issues, such as university examinations, increases in tram fares or academic fees, or less important questions. In a few cases, such as the language controversy in Madras and in several states during the 1967 general elections, students have organized around broader political questions. The level of indiscipline remains high, and in some institutions it has forced the closing of the university. But in general it is sporadic, unorganized, and leaderless. In a sense, it is more difficult to deal with precisely because it is directionless, because university personnel cannot really meet the concerns of the students. But it must also be said that in most cases, administrators have dealt with the students with a combination of arrogance and indecisiveness which has not stimulated confidence or respect. It is likely that indiscipline will continue as long as the situation in the universities is difficult for many students and as long as there is a problem of finding adequate employment after graduation. In India, student activism is directly linked to the organizational problems of the university and the contradictions in the broader society.

It is perhaps surprising that more universities are not seriously affected by unrest. A number of recent studies, e.g., *Survey of Living Conditions of University Students* (1961), indicate that a substantial proportion of college students are undernourished. Many live in poor conditions, either with their families or independently in large towns or cities where housing is expensive and scarce. There is little provision of extracurricular activities. The university system is impersonal and highly bureaucratic. Changes in the social class composition of many colleges have meant that new elements of the population are entering the colleges with increased frustrations and anxieties. The continuing problem of educated unemployment causes worry. It is significant that in the past several years, many engineering graduates (one of the more favored faculties) have waited a year or more for a suitable position. The situation for arts graduates is considerably worse, and a very large proportion must in the end lower their aspirations in order to obtain any employment at all.

PROBLEMS FACING INDIAN UNIVERSITIES One of the most critical issues for both the students and the institutions themselves is the language question (Shah, 1968). Indian universities are now in the process of shifting the medium of instruction from English to Hindi or one of the 15 official regional languages. Some institutions still retain English, while others have already made the switch. Graduate instruction is still in English in almost all the universities. The traditional language of university education in India has been English. This was workable as long as the student population remained small and limited to children of elite families which spoke English and who had generally been educated in English-medium secondary schools. As the student population shifted, however, many students had an inadequate command of English and could neither follow lectures nor write examinations in English.

The decision to shift the medium of instruction involved a long debate and was as much the product of political pressure as of academic argument. Newly articulate elements of the population who aspired to university education but did not have command of English demanded a shift. Nationalist politicians joined in, and the sense of regionalism which became particularly important after the creation of linguistic states in the late 1950s added to the pressure. While the debate continues, the decision seems to have been made in favor of regionalization of higher education as well as the schools, which have already adopted the regional languages. English will probably remain the language of graduate education in the sciences for an indefinite period and will continue to be important in graduate arts programs. Undergraduate education, except for a few of the elite colleges, will gradually shift entirely to the regional languages, with some emphasis on English and on Hindi in the non-Hindi-speaking areas.

This largely unheralded revolution in the language of higher education in India has substantial importance for the universities. Regionalization will mean that higher education will become more democratic in that students from lower socioeconomic groups who have not had secondary education in English will have access to the universities. It will also mean that standards will perhaps continue to decline, at least during the short run, since books and other documentary sources do not exist in many of the regional languages of India. The Indian universities will also become more insular and less cosmopolitan.

Another crucial issue involves the examination system and the related questions of wastage in the universities (*Report on Examination Reform,* 1965). Practically all commentators, Indian and foreign, have criticized the system of centrally administered examinations and the rigidity which this system entails. Examinations are, in almost every university, administered and set by the university through boards of study in each discipline. The individual colleges, in which more than 80 percent of the students are located, have little or no control over the examination, and the individual teacher has even less control. Examinations stress memorization, require little critical thought, and are often considered irrelevant. It is common, when too large a proportion of the students fail an examination, to give "grace marks" and simply to add a given number of marks to each examination which permits a higher percentage to pass. This practice has also come under attack in recent years.

While it is not possible to discuss the complicated question of examinations in full here, there is also a case in favor of the present system. The main argument is that the system ensures at least a minimal standard of quality which all students must meet. In a university system with widely diverse colleges and differing standards, the examination provides a kind of floor below which the colleges cannot go. The examination system is linked to another crucial question—the problem of wastage in higher education. On the undergraduate level, the wastage rate is quite high; in some universities which give two external examinations during the undergraduate career, it is as high as 80 percent, and the usual national figure (*Report on Standards of University Education,* 1965) given is around 50 percent. The general graduate percentage of failure is around 20 to 30, with the proportion of failure declining slightly in recent years (*Report on Standards of University Education,* 1965, p. 40). On the undergraduate level, science students are more successful in their examinations than arts students, perhaps due to their better preparation and the fact that all science students are enrolled full-time.

The undergraduate wastage rate in India is quite high by international standards, and certainly is a costly factor, both in individual and institutional terms. One of the main recommendations of both the Education Commission and several UGC Committees on Examination Reform was to institute a more selective admissions policy and by this means seek to exclude from the colleges individuals who will obviously have difficulty in completing their studies. Thus far, however, these measures for reforms have not been implemented. Another result of the high rate of failure in examinations is that only 25 percent of the students in some universities are able to finish their education in the prescribed time (*Report on Standards of University Education,* 1965, p. 19). Students are permitted to retake examinations, and many are forced to drop out of college in order to work.

PROPOSED REFORMS In its recent major report on education in India, the Education Commission made the following recommendations, among others, regarding higher education (*Report of the Education Commission,* 1966):

1 While expansion of higher education is necessary for India's economic development, the rate of expansion should be slower in the coming period.

2 There is a great need for selective admissions to higher education. To provide selectivity in admissions, a Central Testing Organization, similar to the Educational Testing Service in the United States, should be set up, and the universities themselves should set more stringent standards for their colleges.

3 The standards of the colleges should be improved, and the least adequate of existing colleges should receive special attention.

4 The UGC should undertake to select and appropriately fund a number of "major universities" which would provide education of an international standard and would be able to contribute first-rate research. Such institutions, by their example, would have a salutary effect on the whole of Indian higher education.

5 Colleges should be allowed more scope for improvement and experimentation, and some of the best colleges should be identified and permitted a degree of independence from university authorities.

Higher education remains one of the most controversial topics in Indian public life. It is perhaps significant that in the three years since the publication of the Education Commission's report, very little has been done to implement its proposals for reform. Given the pressures on the university system discussed in this essay, substantial reform seems unlikely. Yet, the Indian university will continue to play a critical role in the society and will continue to grow. The debate over the goals of higher education and the effectiveness of the university in meeting these goals will go on, but at the same time higher education will continue its virtually unplanned growth and will continue to train the elite and provide broad social mobility for growing numbers of Indians.

Universities in India

Agra

Aligarh

Allahabad

Andhra

Andhra Pradesh Agricultural

Annamalai

Banaras

Bangalore

Berhampur

Bhagalpur

Bihar

Bombay

Burdwan

Calcutta

Darbhanga Sanskrit

Delhi

Dibrugarh

Gauhati

Gorakhpur

Gujarat

Gurukul Kangri Vishvavidyalaya

Indore

Jabalpur

Jadavpur

Jammu and Kashmir

Jawharlal Nehru Krishi Vishwavidyalaya

Jiwaji

Jodhpur

Kalyani

Kanpur

Karnatak

Kerala

Kurukshetra

Lucknow

Madras

Madurai

Magadh

Maharaja Sayajirao University of Baroda

Marathwada

Meerut

Mysore

Nagpur

North Bengal

Orissa University of Agriculture and Technology

Osmania

Panjab

Patna

Poona

Punjab Agricultural

Punjabi

Rabindra Bharati

Rajasthan

Ranchi

Ravi Shankar

Roorkee

Sambalpur

Sardar Patel

Saugar

Saurashtra

Shivaji

S.N.D.T. Women's

South Gujarat

Sri Venkateswara

Udaipur

University of Agricultural Sciences,
Bangalore

Utkal

Uttar Pradesh Agricultural

Varanaseya Sanskrit Vishwavidyalaya

Vikram

Visva-Bharati

References

Airan, J. W. (ed.): *College Education in India,* Manaktalas, Bombay, 1967.

Altbach, Philip G.: "The Permanent Crisis of Indian Higher Education," *Quest,* no. 60, January–March 1969.

Altbach, Philip G.: "Student Politics and Higher Education in India," in P. G. Altbach (ed.), *Turmoil and Transition,* Basic Books, Inc., Publishers, New York, 1968, pp. 17–73.

Ashby, Eric: *Universities: British, Indian, African,* Harvard University Press, Cambridge, Mass., 1966.

Estimates Committee, Lok Sabha: *Report on the University Grants Commission,* Lok Sabha Secretariat, New Delhi, 1966.

Gaudino, Robert: *The Indian University,* Popular Prakashan, Bombay, 1965.

McCully, Bruce: *English Education and the Origins of Indian National Development,* Columbia University Press, New York, 1940.

Report of the Education Commission, 1964–66: Education and National Development, Ministry of Education, New Delhi, 1966.

Report on Examination Reform, University Grants Commission, New Delhi, 1965.

Report on Standards of University Education, University Grants Commission, 1965.

Shah, A. B. (ed.): The Great Debate: *The Language Question in Indian Education,* Lalvani, Bombay, 1968.

Singh, Amar K.: "Academic Politics and Student Unrest," in P. G. Altbach (ed.), *Turmoil and Transition,* Basic Books, Inc., Publishers, New York, 1969.

Survey of Living Conditions of University Students, Ministry of Education, Government of India, New Delhi, 1961.

University Development in India, 1965–66, University Grants Commission, New Delhi, 1966.

12. Commentary

by James A. Perkins

It may be small comfort to American educators to realize that their opposite numbers in other countries are wrestling with the same problems they are. But comfort for educators comes in small doses these days, and from the preceding chapters they will undoubtedly learn from the experiences common to all in higher education.

The first general experience is surely that of handling overwhelming numbers with inadequate resources. Despite the already considerable expansion of facilities for higher education in the nine countries surveyed in this volume, there are still many more applicants than places. And the surge of applicants has by no means reached its peak. Clearly the democratization of secondary education has led to increased demand for college and university entrance, and this demand has been encouraged by the need for trained manpower. The combination has been lethal where, as in France and Germany, there has been inadequate preparation for these irresistible claims. The lesson is clear: the problems of higher education are embedded in the policies for secondary education.

The second general experience is rising costs. Rising costs are the inevitable consequence of rising numbers. And costs have gone up so fast that financial policies have not kept income and expense in balance. Systems of taxation have had to be revised; colleges and universities have had to adopt unfamiliar (and generally distasteful) arrangements for public cost accounting and to search for new money from every possible source.

The third general experience is that the increase in numbers and costs has led to a variety of public and private systems for planning and coordinating the growth of higher education. Though none of these systems is working very well, they all are struggling with the difficult problems of allocating resources in a way that will both serve the public purpose and preserve institutional autonomy. This, clearly, is no small trick.

Some systems have been designed to coordinate the interests of the universities: the University Grants Committee in Great Britain functions in this way. Some have been designed to bridge the state-federal relationship (and to bring in academics and private citizens as well), as in the case of Germany. Others leave their planning and coordination pretty much up to the central ministry of education, as in France and Japan. All, however, are faced with the need for bringing into some kind of harmony the increasingly interlaced interests of prospective students and their families, university faculties, employers of university personnel, and others. Only in this way—with adjustment of conflicting priorities—is it possible to allocate resources sensibly. One of the most interesting tasks ahead for the developed states is the evolution of national systems of higher education in which various interests and demands are both understood and well articulated.

Apart from these three general experiences Dr. Burn and Dr. Altbach provide a gold mine of information on each of the individual countries discussed in this volume. Perhaps it will be useful to highlight some points of particular interest.

In the case of Great Britain, the report identifies, but does not attempt to analyze, the shifts in the balance of power between the government, the University Grants Committee, and the universities and other institutions of higher education. If one can detect a drift of affairs, it is toward consolidation of all the higher education institutions at the university level into a single system, increased control over that system by the UGC, and the beginnings of increased surveillance of UGC affairs by the central government. This trend is understandable since the size of the budget for higher education has heightened public concern and made higher education expenditures a matter of public policy. It is not likely, therefore, that the almost complete autonomy that the UGC once enjoyed could have been maintained for any length of time. As Dr. Burn mentions, the fear that the Treasury's right to "inspect the books" would lead immediately to an invasion of academic freedom has not been borne out. But the basic drift described above is discernible and is a matter of some concern.

Turning now to three countries with federal systems—Australia, Canada, and Germany—one finds, along with a good many individual differences, certain kinds of problems common to federal systems, which are also pertinent to the United States experience. These are relationships between federal government and state governments, universities as a system, and universities as individual institutions.

In all federal countries, with the possible exception of the Soviet Union, relations between the central and state governments are a matter of sensitivity. Australia's problems are typical. One has the impression from this study that the Australian states have taken vigorous leadership in educational innovation. The result has been that while Commonwealth financial support has increased, Commonwealth government control has been kept to a satisfactory minimum. The Australian Universities Commission, established in 1959 as an advisory body, has served as an important balance wheel in the federal-state relationship. And it is balance—between the needs for funding, planning, and coordination on one side and the needs for independence, freedom to innovate, and internal flexibility on the other—that is the critical concern.

In Canada, the split between French Quebec and the rest of Canada is pivotal in national policies and consequently affects higher education. Actually, Canada is four separate geographical areas as far as higher education is concerned: the Western provinces, Ontario, Quebec, and the Maritimes. Geography and, most particularly, culture have created a resistance to national approaches to national problems, and it is hard to see how national approaches can be greatly strengthened until the basic French-English division of the country is in some measure resolved.

Within this decentralized set of systems, however, there is much ferment in both Ontario and Quebec. In the former some interesting experiments are going on, hand in hand with the development of a provincewide system, while in Quebec the struggle for modernization against the more traditional interests of the Church holds the center of the stage. For the immediate future, the report on Canada indicates that the provinces will be the center of planning and of innovation while the federal authorities will hold to a modicum of involvement.

In Germany, another federal system, higher education has been traditionally the concern of the *Länder,* and the university has been the province of the full professor. Once again Germany is an illustration of the complexities of developing national systems that will provide for local autonomy, both political and academic, while at the same time encouraging planning at a national level. The Wissenschaftsrat, a unique body made up of federal and state officials as well as university professors and laymen, is potentially the most powerful coordinating and planning body for higher education in Germany. The process of modernization now finds the Wissenschaftsrat on one end of the spectrum and the students on the other, with state officials and the professoriat acting as factors of powerful resistance.

In Sweden one finds a tight centralized system. Higher education is governed by an alliance between the Ministry of Education and the Office of the Chancellor of Universities, but Sweden's recent reforms involve considerable participation of students and faculty in policy making and planning. One has the impression of a fairly well articulated system, with central planning having anticipated most but not all of the problems. This has been done with an astonishing increase of 600 percent in entrants into higher education over the last 20 years. The discipline that comes from a single state system, with a socialist philosophy to which all the parties in the country are committed, has made possible agreement on forward-looking plans and on means of making them effective. Sweden and Russia, of the nine countries covered in this book, have had the least disruption and the least difficulty expanding their systems in higher education in the face of new social priorities.

France is something else again. A centralized state like Sweden, France has had the benefit of neither effective central planning nor certainly any public consensus about the expansion of higher education and the form that expansion should take. Actually, French higher education is facing the consequences of democratizing secondary education without the proper attention to the consequences of the demands for places in universities. The results are swollen enrollments, little agreement about expansion plans, and wide division within the French system—from peasant to Prime Minister—with respect to the role and mission of higher education in French society. In the middle of this complex, the central institution of the University of Paris, which in many ways is one of the greatest centers of intellectual thought in the world, is in danger of fragmentation and internal destruction if it is not able to develop an acceptable plan for its functioning.

The Faure legislation of November 1968 has not been fully implemented, and Faure himself has not continued in office. Late reports suggest the faint air of discouragement after the vigorous interventions of Faure some time ago. The problem for higher education in France and its universities remains.

In the Soviet Union, as in Sweden, one finds the optimum of effective planning with a maximum of public acceptance of those plans. While problems do remain, they are dealt with outside the public forum and are resolved by appropriate internal decisions involving the Party and government apparatus. As in all carefully planned systems, inaccuracies in projections exist and will continue to exist as long as human beings are fallible and unpredictable. But anyone looking at the Soviet experience cannot help being impressed with the way in which gradations of possibilities for university experience have been made available to potential students. Though Soviet universities have not been able to absorb all qualified applicants, nevertheless, alternatives are present. Those who do not make a university have the possibility of going to a technical school. Those who cannot make a technical school can continue jobs in the provinces or in their home cities with a connection with the university that makes it possible for them to continue studies. The allowance for individual circumstances and the hierarchy of alternatives present have solved for the Soviet Union many problems that are still being wrestled with in other countries. It is the more remarkable that this has been accomplished in a federal system. No doubt this has been made possible by the strong hand of the Party, which can operate with equal force at both federal and state levels.

In India it is a cliché to say there are too many graduates from universities. Next to the United States and the Soviet Union, India is third in the number of students enrolled in universities, today roughly 2 million. Two problems stand out as one reads the report on the Indian circumstance. The first is that 85 percent of students in higher education are in private affiliated colleges, of which there are almost 1,700. Private colleges by definition are not so easily subject to public direction, and this fact is critical when the colleges and universities change the priorities of their attention. The problem of assuring that higher education reflects the new needs facing India for the rest of the century will be difficult to resolve in the face of such a federally decentralized system and such a large proportion of students in small private institutions. Furthermore, while there is a grants commission for India, there do not seem to be any powerful bodies reflecting education interests that can bring their weight to bear on both public and private authorities involved in the Indian experience.

As in the case of India, Japan, though a unitary and not a federal state, has a large part of its institutions of higher education in the private sector. About 75 percent of all students in higher education are in private rather than public institutions, which has made national planning a complexity. The result has been great autonomy on the part of individual universities and therefore inability to deal with crises, like the current student difficulties, that are national in scale. In Japan, again as in India, the observation must be that the private system with its institutional independence provides the possibility of great flexibility but it also provides the possibility for great resistance to change. Surely, unless the private institutions use their independence for imaginative planning and for concerted action in the national interest, their days are numbered and they will be replaced by public institutions or brought under some national control. In the meantime, national problems that affect all the institutions will be dealt with in sporadic fashion. Those groups which are nationally organized — religious, student, or private — will be able to bring unmerciful pressure to bear on individual and uncoordinated university activities. As in India, there is no promising sign that those immediately concerned with higher education in Japan are organized to offer effective guidance and control to either public or private authority. No more urgent task faces these two countries.

Now to draw some conclusions for the United States from this survey of higher education in nine countries.

First we see that, in the United States as well as abroad, as the costs of education rapidly increase, financial support is sought from the highest political (taxing) power. In every country studied, support for higher education and research has shifted, and will shift further, from local to central governments, from state to federal authorities, from private to public funding. In the United States, with its heavy commitment to almost universal higher education, the emergence of this trend comes as no surprise. (That the shift to federal support has not been more marked here than elsewhere may be explained by the relative wealth of this country and the vitality of the federal idea.) The last half decade has seen an enormous increase in the federal budget for higher education, and the Carnegie

Commission has already projected the need for an increase in federal financial responsibility, along with increases in state and private contributions. But clearly the largest percentage increase will involve federal funds.

In the United States, if anything like the increase in federal support that has been projected turns out to be available, the balance of responsibility between federal and state governments will be drastically changed. We can anticipate, on the basis of experiences abroad, that state and local governments will react strongly against the usurpation of their prerogatives in higher education and will argue that they should be the managers and disbursers of federal funds for education. For the individual institutions, which increasingly will be the direct recipients of federal support, the biggest change will be occasioned by their becoming publicly accountable for the ways in which that money is spent. In the opinion of this observer, neither the states nor the colleges and universities have even begun to think of the impact on established ways of doing business that is bound to accompany this shift in the financing of higher education.

A third conclusion applicable to the United States is that when the drive toward national cohesion is accompanied by a drive for equality of opportunity, central governments are expected to offset inequities.

In almost every country studied, there is a tendency to widen the range of admissions by establishing increased scholarships, new institutions, and instructional programs relevant to widely divergent needs. Even though the United States has been a leader in the development of flexible and differentiated systems of higher education, it could study with profit the experiences of others: for example, in the Soviet Union alternative arrangements of part-time study and home correspondence courses for those who are not admitted as full-time students; in Germany, the range of institutional choice open to students throughout their academic career. We could give special attention to increasing flexibility in our system in order to enhance the opportunity for the disadvantaged and the talented to enter the institutions of their choice. And we could make that choice more meaningful if we devised improved information systems that would give the individual a sharper view of his needs and a clearer picture of institutional offerings.

In order both to equalize opportunities and to reduce costs, higher education in the United States requires greater interinstitutional coordination. Here, there is much to be learned from the coordinating efforts in other nations.

It is apparent that the coordinator's lot is not a happy one. First, those who are being coordinated are rarely pleased with the coordinator or with the very fact of being coordinated. The head of an institution, whether president, vice-chancellor, or rector, is rarely inclined to greet the coordinator with unreserved enthusiasm. Further, a president has all sorts of pride and responsibility tied up with the notion of institutional autonomy and its importance as the shield for academic freedom. Thus, the coordinator must deal from the first with emotional factors of a special order.

Another problem in coordination is a critical one but is rarely acknowledged in discussions of the theoretical premises and problems associated with the task. That problem is one of staff—the people working under a coordinator who are to carry out the delicate day-to-day business of coordination. Whether on a German, British, Canadian, Australian, or Californian campus, administrators will, and do, say with equal feeling: "The coordinator is a fine well-meaning fellow—but those mice around him are impossible!" The staff rarely have the coordinator's prestige or experience; they are generally underpaid and unprepared for the kind of diplomacy needed to deal with touchy academics, and they almost always receive the blame for the coordinator's actions. In the United States as well as in other systems faced with the desperate need for coordination, ways must be found to attract talent and skill—not just in the man at the top, but in the entire group involved in the coordinating process.

A further difficulty becomes clear on examining the overseas experience. It is that bureaucracy in the private sector is no more benign than its counterpart in the public sector. The University Grants Committee in Great Britain is an appropriate example. As the UGC's staff expands, their surveillance causes as much anguish as if they were Treasury officials—and sometimes more, because they cannot be so easily dismissed as government Neanderthals. The UGC is, after all, a venture of the universities themselves.

The United States would also do well to study the strengths of the methods of coordination undertaken in various countries. The British involvement of faculty and the German involvement of faculty plus informed laymen outside the government and government officials are the distinctive features of their coordinating bodies. Both methods reveal a recognition of the fact that coordination is more than just an administrative problem. The adoption of approaches such as these would undoubtedly benefit American experiments in coordination and cooperation.

Acknowledgments

The writer is indebted to a great many people for assistance with this survey. They are listed in Appendix B. For most of the countries, special debt must be acknowledged to individuals for their interest, counsel, and comment on preliminary drafts of country chapters: Prof. Friedrich Edding of the Max Planck Institut für Bildungsforschung, Berlin (for the chapter on Germany); Prof. Edward F. Sheffield of the University of Toronto (for the chapter on Canada); Mrs. Stella M. Greenall, research officer of the National Union of Students in Great Britain (for the chapter on Great Britain); Dr. Robert S. Schwantes of the Asia Foundation (for the chapter on Japan); Prof. Harold J. Noah of Teachers College, Columbia University (for the chapter on the Soviet Union); and Miss Lizzie Gibson of the Organization for Economic Cooperation and Development (for the chapter on Sweden). For the chapters on Australia and France, particular individuals cannot be singled out for special thanks as so many were helpful.

The patience and interest of my husband and children were essential to the completion of this survey. To Dr. Clark Kerr this survey owes its inspiration and direction. It was because he thought I might do it that I tried.

Barbara B. Burn

355

Appendix A: Annotated Bibliography

FRANCE   The Orientation Act of November 1968 changed the structure and functioning of the universities so radically that many general works on these subjects have more historical interest than contemporary validity. As with most of the other countries surveyed in this volume, appendix V of the Robbins Committee Report (Robbins Committee, *Higher Education: Report of the Committee Appointed by the Prime Minister under the Chairmanship of Lord Robbins, 1961–63,* Cmnd. 2154, HMSO, London, 1963) and UNESCO's *World Survey of Education,* vol. IV (Paris, 1966) give a broad overview of higher education in the early 1960s. The sections on higher education in *Encyclopédie Pratique de l'Éducation en France* of the French Ministry of Education (Paris, 1960) present a comprehensive factual survey, including considerable historical background.

Since the beginning of this decade, the rising pressure for university reform has been paralleled by an expanding volume of publications on the subject. Raymond Aron in his "Quelques Problèmes des Universités Françaises" (*Archives Européenes de Sociologie,* vol. III, no. 1, Paris, 1962) criticizes the conservatism and inflexibility of the universities in the face of the changing higher education needs of society. Gerald Antoine and Jean-Claude Passeron (*La Réforme de l'Université,* Calmann-Levy, Paris, 1966) call for wide-ranging reforms in structure, governance, and teaching and research functions and, in particular, in the rigid requirements of the *agrégation,* which caused excessive specialization and was losing its value as a professional qualification for *lycée* professors because of changes in the *lycées.*

The 1966 reforms of the three cycles of university education are comprehensively evaluated by Raymond Aron in his series, "La Crise de l'Université" (*Le Figaro,* 140ᵉ année, nos. 6703–6706, March 17-21, 1966), and Bert M-P. Leefmans analyzes their impli-

357

cations for American students in "French Educational Reform and the American Student" (*Liberal Education,* vol. LIII, no. 2, May 1967). Jean Capelle discusses the whole spectrum of higher education, problems and strengths of the universities, and the 1966 reforms in *Tomorrow's Education: The French Experience* (Pergamon Press, Ltd., Oxford, 1967). The Caen Colloquium, at which reform-minded professors, administrators, and other educationists debated and put forward recommendations for university reform, is reported in "L'Université Face à sa Réforme" (*Revue de l'Enseignement Supérieur,* no. 4, Paris, 1966). The Orientation of Higher Education Act (no. 68-978, November 12, 1968) was published in the *Journal Officiel* (Paris, November 13, 1968).

For studies of scientific and technical training and research see OECD, *Reviews of National Science Policy, France* (Paris, 1966) and *Scientific and Technical Personnel: The Education, Training and Functions of Technicians, France* (Paris, 1967). An excellent study of financial assistance for students is Marianne von Rundstedt's *Studien und Berichte: Die Studienforderung in Frankreich 1950–1962* (Institut für Bildungsforschung in der Max Planck Gesellschaft, Berlin, 1965). The system for financing public education, including higher education, is described in "The Financing of Education under a Centralized System: France," by André Garcia (OECD, *Financing of Education for Economic Growth,* Paris, 1966).

On educational planning and the Fifth Plan, 1966-1970, on all education, the major reference is the plan itself (Commissariat Général du Plan d'Équipement et de la Productivité, V^e plan 1966–1970: *Rapport Général de la Commission de l'Équipement Scolaire, Universitaire et Sportif,* Paris, 1965). Two studies which give the history of educational planning and its relationship to the total investment plans for the development of the French economy are Claude Vimont's "Methods of Forecasting Employment in France and Use of These Forecasts to Work Out Official Educational Programmes" (in Seymour Harris (ed.), *Economic Aspects of Higher Education,* OECD, Paris, 1963), and "Integration of the Educational Plan within General Economic and Social Planning in France," an unpublished address by J-P. Guillard of the Commissariat Général du Plan, presented at the National Seminar on Educational Planning held by the Australian National Advisory Committee for Unesco, Canberra, 1968.

Among the spate of publications on the May 1968 student revolt, the recent book by Daniel and Gabriel Cohn-Bendit, leaders in the revolt, has special interest: *Obsolete Communism: The Left-Wing Alternative* (McGraw-Hill Book Company, New York, 1969).

Two journals of the Ministry of National Education, *Informations Statistiques* and *Éducation Nationale,* are useful references for statistical and other information. *Éducation in France,* published periodically by the Cultural Services of the French Embassy (in New York), prints articles and translations of official reports on all educational levels and includes statistical data. The annual *Tableaux de l'Éducation Nationale* of the Ministry of National Education is another basic official reference.

GREAT BRITAIN
Sources on higher education in England and Wales are abundant and outstanding in quality and detail. The problem is mainly one of selection rather than identification.

For the period up to 1962 the Robbins Committee Report (*Higher Education: Report of the Committee Appointed by the Prime Minister under the Chairmanship of Lord Robbins 1961–1963,* Cmnd. 2154, HMSO, London, 1963) is an encyclopedia of information on universities, teacher education, and advanced further education since the early 1950s. Its chief weaknesses lie in methods for predicting future demand for higher education and in its neglect of future needs for highly trained manpower in setting expansion goals. On the University of Oxford only, the Franks Report (*Report of the Commission of Inquiry under the Chairmanship of Lord Franks,* 2 vols., Clarendon Press, Oxford, 1966), which was prompted by the Robbins Committee Report, makes a detailed review of governance, the collegiate system, staffing, finance, students, and the role of this university in the total university system.

Several University Grants Committee publications report periodically on university affairs. The annual *Returns from Universities and University Colleges in Receipt of Exchequer Grants* provides comprehensive statistics on enrollments, degrees awarded, academic staff, and finance. The *University Grants Committee Annual Survey,* published in the *Returns* until 1960 and separately since, reviews UGC activities and gives guidelines for future developments. Every five years the quinquennial report of the UGC, *University Development,* summarizes developments for a five-year period and sets forth the UGC's recommendations for finance and expansion in the next quinquennium. The most recent is *University Development 1962–67* (Cmnd. 3820, HMSO, London, 1968).

Reports of special committees appointed by the UGC, sometimes jointly with other bodies, to study and recommend on special fields give in-depth studies of selected fields: computers (*A Report of a Joint Working Group on Computers for Research,* Cmnd. 2883, HMSO, London, 1967); Latin American Studies (*Parry Committee Report,* 1964); audio-visual aids in higher scientific education (*Brynmor Jones Committee Report,* 1965); and the report on the success rate of university students *(Enquiry into Student Progress,* 1968).

The annual report of the Department of Education and Science, *Education and Science in 1967* (Cmnd. 3564, HMSO, London, 1968), which replaced the earlier report *Education in 19 . . . ,* together with the annual *Statistics of Education* of the DES, present detailed statistics on all education falling under the further education and teacher education rubrics: enrollments, staffing, finance, awards to students, numbers of institutions, and degrees, diplomas, and certificates awarded. These publications also contain information on university finance and awards to university students. Special DES reports treat particular aspects of higher education: the *Report of the Committee on Social Studies* (Cmnd. 2660, HMSO, London, 1965); the landmark Anderson Committee study on student finance (*Grants to Students,* Cmnd. 1051, HMSO, London, 1960); *A Plan for Polytechnics and Other Colleges* (Cmnd. 3006, HMSO, 1966); the Weaver Report on *The Government of Colleges of Education* (HMSO, London, 1966). DES reports also discuss research, science education, and manpower needs and problems: *Statistics of Science and Technology* (prepared jointly with the Ministry of Technology, HMSO, London, 1967); *The Brain Drain* (prepared jointly with the Ministry of Technology, Cmnd. 3417, HMSO, London, 1967); and the Dainton Committee *Enquiry into the Flow of Candidates in Science and Technology into Higher Education* (Cmnd. 3541, HMSO, London, 1968). The *Report on Science Policy* by the Council for Scientific Policy (Cmnd. 3007, HMSO, London, 1966) summarizes needs and developments in scientific training and research.

The *Commonwealth Universities Yearbook* (annual), published by the Association of Commonwealth Universities, includes a general survey of universities followed by subsections on each institution, giving general information, personnel, fields of study, and statistics. UNESCO's *World Survey of Education,* vol. IV (Paris, 1964) is a useful general summary, now somewhat outdated. An excellent account of the role of higher education in research is OECD, *Reviews of National Science Policy, United Kingdom, Germany* (Paris, 1967), which contrasts research organization and the research effort in the two countries and has separate sections on each.

British Universities, by Sir James Mountford (Oxford, University Press, London, 1966), combines some historical background with an exposition of the university scene in the mid-1960s including expansion in the post-Robbins period and attendant problems. Two excellent accounts of the thinking and planning of the new universities of Essex and Sussex, respectively, are Albert E. Sloman, *A University in the Making* (Reith Lectures, 1963) and David Daiches (ed.), *The Idea of a New University* (Andre Deutsch, Ltd., London, 1964).

A major recent study of the growth in enrollments in higher education in England and Wales since the Robbins Committee Report is *The Impact of Robbins: Expansion in Higher Education,* by Richard Layard, John King, and Claus Moser (Penguin Books, London, 1969). This study predicts a sizable shortfall of places in higher education by 1971-72 as a result of changes in enrollment demand in the post-Robbins period.

Among periodicals the main sources on higher education are *Universities Quarterly, Reports* of the Home Universities Conference (annual), and the *Times Educational Supplement.*

CANADA   The rapid change in Canadian universities and colleges in the last decade has been accompanied by the publication of increasing numbers of volumes on the subject. Those produced before the mid-1960s are given in R. S. Harris and A. B. Tremblay, *A Bibliography of Higher Education in Canada* (University of Toronto Press and Les Presses de l'Université Laval, 1960), and R. S. Harris, *Supplement* (1965). More recent select bibliographies can be found in the Canada section of the *Commonwealth Universities Yearbook* published by the Association of Commonwealth Universities (London, annual volume).

Useful summaries appear in the ACU *Yearbook,* in vol. IV of UNESCO's *World Survey of Education* (Paris, 1966), and in appendix V of the Robbins Report (*Higher Education: Report of the Committee Appointed by the Prime Minister under the Chairmanship of Lord Robbins 1961–63,* Cmnd. 2154, HMSO, London, 1963). *Canadian Universities and Colleges,* published by the Association of Universities and Colleges of Canada (Ottawa, annual volume), also summarizes the higher education scene and presents basic information on individual institutions. Recent developments are annually reported in sections of the *Canadian Annual Review* (University of Toronto Press), the *Canada Yearbook* of the Dominion Bureau of Statistics (Queen's Printer, Ottawa) and the *Survey of Higher Education,* also prepared by the Dominion Bureau of Statistics. Also useful in presenting information and some critical discussion on the total situation in the first half of this decade are a series of five articles in the *Canadian Geographical Journal* on universities and their environments in five regions (1965-66); R. S. Harris (ed.), *Changing Patterns of Higher Education in Canada* (University of Toronto Press, 1966), whose four chapters discuss the Atlantic Provinces, the West, Quebec, and Ontario in turn; J. E. Hodgetts (ed.), *Higher Education in a Changing Canada* (University of Toronto Press, 1966), which deals in part with the future of higher education; and D. F. Dodson (ed.), *On Higher Education: Four Lectures* (University of Toronto Press, 1966).

For detailed statistics on recent enrollments, the annual Enrollment in Universities and Colleges (part I of *Survey of Higher Education*) and *Preliminary Statistics of Education* (Dominion Bureau of Statistics, Queen's Printer, Ottawa) are basic references. Data for as early as 1951 and projections to 1975-76 (now considered too low) are combined in *Enrollment in Schools and Universities 1951– 52 to 1975–76,* prepared by Wolfgang M. Illing and Zoltan E. Zsigmond for the Economic Council of Canada (Staff Study 20, Queen's Printer, Ottawa, 1967). Copious information on past and projected enrollments can be found in the report of a commission to the Association of Universities and Colleges of Canada under the chairmanship of Vincent W. Bladen, *Financing Higher Education in Canada* (University of Toronto Press and Les Presses de l'Université Laval, 1965). An official source on the financing of higher education which provides statistical data assembled since the Bladen Report is *Canadian Universities, Income and Expenditure,* an annual publication since 1961 of the Dominion Bureau of Statistics (Queen's Printer, Ottawa).

The main study of governance is Sir James F. Duff and Robert O. Berdahl, *University Government in Canada: Report of a Commission Sponsored by the Canadian Association of Universities and Colleges of Canada* (University of Toronto Press, 1966). Much of the discontent with governance which prompted this report is articulated by 11 scholars in George Whalley (ed.), *A Place of Liberty* (Clarke, Irwin, and Company, Ltd., Toronto, 1964).

Scientific education and research in Canadian higher education is the subject of W. P. Thompson, *Graduate Education in the Sciences in Canadian Universities* (University of Toronto Press, 1963) and OECD, *Training of and Demand for High-level Scientific and Technical Personnel in Canada* (Paris, 1966). The Frank Gerstein Lectures at York University in 1965 also focused on *Science and the University* (Paris, 1966).

Among periodicals, *University Affairs,* published quarterly by the AUCC, is an indispensable source of current information. The CAUT Bulletin, published six times a year, deals with current topics, particularly those pertinent to teaching staff. The *Proceedings* of annual meetings of AUCC similarly presents discussions of contemporary issues and developments.

AUSTRALIA It is only in the last ten years that much has been published on Australian higher education. Official sources still predominate. The Murray Committee Report (Commonwealth of Australia, *Report of the Committee on Australian Universities,* Canberra, 1957) reviews the rapid increase in university enrollment in the postwar period; its recommendations set the stage for many developments in this decade. The three-volume Martin Committee Report (Committee on the Future of Tertiary Education in Australia, *Tertiary Education in Australia: Report of the Committee on the Future of Tertiary Education in Australia,* Melbourne, 1964–65) takes in all postsecondary education. Volume I reviews enrollments and staffing and the financing of the institutions and students. Volumes II and III describe the higher education situation in a series of major disciplines. This report was a landmark in Australian higher education comparable to the Robbins Committee Report in Great Britain.

The several reports of the Australian Universities Commission (*First Report 1958–63,* 1960; *Second Report 1961–66,* 1963; *Third Report 1964–66,* 1966; and *Fourth Report,* published in March 1969) have provided periodic reviews of university developments and set forth funding requirements for the future. The major official publication on advanced education is the Wark Committee's initial report (Commonwealth of Australia, *First Report of the Commonwealth Advisory Committee on Advanced Education,* Canberra, 1966). Nearly all its recommendations have been implemented. These documents constitute the basic official record of

Australian higher education since the early 1950s except that, apart from the Martin Committee Report, teacher education is omitted as there is no national body with jurisdiction over it.

Additional official sources, especially for statistics on enrollments and finance, include *University Statistics* published periodically by the Commonwealth Bureau of Census and Statistics, the *Official Year Book of the Commonwealth of Australia,* and the *Universities (Financial Assistance) Acts* of various years. *A Brief Guide to Australian Universities,* published periodically by the Australian Council for Educational Research, is a useful handbook.

At the state level, sources include a number of special studies carried out in the last several years: the 1963 Ramsay Committee Report on tertiary education in Victoria, the 1966 Heath Report on advanced education (nonuniversity) in New South Wales, the 1966 Burton Report prepared by the Committee of Inquiry chaired by Herbert Burton on advanced education in the Australian Capital Territory, and the 1966 Jackson Committee Report in Western Australia (committee chaired by Sir Lawrence Jackson). Reports of state departments of education and of the educational institutions themselves provide additional information.

The main periodicals treating higher education include *The Australian University* (published by the Vice-chancellor's Committee, Melbourne University Press); *Vestes* (Federation of University Staff Associations); E. L. French (ed.), *Melbourne Studies in Education,* (Melbourne University Press [annual]), *Australian Quarterly,* and the *Australian Journal of Education.* Useful international sources include the Unesco *World Survey of Education,* vols. I to IV (Paris, 1955, 1958, 1961, 1966) and the Robbins Committee Report, appendix V (Robbins Committee: *Report of the Committee Appointed by the Prime Minister under the Chairmanship of Lord Robbins 1961–63,* Cmnd. 2154, HMSO, London, 1963).

Among relatively recent nongovernment publications focusing on the problems, current developments, and future projections of higher education are A. P. Rowe, *If the Town Fits* (Melbourne University Press, 1960), which outlined university problems as seen by the then vice-chancellor of the University of Adelaide, ignited controversy, and probably shares much credit for the greatly increased public attention to universities; John Wilkes (ed.), *Tertiary Education in Australia* (Angus and Robertson, Sydney, 1965), which includes articles on the different sectors of higher education by outstanding authorities at a time of major change; and E. L. Wheelwright (ed.), *Higher Education in Australia* (Federation of Australian University Staff Associations, Melbourne, 1965), which includes a useful bibliography, comprehensive statistical tables, and articles highlighting contemporary developments.

David S. Macmillan, *Australian Universities* (Sydney University Press for Australian Vice-chancellors' Committee, 1968) gives historical background, descriptions of the individual universities, and general comment on the university sector. Several papers presented at the National Seminar on Educational Planning held in Canberra in 1968 by the Australian National Advisory Committee for Unesco analyze future higher education development and national planning. Among these papers "Demographic Trends" by the demographer W. D. Borrie, who has often published on enrollment projections and population trends, estimates higher education enrollments to 1986; these estimates are being referred to as guidelines by national authorities.

FEDERAL REPUBLIC OF GERMANY Publications in English on German higher education are relatively few, but their number is increasing. Among recent general publications are *Higher Education in the Federal Republic of Germany: Problems and Trends* (German Academic Exchange Service, Bonn, 1966); the appropriate sections of UNESCO's *World Survey of Education,* vol. IV (Paris, 1966); appendix V of the Robbins Committee, *Higher Education: Report of the Committee Appointed by the Prime Minister under the Chairmanship of Lord Robbins 1961–63* (Cmnd. 2154, HMSO, London, 1963); and UNESCO, *Factual Background Document on Access to Higher Education in Europe,* vol. III (Conference of Ministers of Education of European Member States of Access to Higher Education, MINEUROP/3, Paris, Oct. 6, 1967). The OECD, *Reviews of National Science Policy: United Kingdom, Germany* (Paris, 1967), although focusing on research, gives considerable information on contemporary higher education.

The periodical *Education in Germany* (Inter Nationes, Bad Godesberg) reports on current developments at all levels of education. In *Educational Record,* Fall 1968, Wolfgang Brezinka's "German Universities: Crisis and Reform" (vol. 49, no. 4) reviews current problems and efforts to reform university structures, curricular organization, and student participation.

Educational planning is a recent development in the Federal Republic. Informative articles on this subject include "West Germany's Turn to Bildungspolitik in Educational Planning," by Ursula K. Springer (*Comparative Education Review,* vol. 9, no. 1, February 1965) and two articles by Friedrich Edding, an international authority on the economics of education: "The Planning of Higher Education in the Federal Republic of Germany," in Seymour Harris (ed.), *Economic Aspects of Higher Education* (OECD, Paris, 1964) and "Educational Planning in Western Germany," *The World Yearbook of Education 1967* (Evans Brothers Ltd., London, 1967).

Since 1960 several major reports have been published by the Wissenschaftsrat (in German only) which provide a wealth of information, review past developments, and set forth recommendations on the future development of higher education: *Empfehlungen des Wissenschaftsrates zum Ausbau der Wissenschaftlichen Einrichtungen, Teil I, Wissenschaftliche Hochschulen* (Bundesdruckerei, Bonn, 1962), *Anregungen des Wissenschaftsrates zur Gestalt neuer Hochschulen* (1962), *Abiturienten und Studenten (Entwicklung und Vorausschätzung der Zahlen 1950 bis 1980)* (1964), *Bericht des Vorsitzenden über die Arbeit des Wissenschaftsrates 1961 bis 1964* (1965), and *Empfehlungen des Wissenschaftsrates zum Ausbau der Wissenschaftlichen Hochschulen bis 1970* (1967). The last of these reports surveys university growth since 1960, estimates future enrollment demand and the costs of expansion required to meet this demand, recommends measures, including a *numerus clausus,* to enable the universities to handle rising enrollments, and has a vast amount of statistical material. A study of the Permanent Conference of Ministers of Education, *Bedarfsfestellung 1961–1970 für Schulwesen, Lehrerbildung, Wissenschaft und Forschung, Kunst and Kulurflege* (Stuttgart, 1964) also forecasts higher education developments.

Two reports of the Ministry for Scientific Research, *Bundesbericht Forschung I, II* (Bonn, 1964 and 1967), describe the research effort in the Federal Republic and include discussion of university development, reform, and finance. Another major and massive official study, *Bildungsplanungbericht 1967: Bericht über den Stand der Massnahmen auf dem Gebiet der Bildungsplanung* (V/2166, Bonn, 1967), presented by the Federal Chancellor to the Bundestag, reviews measures taken in educational planning at all levels and forecasts future developments. Its two sections were prepared, respectively, by the federal and *Länder* governments.

SWEDEN Surprisingly little has been published in English on Swedish higher education apart from studies by UNESCO, the OECD, and organizations in Sweden. The OECD, *Educational Policy and Planning, Sweden* (Paris, 1967) treats all education in Sweden. Chapters on higher education, educational expenditure, and planning review recent trends, reforms in structures and teaching methods since 1955, enrollments, staffing, and the relationship of educational planning to manpower forecasting. More general surveys of higher education may be found in UNESCO, *World Survey of Education* (vols. I to IV, Paris, 1955, 1958, 1961, and 1966; vol. IV in particular concentrates on higher education), and the Robbins Committee Report: *Higher Education: Report of the Committee Appointed by the Prime Minister under the Chairmanship of Lord Robbins 1961–63* (Cmnd. 2154, HMSO, London, 1963, appendix V). The *International Handbook of Universities* (International Association of Universities, Paris, 1968) lists all the institutions of higher education together with their faculties, enrollments, staff, degrees awarded, and admissions requirements.

The Information Department of the Office of the Chancellor of Swedish Universities publishes (in English) occasional papers on aspects of higher education: academic degrees, enrollments, current trends, and other topics. Its *Report on Higher Education in Sweden* (Stockholm, 1966, 28 pp.) summarizes post-World War II expansion and change in the universities and other postsecondary institutions.

The OECD, *Reviews of National Policies for Science and Education, Scientific Policy in Sweden* (Paris, 1964) gives an excellent account of scientific research, its organization and financing, and its relationship to the higher education system.

For statistical information, the best single source is the annual issue of *SOS Högre Studier* (National Central Bureau of Statistics, Stockholm). Each issue contains a summary (in English) of developments during the year and English translations of the titles of tables. The annual *Statistical Abstract of Sweden* is another essential source for statistics. Some of the *Statistical Reports* issued from time to time by the National Central Bureau of Statistics also contain recent information on enrollments, graduations, and related matters. In another report series of the Bureau, *Forecasting Information,* the issue of Apr. 10, 1968, projects graduates from universities and specialized colleges until 1980. *Högre Utbildning och Forskning i Sverige (Higher Education and Research in Sweden)* published by the Department of Education in 1967 (in Swedish only) gives statistics on enrollments, examinations, recurrent expenditures per student, and teaching staff. Although the annual report of the Office of the Chancellor of Swedish Universities *(Högre Utbildning och Forskning)* is also published only in Swedish, its statistical tables on enrollments and staffing can be understood by the non-Swedish-speaking reader.

Introducing SFS (Swedish National Union of Students, Stockholm, 1966) describes the organization and aims of the National Union of Students. The January 1968 issue of *Fact Sheets on Sweden* explains the system of financial aid for students in higher education: "State Study Assistance in Sweden."

A major cause of recent university reform in the universities is the extended period students have tended to spend at university before taking their examinations, especially in the free faculties. Tables showing study periods in different faculties can be found in a special report prepared in 1966 by the Office of the Chancellor of Universities: *Universitetspedagogiska Utredningen (UPU) II, Studieresultat för en Inskrivningsargang vid Universitet och Högskolor.*

JAPAN The involvement of the United States in the reform of education in Japan after World War II and the interest of both educators and Japan area specialists in these developments resulted in a wealth of publications on Japanese education, including higher education, in the postwar period. Herbert Passin's bibliographical guide of 1965 ("Japanese Education: Guide to a Bibliography of Materials in the English Language" in *Comparative Education Review*, vol. IX, no. 1, February 1965) provides a useful and comprehensive compilation of 466 sources in English dating from 1872 to the early 1960s and is organized under eight different categories. On the institutions themselves and their comparability to American higher education institutions, Vroman, *Japan: A Study of the Educational System of Japan and Guide to the Academic Placement of Students from Japan in United States Educational Institutions* (American Association of Collegiate Registrars and Admissions Officers, 1966) is a relatively recent guide, useful not only to American admissions personnel but also to the comparative educationists.

More than many non-English-language countries, Japan has published a number of official studies on its higher education system in English. Preeminent among them are the white papers and annual reports and surveys. The white papers tend to be studies in depth, while the reports and surveys are laden with statistical and organizational data. Also useful as official sources are the publications of the Japanese National Commission for Unesco, which explain Japanese education to the non-Japanese and analyze its role in national development. The section on Japan in Unesco's fourth volume of *World Survey of Education* provides a slightly outdated but comprehensive summary. The periodic catalog of institutions of higher education in Japan, published by the Overseas Advertiser Company, Ltd., gives basic data on all institutions and also lists national research institutes. *Japanese Universities and Colleges,* prepared by the Japanese University Accreditation Association (Tokyo, 1967), includes a directory of universities and colleges, a brief history of these institutions and the Association, and statistics on students and faculty.

The UNESCO–International Association of Universities study of university entrance problems worldwide ("Japan," in *Access to Higher Education*) describes the highly competitive situation in Japan in its section on that country. A basic study, which includes the postwar period, is Ronald S. Anderson, *Japan: Three Epochs of Modern Education* (U.S. Office of Education, Washington, D.C., 1959). Although Herbert Passin, *Society and Education in Japan* (Teachers College Press, Columbia University, 1965) deals with all education, not just higher education, it is very valuable in explaining the social attitudes toward higher education which have been a major factor in the competitiveness of university admissions. Two recent publications which also relate education to political and social forces in Japanese society are John W. Hall and Michael K. Beardsley (eds.), *Twelve Doors to Japan* (McGraw-Hill Book Company, New York, 1965) and Ronald P. Dore, "Education: Japan," in R. E. Ward and D. Rustow (eds.), *Political Modernization in Japan and Turkey* (Princeton University Press, Princeton, N.J., 1964).

Although it focuses on research and science policy, the OECD study *Reviews of National Science Policy: Japan* (Paris, 1967) devotes a chapter to higher education, including university organization, education and manpower policy, and the role of universities in research. The journal of Hiroshima University's International Educational Research Institute *(Education in Japan: Journal for Overseas)* discusses higher education in some of its issues.

For current reporting of the rapidly moving university situation, the English-language Japanese newspapers, including the *Japan Times* and the *Mainichi Daily News,* are useful sources.

SOVIET UNION   *Soviet Education: A Bibliography of English-language Materials* by Nellie Apanaswicz in collaboration with Seymour M. Rosen (U.S.

Department of Health, Education, and Welfare, Office of Education, Studies in Comparative Education, OE-14101, Bulletin 1964, no. 29, 1964) provides a well-indexed annotated listing of publications since the late 1950s, including several dozen relating to higher education.

The two most comprehensive works on higher education since World War II are Alexander G. Korol, *Soviet Education for Science and Technology* (Technology Press of Massachusetts Institute of Technology and John Wiley & Sons, Inc., New York, 1957) and Nicholas DeWitt, *Education and Professional Employment in the U.S.S.R.* (National Science Foundation, Washington, D.C., 1961). They analyze both specialized secondary and higher education and focus particularly on the relationship between manpower needs and education.

Two brief general surveys of higher education are found in UNESCO, *World Survey of Education,* vol. IV (Paris, 1966) and the Robbins Committee Report (*Higher Education: Report of the Committee Appointed by the Prime Minister under the Chairmanship of Lord Robbins 1961–63*, Cmnd. 2154, HMSO, London, 1963, appendix V). V. A. Kitaitzev, "Union of Soviet Socialist Republics," sec. IX in International Association of Universities and UNESCO, *Access to Education* (Paris, 1965) is concerned mainly with admission to higher education and student background. *Higher Education in the USSR: Curriculums, Schools, and Statistics* by Seymour M. Rosen (U.S. Department of Health, Education, and Welfare, Office of Education, OE-14088, Bulletin 1963, no. 16, 1963) presents, in compressed form, information on higher education and its relationship to national planning and the economy.

Although the emphasis in Harold J. Noah, *Financing Soviet Schools* (Teachers College Press, Columbia University, New York, 1966) is on elementary and secondary education in the 1950s, he reviews higher education expansion and financing, the growth of part-time enrollment, and the extent of private, mainly parental, support of students in higher education. A recent volume translated and edited by Harold J. Noah, *The Economics of Education in the U.S.S.R.* (Frederick A. Praeger, Inc., New York, 1969), testifies to the growing concern in the Soviet Union with the cost of education and its impact on economic growth. The book grew out of a conference held in Moscow at which specialists from government, higher education institutions, and enterprises discussed economic aspects of education and problems of planning.

The lengthy and somewhat repetitious *Planification de l'Éducation en URSS* by K. Nozhko et al. (International Institute for Educational Planning, Paris, 1961) presents a more doctrinaire discussion of educational planning. This study also discusses the relationship of higher education institutions to government, governance, enrollments, the socioeconomic background of students, and various other topics. For a concise description of the Soviet educational planning process see K. G. Nozhko, "Methods of Estimating the Demand for Specialists and of Planning Specialized Training within the USSR," *UNESCO Statistical Reports and Studies* (ST/S/9, Paris, 1964).

The most recent English-language study of the relationship between educational and government is Herbert C. Rudman, *The School and State in the U.S.S.R.* (The Macmillan Company, New York, 1967). It describes and analyzes the role of government at the national and republic levels and makes clear the supreme authority of the Communist Party in decision making at all levels, both in the organs of government and in the governance of higher education institutions. Rudman finds little evidence of any independence of the union republics from the national Ministry of Higher and Specialized Secondary Education.

On the subject of students, Murray Yanowitch and Norton Dodge, "Social Class and Education: Soviet Findings and Reactions" (*Comparative Education Review,* vol. 12, no. 3, October 1968), drawing on the increasing number of sociological studies of Soviet higher education by Soviet specialists, points out that the Soviet Union, like Western countries, not only continues to have difficulty in providing equal access to higher education for all sectors of society but also is becoming more concerned by the conflict between effective implementation of this principle and the more economic system of admitting to higher education on the basis of intellectual ability.

A major recent study of Soviet research sponsored by the National Science Foundation is Alexander G. Korol, *Soviet Research and Development: Its Organization, Personnel, and Funds* (M.I.T. Press, Cambridge, Mass., 1965). It traces the rapid expansion of research in the 1950s and discusses its organization and the limited but enlarging role of higher education institutions in research and development. C. Freeman and A. Young, *The Research and Development Effort in Western Europe, North America and the Soviet Union* (OECD, Paris, 1965) draws on the Korol study for its international comparison of research in 1962; the difficulties in interpreting Soviet statistics are emphasized.

The U.S. Department of Commerce report, *Estimates and Projections of Educational Attainment in the USSR 1950–1985,* prepared by Ann S. Goodman and Murray Feshbach in *International Population Reports* (ser. P–91, no. 16, 1967) focuses on the increase in educational attainment of the population ten years old and includes a number of statistical tables. A major official Soviet source for statistics is the annual *Statistical Yearbook* (*Narodnoe Khoziaistvo SSR, Statisticheskii Yezhegodnik,* Moscow).

An essential journal for any study of Soviet education is *Soviet Education,* a monthly published by the International Arts and Sciences Press (New York) which gives official translations of selected articles from Soviet education journals.

INDIA[1] Unlike many industrialized countries, the literature on higher education in developing countries in general is thin to the point of nonexistence. For some nations, even basic statistical data are lacking, and careful studies of virtually any aspect of higher education are in general unavailable. So-called "underdeveloped nations" are indeed underdeveloped in terms of research on most topics of importance to modernization, higher education among them. India is more fortunate than many developing areas in that its university system is large and well developed and some emphasis on research goes back for at least 50 years. The most comprehensive listing of materials concerning Indian higher education can be found in Philip G. Altbach, *Higher Education in Developing Countries: A Select Bibliography* (Harvard Center for International Affairs, Cambridge, Mass., 1970), pp. 63–73. Approximately 200 books and articles in English are listed in this bibliography.

One of the richest sources of statistical data concerning Indian higher education can be found in official government publications, and particularly in those of the University Grants Commission, a semigovernment agency responsible for research on universities as well as for the disbursement of funds from the central government to institutions of higher education. The annual reports of the UGC and their annual publication, *Universities in India,* provide basic statistical information of an up-to-date nature. UGC reports on *Examination Reform* (Delhi, 1962), on *General Education*

----

[1] Prepared by Philip G. Altbach.

(Delhi, 1967), on *Standards of University Education* (Delhi, 1965), on the *Medium of Instruction* (Delhi, 1961), and on other topics are usually thorough and informative documents. The semiannual *Universities Handbook,* published by the Inter University Board of India and Ceylon, is also a key source for statistical data.

Various official Government of India commissions on higher education provide a rich source of data both of an interpretative and statistical nature. Among the most important of these documents are the *Report of the University Education Commission, 1948–49* (Manager of Publications, Delhi, 1950) known as the Radhakrishnan Report, and the *Report of the Education Commission, 1964–66* (Manager of Publications, New Delhi, 1966). The recommendations of these reports are comprehensive, although their implementation has been slow due to lack of resources and other problems.

The best analysis of the transfer of higher education from Britain to India can be found in Eric Ashby's *Universities: British, Indian, African* (Harvard University Press, Cambridge, Mass., 1966). Robert Gaudino's *The Indian University* (Popular Prakashan, Bombay, 1965) is the most adequate overall description of modern Indian higher education, although it is now somewhat outdated. There is no adequate historical account of Indian universities, but Syed Nurullah and J. P. Naik, *A Students' History of Education in India* (Macmillan, Bombay, 1962) remains the best overall account. Histories of specific universities, such as S. R. Dongerkery, *History of the University of Bombay* (University of Bombay Press, Bombay, 1957) and *Hundred Years of the University of Calcutta* (University of Calcutta, Calcutta, 1957), also exist for a number of institutions. Most of these accounts are descriptive and of only limited use to anyone but a specialist.

There have been several studies of specific aspects of higher education in India. A. R. Kamat's *Two Studies in Education* (Asia Publishing House, Bombay, 1968) deals with the problem of wastage in higher education. The volume edited by Philip G. Altbach entitled *Turmoil and Transition: Higher Education and Student Politics in India* (Basic Books, Inc., Publishers, New York, 1969) is probably the best overview of this key aspect of Indian higher education. *The Great Debate: Language Controversy and Higher Education,* edited by A. B. Shah (Lalvani, Bombay, 1969), provides an analysis of this key issue of policy in Indian higher education. A. B. Shah (ed.), *Higher Education in India* (Lalvani, Bombay, 1967) provides a series of articles on various aspects of higher education by experts in the field. One of the most significant overall analyses to appear recently is Lloyd and Susanne Rudolph (eds.), *Politics and Education in India* (Harvard University Press, Cambridge, Mass., 1970). This collection includes case studies concerning the relationship of higher education to politics on the central and state levels. A. B. Shah (ed.) *Education, Scientific Policy, and Developing Countries* (Manaktalas, Bombay, 1967) includes a number of perceptive articles on Indian universities in addition to a series of analyses concerning higher education in developing areas generally. A classic of historical analysis of the role of education in the nationalist movement in India is Bruce McCully, *English Education and the Origins of Indian Nationalism* (Columbia University Press, New York, 1940). A number of other studies concerning specific aspects of Indian higher education combine analytical rigor and relevance to current problems. Much of the writing on Indian universities, however, is characterized by a lack of data and overly general commentary.

Many areas have received virtually no attention from scholars or analysts. The whole question of academic reform in India has been treated mainly in government reports and has not received much independent scholarly attention. Studies of the extremely important and complicated language question remain to be conducted, although there is a good deal of commentary on this topic. Studies of student activism are not numerous, and there are only a few articles on the key question of university-government relations.

Several journals deal regularly with Indian higher education and are worthwhile in analyzing aspects of universities. *Minerva,* the excellent quarterly journal edited by Edward Shils, devotes substantial attention to India. Shils' own recent article, "The Indian Academic," *Minerva,* vol. 7, Spring 1969, pp. 345–372, is an example of this attention. The *Journal of University Education,* published from Delhi and unfortunately no longer being issued, also has some valuable articles. Analytical articles concerning higher education appear from time to time in the *Economic and Political Weekly* (Bombay) and in the *Education Quarterly,* an official publication of the Ministry of Education. *Quest,* an independent quarterly published from Bombay, also contains occasional articles of high standards on university issues.

Appendix B: Individuals and Organizations Consulted in the Country Surveys

AUSTRALIA B. R. **Williams,** Vice-chancellor, University of Sydney

W. H. **Maze,** Assistant Principal, University of Sydney

Graeme E. **de Graaf,** Director, International House, University of Sydney

V. J. **Truskett,** Executive Officer, College of Advanced Technology, Bathurst, N.S.W.

H. L. **Craig,** Executive Director, Universities Board, N.S.W.

G. W. **Muir,** Director of Teacher Education, Department of Education, N.S.W.

New South Wales Institute of Technology

R. **Dunbar,** Director, Department of Technical Education, N.S.W.

A. G. **Mitchel,** Vice-chancellor, Macquarie University

S. W. **Cohen,** Deputy Vice-chancellor, Macquarie University

H. W. S. **Philp,** Head, School of Education, Macquarie University

W. D. **Borrie,** Director, Research School of Social Sciences, Australian National University

Norma **MacArthur,** Australian National University

I. W. **Wark,** Chairman, Commonwealth Advisory Committee on Advanced Education

James **McCusker,** Secretary, Commonwealth Advisory Committee on Advanced Education

J. K. **Kaye,** Secretary, Australian Universities Commission

F. S. **Hambly,** Secretary, Australian Vice-chancellors' Committee

P. H. **Partridge,** Australian National University

L. F. **Crisp,** Deputy Chairman of Council, Canberra College of Advanced Education

President and other students, Graduate Student Union, ANU

Secretary, Australian Research Grants Committee

Department of Education, Victoria

R. E. Parry, Registrar, Victoria Institute of Colleges

R. Marginson, Vice-principal, University of Melbourne

Barbara Falk, Chairman, Center for the Study of Higher Education, University of Melbourne

Tom Roper, Education Vice-president, National University Students Association

J. Frederick, Student Counsellor, University of Melbourne

C. S. Birkett Clews, Deputy Vice-chancellor, University of Western Australia

H. S. Williams, Director, Western Australian Institute of Technology

Neil G. Traylen, Director of Teacher Education, Western Australia

CANADA Edward F. Sheffield, Professor of Higher Education, University of Toronto

Robert O. Berdahl, Co-commissioner Duff-Berdahl Report

Donald C. Rowat, Co-commissioner, Commission on Relations between Universities and Governments

G. C. Andrew, Director, Association of Universities and Colleges of Canada

David G. Fish, Director of Research, AUCC

Ralph D. Mitchener, Division of Educational Support, Department of the Secretary of State

Davidson Dunton, President and Vice-chancellor, Carleton University

J. Percy Smith, Executive Secretary, Canadian Association of University Teachers

N. LeSeeleur, Acting Director, Education Division, Dominion Bureau of Statistics

Zoltan E. Zsigmond, Higher Education Branch, DBS

R. W. Jackson and staff, Science Council of Canada

Economic Council of Canada

Teresa R. Harmstone, Carleton University

Normal Walmesley, Director of University Resources Study, AUCC

Canadian Union of Students

Robert M. Pike, University of Alberta

GREAT BRITAIN

S. M. Greenall, Research Officer, National Union of Students

P. M. O'Bryan, Education Officer, British Embassy, Washington, D.C.

E. R. Copleston, Secretary, University Grants Committee

R. H. J. Thorne, Committee of Vice-chancellors and Principals

R. J. Guppy, Universities Branch, DES

H. W. French, H. M. Chief Inspector, DES.

A. G. Atkinson, Planning Branch, DES

G. Williams, Deputy Director, Unit for Economic and Statistical Studies in Higher Education, London School for Economics and Political Science

Alan Evans, Vice-president, NUS, 1968–69

Douglas A. Baker, Director, Education and Welfare, NUS

Lucy S. Sutherland, Principal, Lady Margaret Hall, Oxford University

A. H. Halsey, Head, Department of Social and Administrative Studies, University of Oxford

The Schools Council

Science Unit, American Embassy, London

Earl L. Griggs, Director, University of California Study Abroad, U.K.

FRANCE

Edouard Morot-Sir, Cultural Counselor, Embassy of France (New York) and Representative of French Universities in the United States

Raymond Poignant, Directeur par interim, International Institute for Educational Planning

Jean Capelle

Bert M. P. Leefmans, Director, Institute of International Education, Paris

M. Trincal, Head, Higher Education Statistics, National Ministry of Education

Institut Pédagogique National

U.S. Information Service, American Embassy, Paris

Organization for Economic Cooperation and Development

UNESCO

Union Nationale des Étudiants

Centre de Sociologie Européene

FEDERAL REPUBLIC OF GERMANY

Friedrich Edding, Max Planck Institut für Bildungsforschung; also Marianne von Rundstedt, Mssrs. Ernst Georg Schleifer and Wolfgang Nitsch

K-G. Hasemann, Secretary General, Wissenschaftsrat, and Mr. **Heim,** Chief Statistician

Elmer Freund, Federal Office of Statistics, Wiesbaden

R. Moeller, Deutsches Studentenwerk

Dagmar Moellenkamp, Permanent Conference of Ministers of Culture and Education Affairs

Wolfgang Paulig, Federal Ministry for Scientific Research

Johannes Thomas, Rectors' Conference

Verband Deutscher Studentenschaften

K. Scheuch, University of Cologne

Edward J. Joyce, Cultural Attaché, U.S. Embassy, Bonn

West German Permanent Representative to UNESCO

Free University of Berlin

University of Freiburg

Deutscher Industrie und Handelstag

Joseph B. Cox, Cultural Affairs, Department of State

JAPAN

Robert S. Schwantes, The Asia Foundation

Robert S. Barendsen, Comparative Section, Education, Office of Education, Department of Health, Education, and Welfare

Ray A. Moore, Amherst College

Ronald S. Anderson, University of Hawaii

Edwin O. Reischauer, Harvard University

Shigeharu Matsumoto, Chairman of the Board, International House of Japan

Masumori Hiratsuka, Director, National Institute for Educational Research; also **Mr. Narita,** Chief, Third Research Section, First Research Division, National Institute

Tatsuo Morito, President, Japan Scholarship Foundation

Shigeo Minowa, Director, University of Tokyo Press

Graham Lucas, Japan Representative, The Asia Foundation; also **Allen G. Choate,** Assistant Representative

Delmer M. Brown, Director, University of California Study Center, International Christian University

Seizaburo Sato, Associate Professor, University of Tokyo

Junichi Natori, Director, International Division, Waseda University

Juro Horiuti, President, Hokkaido University

Yoshihki Ishizuka, Faculty of Agriculture, Hokkaido University

Nobuo Suzuki, Secretary, Hokkaido University

William D. Eddy, Hokkaido Student Center, Hokkaido University

Alice Cary, Amherst House, Doshisha University

Issei Kato, Secretary General, Japanese University Accreditation Association

Ministry of Education, Statistical Branch

Isao Saito, Acting President, Doshisha University

SWEDEN   Lizzie Gibson, Organization for Economic Cooperation and Development

Ingvar Svennilson, Institute for International Economic Studies, University of Stockholm

Lennart Sandgren, Under-secretary of State, Ministry of Education

Bengt Hultin, Head, Information Section, Office of the Chancellor of the Swedish Universities

Torgny Segerstedt, Vice-chancellor, University of Uppsala

Ulf Fornstedt, Secretary General, Swedish Student Union

K. Wallberg, Head of Division, National Bureau of Statistics

Goran Svanfeldt, National Bureau of Statistics

Raymond Lindgren, Resident Director, California State Colleges International Program, University of Uppsala

A. Harry Passow, Fulbright Professor, University of Stockholm

Swedish Institute for Cultural Relations with Foreign Countries

United States Embassy, Stockholm

Margareta Vestin, Board of Education

Central Organization of Salaried Employees (TCO)

Swedish Professional Association (SACO)

SOVIET UNION   Harold J. Noah, Teachers College, Columbia University

Seymour M. Rosen, Comparative Education Section, Office of Education, Department of Health, Education, and Welfare

George Z. F. Bereday, Teachers College, Columbia University

Detlef Glowka, Max Planck Institut für Bildungsforschung, Berlin

Klaus Meyer, Osteuropa-Institut, Free University of Berlin

Robert Allen, Soviet Specialist, Library of Congress

The Directorate for Scientific Affairs of the Organization for Economic Cooperation and Development provided assistance with the surveys on countries which are members of the OECD (thus excluding Australia and the Soviet Union). The writer is indebted particularly to Mr. Ladislav Cerych and Miss Lizzie Gibson.

Index

This book was set in Vladimir by University Graphics, Inc. It was printed on Vellum Offset and bound by The Maple Press Company. The designer was Elliot Epstein; the drawing was done by John Cordes, J. & R. Technical Services, Inc. The editors were Herbert Waentig and Laura Givner for McGraw-Hill Book Company and Verne A. Stadtman and Margaret Cheney for the Carnegie Commission on Higher Education. Frank Matonti supervised the production.